THE GREAT AMERICAN BIRTH RITE

THE GREAT AMERICAN BIRTH RITE

WILLIAM
AND
JOANNA
WOOLFOLK

THE DIAL PRESS   1975   NEW YORK

Library of Congress Cataloging in Publication Data
Woolfolk, William.
  The great American birth rite.
  Includes index.
    1. Children—Management—Economic aspects—United
States. 2. Infants—Care and hygiene—Economic aspects.
3. Childbirth—Economic aspects—United States.
I. Woolfolk, Joanna, joint author. II. Title.
[DNLM: 1. Child care—Popular works. 2. Family
planning—Popular works. 3. Illegitimacy—Popular
works. 4. Pregnancy—Popular works. WQ150 W913g]
HQ769.W876   338.4′7′6491   75-12745
ISBN 0-8037-5232-6

Manufactured in the United States of America

First printing

CONTENTS

For DONNA
the most fortunate birth
in 2,000 years

SPECIAL ACKNOWLEDGMENTS

To ROY NEWQUIST, and the team of interviewers, professional and volunteer, who helped us to compile the testimony in these pages.

Above all, to the hundreds of people who gave so generously of their time to share with us their opinions and expertise.

So long as one has the desire to discover the truth and say it, one goes on trying to discover and say it. That is all that remains of morality.

LEO TOLSTOY

THE
GREAT
AMERICAN
BIRTH
RITE

In this book you will learn nothing about how the fetal nervous system develops. You will not discover how a baby's physiological competence registers at sixty seconds after birth, or five minutes, one day, one week, one month or one year. You will hear nothing about that ultimate miracle in which, still dependent on mother, unable to breathe, kept alive by oxygenated blood coursing through the umbilical cord, the newborn infant is cut loose to pursue its precarious separate way. Nor will you gain much insight into subsequent infant and child behavior.

What interests us is a wholly different aspect of birth and baby.

There is a good deal of useful, practical, dollars-and-cents information about birth practices—from what obstetricians and pediatricians charge to what it costs to outfit Mother and Baby, from the most efficient, least expensive method of birth control to how much you need to pay in a maternity home or at a day-care center. And there is also some good medical advice and some sensible information about how to raise a Baby.

However, the book is not intended to be an index of prices or a guide to medical practice. We did not set out to write a sociological study, a handbook for parents, or an exposé. Before you ask what is it, we will tell you. It is as direct, thoroughgoing, and in-depth a survey as we could possibly devise on the current American way of having babies and raising them. It is an attempt to report to you on exactly what is going on out there.

We began with a determination to uncover the facts and to follow them wherever they might lead. As Thomas Huxley once did, we prayed that God would give us the strength to face a fact.

Our method was basically simple: we sat down and talked with people engaged in the birth business, and with the customers who bought their products and services. That required a good deal of reading beforehand in books, magazines, newspapers, government reports, pamphlets and theses, chiefly to equip us to ask the right questions and decide whether we got the right or at least the relevant answers.

The interviewing covered a period of two years, in which we recorded on-the-spot impressions and opinions of more than six hundred people and ran through three hundred hour-long reels of tape. (This does not include those who responded to our written questions.) An interview might yield only a minute or two of worthwhile material, often no more than a single line, and the entire experience taught us compassion for the lawyers who had to listen to those endless hours of Presidential tapes. They are the real heroes of Watergate.

Our procedure with any material gathered during interviews was to allow a direct comment to stand on its own, circumscribed only by quotation marks, so the reader could judge its value for himself. If statistics were quoted during an interview, we checked with at least two other sources. If the figures then jibed, fine. If they fell within parameters set by the other two sources, we included them. If they failed to do either, we simply left them out.

Our interviews were conducted with obstetricians, midwives, pediatricians, newspaper columnists, businessmen, lawyers, consumer experts, authors, hospital and day-care center personnel, baby-sitters, sociologists, psychologists, politicians and, of course, parents. Wherever possible, we allowed them to speak in their own voices.

Quite deliberately, there is no emphasis on the atypical or the quaint. Our main concern is with the ordinary ways that this generation of Americans is having and raising babies. (We recognize that for most new parents there is nothing ordinary about the birth of their baby.)

Baby is also big business.

Birth is a process which produces a highly valuable consumer—a consumer who never goes to market, but nevertheless devours innumerable products. A large segment of American business is devoted to satisfying the needs, real or imaginary, of Baby and those conveyor belts to Baby otherwise known as parents.

We define a businessman as someone who has something to sell, whether a service or a product. Therefore the first businessman to deal with Baby (if we omit the abortionist) is the obstetrician. Like his brethren in the medical fraternity, the obstetrician is devoid of that type of sentiment featured in Hallmark cards (a company which happens to be in business to exploit sentiment). Medicine is only partly a science, and less an art—it's mostly a business. If we regard a doctor as anything but a businessman, we will not be able to bargain properly for the very special services he is selling.

Let's not forget this simple but serviceable definition: the obstetrician is a businessman. So is the pediatrician. So is the midwife. So are the doctors who offer professional advice in newspapers, magazines and books.

Baby-sitting and day-care centers have an obvious "consumerist" side. This is where government also becomes involved. Politicians with an eye to the parent vote have lately been tenderly concerned with the problems and rights of the very young. But they are not motivated exclusively by a desire to promote the physical and emotional well-being of children or to provide them with a comfortable, beautiful, and culturally enriching background.

In other chapters we deal directly with the producer-consumer, profit-and-loss relationship between Baby and those making baby products.

The mighty wheels of American business grind out what Baby needs—or what parents can be persuaded that Baby needs. This is where sentiment is most commercialized, although in the multibillion dollar industry devoted to meeting Baby's needs, true sentiment is as hard to find as an Arab sheik at a bar mitzvah.

If you, the reader, take away only one message from this book, we hope it is that.

Many problems indigenous to The Great American Birth Rite affect everyone, even those who are not proud new parents of a little miracle. Illegitimacy, adoption, child abuse, abortion, the declining birthrate, the special perils that confront children in our highly industrialized, technological society are all pervasive social concerns. The government giveth with one hand, but taketh away with the other. Politicians count votes. You must count costs.

Mark Twain, who never spoke entirely in jest, once advised a reporter to "get your facts first—then you can distort 'em all you want." What he meant, at least in part, is that facts are more important than opinions and must always take precedence. The earth did not go around the sun merely to prove Copernicus was right.

But when you have acquired a certain critical mass of fact, as we did in the course of our long research, you inevitably develop certain opinions, a bias, if you prefer. Let us state now what bias we have acquired so that you may identify it when it appears, as it will, on the following pages. It is not stupendous. It is no more than a conclusion any reasonably well-disposed person might have come to without having gone to as much preliminary trouble.

We believe that the Great Campaign of businessmen is directed not only at, but against the consumer. And the struggle between the consumer and the businessmen in medicine, in commerce, in government, is most unfairly weighted. The average consumer-parent is far too preoccupied with day-to-day living to offer real resistance to the formidable batteries of persuasion brought to bear on him. He is like a country rube at a carnival, and before the sharpsters are through with him, he will be making change for a three-dollar bill.

Of course it will come as no surprise to anyone to learn that the struggle is also weighted most unfairly against those least able to defend themselves: the poor.

The economics of the birth business are rooted in our social order. The birth business is a segment of American capitalism and cannot be studied apart from its environment, any more than you can take a fish out of water to watch it swim.

Let us close with this pragmatic word: in addition to being the most miraculous of human creations, Baby is big business. And sometimes the professionals in medicine, in business, and in government act as if the consumer must be the one Abraham Lincoln meant when he said you *can* fool some of the people all of the time. To protect himself, the consumer must try to judge whether a need is real or provoked, whether the price charged for a service is reasonable or inflated. In buying products and services, difficult as it is to choose, ill-equipped as he may be to choose, he must. Or he will be victimized. He will be victimized so artfully that he may not even be aware of it.

THE OBSTETRICIAN: HOMO SAPIENS MORIBUNDIS

1

He is 5 feet 11 inches tall and fifty-four years old. He drives a Cadillac, belongs to at least one country club, has three children and a wife who is prominent in local charities. He pays taxes on $82,000 a year.

He is the average American obstetrician.

Color him carefully. He may not be around long.

But before we consign this overpaid underachiever to the dustbin, let's find out what sort of creature he is and how he functions on today's birth scene. Let's talk to one who fits as closely as possible the profile delineated in the first paragraph.

Dr. William F. is a dark, slim, fifty-year-old obstetrician who has practiced from his Chicago Heights office since completing his hospital residency in 1948. His earnings, in excess of $85,000 per year, are very close to the national average for obstetricians.

"I became an obstetrician," Dr. F. says, "because I found out when doing my internship that ninety percent of women will cooperate with a doctor, whereas the male patient seems by nature inclined to make his own diagnosis, to disobey rules."

Though he lived at home, he was $18,000 in debt when he opened his office the day after his residency ended. He charged $75, at most, for attending a woman through pregnancy, and the hospital bill hovered near the $100 mark.

He has served the same south suburban area since, despite two moves of offices. Today he charges a minimum of $600 and feels that a patient is fortunate to get out of the hospital for less than another $600.

If a couple is covered by one of the more generous group or private policies at Blue Cross, they will get up to $200 for the obstetrician and $25 per day for hospitalization, a poor contribution toward the ob.'s charge and a hospital tab of over $100 per day.

What does Dr. F. offer for what he is paid?

"I don't want to make it seem as though my ministrations to each patient are the same because no pregnancy *is* precisely the same. But let's generalize as much as we can.

"A woman comes to me when she knows, or suspects, that she is pregnant. She will receive a thorough physical examination, the appropriate blood and urine tests, and be placed on a diet corresponding to the amount of weight she should gain during pregnancy and whatever deficiencies existing within her body which might affect the welfare of the fetus. She will visit me at least once a month until the seventh month, after which I require a visit every two weeks until the ninth month, when I see her every week or ten days depending upon her welfare and the development of the child. I would say that seventy percent of my patients fall into this routine of handling, with potential complications either non-existent or averted. But thirty percent have problems, either physical or psychological, which require more frequent visits or even house calls.

"I attend her delivery at the hospital—only one out of fifty of my patients is delivered by anyone other than myself. I check out her and the baby immediately after birth, on the day after, and normally once more before they leave the hospital. In the meantime I have consulted with the pediatrician or g.p. she has selected to care for her child, turned all pertinent records over to him, and made sure as best I can that proper care will continue as the child grows."

What does this amount to in annual income?

Dr. F. shrugged. "Since I deliver two hundred women each year, the total should be a hundred and twenty thousand dollars. But in making allowances for the special cases, problem pregnancies, charity cases either imposed on me or those I wish to handle, it ends up at eighty-five thousand. After taxes, office rent, the heavy load of malpractice insurance every doctor must have, my receptionist and utilities, I don't end up poor, but on the other hand I don't end up rich. I could handle more cases and make more money above the line, but I'm not young any more, I have an ex-family to support and a present family to maintain, and I can do more for everyone involved by working moderately rather than wearing myself into being the victim of a stroke or cardiac arrest."

What is life like for a successful, prestigious obstetrician?

"I know that most people think of an obstetrician as a man who has it easy, attending woman in her most natural function. The truth of the matter is that half of my meals—breakfast, lunch or dinner, at home or out—are interrupted by phone calls from my answering service, the hospitals, or my patients. Usually it's a storm in a teacup—spotting, a fight with the husband, hysteria on the part of husband or wife, or false labor—and all that's needed is reassurance. At least a hundred and eighty of the three hundred sixty-five nights of the year are interrupted the same way; a full night's sleep is a novelty."

Dr. F.'s wife, a comely brunette of forty-five, isn't as tolerant as the doctor.

"My husband is a very patient man," she explained, "and I wish he could put his foot down. Why can't he ever finish a meal while it's hot? Why can't he ever get a full night of uninterrupted sleep unless we're on vacation? Most of the calls he gets on his so-called private time are from women who just need reassurance, not help."

Most obstetricians feel harassed by their patients. The theme runs through all our interviews (with a total of forty-six obstetricians) like an obsession: "Twenty years ago my patients were not as bothersome as they are now." "Your modern woman is an over-indulged, spoiled, hysterical brat." "You take a woman who dominates her husband, and she'd like nothing better than to do the same to her doctor."

Dr. F. says, "I could handle twice as many patients if I could cut out pseudo-emergencies and hystericals. I could even cut my fees proportionately."

A Los Angeles obstetrician offers a more balanced appraisal. "I don't think an obstetrician can be impersonal. He's not only the woman's doctor, he's her friend and confidant and psychiatrist. A pregnant woman needs someone to confide in and rely on, and her ob. is elected. Sure, I could handle more patients if I could cut out the hand holding, but it's part of my job."

GETTING WHAT IS PAID FOR

That first visit to an obstetrician's office is often discouraging to women. Three out of twenty prospective patients, after getting the sermon, take their business elsewhere.

However, whether she is one of the seventeen who remains with the first obstetrician or one of the three who moves on, she will need all the assurance her doctor can give her. This is part of what she is paying for. She is uncomfortable, worried, and beginning to wonder how painful and difficult the delivery will be.

"We tend to think," says the blunt spoken Dr. F., "that bearing a child is so normal and natural for a woman that she can take it in stride, almost casually. If it were all that natural she would eat her afterbirth like animals do and conceive only when in heat."

What she pays for besides reassurance and periodic examination during her nine months is counsel. Some obstetricians are stricter than others on the question of what is ingested by the mother during pregnancy, although recent research increasingly indicates that anything she ingests, even in miniscule amounts, has some effect on the fetus. "It's inevitable," one doctor said. "A mother is supplying the fetus with blood and oxygen and every nutrient that promotes development. She's the *only* source of supply."

There are certain valuable byproducts that derive from a woman's putting herself under the care of an obstetrician.

Most obstetricians try to persuade a mother-to-be to stop smoking. The chances of infants contracting pneumonia or bronchitis in their first year of life are nearly doubled if the mother smokes. However, if a woman is a confirmed smoker the doctor will not succeed too often, for the odds are seven out of ten that she will continue puffing away throughout her pregnancy.

The percentages on heavy drinkers are somewhat more encouraging. Almost one out of two will moderate their consumption of alcohol or give it up for the duration of the pregnancy.

Well they might. "Fetal alcohol syndrome" can be as compelling a reason for ending a pregnancy as the more feared genetic defects. Typical physical signs of the fetal alcohol syndrome: smallness at birth, slowness in gaining weight, and cheekbones, eye slits and heads that are disproportionately small even for the baby's size.

Of course, if a pregnant woman is on barbiturates, marijuana or hard drugs, her obstetrician will warn her to get off them. Many obstetricians make this a condition of accepting such a patient.

Says Dr. F.: "I know that extensive research involving hard drugs, marijuana and birth defects is going on—particularly in Britain, Canada, and the U.S.—and that we still don't have all the answers. But I also know the kind of babies I have delivered from women who were heavy smokers of pot or hash, or who regularly took the so-called uppers and downers. To coin a cliché, it ain't pretty. Brain damage, sometimes actual body impairment, is far too common. So I tell my patients on their first visit that drugs of any kind are out. It's true a woman will sometimes need drugs during pregnancy, but I'll be the one to prescribe them—and then only when absolutely necessary."

Rapidly accumulating evidence proves that when a pregnant woman is, or becomes, addicted, her baby will also be born an addict. TV reporter Geraldo Rivera did an alarming documentary on this subject, "The Littlest Junkie." He says there were an estimated two thousand cases of addicted newborn infants last year, but that no one knows how many other cases went unidentified at private hospitals.

A number of the infant addicts won't survive. "They have to go through withdrawal, just like adults," Rivera says. "When they're not treated, the death toll is around ninety-three percent. Even when doctors attempt treatment, thirty-four percent still die. The tremors, the diarrhea, the vomiting and the convulsions are just too much when the addict weighs only six or seven or eight pounds."

Paying the obstetrician an exorbitant fee does not insure the birth of a living child. Despite the advances of modern obstetrical medicine, approximately 15 percent of conceptions end in miscarriage and approximately one out of every four women will encounter a serious problem during pregnancy. Some of these problems endanger her life and that of the fetus—such as the edema or water retention common in kidney disorders, liver diseases, and many organic infections.

Stillbirth is far less common now than even a few decades ago. Improved diagnostic techniques and the general increase of medical knowledge have played their part in keeping down the number of babies who die in the womb. In most miscarriages, the fetus is discharged from the womb before it's developed to a point at which the doctor can tell why it did not develop normally, but there is still the unexplainable tragedy in which a big, perfectly developed baby is born dead.

The magnitude of the tragedy for the parents obscures the fact that the obstetrician, a businessman, will neither cancel nor reduce his customary fee. A lawyer may offer his services on a contingent fee basis—if you don't collect, neither does he—and manufacturers in a broad spectrum of other businesses will refund a customer's money if the product or service is unsatisfactory; a writer or a composer or a painter will expend his best professional efforts and receive no compensation if the final result is deemed unworthy. But when a doctor fails, the blame goes to God. The bill goes to the patient as usual.

On the other hand, obstetricians work at night—and don't collect overtime.

Most labor pains begin at night. Seventy percent of patients begin labor after the sun goes down, and 50 percent of deliveries occur between 6:00 and 9:00 A.M.

We asked obstetricians why. A Seattle-based doctor found the answer in psychology: "The day's work is done and the other kids are in bed, her husband's at home and a sitter's available, so why not throw a few things in a bag and head for the hospital? Her contractions are so far apart there's not much danger of delivery before morning, but it's more convenient and dramatic to go at night."

A Los Angeles obstetrician doesn't agree: "I think it's purely physical. She's most likely had a busy day, housework, shopping or whatever, and she's exhausted herself to a point that just naturally induces labor."

There's no doubt that labor pains starting at night present a major problem to the harassed obstetrician. Doubtless this is the reason that the number of women receiving induced labor has increased so sharply during the past decade.

"I see nothing wrong with inducing labor if the pregnancy has proceeded normally," states the Los Angeles ob. "It may be more convenient for her or her husband to have the baby at, say, midnight on Tuesday instead of ten o'clock Wednesday morning. It is better for the hospital to be able to schedule its delivery rooms with some degree of certainty. And it's certainly better for me."

What is left out of this summary is as interesting as what is included. Omitted is any mention of those parents, who must be in a majority, who would prefer to have their baby born at nature's prompting rather than the doctor's.

One problem cited frequently by obstetricians who deal with middle- and upper-middle-class patients has nothing to do with the actual birth process. A Portland, Maine, obstetrician put it this way: "It's safe to say that a good percentage of pregnant women are borderline neurotics. They simply can't cope with the stress of carrying and delivering a child, so they take it out on their doctor. They barrage him with phone calls, prolong their appointments in his office, summon him out of bed at night to a false labor and, in the end, if anything goes wrong, file a malpractice suit."

Malpractice is a word that is anathema to the practicing physician. What constitutes malpractice, according to Mr. Webster, is, "criminal neglect or unprofessional treatment of a patient by a doctor; 2, wrong practice or conduct in any official or professional position." Since 1960 the number of malpractice suits filed against physicians and surgeons has risen a spectacular 900 percent!

Doctors say that patients have an unrealistic idea of what medical treatment can accomplish.

"Medicine is not an exact science," says one ob., "and the outcome of a pregnancy may depend on many factors not under a doctor's control. A woman's pelvic structure may not allow for normal procedure, or her cervix may not dilate the required ten centimeters, thereby making surgery or an emergency Caesarean section necessary. In some cases a woman becomes physically ill during pregnancy because her body tends to reject the presence of a fetus and can't accomodate it chemically. There are breech births in which the baby is positioned incorrectly in the womb and emerges any way but head first. We can deal with most of these problems, but they do increase the chance of something going wrong. And the doctor gets the blame."

Whatever the reason for the upsurge in malpractice suits, the medical profession is understandably bitter about the phenomenon, for malpractice insurance costs have risen correspondingly. According to Malcolm C. Todd, president of the American Medical Association, about $1.58 of every $10 you pay to your doctor goes to cover his malpractice insurance. And of each dollar awarded in a malpractice suit, only 28 cents finds its way into the plaintiff's pocket. The other 72 cents goes for lawyer fees and court costs.

The average obstetrician now pays about $7,000 a year for $250,000 worth of malpractice insurance. This can go higher if the obstetrician wants more coverage—or if a previous malpractice claim has been filed against him. Insurance costs of $10,000 to $12,000 a year are not uncommon, and doctors who have recent claims against them may pay as much as $20,000 a year. The average physician is sued once every seven years, and the incidence is even higher for certain high-risk specialties.

No one doubts that there are incompetent doctors, some of whom bear distinguished reputations. We asked doctors to tell, in strictest confidence, instances they knew of personally in which there were good grounds for a malpractice suit. We accumulated enough examples to fill another and thicker volume than this one.

There was, for one example, the true story of a high-priced society obstetrician, a handsome man with an active social life. One night he was called away from a cocktail party to an emergency delivery when he was in no condition to do anything but go to bed and sleep it off. The patient had a placenta previa —a condition in which the placenta partially or completely covers the opening of the cervix. The obstetrician clumsily punctured it, causing uncontrollable bleeding. Only prompt action by the intern present in the delivery room saved the mother, but there was no way to save the baby.

Many obstetricians are known by their colleagues to be unqualified, and other doctors cover for them during their deliveries. They have code phrases so that the patient won't guess what is happening. Like: "Doctor, do you mind if I finish up these last few stitches?" Or: "Shall I apply the forceps now, Doctor?"

Most of the physicians we interviewed, however, insisted that genuine malpractice incidents are *statistically* insignificant. They firmly believe most lawsuits are conceived in ignorance and born out of malice and greed. The view is not unbiased, but there's no denying the near-unanimity of the responses.

Dr. F. sums up the general attitude. "The multiplying lawsuits are a manifestation of the get-something-for-nothing syndrome. I know people who exult in how they got so many thousands of dollars in an accident settlement by pretending to a whiplashed neck or a back injury they didn't really have. That's the attitude of those who file malpractice suits. And the result is that right now in the courts doctors are accused of at least twenty times the number of errors they actually make."

A Los Angeles obstetrician had a different view. "I blame it all on inflation. People expect prices to go up for food, cigarettes, liquor, or houses, but they damn the doctor as a profiteer because he raises his fees. So when anything goes wrong, they think this is their chance to get some of their own back. And when a malpractice suit comes to trial, the jury, if not the judge, is completely on the side of the person suing."

Doctors who work mostly in low-income or poverty areas are most affected by the rising cost of malpractice insurance, for they cannot pass on the added expense to their patients. Dr. Carl Goetsch, of the California Medical Association, predicts any further increase in liability premiums will drive these doctors from their practices.

An obstetrician-gynecologist who practices in a low-income area of Oakland, California, confirms this. "I have reached the point where I can't break even financially. My fees are more or less frozen. Eighty percent of my practice consists of Medicaid patients. My insurance payments will go up over three thousand dollars in the coming year. I've seriously got to consider whether I can continue practicing medicine. If I do, I will certainly have to look for patients who can afford to pay better for my services."

MONKEY BUSINESS

There is one problem that obstetricians are very willing to discuss. In fact, they display almost the same fascination with this topic that the physically ill have with their ailments.

If the doctors are to be believed, the phenomenon of "transference" is as common among their patients as among those of psychoanalysts.

Dr. F.'s wife says, "I worked as a doctor's receptionist for five years before I met my husband, and I can tell you that an amazing number of women develop an openly seductive attitude toward their obstetrician. First he becomes a father figure, then a potential lover. I'll wager that half the women my husband treats develop some sort of romantic fixation on him."

A number of our interviews with obstetricians confirm this.

"I shudder when I get one of these women as a patient because I know what I'm in for. It will start out with innuendos and kidding, and progress to covert suggestions and frank invitations. Then the phone calls begin at my office and at home. Sometimes I wonder if my wife really believes me when I tell her I do nothing to encourage these women."

This is a subject on which every doctor we interviewed seemed to have an opinion. Medical men are no different from other males: they like to think about, talk about, dwell upon the possibility that they are the secret object of women's erotic fantasies. The difference is that physicians obscure their own interest in a veil of scientific jargon or rationalizing.

One doctor, obviously of a mystical turn, thought the reason was that women patients believed he was doing "holy work" and revered him for what they considered an almost priestly dedication to his task. He saw himself as a kind of worker of miracles, remarking that "after all, we are bringing life into the world, and what is more marvelous than that?"

Another doctor thinks the reason is "we're always handling their private parts, and not too many men do. Women have been taught ever since they were little girls they shouldn't allow a man to do that unless it was someone they cared for. So when they undress for you and you start looking where you're not supposed to look and touching what you're not supposed to touch, they think it's proper for them to fall in love with you!"

A concluding opinion from Dr. F.: "When you come right down to it, an obstetrician has more to do with the making of the baby than the father. The father spent ten minutes doing his part of the job. The woman has to do hers for nine months, and during all that time who is the man worrying about her, helping her, advising her? The obstetrician. He's also the guy who's going to share the whole final delivery-room trauma with her. Naturally, she considers him as having more to do with her baby than the 'technical' father. A little sperm can't equal all that consideration, nor replace the fact that she knows when it comes down to the wire she's going to be dependent on her doctor, not her husband!"

Just to round out our sampling with a more objective opinion, we consulted a well-known woman psychiatrist. She was willing to speak frankly if her identity was concealed. "Listening to the tapes of these interviews, I can't help being a little suspicious. More than a little, in fact.

"It strikes me that many of the ob.s you interviewed are suffering from what I call countertransference. They are getting ego satisfaction out of telling stories about how their patients fall in love with them. Maybe they really believe it, but I would be inclined to think that in many cases it's their own thing.

"Which of course brings up the question of who chooses to be an ob-gyn man to start with. The choice of specialty is significant. Many choose it because they like women, a healthy reason, I'd say. In that event, though, and when you consider how busy and harassed they claim to be, it must be pretty frustrating not to be able to do much about it. Wouldn't it be perfectly natural for them to fantasize what is not happening to them in reality?

"Add to this the number of ob-gyns who dislike or even hate women, and there must be lots of anti-women types here. They would like to degrade women, talking about them as brainless helpless creatures of ungovernable libidos.

"And how about the lechers and sadists in the field? Obstetrics would be a natural choice for them. The lechers would have a field day, and the sadists could get their kicks hearing women scream during labor. And how would these types tend to describe their experiences? You guessed it.

"On the whole, I wouldn't be surprised if countertransference weren't as plausible an explanation as what they say is going on—and I would certainly like to bet that there isn't as much going on as you've got down on those tapes!"

WHO INVENTED HIM?

It is difficult to determine whether the obstetrician came into being through necessity or invention. Some cynics maintain that all we needed to know about obstetrics was discovered nine months after Eve first ate that apple in the Garden of Eden.

In the nineteenth century there was some press mention of "special" doctors who attended Queen Victoria during her confinements. This immediately created a demand for "special" doctors among those who, while not of royal or even noble birth, had arrived at a station in society in which what was good enough for Queen Victoria was not too good for them. In Europe, this included not only families of the still affluent aristocracy, but newly affluent "commoners," such as the Rothschilds and the Krupps, who were forming a powerful aristocracy of wealth. Why should their heirs be delivered into the world by the gross and clumsy hands of "ordinary" physicians?

The question was no sooner posed in Europe than it was answered in America. Why, indeed, asked the wives of Woolworth, Morgan, Biddle, Astor, Rockefeller, Cabot, Lodge, and Duke. Nor were the wealthy families in the hinterlands to be outdone. By the time World War I began, the "special" doctor was in demand by rich women in Chicago, Omaha, Minneapolis, and Memphis. And on Park Avenue, in Newport and Boston and Philadelphia, a number of doctors who restricted their practice to women in confinement were being openly referred to as "baby doctors."

"There is no man other than Dr. Ruskin I would trust with myself or my baby-to-be," Mrs. Philip Pillsbury wrote in 1912. "He has charm and distinction and respect for my privacy."

During the great shift of population to the West, the shortage of doctors became critical in certain areas. All kinds of inducements were offered, including free homes, horses, and office space. The general practitioner who answered the call was typically a hard-working, undertrained professional who traveled long distances to make house calls, operated without the aid of hospital facilities, and generally had more compassion than competence. In many respects he is one of the few real heroes of the American frontier, but the family of means, especially when contemplating the infant mortality rate of the times, could not be blamed for seeking out a doctor who would offer something "special"—i.e., see the mother-to-be frequently during the course of pregnancy, soothe her alarms, banish her fears, and guarantee that the very latest medical expertise would be available to insure the safe arrival of her baby.

It wasn't until 1920, however, that medical schools and hospitals began to turn out trained "baby doctors," and the new specialty became a fixture in American life. As a nation, we were suffering simultaneously from a doctor shortage and a postwar baby boom. New hospitals and hospital complexes were being built that included delivery rooms, and entire floors were set apart for maternity cases. Here the "special" or "baby" doctor worked in antiseptic sanctity. During this period, the obstetrician-gynecologist was created: the "baby" doctor and "women's" doctor merged into one.

As with any specialization within the medical field, fees became the distinguishing mark of the trade. In 1900, $150 was paid to a "baby" doctor instead of a customary $60 to the family doctor. The fees didn't change appreciably until 1945, when the ratio climbed to a mere $200 vs. $90.

There were notable exceptions: John Jacob Astor paid $2,000 for the birth of his eldest son, and Sarah Delano Roosevelt paid $850 for the birth of Franklin D. Often, however, this was largesse from grateful parents, a revealing sidelight on the status of the doctor who visited the homes of the rich. The money paid to him was in a sense a gift from the upper class to a servant for a job well done rather than a fee charged by a professional person in accordance with the standards set by his profession. That tells us a good deal about how social America looked at the "professionals" in that day. Doctors, including obstetricians, still charge variable fees, but the charge is decided by them and usually discussed with the patient beforehand. A "baby doctor" would not for a moment consider the payment he receives to be a mark of gratitude from his social superior.

The simple justification for the additional fee charged by the "special" or "baby" doctor—whose increased dignity and status entitled him to the impressive designation of "obstetrician"—was that he would make the whole process of birth easier for his patients. Sedatives and sleeping pills were routinely prescribed for any patient who complained of being "nervous." Anesthetics, ranging from ether to spinal or cervical blocks, began to be administered, even when a woman's contractions were as much as ten minutes apart. If a patient developed, during pregnancy, a kidney infection or a cold, the miracle-performing wonder drugs (such as sulfanilimide and sulfathiozole, then penicillin, then antihistamines) were freely prescribed. Everything possible was done to insure that the Modern American Mother would sail through a smooth pregnancy and an anesthetized birth. Everything possible was done to insure that neither Mother nor Father would regret for a single instant the choice of a skilled specialist over the perfunctory services of a mere general practitioner.

The first serious threat to this idyllic arrangement came when the Lamaze Natural Childbirth techniques first became known in this country. Dr. Grantly Dick-Read's best-selling book, *Childbirth Without Fear,* captured the imagination of hundreds of thousands of American women, many of whom came to the conclusion that having a baby might just possibly be an experience worth remembering.

"There's a big difference," an obstetrical nurse in Ashland, Wisconsin, remarked, "between babies born to a mother who hasn't been doped up and one who's practically knocked out of the scene. The mother who isn't drugged is likely to have a baby that has a better color, cries louder, responds better, and seems just plain healthier, both at the time of birth and later when it's taken home."

The Natural Childbirth movement did not directly oppose the obstetrician, nor his methods, but they did subtly undercut the patient's faith in anesthetics and sedatives at the time of birth. They claimed that a woman who had exercised properly during pregnancy, who learned breathing techniques to apply at labor, and knew how to push with her contractions, could both give and experience birth with no difficulty.

This new challenge to the obstetrician might be compared to a well-established product suddenly being challenged in the marketplace by an upstart newcomer. Entrenched in public favor, neither the obstetricians nor the AMA bothered to take a direct stand against Natural Childbirth. They loftily ignored it. Their attitude is best summed up by an obstetrician's remark, "If a woman wants to have it Natural, fine. I'll go along as far as she wants to go. But I know from experience that she won't go very far before she wants the pain killed."

Another challenge to the omniscience and infallibility of the obstetrician appeared. In Europe and America, scientists discovered that many drugs intended to make childbirth easier for the mother were actually causing physical and mental damage to the baby. The obstetrician's right to make childbirth "easy" at such dreadful cost was questioned. The tragedy of thalidomide became a worldwide scandal.

Still another challenge comes from within the medical profession itself. A controversial French doctor, Frederick Leboyer, begins with the premise that babies have been entering the world much too abruptly and violently. He believes that what obstetricians consider a "normal" delivery is actually a very traumatic experience for a newborn infant.

In order to reduce the impact, or trauma, for baby, Dr. Leboyer insists on dim lights in the delivery room. Everyone must speak in whispers. In the womb, Dr. Leboyer points out, all sounds are absorbed and muffled by amniotic fluid, so when a baby is born, the sound level appears to it as explosive.

Instead of immediately cutting the umbilical cord and slapping the child to compel its first breath, Leboyer lets the infant slowly become accustomed to a new way of breathing. By not cutting the umbilical cord at once, he allows the infant two ways of breathing, for it still receives oxygen from the blood coursing through the cord.

He places the infant on its mother's abdomen. "It is considered normal to put a baby into cloth wraps straightaway. But, after having been in such a slippery environment, the contact with clothes for the infant is as if he were being scorched. I put the newborn on the mother's abdomen, naked, since only skin is alive and sensitive enough to be bearable."

Finally, the newborn baby is immersed in a lukewarm bath. Water temperature is a little above body temperature, and the infant is immersed up to its neck. In this way, it experiences some of the liquid weightlessness it used to know while floating in amniotic fluid. Then he is taken out, dried, and wrapped in a warm cloth.

Dr. Leboyer claims this gentle way of introducing baby to the world makes a difference in its later physical and emotional development.

The actual development of babies delivered by the method is now under study in France, to test this claim.

After three decades of unchallenged reign, not only the obstetrician, but his time-honored methods, are being seriously questioned.

MOTHER SPEAKS OUT

In the course of researching this book, we interviewed a total of eighty-five new mothers. One question we invariably asked was their opinion of their obstetrician.

Twenty-eight women were enthusiastic about their ob.s and apparently pleased with everything from their initial visit to the birth process to the fee paid. Fifty-seven women rendered negative judgments. On a scale ranging from mild to vehement, they resented the ob.'s perfunctory or impersonal treatment, or blamed him for a traumatic experience of one kind or another. Most had complaints about the impossibly high cost of having a baby.

Christine Johnston is one of the latter. She gave birth to a 7-pound boy at 11:40 P.M. on April 29, 1973. Her labor was relatively easy as far as pain level and length were concerned, and the baby was healthy.

Today she is furious. "It cost me a thousand and ten dollars to have my baby. That includes charges for the obstetrician, the hospital, the anesthetist, and everything else including the few aspirin they gave me. My husband is a cab driver. We can't afford to have another baby—much as we want one."

The fee charged Christine Johnson is classified as low to moderate by those obstetricians who charge variable fees. Although the charges are discussed with each patient beforehand, the obstetricians were notably reluctant to discuss the variation in fees with an outsider. They treated the subject with the delicacy of men playing croquet with live bombs.

"I wouldn't want any of my patients to get the idea that my variable fees include any kind of extra services for people who can afford them," one doctor anxiously explained.

A pregnant woman in a maternity ward expressed what must be a common apprehension. "Here I am, having a baby, shoved into an ugly white smockish outfit and some resident's cap over my beautiful hair, and I'm wondering if Jackie Onassis didn't have a more attractive arrangement when she was having her babies. I'd sort of like to feel she didn't, even if she can pay more, because my baby is going to be just as important as hers."

Many women we interviewed had complaints about the brusque and hasty treatment they received. "He made me feel like I was on an assembly line," said a woman in Richmond, Virginia. "If he was so busy, why did he take me as a patient? Every time I came into his office, it was packed to the wallpaper with women in all stages of pregnancy. I never got to see him at the time my appointment was scheduled; sometimes I waited a whole hour.

"When I finally did get in, I had questions that I never got a chance to ask. He was always too busy. I climbed in and out of those darn stirrups and that was about it.

"I tried calling him once. It was an emergency, I thought. I was spotting and I couldn't keep anything on my stomach. When his answering service finally had him call me, he sounded irritated. He asked me what I'd done before the spotting, and I told him I'd hung draperies. Then he got really mad and told me to stay in bed and if I wasn't better in four hours to call him back. He didn't explain anything. I called a friend of mine who'd had a baby last year and all she did was laugh and say it wasn't unusual for this to happen in the fourth month.

"At least he could have told me *that* much! I almost went crazy, figuring I was miscarrying or something."

Most women think they do not get the time and attention they pay for. They wish the doctor would treat not only their physical condition but their mental and psychological state. Perhaps they are asking too much. Obstetricians are only human. Many are simply not capable of this kind of understanding and compassion. They can deliver a woman of a baby but not of her anxieties.

The one central obligation the obstetrician must never shirk, in the opinion of women we interviewed, is to be present with her at the time of delivery.

Sandra, who lives in Westminster, Illinois, had a normal pregnancy without incident, and was satisfied with the attention she received from her ob. When it was almost time, he warned her that she might "go fast" after labor started, due to her generous pelvic structure and to a noticeable dilation that had begun in the seventh month.

On a Wednesday morning, promptly at eleven o'clock, her contractions began. She phoned her obstetrician and the nurse told her to have her husband bring her to the hospital. The nurse said she'd locate the doctor quickly.

On Wednesday afternoons, her obstetrician always played golf at the Westminster Country Club. But on this Wednesday, the course had been appropriated for a professional tournament and regular members were barred from the greens. The ob. neglected, however, to inform his secretary that he had gone to play at another club.

A short chronology of what followed: Sandra arrived at the hospital at 11:40 A.M. Her baby arrived at 4:45 P.M. And the obstetrician arrived at the hospital to congratulate Sandra upon her fine baby boy at 7:55 P.M.!

"Four hundred seventy-five dollars he charged me, and he couldn't be found the very day he predicted I'd deliver!" she exploded. "Believe me, I wouldn't let my husband pay him the last seventy-five dollars I owed. He threatened to turn it over to a collection agency, but in the end he never did."

Rachel, who lives in San Francisco, is particularly bitter about the way she was handled.

"I suppose you'd call my ob. a society baby doctor. He charges the highest fees and he delivers the best-heeled ladies in the Bay area, but that isn't why I went to him. I was told he was good, maybe even the best, and I felt I might need the best because I've got hardly any pelvis at all.

"Anyway, I became pregnant in January and went to him. No getting around it, I felt I was getting the best possible care. He put me on some exercises he thought might widen my pelvis, and assured me that he'd be able to tell, three weeks before the baby was due, whether or not my pelvis would widen far enough and if I'd dilate properly so I could have a normal birth without any cutting." She blushed. "You see, my husband and I have such good sex—I mean, we fit so well together—that I didn't want my vagina stretched out of shape if I was going to have a difficult birth. I'd prefer a Caesarean section to any cutting or stitching.

"The thing he didn't do was tell me he was taking his vacation from September first to twentieth, completely covering the time when I was supposed to deliver. I was due on the tenth. I didn't learn about this until late August when I came for my appointment—I had a weekly appointment by then—and the nurse gave me a list of five obstetricians and asked me which one I wanted to deliver my baby!

"I got hysterical. I mean, there I was, three weeks away from delivery, with an acute pelvic structure problem, and she's telling me another doctor is going to take over! I'd paid for the best and I was going to end up, when it counted, with second-best! If he'd told me when I came to him that he'd be on vacation when I terminated my pregnancy, I'd have taken another ob., probably one just as good. But there I was, with *my* doctor knowing all the details of my case—intimately, to say the least—and at the last minute some other doctor would take over, someone who'd probably use forceps (I hate the idea of forceps!) the minute I passed out!

"Well, they calmed me down, and my doctor apologized for the bad timing but said he had to take his vacation then to enroll his kids in a boarding school in Switzerland. He told me to come in the next Monday and he'd have the other ob., the one I picked, with him to make a thorough examination, and he'd pass on all the details, the vagina and forceps and all that. I left his office still angry, but there was nothing I could do about it.

"The new doctor was all right—but it wasn't the same. I only had two weeks with him to really let him get to know me and my problems, how uptight I was about the things I mentioned. And he had sort of a distant personality so I never felt as though I got to know him.

"I had my baby—a six-pound girl—by Caesarean section. I had terrible pains, and the cervix wouldn't dilate. I wouldn't let them give me drugs because I didn't want to pass out and have them stretch me out of shape or cut me. Later the nurse in the delivery room told me I'd have had a pretty easy birth, only a few stitches, if I'd let them give me a cervical block and waited another half hour. But the doctor I depended on wasn't there, and I really couldn't take any chances."

A more bizarre case involves a woman we will call Charlotte Ames. In a large midwestern city, her doctor—we'll call him Clayton Smith—is known as (a) the most "exclusive" ob. in town, and (b) a temperamental martinet who often will reduce a head nurse to tears in seconds. Several years ago he established a definite rule: no other doctor, or any member of the hospital staff, is to deliver one of "his" babies.

Charlotte is a soft-spoken brunette, perhaps thirty, obviously well-to-do. "I suppose we paid a lot for Dr. Smith, more than we should have, but my husband always has to go first class. I liked Dr. Smith very much. He was a very brusque man, but very much like my father. I followed his orders, which were simple—the diet, rest, some exercise, moderation in liquor and drugs. I even quit smoking.

"I started into labor at eight o'clock on a Saturday night—I remember that because Doreen, our housekeeper, was off, and I was loading the dishwasher when the pains started. My husband called Dr. Smith's answering service and took me right downtown to the hospital.

"When I got to my room the pains were twenty minutes apart and not really much worse than menstrual cramps. Everything proceeded normally; I was treated like a queen because I was Dr. Smith's patient. Nurses and residents came around every few minutes.

"By eleven o'clock the pains were five minutes apart, and even though nobody said anything I could tell everyone was nervous, especially the nurses. I heard a lot of whispering out in the hall, and finally a resident and two nurses came in and told me they'd take me to a labor room where I'd be more comfortable and closer to the delivery room when Dr. Smith arrived.

"It was odd, but that was the first time I was aware that Dr. Smith wasn't around. I asked the resident and he told me Dr. Smith was probably en route to the hospital. My husband was pretty nervous by then, but I told him not to worry—the baby was bound to show up even if the doctor didn't.

"By the time they wheeled me into the labor room, the contractions were just a couple of minutes apart and I was beginning to push. The resident looked under the sheet and he went white. There was Muzak being piped into the room, so I guess he and the nurses thought I couldn't hear them when he muttered, 'Christ, I can see the head!' Then a nurse said, 'We'd better give her a shot to hold back labor,' and the other nurse went away for a few seconds and came back with a syringe, and just when they put the needle in my arm my water broke. Some had come out before, but this was like a flood.

"I don't remember much after that. I guess I was out most of the time. When I came to I was in my room and my husband looked awful and the nurses were hovering the way they do when something's wrong. Before I could even ask what had happened, my husband took my hand and told me the baby had been born dead. I cried, quietly at first, but then it hit me: that baby had been alive in me, alive coming out of me in the labor room. How *could* it have been born dead?

"It took a few days to find out what happened. They had killed the baby, suffocated it, by holding me in an inert state of labor until Dr. Smith could get to the hospital from his home, about fifty miles away. The staff was too terrified to deliver one of his patients. So, in effect my baby died to avoid one of his tantrums.

"I told you that my husband goes first class. Well, the hospital got a first-class lawsuit filed against it!"

In this case, the hospital and the on-duty physician seem to be at fault for the tragedy. Though a lawsuit is pending, attempts are being made by the hospital to settle out of court. Legally, Dr. Smith is not involved. The phone in his car was not working that day and he did not learn of Charlotte's confinement until she was taken to the labor room. He did *not* give a direct order to delay birth.

More publicized, and in some respects more tragic, is the case of Mrs. Emery Deutsch. Her baby was born in New York's fashionable Doctor's Hospital. Her obstetrician (equally fashionable) was Dr. Emanuel Klempner.

Mrs. Deutsch started labor that Sunday morning, and her doctor ordered her, by phone, to go to a private room in the hospital. She complied, and at four o'clock he examined her. He told her that birth was several hours away and that he would go to his apartment a few blocks away to take a nap, returning when labor progressed to the point where a nurse should call.

It is impossible to predict absolutely the course of labor or the precise moment of birth, and Mrs. Deutsch progressed more quickly than was anticipated. Before the doctor could rush back to the hospital, the baby's head started to emerge. She claimed that the obstetrical nurses applied pressure to hold back birth until the doctor arrived.

Hospital records put the time of birth at 6:47 P.M. Mrs. Deutsch had been wheeled to the labor room, with pains only three minutes apart and birth imminent, at 6:25. Dr. Klempner's arrival is estimated at 6:32.

The baby, a boy, was born mentally retarded. The Deutsches sued and, after a complete airing of the minute-by-minute events, a jury awarded them $280,000.

Has the obstetrician made, in effect, a business contract with his patient that *guarantees* the care she needs during pregnancy, no matter how far beyond normal anticipation that care may go? Does that contract include the climactic moment of birth?

Not necessarily. An obstetrical nurse in Atlanta says, "The panic most women go through when their ob. doesn't show up is incredible. It's hysteria on top of hysteria. They'll try to hold up on their contractions, they'll fight every minute of the normal birth process. Sometimes they even hurt themselves, and the baby, trying to hang on until their doctor comes. She's gotten so dependent on him that she believes he's *got* to be there or things will go wrong.

"If the patient was told, simply and honestly, that half the firemen and policemen in the city are just as capable as an ob. of delivering a baby, she wouldn't go through the 'Where's my doctor?' trauma. After the seventh month, it doesn't matter who actually does the delivery because nine times out of ten the birth is totally without complications. In the delivery room we're ready, whether the doctor is or not. Any intern, any obstetrical nurse, and certainly the resident physician, is fully qualified to deliver a baby. There's the dilated cervix, there's the baby's head, here are our hands. Bing, bing, bing.

But no. I don't know if it's ego or carelessness or the don't-give-a-damn attitude just about everyone has these days, but the ob. has her convinced that only *he* can see her through birth. He pulls this psychological act with her to give the illusion that he's earning his fat fee."

The obstetrician likes to give the impression to his more affluent patients that he is working out of a cave in Delphi. But when a patient does not have money, his services quickly become less essential, not to say superfluous.

When Mrs. Shirley Jean Abrams of Latta, South Carolina, became pregnant, her family owed the obstetrician, Dr. Dan F. Moorer, $350 for previous treatment. On the day she was ready to deliver, Dr. Moorer would not order Mrs. Abrams admitted to the Marion County Memorial Hospital. And the hospital refused her admittance because obstetrical cases are not considered emergencies.

With the birth of her baby impending, she was driven around for seven hours in an ambulance by Jamie Mozingo of the Marion County Rescue Squad. Mozingo took her to twenty other doctors, but none would order her admitted to the hospital for delivery.

Finally, with instructions from a midwife, Mozingo himself delivered Mrs. Abrams of a seven-pound, two-ounce girl. Mother and child survived the ordeal in good shape.

Dr. Dan F. Moorer justifies his refusal to deliver the baby because of an outstanding bill. "If I started taking cases for free, I'd have five hundred in a month."

Barbara Seaman, author of *Free and Female,* says emphatically, "about fifteen percent of obstetricians are very nice, another fifteen percent are tolerable, but the rest are bad." Interviewed in Los Angeles, the outspoken Ms. Seaman, who is also the child-care and education editor for a woman's magazine, *Family Circle,* adds that, compared to most physicians, obstetricians are stupid. One factor that contributes to their stupidity, she says, is that though their patients are women, most of the textbooks they read are written by men and contain such non-illuminating passages as "The traits that compose the core of the female personality are feminine narcissism, masochism and passivity."

"Is it any wonder," she asks, "that most obstetrician-gynecologists believe women are just silly creatures with a lot of psychosomatic complaints who are not to be taken seriously?" She refers doubters to the advertisements in medical journals that ob.s read. "Even the ads for tranquilizers show shrewish-looking women and say, in effect, 'Doctor, here's how to get her off your back or off her husband's back. Just shoot her up with our product and she'll shut up.' "

Ms. Seaman even has doubts about the kind of men who go into obstetrics and gynecology:

"I have yet to go to a gynecological meeting where every other paper presented doesn't start with some sort of dirty joke about women. You probably know the kind of guy in school who was called Dirty Eddie, who's very smart but who's always looking at dirty pictures. Dirty Eddie ends up in gynecology."

Wouldn't the solution be to have more women obstetricians and gynecologists? Ms. Seaman points out that women medical school graduates are channeled into specialities that are considered "feminine": anesthesiology, psychology and pediatrics. Few women are accepted for surgical specialities—such as obstetrics and gynecology. At best, medical schools are practicing tokenism, she adds.

WHAT'S NATURAL ABOUT IT?

We spoke with the head of a Natural Childbirth Clinic in Oakland, California, an ex-obstetrical nurse who has operated her clinic for fifteen years, enrolling over one hundred couples per year in her classes. She also supervises other independent groups in the Bay area, lectures before Women's Clubs and PTAs, and may be the foremost exponent of Natural Childbirth in the U.S.

"To be brutally frank," she says, "I'd eliminate the obstetrician altogether. He's overpaid, overworked, and unnecessary. He had his day, and now it's high time his medical training and skills were transferred to areas of research and treatment and surgery that need him. My God, if all the doctors who become ob.s in this country had turned their attention to cancer, we'd have cured it by now.

"When a woman gets pregnant, she can go to a regular doctor, a general practitioner, to make sure of blood types, blood pressures, organic health, all the metabolism stuff. Then she can check with him maybe three times during those nine months. At the most, that's twenty dollars a visit including everything. Total: sixty dollars.

"Meanwhile, as soon as she knows she's pregnant, she enrolls with her husband—who doesn't have to come to all the meetings—in a Natural Childbirth class. There she'll learn everything she needs to know about the course of pregnancy and the process of birth and then some. That's seventy-five dollars.

"While she's in the class, we'll arrange for a midwife to counsel her and to attend her at birth. That, at the outside, is one hundred dollars. She ends up spending a grand total of two hundred thirty-five dollars as opposed to the much larger fee the ob. would have charged. She's had ten times the attention the ob. would have given her, ten times the assurance and reassurance, and her baby is delivered by a midwife she's gotten to know and trust."

A Seattle obstetrician-gynecologist rebuts this: "My complaint with the Natural Childbirth people is that they just don't tell the truth. In effect, they lead a woman to believe that childbirth is a routine thing. It isn't. And the trauma of discovering that will last her the rest of her life.

"It's time to get a few facts on the line. The American woman is a pampered creature. She has her home appliances, her quick and easily prepared foods, her sprays and powders and lipsticks and skin conditioners. Our society has made her a pet pussycat, and she knows it. And she's guilty about the easy life she has compared to her parents and grandparents. That's why the Natural Childbirth thing appeals to her. She thinks she's getting back to real basics. I'm not saying she doesn't get something good out of it—the attitudes they teach may help her during pregnancy, the exercises are fine, the breathing techniques very sound. And the rapport she establishes with her husband during the rather trying pregnancy period is perhaps the biggest plus of all.

"But—and this is the important but—she is misled into believing that the labor contractions are going to be no worse than menstrual cramps. She thinks if she grits her teeth and breathes right, it will be over and the baby will be born with no more trouble than having a tooth extracted.

"Baloney! The pains are far worse than she bargained for. By the time the contractions are three or four minutes apart, she's likely to want anything from a general anesthetic to a paracervical block to put her out of her misery. It's not fun anymore. And if her poor husband is unlucky enough to be in the delivery room with her, he'll get the blame for having got her into such a mess."

All but two physicians we interviewed were opposed to Natural Childbirth, most of them regarding it as a noble concept that simply doesn't work.

A doctor who emphatically favors it is Robert A. Bradley, author of *Husband-Coached Childbirth* (Harper and Row), who has taught Natural Childbirth for more than a quarter century. He believes that husbands ought to be in the "birth room" (he objects to the term "delivery room"). The doctor even provides a "daddy stool" on which the husband sits wearing a white intern's coat.

Dr. Bradley coaches young mothers in exercises to ease the experience of childbirth, and gives the husbands detailed instructions on how to help their wives during pregnancy and later in the "birth room." He is convinced that the event of birth provides a kind of fulfillment for a marriage and should be shared as fully as possible.

And he's so confident his "natural" methods work that he presses nurses into service to start taking pictures of the new threesomes at the moment of birth. The pictures all show very happy mothers and proud fathers.

Dr. T. Berry Brazelton, an outspoken pediatrician and a recognized authority who has written several best-selling books, put himself on record that "In our medicated society we have eradicated some of the pain and anxiety, but I'm afraid we have eradicated more of the excitement and joy. Pregnancy, labor and delivery are thought of as essentially a disease. . . . As a result, the anxiety and fear and pain are medically treated as if they were evil and destructive symptoms."

"I'm not against Natural Childbirth per se," says our Seattle ob. "Anything that makes childbirth more tolerable is a boon to anyone. But I object to a couple paying seventy-five to one hundred fifty dollars to be told they should ignore much of the advice I give them as part of my fee." Nor does he agree with allowing husbands to "help" in the delivery. "When the woman starts having contracting pains that make her worst menstrual period seem like a hangnail, hubby is there to mop her brow, but they're both angry and frightened. She refuses the demerol which would make the pain a lot more tolerable, and when things get more intense she won't accept a paracervical block to spread both sides of the cervix to aid dilation. So she suffers unnecessarily, and her husband too, all because some Natural Childbirth counselor assured them that birth would be as natural for her as for Daisy the cow out in pasture having her fifth calf. Usually when the pains get really bad, I'm able to convince my patient to take the demerol shot and the paracervical block, both of which are harmless aids to safe birth. But by then a lot of pain has been needlessly endured."

Back to Oakland and to our Natural Childbirth lady for a reply: "There's beauty in birth, even in the pain of it. Nothing worthwhile ever comes along without involving pain. We try to teach the mother-to-be to accept the pain as natural, as nature's way of introducing a new life to the world. We don't want instruments and shots and knives to interfere if they can be avoided. Ninety-nine times out of a hundred they *can* be avoided.

"Also, we teach her husband to be a help, to stay with her through the process of birth, to understand what is going on and to do everything he can to suffer it through with her. After all, he's responsible too.

"We put in nine months of conditioning to take the fear out of having a baby, to normalize the whole procedure to the point where the mother will become like an Italian peasant woman who has her baby in the field and goes back to work. And what happens? The average ob. flashes a condescending smile when a woman mentions she's attending a Natural Childbirth clinic. He doesn't come right out and tell her she's wasting her time, but he's so patronizing he begins to destroy her confidence. He warns her that her husband will not be able to take the delivery room scene. He'll faint or throw up or simply run out on her at the crucial moment.

"Then he plants doubt in her mind about her ability to go through Natural. It's easy to scare anyone when you're a doctor talking about a subject like pain. If she still wants to try it, then at her last appointment he tells her how much this or that type of shot or medicine will ease her labor and dilate her automatically so she won't have to go through 'torture.' In other words, if she follows his advice, she can have the baby as easy as mixing up a Betty Crocker cake mix. If she doesn't, it's straight to the rack and the stake.

"Okay, maybe she gets to the labor room in good shape. But that's where the months of good, healthy Natural Childbirth conditioning are shot to hell. When the contractions get rough, all she can remember is what the doctor said about easing her pain. If the ob. is there with her, he makes the point again.

She's in no condition to argue at that moment. So, wham, she takes the shot and she's half out of it when that thing of beauty, childbirth, comes to pass. The ob. and the hospital have won again.

"Like I say, it makes me mad. We've ended up doing only one tenth as much for that couple as we could because the ob. didn't want to spend an extra fifteen minutes with her during birth and because the hospital, no matter what they tell you, doesn't want the delivery room cluttered up with a husband.

"The truth is, the ob. is redundant. He should disappear the way of the dodo.

"Birth *is* beautiful."

MIDWIVES AND OTHER WITCHES

In Santa Cruz, California, a young husband telephoned the Birth Center, where a group of seven women offered midwife assistance. Midwives are forbidden to make home deliveries in California, but the young husband pleaded that his wife was in labor and needed help at once.

Two women from the Birth Center responded to the call. They discovered that the "husband and wife" were actually special investigators for the California Department of Consumer Affairs. The two young women were arrested and charged with practicing medicine without a license.

The constitutionality of the statute under which the women were charged is currently being challenged, and attorneys on both sides predict that the issue will ultimately reach the Supreme Court.

"Birth is normal," said one of the women arrested. "It doesn't need drugs and it does need equipment. It's not a disease. We're only there to aid nature."

Anne Flower Cumings, an attorney for the accused women, said the case symbolizes the opposition that midwives encounter from the medical profession. "It's because of money, money, money. In the vast majority of cases, births attended by midwives are not dangerous. And when they are, they can be separated out. Nobody wants to hurt anyone."

State Senator Anthony C. Beilenson of Los Angeles, who sponsored a bill legalizing midwifery, believes that licensed nurse-midwives are less expensive and more accessible to the estimated ten thousand women in California who each year give birth without receiving prenatal care.

But Dr. Thomas Elmendorf, past president of the California Medical Association, warns: "We're aware that normal childbirths can be performed without problems and that taxi drivers, policemen, and husbands can help in the delivery. The trouble is that too often you don't know you're going to have a problem until you're into the problem itself. And then it's too late."

So the dispute continues, while the gap increases between the hospital and medical costs of childbirth, and the parents' ability to pay. Today, only middle- and upper-middle-class women can afford to pay for an obstetrician. Only 51 percent of the approximately three million babies born each year are delivered by obstetricians. The rest are delivered by general practitioners, residents, interns, and "others."

Each year our medical schools turn out fewer obstetricians (only 6 percent of the number of new doctors), and hospitals report that 15 to 20 percent of their ob-gyn residencies are unfilled.

Soon there won't be enough obstetricians to go around even if you could afford to pay for them.

One might wonder why, under the circumstances, there is still so much opposition to the nurse-midwife. Is it really because we have, and wish to maintain, the highest standards of health care?

When Dr. Louis M. Hellman was chairman of the obstetrics department at State University of New York Medical School, he decried "the simplistic assumption that our maternity care is good simply because our maternal death rate is low and because we obstetricians may be doing a good job personally . . . If we had equalled Norway's decline in baby deaths, some twenty-five thousand more of our babies might have been saved."

In Norway, 99 percent of births are attended by midwives.

THE PATIENTS TESTIFY

We asked many patients how they regarded the services of nurse-midwives.

Mrs. Carolyn McNab, thirty-four, of Westbury, Connecticut, gave a typically enthusiastic reply. "They are more concerned, more compassionate, and they ask more questions. You can be more frank with them because they're women and they understand. You're not just another thousandth person. A male doctor feels you're just another bitchy woman."

An unmarried actress, twenty-eight, of Hollywood, who had switched from an obstetrician: "No matter how good the professional quality of a doctor's service, it doesn't mean anything if the emotional support isn't there. What I like is the personal approach here at the prenatal clinic. In my obstetrician's office I felt like a human cipher. There were signs on the wall: Take A Cup, Get Urine, Be Seated Until Your Name Is Called. The receptionist asked if

I had my pink card with me. I had a feeling I was just something ready to be folded, stapled, stamped—and put away into a filing cabinet until I was ready to deliver."

The California Medical Association and the State Board of Examiners do not believe that the average woman is informed enough to judge the quality of medical care. They continue to believe that midwifery is a step backward.

"It's throwing out the window all the new advances in medicine," says an examiner for the State Board. "The most dangerous hours in an infant's life are the ones he spends being born. Even in what seem to be routine deliveries, seven out of a thousand babies die during labor. And the Lord only knows how many more suffer brain damage or oxygen insufficiency during passage down the birth canal. A qualified obstetrician working in a hospital with the latest equipment can help some of those infants.

"Take a simple yet marvelous thing like fetal monitoring. Less then ten years ago fetal electrocardiograms were unsatisfactory. They were just electrodes placed on the mother's abdomen. Then they developed a method in which the obstetrician inserts a half-inch silver electrode on a thin wire right through the cervix and onto the infant's scalp. That fetal monitoring system—and the newer methods now coming into use—alerts doctors to problems in delivery. And then he can do something about it. If everything else fails, he can deliver the baby by Caesarian. Can a midwife do that?"

"Maternal mortality is now practically zero in this state," adds a spokesman for the California Medical Association, "and newborn-infant mortality has been reduced from about twenty per thousand live births to about fourteen per thousand in the past five years. As professionals, we have to recommend what we think is the highest quality care. An individual has to make the judgment of whether to pay for that high quality or buy something less."

HOSPITAL DUTY

Is it something less?

Unlike the "granny-midwife" of an earlier era, these women are registered nurses trained in midwifery. The training for registered nurses who wish to qualify can run from eight months to two years, and then the candidate must pass the certification exam given by the American College of Nurse-Midwives.

The nurse-midwife is qualified to deliver a baby and also to provide for prenatal care, including vaginal examination, to administer pain-killing drugs and medication for nausea and vaginal infection, etc., and even perform and repair episiotomies (small incisions made between the vagina and the anus to ease the baby's entrance into the world). She also can provide medical care to the newborn, supervise the postpartum period, and disseminate and prescribe birth-control information and devices.

At Roosevelt Hospital in New York, nurse-midwives now perform almost half of the total baby deliveries each day.

"We perform like a team," says one of the five nurse-midwives currently on duty. "And we're invaluable because we understand both the medical and nursing problems. A doctor doesn't have to tell us what to do for a patient. We know what to do as well as he does. It's true we work mostly with the clinic patients. But you'd be surprised how many doctors prefer us to the residents and ask us to be around for the initial examinations during labor.

"We work eight-hour shifts, although we don't have enough staff for around-the-clock duty. We cover midnight to eight A.M., and eight A.M. to four P.M. I'd say more than nine out of ten of our deliveries have no complications at all. No stimulation of labor, hardly any medication. That's a better record than the obstetricians around here. One reason is that when a woman is in labor she wants someone really sympathetic. Then she doesn't need as much anesthetic. And the less anesthetic, the less chance of a forceps delivery and the safer for the child."

Another: "The whole thing isn't just delivering the baby. Most of the time is spent in clinics or talking with the women in labor. Just by talking to them you can help to direct the ante and intrapartum (labor and delivery) periods. And, to be perfectly frank, we're more expert in our examinations than any first-year resident or intern."

A doctor at the hospital: "I suppose a nurse-midwife can get more personally involved with a birth than a man does. The patient senses this. She feels that when the nurse-midwife talks to her, she's hearing from somebody who knows what it's like, and trusts her more. And I notice that women understand the importance of touching. Men doctors are naturally more reluctant to rub a woman's abdomen and back during labor. But the simple touch of a hand on a shoulder can often do more than medicine."

Some hospitals currently employ nurse-midwives simply as regular nurses, others allow them to do clinic practice but don't allow them to do deliveries. Many more hospitals would be willing to hire nurse-midwives if they could find them. The American College of Nurse-Midwives lists only 1,200 members.

"The real problem," said a spokeswoman for the College, "is that there aren't enough schools to train nurses in midwifery. And there aren't enough people qualified to teach. A student has to do twenty deliveries before being certified, and how can she when there aren't enough hospitals and midwives to supervise her?"

In addition to opposition from doctors, the new breed of nurse-midwives also confronts opposition from nurses, who resent taking orders from them. In a way, the nurse-midwife is in a buffer position between the doctors and nurses, the residents and the patients. She has no desire to handle a difficult problem when it arises, but she can, whereas the average nurse has been trained *not* to handle anything. Doctors have warned them that they are not competent to handle certain situations.

"The trouble is, too many RNs are in awe of doctors and accept their every word as if it just came out of a burning bush," says one outspoken nurse-midwife. "They stand by mutely in the face of his cursory examinations, shrug at his inflated bills, sell their souls to please his inflated ego, and worst of all play ignorant of the merest surface information that might tread on the M.D.'s sacred turf."

One young nurse-midwife complains that "I have more responsibility than a nurse, but no real authority. I can do things that are written in our standing orders and that's it. Beyond that, I only make suggestions. But that has its advantages. Even if I got into real trouble in the delivery room, I have an easy out. The doctor is the one in charge. That means he's responsible for what I do. As a result, I only pay about ten dollars a year for malpractice insurance. I can't do anything that anybody would be likely to sue about."

AMONG THE WITCHES

Primitive societies had two tribal members whose official duties consisted of caring for the health of their members. One was the witch doctor and the other the midwife. The former was feared and honored and often ranked second in the tribal hierarchy after the chief. But the midwife, assigned to attend mere women during the "unclean" birth process, was regarded only as a necessary evil. In primitive groups men could not approach women during the menstrual period or at birth (a practice that endures among the Hasidim), and so all pregnant women had to be looked after by other women.

In these early days the midwife was forced to live by herself. She was seldom praised if a birth went well, but always was suspected or condemned when things went badly. She was a convenient scapegoat since no one knew quite where to put the blame for anything.

The midwife began to fare better when some degree of obstetrical knowledge came to the empires of Egypt and the Middle East. The royal or wealthy ladies of ancient Egypt and Sumeria paid handsomely to be guided through a safe delivery.

In Rome she maintained her status and under the Empire was frequently rewarded when an emperor's or senator's child was successfully delivered.

With the fall of the Roman Empire, however, the midwife's fortunes declined. Her social status in Christian Europe fell so low that only the most ignorant and "unwanted" outcast would assume the role.

Her nadir extended from 1300 to 1800, a five-hundred-year span. Uneducated, slovenly, knowing nothing of hygiene, the midwife was deemed unfit for normal social intercourse. She could be put to death as a murderess if a noble birth went badly, or as a witch if the slightest suspicion attached to her conduct. As a profession it was fully as precarious, if less rewarding, than that of a highwayman.

On the other hand, the midwife wasn't much help to anyone. She did nothing to alleviate the pains of labor, for mothers were supposed to bring forth children in sorrow. Pain was sent as a punishment from God and was to be accepted willingly. Under the midwife's ministrations, as late as 1600, infant mortality had "stabilized" at 60 percent and mothers' deaths per delivery at 35 percent.

Dr. Llewellyn Cox, author of *British Medical Practice,* estimates that the practicing midwife made "perhaps eighty pounds per annum from helping with the delivery of mothers placed in her charge, and one hundred forty pounds per annum from advice given and charms sold during the course of pregnancies." In all fairness, considering the results, she should have been paid something by the local undertaker.

Treatment administered by both the midwife and the medieval physician was based as much on superstitition as on any valid concept of what would benefit mother and child. Purgatives, emetics, and bleedings were recommended for women having trouble carrying a child or feeling merely "out of sorts" during the course of pregnancy. Perhaps it is not surprising that, by the twelfth century, doctor and midwife were more feared than revered.

Childbearing and childbirth were conducted under what might be called normal conditions and normal auspices until the mid-nineteenth century. Ironically, it was Queen Victoria who gave the impetus to the change. In 1853, while being delivered of her eighth child, she took chloroform to ease the pain. She was so delighted with the result that she told everyone about it, and for the first time it became quite proper for decent people to talk about such matters and even to write about them. The use of anesthetics was no longer considered "unnatural." Indeed, anyone who dared call it so would have been guilty of treason.

A little more than two centuries earlier, an unfortunate midwife was found guilty of witchcraft for having dared to try to ease the pains of a childbirth. Times, as someone has remarked, change.

A NEW ERA

In the United States, the midwife suffered an ambiguous history. Present from the earliest colonial days, she has delivered untold millions of women during our three-hundred-year history. Only during the Puritan witch hunts of New England was she persecuted, but on the other hand, she was never fully recognized. She continued to practice and flourish, particularly in the rural areas of Kentucky, Tennessee, and Virginia, outposts of the west, and in minority ghetto areas in major cities. Elsewhere, the physician—first the general practitioner, then the obstetrician—was recognized as "the" baby doctor. The midwife was legally classified as "a person who attends, or who bargains, contracts or agrees to attend, any woman at or during childbirth and who is not licensed to practice the healing arts generally or obstetrics in particular."

Through the early decades of the twentieth century, the midwife steadily lost favor in America. "In 1920," the *Encyclopaedia Britannica* reports, "Massachusetts was the only state in which midwives had no legal status; by the mid 1960s they had no status in ten other states." But the mid 1960s saw a startling reversal of this trend. Thousands of women, discouraged with the offhand treatment they received from obstetricians and hospitals, undoubtedly played a part in the midwife's renaissance. The obstetrician himself, faced with an overwhelming workload, no longer opposed the midwife as a threat to his practice. Women's Lib—turning the attention of the American woman toward the intimate details of her own psyche and body—diminished the mystique of the male ob., as did the training of the various Natural Childbirth groups.

Nor can one discount the power of the press. Beginning in 1961, magazines and newspapers literally bloomed with accounts of the midwife's return to favor in most of the Western world.

In Sweden, as almost everyone soon learned, when a woman suspects she is pregnant, she is examined first by a physician. If she has no organic malfunc tion, blood problem, or psychological aberration, she is promptly passed on to a registered midwife who becomes her obstetrician, counselor, and friend during the course of pregnancy and through delivery.

The Swedish midwife's annual income ranges between $9,500 and $15,000 —not markedly below the earnings of the average Swedish doctor. She is thoroughly trained as an obstetrical nurse, an exacting course which includes the equivalent of two full (American) years of medical school. In addition, she employs the Lamaze psychoprophylaxis approach to labor (similar to our Natural Childbirth) which teaches the prospective mother via attitude, breathing orientation, and exercise to have her baby with a minimum of emotional distress and a subjugation of pain.

A logical question arose in the wake of these surprising facts. Why not let the midwife play a similar role here, in a country beset by a shortage of obstetricians and hospital rooms?

UP TO THE MINUTE

Today there are 1,200 nurse-midwives practicing in the U.S. Training is offered at Downstate Kings County Hospital and the Columbia Presbyterian Medical Center in New York; Johns Hopkins Hospital in Baltimore; Yale-New Haven Hospital in New Haven; the remarkable Frontier Nursing Service in Hyden, Kentucky. Similar specialized nurses' training leading to an RN or a B.S. degree is rapidly being introduced in other large hospitals. Duke University's Medical School is the first to offer nurse-midwife training at the college level. It is estimated that by 1975 at least fifty hospitals and forty universities will be offering a specialized course (ranging from eighteen months to two years) that will qualify registered nurse-midwives.

Rose Taylor is an example of a nurse-midwife conducting her own practice in New York City, though she is loosely affiliated with Downstate Kings County.

"I became a nurse-midwife because as an obstetrical nurse I found I was delivering as many babies as an obstetrician. I even considered becoming an ob., not because of the money, but because I envied the way he could establish rapport with his patients over nine months. I say 'could' because he didn't do it often. All the ob.s I knew were too busy."

Now Rose Taylor administers to two hundred patients each year. The patient pays a flat fee of $150, which includes prenatal care and delivery, plus six home visits, and the majority of her patients are blacks or Puerto Ricans who prefer, not just because of their economic strictures but because of tradition, to have their babies at home. A mere 20 percent of her patients go to the hospital for delivery.

"Most people don't realize it, but there have always been midwives in every ghetto area in every city in the U.S. People there can't afford obstetricians and hospitals. The AMA and the individual doctor have always looked the other way because the illegal or extra-legal midwife took a bulk of charity cases off their hands. The trouble is, many of the ghetto midwives lack proper training. God knows what the mortality rate is on the babies they deliver. I don't think we have those statistics. But we should remember that of the 2.1 million babies born annually in the U.S., at least 450,000 arrive *unattended by any licensed physician or nurse-midwife.*

"I think," Rose Taylor concludes, "we're coming to the end of the period in which American women depended solely on the obstetrician. He's gotten too busy to give them the attention they want and his fees are too high. Also, hospitals have become so costly, crowded, and dehumanized that women hate to go there." She shrugged. "Ten years ago the obstetrician was a prestige symbol, like a Cadillac. Now the American woman has grown up. She realizes that the main job of a Cadillac or a Volkswagen is simply to get us where we're going."

There is an increasing tendency among higher-income women to seek out a member of their own sex.

Dora Cahill, a nurse-midwife who has practiced on an outpatient basis for ten years in Manhattan, says: "It used to be that only women who couldn't afford to see a doctor would call me. In my professional capacity, I didn't go inside a middle-class house for years. Lately it's changed. Last year I delivered twelve women who could have afforded any ob. they wanted. They just didn't want any ob."

One reason, cited by most women in our survey, is that nurse-midwives *care* more than a male obstetrician does. This is tacitly conceded even by obstetricians. One doctor told us frankly, "Obstetrics is incredibly boring. To relieve my boredom, I conduct a little race when I deliver a baby boy. I rush to see if I can cut the cord before he has an erection. I win about fifty percent of the time!"

SCHOOLS FOR MIDWIFERY

Today's nurse-midwife is a highly trained specialist, apt to be in her late twenties. She puts in a busy forty-hour week and earns (in New York) between $10,000 and $15,000 per year. A rapidly increasing number of hospitals offer training for nurse-midwives, but a candidate may begin her midwifery course only after obtaining her RN. (To qualify at Columbia University, she must also have a Bachelor of Science degree in nursing.)

In some hospitals the certified midwife is required to take a six-month internship in maternity wards. The average physician delivers ten or twelve babies during medical school and another one hundred in two months of obstetrics during his internship. At most hospitals offering nurse-midwife training, the woman usually performs 120 deliveries by the time her training is completed. At the end of her training, therefore, she actually has more experience than most doctors!

A trainee at the Frontier Nursing Service in Hyden, Kentucky, told us— not resentfully—that only after seven months of rigid instruction and the close observation of twenty deliveries was she deemed qualified to make a delivery herself. And even then she had a supervisor monitoring her.

The Frontier Nursing Service, for a fee of only $150, provides a complete maternity package that includes prenatal care for the mother, delivery in the home or hospital, postpartum care, and five home visits.

Nurse-midwife training programs are scarcely ten years old, but some remarkable results should be noted. At Baltimore City Hospital nurse-midwives instruct medical students in obstetrics. At Downstate Kings County Hospital in Brooklyn they supervise a clinic for teen-age mothers. In at least ten hospitals, nurse-midwives are in charge of family planning clinics.

If the trend continues, another decade may move us much nearer to the kind of medical care in childbearing that is practiced in Norway and Sweden— countries that have the least expensive and safest methods in the civilized world.

NO DRUGS

Avoidance of drugs during pregnancy is part of the credo of the modern nurse-midwife, and although she is permitted to prescribe pain-killing drugs during a delivery, she is less likely to do so than a physician. She relies much more on psychoprophylaxis—the prevention of pain by psychological means.

Simply talking to the patient, explaining what is happening at each stage of labor, offering comfort and sympathy can completely eliminate pain for some women and greatly reduce it in others.

The obstetrician, on the other hand, employs an arsenal of drugs, and is all too likely to use them as the patient's contractions grow stronger, more frequent, and of longer duration. Medication will often start during the first stage of labor, when the cervix starts to dilate and produces low back pain somewhat akin to a menstrual cramp. As the uterus contracts more strenuously, and the abdominal and respiratory muscles operate to expel the baby, the obstetrician turns to pain killers, sedatives, and tranquilizers. In varying degrees these will relax the patient, decrease her awareness of pain, and produce rest or sleep. Sometimes he will combine the pain killer with an amnesic, such as scopolamine, which operates to make her forget any pain she may have felt.

The analgesics do their work by depressing the patient's nervous system. This is no problem for the mother, but can be a problem for her unborn baby. Drugs taken by a pregnant woman can cross by way of the placenta into the bloodstream of her fetus, thereby depressing the respiratory center in the unborn child's brain and causing breathing difficulties.

Like the analgesics, anesthetics can also pass through the placenta. A general anesthetic, which completely eliminates pain by producing unconsciousness, can cause an infant to be born sleepy, and this in turn may make some of his vital responses sluggish at a time when the infant needs to have everything going for him. Even a full-term normal baby may have difficulty shaking off the depressive effect, and a premature baby is in real danger.

Nurse-midwives urge their patients to learn as much as they can about childbirth. "A woman who understands her own anatomy and the physiological process of birth is less likely to experience discomfort or pain than a woman who doesn't know what to expect," one nurse-midwife wrote to our interviewer. "A large measure of the success of 'natural' or 'prepared' birth is due to the extensive prenatal education and attention given to the women patients. . . . Realistically, she cannot expect birth to be painless, but there is equally no reason for the experience to be fraught with suffering. Without undue reliance on analgesics, anesthetics or amnesics, the average woman can certainly expect a safe and relatively comfortable delivery.

"And she will improve the chances of having a normal, healthy baby."

HOME DELIVERY

Harriet Horne is an attractive blonde in her late twenties who lives in a comfortable home fronting the beach at Santa Barbara, California. She breast-feeds her week-old daughter.

"I had my first baby, Jimmy, at the hospital, and I made up my mind that

I'd have my next baby at home. A new mother needs her baby more than the two fifteen-minute stretches per day I was allowed in the semi-private ward. And she needs flexible visiting hours—she's at an emotional point in her life where there's some mighty special communication she wants with her husband."

Harriet Horne is one of a rapidly growing number of young mothers of all economic levels who are having their babies at home.

"You associate a hospital with having an operation, and when you're having a baby you're not sick," observes Linda Ahles of Laguna Beach, California. "At home you feel as if something pleasant is going to happen to you. There's a nesting instinct you feel."

Margaret Wright, from Dana Point, California, describes her experience having her baby at home enthusiastically. "I fell in love with my husband all over again. There's a tremendous amount of ego trip tied up in this for the father, too. At home, he didn't feel he was competing with the obstetrician."

Dr. Fred Osterman, an obstetric resident at the University of California, takes the opposite view. "If you tied ninety-five percent of women in labor to a tree in Golden Gate Park, the baby would fall out. But I would never do a home delivery because it wouldn't be safe. You can't resuscitate a baby at home. There could be brain damage."

Dr. Robert McNeil, a Los Angeles obstetrician, opposes home delivery even more vehemently. "We know that six percent of births are Caesarean, three percent require blood transfusions, and one percent involve infections. There is also a danger of hemorrhage, and there's no way to replace blood at home."

A few obstetricians, such as Dr. John S. Miller, of San Francisco, think there are psychological reasons that outweigh these objections. He predicts that the trend toward home delivery will continue and almost 40 percent of births will take place in the home by 1980. "Today's young people see in birth an exciting experience. They don't want it to take place in a medical factory like a hospital." And he is opposed to the hospital practice of keeping infant and mother separate, except for short periods, in those crucial first few days.

There is important new evidence to support this in the discoveries of Dr. James Prescott, of the National Institutes of Health. Dr. Prescott, a national authority on behavior study and brain development, says it is now clear that infants, particularly in the first few days after birth, need touching and physical affection as much as they need food. Dr. Prescott believes the sensory treatment given a child in the first twenty-four hours of its life may have permanent effects on the way the child—and the adult—thinks and acts.

"We should not be separating infants from their mothers at birth. There is no other mammal in the world that is separated this way. It's biologically, psychologically and socially abnormal. And it's done for the convenience of the hospital."

In Dr. Prescott's work with institutionalized infants deprived of sensory stimulation and affection, he observes that "when infants are separated from their mothers, they protest. But gradually they become passive and then withdrawn. Functional mental retardation develops as well as severe emotional disabilities. . . . We consistently find that a lack of touching, a lack of bodily and physical pleasure leads to emotional disturbance."

A Los Angeles obstetrician, who asked that his name not be used, favors home births in principle, but recommends hospitalization for women whose Rh blood factor is incompatible with the husband's, women with diabetes, first babies, or problem pregnancies. He insists that any woman contemplating home delivery be trained in methods of Natural Childbirth, involving at least six weeks of prenatal training in rhythmic breathing for the labor period. "Childbirth at home is fine as long as it is done with up-to-date methods and the mother is trained for it."

All nurse-midwives we interviewed favored home delivery over hospitalization, except in those cases where problems are anticipated.

"Good hospital care costs money," a Syracuse, New York, nurse-midwife said. "The poor can't pay for it, and that means they don't get the care and attention they need. Poor mothers and their babies are victimized by the understaffing and overwork at the clinic level. To be perfectly frank, they don't have the same chance of survival as people who can afford to pay. And that means a price tag is being put on human life!"

A price comparison was made by a research team in Rochester, New York, in 1972. In a study of almost 4,000 patients, the costs were put at $16.10 a day for home delivery and $96.41 in area hospitals.

A Stamford, Connecticut, nurse-midwife: "I know of six patients in recent years who died of staph infections and septicemia directly caused by the lack of proper hygienic standards at hospitals. The most virulent and deadly bacteria are found in hospitals because the constant use of antibiotics have made some bacteria almost insensitive to all forms of therapy. Where else are antibiotics used as frequently as in hospitals? The public isn't aware of the very real danger. If they were, more women would be demanding that their babies be delivered at home!"

"Maternity patients take up too much of the hospital load right now," adds a New York City nurse-midwife. "If we could convince more mothers to have their babies at home, we could solve the shortage of hospital beds and bring down costs overnight."

One ingenious Salt Lake City woman found a way to get around the $75 per day charges at the Latter-Day Saints Hospital. Ruth Egan was told by her doctors that she had dangerous potential complications in her pregnancy concerning the lifeline that fed the developing fetus, and for this reason couldn't have her baby at home. On the other hand, she couldn't afford to pay the hospital charges while waiting for her baby to be delivered.

Her solution: she moved the family truck and camper unit into the hospital parking lot, a few steps from the emergency entrance. Her doctor, nurses, and other hospital employees made daily visits to the camper.

"Everyone was caught up in the romance of the unique case," said L. Brent Goates, chief administrator of the Latter-Day Saints Hospital.

The possibility exists, however, that Ruth Egan's solution was considered so romantic simply because it *was* unique. It's hard to imagine most hospitals looking with favor on their parking lots filling up with pregnant women in campers, nor will doctors and nurses be cooperative if the practice becomes widespread.

A happy medium between the costly impersonality of hospital delivery and the potential danger of home delivery is the lying-in facility. Before this book goes to press, the first one of its kind will have opened in a major city. (Location and personnel cannot be disclosed because two more licenses must be secured and the planners fear AMA opposition if their plans are made known beforehand.)

Five nurse-midwives, two paramedics, one g.p. and two obstetricians have raised $75,000 to construct a forty-bed, one-story lying-in hospital. Because the hospital will be limited exclusively to obstetrics, that $75,000 includes all equipment for the delivery room, post delivery room, kitchen, etc. (*If* it were designed as a general hospital, the equipment alone, without the building, would cost $65,000!) Full-care rates for semi-private rooms will vary between $20 and $35 per day. No problem is anticipated in obtaining health insurance coverage from the few plans that allow maternity benefits.

"We think it's *the* solution," one of the obstetricians engineering the project stated. "We'll be fully equipped to handle ninety-nine out of one hundred women, and we'll make sure that hundredth woman is directed to a facility where her special birth problem can be handled. Our patients will pay from a third to a half of what they'd pay in a general hospital, have their baby and recuperate in an informal and friendly atmosphere. And they'll enjoy more comforts than at home.

"Frankly, we're going to duplicate the Swedish nurse-midwife arrangement as closely as we can. The patient will consult with one of three doctors, then if everything's okay, she'll be turned over to the nurse-midwives for prenatal care and Lamaze training and all the rest of it. The state requires that an M.D. be present at birth, so one of us will be in the delivery room looking on.

"We don't even want to call it a hospital. 'Lying-in Home' is more like it. If it works the way we think it will, you'll see them springing up like mushrooms all over the country."

As our nation nears its two-hundredth birthday, we have come to a crisis: of the babies who will be born this year, obstetricians can deliver only half. There are simply not enough ob.s to deliver more.

The cost of having a baby, including obstetrician and hospital, hovers near an outrageous $1,500 figure. Nurse-midwife attendance can reduce this to under $200 with home delivery. Even the proposed lying-in clinic-hospital, if utilized for the five-day postnatal period, would cut the costs to less than $400.

In addition, at least 100,000 more hospital beds are needed to care for Americans who actually require hospital care. Nine out of ten obstetrical cases do *not* require hospital care. So if we place 90 percent of our obstetrical cases in the hands of nurse-midwives, we can keep that same 90 percent out of our hospitals and solve the shortage in a single bold stroke.

If we can rid ourselves of some of the prejudice that has been nurtured to the present day by selfish men for their own interests, we can make childbirth once again the untraumatic, inexpensive and "natural" process it should be.

THE PEDIATRICIAN: HOW TO TREAT A "MUMMY-ACHE"

3

Dr. Gordon Binsfield came to the hospital at 8:30 A.M., the usual hour for his rounds. He briefly checked two infants scheduled to accompany their mothers home that morning, then went to see newborn Jamie Ferguson.

For several minutes he studied the charts and records that began the previous night when Eunice Ferguson was wheeled into the labor room. She had given birth to Jamie, a six-pound, two-ounce baby, at 11:40 P.M. Dr. Arnold Nichols, the obstetrician, had checked both mother and child immediately after birth, then left a message for Dr. Binsfield, a pediatrician.

Dr. Binsfield crosschecked with a sheaf of records labeled "Ferguson" he had brought with him. Then he ordered blood and urine samples taken and analyzed. He looked the baby over, nodded with a degree of satisfaction, and left two messages at the desk. He asked to be notified immediately when the specimens were analyzed, and informed Eunice Ferguson that he would see her later in the day.

This type of "immediate" pediatrics is not uncommon today. In fact, neonatology—the branch of pediatrics that deals exclusively with the first thirty days of a child's life—is one of the "hottest" new medical specialties. Normally, the selected pediatrician will see mother and child twice in the hospital—once shortly after birth and once near the hour of discharge.

Therefore he becomes the next in a long sequence of those who minister to the needs of mother and baby, and we will now look at what he does in return for what he is paid, and try to determine if the transaction is a fair one.

In Jamie's case, there was a valid reason for blood and urine tests. What concerned Dr. Binsfield was that the obstetrical records showed Jamie's mother was a borderline diabetic. Diabetic women have 25 percent fetal mortality. In Eunice Ferguson's case, diabetes also ran rampant in her family, indicating to Dr. Binsfield that his new patient would probably have to be watched carefully, particularly in the months immediately after birth.

A further danger signal was the erratic way in which Eunice's blood sugar level had behaved throughout the course of her pregnancy. All pregnant women endure changes in metabolism during pregnancy, but a woman with an organic malfunction or a blood problem is apt to suffer metabolic change of potential danger to herself and the child.

"Diabetes in a pregnant woman really bothers me," Dr. Binsfield says. "The diabetic mother's baby has to be carefully watched. Metabolically, they are weaker, more prone to disease and infection, and short of natural resistance. You can't order a diabetic woman *not* to have a baby, but she should think twice before getting pregnant. She's sure to have a rougher time with pregnancy than most women, and her baby will have a rougher go, physically, than other kids."

Under careful medical supervision, Jamie Ferguson eventually survived, not as robust as he should be, yet capable of a normal and happy childhood.

Had Jamie been born in 1923 instead of 1973, he probably wouldn't have lived twenty-four hours!

WHO IS THE PATIENT?

Like the airplane, motorcar, and obstetrician, the pediatrician is the product of our century. In 1890, the word "pediatrician" was unknown. The family doctor treated child, parent, and grandparent, bringing a baby into the world and (too often) administering to him on the way out. In our western world, 20 to 40 percent of children died during their first year of life.

No one can identify the first pediatrician. Need seemed to create him, as it were, simultaneously in several nations. In the final years of the nineteenth century, the medical world began to recognize the profound differences between adult and child. "Little people" were no longer thought to be mere minatures of their creators.

In truth, the child varies from the mature person physiologically, psychologically, immunologically, and anatomically. He is less vulnerable to the diseases and infirmities that come with aging, but more vulnerable to infectious diseases that pass the adult by.

"I am always pleased when a patient reaches the age of twelve," a famous physician once remarked, "because then I know what his body is about. Before that, there are too many mysteries."

Contributing to the mystery is the fact that most doctors rely on the patient's history and description of symptoms in making their diagnosis. This constitutes 80 to 90 percent of the evidence available to them, with the balance being supplied by actual physical examination and appropriate lab tests.

When the patient is a child, the crucial evidence of a medical history is missing. A mother may be able to tell a doctor that her child has a sore throat, but she can't tell exactly how he is feeling, exactly when it began or the course of development. And very young children can't even tell the doctor that simplest of all preliminaries—where it hurts.

By 1910, the pediatrician was reasonably well known in Scandinavia, England, Germany, Switzerland, and the United States. In these nations the death rate among children was reduced to one tenth of the appalling figure previously quoted. From 1910 on, the establishment of the pediatrician as a fully qualified medical specialist matched the rise of the obstetrician gynecologist.

Today, the average pediatrician's case load is 20 percent more than he would prefer to handle, and therefore a child does not get all the attention and treatment required. One reason is the bewildering rate of medical progress.

"We're on the spot," a UCLA pediatrician remarked, "because we're in the forefront of preventive medicine—the most innovative and experimental type of medicine there is. New immunizations, new drugs, keep coming in. No doctor can hope to keep up. If we could trust the drug companies and the FDA, we'd be all right. But we can't trust either of them enough to go gung-ho on any drug, prescription or patent, at the time it comes into vogue. And we are pressured by the drug companies to prescribe their latest 'miracle.' "

"Parents get into the act," complains another doctor. "Can you imagine what happens when a new decongestant or suppressant is advertised on television? The next day in my office I have to cope with a dozen parents who've been prescribing what's going to make their child well. Absolutely guaranteed —on TV!"

One pediatrician calls this "the side effects of medical technology. Parents not only demand the newest 'miracle drug,' but they are quick to panic when they read about some new drug being taken off the market. Parents become needlessly alarmed that their children are going to turn into freaks or inherit some awful disease."

The "parent problem" is one that bothers most pediatricians. Although the child is their patient, most of their time is spent dealing with the parents. Dr. Lendon Smith, the well-known pediatrician and author of several best-selling books on the subject of child care, ruefully answered when asked if children make good patients: "Yes, but they bring their parents along." Dr. Smith cited the case of one mother who burst into his office late for an appointment, telling the nurse she hoped the doctor wouldn't be upset. It turned out she'd forgotten to bring her child with her!

Dr. Barbara Korsch, a professor of pediatrics at USC Medical School, is working toward improving relationships between parents and their children's doctors. In talking with hundreds of mothers, she found many who feel shut out by the doctor-child relationship. Mothers who are hurried, put down or brushed off by the doctor are less willing or perhaps even less able to follow the doctor's instructions. This tendency is increased when the pediatrician who's been kind and smiling to the child turns brusque and authoritarian to the parent. "This only reinforces feelings of guilt and inadequacy. Warmth can make a difference. Unfortunately, our medical schools teach technology and not communication."

"If I had to do it over, I don't think I'd have specialized in pediatrics," a Chicago doctor replies bitterly. "It isn't the kids. I love them, even the spoiled brats. It's the mothers who get frantic when Junior has a sore throat, and expect me to give the kid a shot of penicillin or tetracycline before I can even prove a throat culture.

"They pass on their hysteria to the kids. More kids suffer from 'mummy-aches' than 'tummy-aches.' I'm not a diagnostician any more. I'm supposed to give the shot and perform the miracle."

More exasperating is the fact, reported by medical journals, that 90 percent of parents do not follow the full course of recommended treatment. "They will either stop treatment too soon because they think the child is showing improvement," says a New York City pediatrician, "or will decide for themselves that if two teaspoons of the prescribed medicine is good for their child, three must be better, and four will certainly effect a cure. What they don't understand is that medicines become toxic in large dosages, and they may be actually giving their child a poison instead of a medicine. What I find even harder to explain is why a substantial percentage of parents never even bother to fill the prescription I give them. Apparently the anxiety that brought them to my office in the first place is cured by the simple act of prescribing—without having to use what was prescribed!"

A Cincinnati pediatrician has an even more serious complaint: "This will sound as though I'm against patent medicines per se, so I'll preface by saying that I'm not. Aspirin proves its value daily, so do the antacids and one or two of the hemorrhoid relief products, and there's nothing wrong with rubbing Vicks on the chest. I'm not even against some home remedies, like a combination of hot water, lemon juice, and honey to treat a cough.

"But here's a problem I come across almost daily. A child is brought in with a very bad cold, the kind settled so solidly in the head and chest that the parent has a right to suspect something more serious—say, pneumonia or a bronchial infection. If I think one of the antibiotics will help, I'll prescribe it. I'll also prescribe palliative drugs, some of them patent medicines, that will help. I'll also try to make sure that the parent will not deviate from the treatment I prescribe because God only knows what can happen when certain drugs or chemicals are combined.

"But the parent takes things into his or her own hands—anxious to cure the child. So she'll also use the decongestant spray she saw advertised on television, or stuff the kid's nostrils with Vicks or use an antihistamine instead of aspirin or—well, God knows what. Their intentions are the best, but they don't realize that nostrils plugged with Vicks can block the passages in the head and promote a serious sinus infection, or that drops of oil from a spray can settle in the lungs and lead to pleurisy or pneumonia if they're not coughed up. Too many times a decongestant becomes a congestant and escalates a simple cold into something very serious. But trying to stop a worried parent is like trying to stop a train by lying down on the tracks."

WHAT HARM CAN IT DO?

Many parent versus pediatrician conflicts are caused by a pediatrician who uses antibiotics too freely.

One viewpoint is expressed by a bitter Minneapolis woman: "When my daughter was five, she came down with infectious mononucleosis, and my pediatrician treated her. He turned her little bottom into a pincushion with penicillin shots. He said he was warding off other infections that can set in when a child is suffering from mono.

"For a whole month after she'd recovered from mono, my daughter was given orally 5,000 units of penicillin per day—still to ward off secondary infections or diseases. Unfortunately, the next year she contracted pneumonia, and when the same pediatrician started her on penicillin again she broke out in a horrible rash and went into convulsions. Now she's eighteen and has to wear a tag which warns against her being given penicillin under any circumstances. One shot would kill her. And all because that pediatrician over-used a wonderful drug to treat an illness it didn't even touch!"

Conversely, the pediatrician is irritated with parents who expect miracles rather than treatment. "If I don't give the kid a shot, they think I'm a lousy doctor," complains one Seattle-based pediatrician. "They all know more about medicine than I do. Most mothers I meet are the kind who would tell Bulova how to make a watch!"

Dr. John Galdamez, of Kansas City, Missouri, warns: "There isn't any more dangerous trend in medicine today than the promiscuous use of antibiotics, or what we call shotgun therapy. A mother comes in with a sick child and wants him or her treated at once with some miracle drug. What should be done is to take a C and S [culture and sensitivity test] to find out what specific drug might be useful against this illness. But that would take forty-eight hours, and Mother isn't going to wait. So the doctor prescribes one of the broad-spectrum drugs useful against many different kinds of bacterial infection. That drug may affect the disease-causing bacteria, but will also affect a number of other bacteria that are in the body not doing any harm but rather, actually doing good. The disease-causing bacteria will mutate and become strains resistant to that broad-spectrum drug. If a later illness is caused by these bacteria, the only way doctors can treat it is by using more toxic harmful drugs.

"We are losing many of our good drugs this way—they are becoming steadily less effective. In my opinion, a doctor would be better off to give a child sterile water or a vitamin pill—and then specific therapy forty-eight hours later. Certainly the child would be better off. But not too many doctors will stand up against an insistent, impatient, often semi-hysterical mother."

It's only fair to say that it isn't just mother who can't wait. Doctors often are not willing to take the time, or to spend their patients' money for lab procedures—many of which can't even be done by the average doctor but have to be done elsewhere.

Dr. Lendon Smith takes a lighter view of the problem of medicating children's illnesses. " 'Go home and take your medicine, and you'll be better.' That attitude inspires confidence. We know that flu lasts three days, and if they come to me after two and a half days and I give 'em medicine that takes eight hours to work, I know I've got 'em!"

Dr. Smith also believes that as children get older, they should, if possible, go to see the doctor themselves. This not only confines the relationship to the doctor and his real patient, but adds to the child's sense of independence and self-worth, as well as encouraging him to speak more openly about his problems. Asked if he often had occasion to tell a parent that a child should really consult a psychologist or a psychiatrist, Dr. Smith admitted it happened several times a day. "But pediatricians are moving into the psychiatrist's field. Psychiatrists are getting smarter too—finding out it isn't always Mother's fault; it could have been a funny kid that came from the father's side of the family. Seriously, genetic factors, hurts to the nervous system, environment— all are tied in together, and it's difficult to sort them out. If I find a kid who's ticklish and has trouble getting to sleep and is a nibbler, I can sometimes help him just by giving him a hamburger for breakfast rather than that junk cereal. If a child's tense and anxious in his classroom at school, why not give him a cassette and let him walk around and learn that way? We've got to stop putting kids down. That's the direction to go in. We need new ideas more than we need new medicines."

For years a large number of parents and pediatricians shared the view that "even if it won't do any good, it won't do any harm." After a quarter century of miracle drug misuse, we know that isn't so. Thousands of young adults carry sharp crystals in their spleen caused by the indiscriminate use of sulfanilimide and sulfathiozole, the first of the miracle drugs, from 1938 to 1944. And it is estimated that over 100,000 young adults and children have been rendered allergic to penicillin because of its overuse from 1949 to 1956, when doctors prescribed it for everything from the simplest cold to more serious infections it could not cure. Scores of miracle drugs have been quietly withdrawn from use when a tendency toward harmful side effects turned up, long after the drugs had received AMA and FDA approval.

In the pediatrician versus parent relationship, the situation is not improved by the confusing changes in medical practice from one generation to the next.

Reports a Houston, Texas, woman: "When I was five, I had a bad attack of tonsilitis and the doctor promptly took my tonsils out. I was eight when I had appendicitis, and out came my appendix.

"Now, when my son David was six, his tonsils became infected. I took him to a pediatrician, who put him on antibiotics. I wondered why he didn't just remove the tonsils, like they had with me. Finally I asked why, and he told me he was making every effort to let my son keep them because tonsils are a sort of clearing house for germs and viruses that might settle in other parts of the body and cause serious illness. The identical thing happened when David's appendix acted up; he told me that unless the appendix was in danger of rupturing, he would leave it in because it acts the same way tonsils do. So, I end up wondering if I am less healthy than I should be because of those expensive surgeries, or if the pediatrician simply doesn't know what he's talking about. It doesn't help that for nearly two years David has had one attack of tonsilitis after another."

We asked her pediatrician to comment: "She's got to realize that we're in a remarkable age of progress," he said. "Preventive medicine has become more important than surgery. We have the drugs now to bring a diseased organ back to health. Not too long ago we had to remove an organ because it could 'die,' so to speak, and bring the whole body down with it. We still don't know the total advisability of keeping tonsils, adenoids, and appendix. But we do know that the shock of unnecessary surgery, no matter how successful the surgery may be, should be avoided if possible."

Nevertheless, among patients the suspicion persists that "doctors always have answers." One father, with obvious delight, told us how his wife had complained that her three-year-old boy wasn't sleeping at night. The doctor told her to give him a glass of warm milk just before going to bed.

"But, doctor," she protested, "just a couple of months ago you told me not to give him anything to eat just before going to bed."

The doctor replied with dignity, "My dear woman, that was two months ago. Science has made enormous strides since then."

PARENTS AND PEDIATRICIANS

Another area of dispute between pediatrician and patients involves economics. The difficulties trace back to the shortage of pediatricians and their consequent need to limit the number of patients. While this disturbs middle-income groups, it most seriously affects the poor, particularly the minorities, who have difficulty in obtaining pediatric care even on the clinic or charity level.

"I should ask you what the hell a pediatrician is, because neither me nor my kids have ever seen one." The interviewee is from Richmond, California, black, and a mother of eight. "Far as I'm concerned, they're only for rich kids. Lord knows I've needed a special kid doctor from time to time, but they just ain't available at the county hospital, not unless you're lucky when you bring the kids in and they happen to have one hanging around."

Lack of child care for county or charity patients is understandable in view of the existing shortage of pediatricians. But it is also understandable that the situation adds fuel to the resentment of minority groups. "Public Health programs make sure our kids get their shots and stuff, but when it comes to anything special, like pneumonia or appendicitis, forget it. It's strictly a county hospital trip, no matter how bad the emergency is." This from a Chicano community leader in Los Angeles. "Our kids don't get the same chance to grow up that other kids do, because we can't afford to buy it for them."

If poverty is a disease, then one of its most serious symptoms is lack of adequate medical care. There is an almost total absence of doctors for the poor. Overall, in the United States, there is one doctor for every six hundred persons. But in ghetto communities, there is only one doctor for every seven thousand to twelve thousand persons. Their "doctor" is the county hospital, often understaffed and poorly financed.

At Los Angeles County USC Medical Hospital, the situation with regard to overcrowding got so bad that the house physicians staged a "heal-in" in a desperate attempt to advertise the plight of patients. They refused to admit any other than extreme emergency cases or to make any discharges. But when the "heal-in" ended, the situation reverted to normal.

The ghetto or inner city resident dwells in a medical no-man's land. In Watts, a black section of Los Angeles where public transportation is extremely difficult to obtain, a resident must travel over six miles to reach the nearest medical assistance. A sick patient often has to pay more in transportation than he does for medical care. And once at the hospital, the long wait for treatment involves the loss of a day's wages. In consequence, the children of working mothers in this area almost never receive such routine health care as pediatric immunizations.

"The fact of the matter is that a clinic is designed for mass production," a pediatrician at the County USC Medical Center told us. "We're supposed to see the greatest possible number of patients in the shortest possible time. This kind of short-order medicine compares with private medical practice like a meal by a short-order cook in a local greasy spoon compares with a gourmet dinner by a master chef in an expensive restaurant. There just ain't no comparison!"

Dr. Lawrence D. Freedman, chief of staff of La Mirada Community Hospital, calls for sweeping changes in medical services to the poor. He believes the federal government should bear all the costs of medical training.

"Free medical education might make it possible for more minority students to get medical training. And it could change the attitudes of America's doctors, who must spend years in expensive training while their contemporaries are already earning a good living.

"All medical and dental graduates whose educations were financed by the government should be required to serve two years in a poverty-area health center or other area of need at reasonable salaries."

Dr. Freedman estimates the total cost of such a program at $40 million a year—about the same as for one new military bomber or a few miles of interstate highway construction.

Escalating medical costs also affect those in the higher income brackets. "I was new in the city when I had my first baby," says Mrs. Kevin Albright of Cudahy, Wisconsin, "so I had no idea which pediatrician to choose. I left it up to my obstetrician. He recommended a doctor who came to the hospital to see my daughter just after she was born, and once again just before we went home.

"Well, we aren't exactly wealthy people, and we ended up with the highest priced pediatrician in the city, whose patients live in Whitefish Bay, not Cudahy. Office calls run us thirty dollars. My neighbors get the very same services from their pediatrician for fifteen dollars. My doctor prescribes drugs by their trade names, and theirs prescribes at about half the price because he uses the generic or chemical name. And what's more, their doctor makes house calls and mine wouldn't think of it. I hate to change doctors because he's got Linda's complete medical record, but I do feel that my obstetrician should have been more considerate in picking a pediatrician for us."

Another complaint of many women we interviewed is expressed by Laura Harkness of San Diego, a mother of three: "Our pediatrician is just plain too busy. I'll make an appointment for two o'clock in the afternoon and bring the kids in, and we're lucky if we can see him by three thirty. The waiting room is bedlam with babies crying and fussing, and older kids fighting or bored.

"The worst of it is I know that my oldest boy, Kenneth, picked up measles at his office because he was exposed to a little girl who was coming down with them. I'm pretty sure my daughter got mumps the same way."

Mrs. Joel Stein of Los Angeles is one of those who has had a happier experience to record, and she offers some insight into what qualities parents would like to find in their pediatrician.

"I have four children, aged three to nine, and two years ago we moved from Seattle to Los Angeles. The pediatrician in Seattle was a very brusque man who never unbent. The kids were actually afraid of him. Down here it's a completely different story. The kids adore their new doctor and look forward to their appointments. It isn't just the lollypops the secretary gives them when they leave. The doctor is warm and friendly, jokes with them and explains everything he's doing. He explains things to me, too. It's very reassuring."

House calls in time of crisis—or the lack thereof—is another source of complaints from mothers. "About a year ago my youngest son became quite ill," says Carol Johnson of Chicago. "He's the sort of boy who just doesn't admit he's sick, but he moped around one full day with a sore throat and a temperature and a queasy stomach—nothing to be alarmed about because so many children's illnesses start off that way. That night, however, he became extremely ill. He vomited and his temperature shot up to one hundred and four degrees. I noticed that his skin was turning an odd sort of parchment yellow, and I guessed what was wrong: he'd been exposed to infectious hepatitis the week before and now he was coming down with it.

"I called the pediatrician—it took him an hour to get back to me after I left an emergency call with his answering service—but he wouldn't come. He told me to give Mark aspirin and to put cold towels on to relieve the fever, and to bring him into his office in the morning.

"Two things really bothered me. In the first place, this pediatrician had assured me he would make house calls in an emergency. Well, we had an emergency, but we didn't get the house call. Second, it isn't the best thing in the world for a child to be hauled around when he's sick with something as serious as hepatitis. And to bring him into a doctor's office, thereby exposing other children, is absurd. Needless to say, I've changed doctors."

"I make house calls as seldom as I can," replies a Denver pediatrician, "not because of the inconvenience, but because almost every time it's a wasted trip. I realize that a sick child is a traumatic experience for a parent. But the parent must realize that a bronchial infection or a bad cold has to run its own course, that it's not a prelude to death."

Most pediatricians we spoke with agree there is hardly anything worse for a child than an oversolicitous parent.

Says our Denver pediatrician: "Parents who can't bear to see their child suffer even a little pain may think they're showing love, but what they're doing is causing long-term psychological problems. Pain and minor illness is a part of growing up for normal children, and they learn how to deal with it themselves without a parent interfering. I'm thinking of giving this particular problem a catchy name so that parents will remember it when they need to. How about 'The Leonidas Complex?'—after that ancient hero of Sparta who saved the day by taking the enemy's spears into his own body. That's what these parents are doing. And what they'll get for their trouble is a spoiled, tyrannical, incompetent child who will never be able to face the harsh realities of life without his parents."

Another doctor quoted a case from his own practice in which a seven-year-old boy, who was afraid of being in the dark with strangers, had so terrorized his parents that they hadn't gone out of the house in years. "They were afraid of the tantrums he'd throw. They thought they were being good parents, but they weren't. They never learned to set limits on their child's demands. So his life will be unhappy as a grownup—and *their* lives are damn near ruined."

Dr. Steven Hersh, of the National Institute of Mental Health, confirms that the child-tyrant syndrome is prevalent in the United States. It seems that many parents feel they are assuming an overwhelming responsibility with the guardianship of a fragile human life, so they go to unnatural lengths to make sure nothing goes wrong.

THE PARAMEDICS ARE COMING

Newsweek magazine once called the pediatrician the "most hard pressed doctor of all." The average pediatrician can hardly handle the traffic through his office, much less concern himself with larger social questions.

But a growing army of "paramedics" is hurrying to the rescue. Increasingly, in rural areas, at outpatient clinics, among the poor and the aged, even in private practice, the "doctor on call" is likely to be a nurse.

As in obstetrics, trained nurse-practitioners are taking over the more routine aspects of pediatric care. Over 80 percent of the pediatrician's workload consists of routine physical examinations, counseling and the handling of minor complaints.

The duties of a nurse-practitioner include the early identification of diseases, physical examinations and immunizations, the treatment of common and minor ailments, and monitoring the conditions of chronically ill patients. In general, their bias is toward "well care," and much of their time is spent simply in counseling, referring, and listening.

This latter phase is becoming more important, for the emphasis in medical care is shifting toward preventive medicine. Dr. Paul Honig, of Children's Hospital in Philadelphia, predicts a much expanded role for nurse-practitioners in this developing area. He believes the future focus in medicine will be the outpatient clinic rather than the hospital bed and that this will require many more trained medical personnel. Since it takes eleven years to train a pediatrician, it is easy to predict that the major burden will fall on nurse-practitioners and paramedics who have been trained less expensively for a much shorter period of time.

Within the broad category of nurse-practitioners, there is a smaller field of nurse-specialists who have taken graduate work in the particular area of their interest. They work even more closely with the doctor. One nurse-specialist in Oklahoma City places the blame for "pediatric panic" largely on the loss in modern society of older female relatives from whom a young woman can learn "the art of mothercraft." She also thinks articles in magazines, newspapers and books that urge mothers to seek a physician's aid in almost any instance are dead wrong. "Never go to the doctor just to be sure. There are going to be twenty other children in the waiting room. You ought to be ashamed to take a doctor's valuable time to talk about your kid's bedwetting. In most problems, a mother knows best, or at least as much as a doctor does. Parents have to wake up to this and so do pediatricians. A good mother may not know how or why she is good, but she practices effective child rearing."

At the hospital where she is currently employed, we interviewed a pediatrician on the subject of whether mother does know best.

"Mothers are not infallible—and neither are we," said our interviewee. "I think a doctor's reputation would be enhanced by an occasional admission he was wrong. And I'm thankful that the majority of sensible parents do not follow our advice as slavishly as supposed. They use their common sense. On the other hand, no parent can do the job alone. They need the help not only of pediatricians, but child psychologists and educators. The stress of modern life makes it almost impossible for a parent to get by without specialized assistance. We all work together on a team in which the parents are included. But don't expect the parents to know it all."

With the advent of these new helpers, it may become possible to grapple with the immense problem of pediatric care in this country.

But there is no way to guard against a catastrophic illness. Barely three years ago, in California, a young hospital resident's wife gave birth prematurely to a 1-pound, 10-ounce baby girl. Given the very best medical care and close surveillance, the tiny preemie seemed to be improving. Then suddenly, just two months after her birth, she died.

The bill: $22,000.

Insurance covered the maternity, but not the neonatal costs. The resident's salary was too high for MediCal and $1,000 too much to qualify for the hospital's clinic-aid program. And the baby was born three months before Crippled Children's Services, a federal-state-county funding service, went into effect.

The California state legislature has since passed a law requiring all insurance companies to cover newborns from their moment of birth on family health insurance policies, regardless of any contrary clauses. Despite the fantastic cost in some individual instances, the insurance companies are actually saving money because with proper medical care they have ended up with fewer handicapped babies.

However, not many states have yet adopted this farsighted policy.

HOW TO GET ALONG

Let's suppose your family's income can stretch to cover the cost of regular visits by the children to a pediatrician.

How do you find a good one?

Your obstetrician can recommend a pediatrician. If you liked and trusted your obstetrician, then the chances are good you'll like the recommendation. Very probably they worked together at the same hospital. The pediatrician will visit the hospital when your baby is born and examine it in the nursery.

Another advantage is that the obstetrician and pediatrician can discuss any of your pregnancy problems that might affect the baby. In fact, this discussion may take place even before your delivery date.

You can also obtain the names of pediatricians from local hospitals, from the local medical society, or from a medical school. Choose one whose office is near you, then set up an appointment. A short preliminary conference can tell you a good deal. Does the doctor work alone, with a partner, or as part of a group? This may give you a clue as to availability of medical help in emergencies. Does the doctor's personality inspire confidence—do you feel you can discuss easily any problems that may arise? Are your questions being answered satisfactorily—as to breast or bottle feeding, for example, or what medical supplies and equipment you should purchase, or any family illnesses you are afraid might affect Baby in the future? What sort of professional training does he or she have? All pediatricians usually have had a number of years of specialized training after completing their internship. But if there is not only an M.D. but an F.A.A.P. after the doctor's name, that signifies a Fellow of the American Academy of Pediatricians. An F.A.A.P. has passed the difficult and comprehensive examination given by the American Board of Pediatrics.

Hospital affiliations are also important. The doctor should be on the staff of an accredited hospital. That helps if your baby becomes ill enough to require hospital care.

Let us suppose that you have found what you think is a good pediatrician. What now? How can you establish a good working relationship, and how can you be sure of getting your money's worth?

Of course, we would all make better patients if we had gone to medical school and learned to ask the right questions and understand the answers. Since that is not possible, here are some rules that may help. Keep firmly in mind that this advice is directed only to those who can afford a pediatrician in the first place.

1. Learn more, by reading books and pamphlets and by asking questions of your pediatrician, about the physical and psychological nature of your child. This will help avoid the type of "pediatric panic" which places excess tension and strain on doctor and child. Two pamphlets published by the U.S. Department of Health, Education and Welfare, *Your Child From One to Six* and *Your Child From Six to Twelve*, are invaluable and are easily obtained from a library or ordered from the U.S. Government Printing Office, Washington, D.C. 20402. They cost 20¢ apiece.

2. Insist that the pediatrician explain to you, at the outset, fees, the appointment schedule to be observed, and the attitude toward house calls. You have a right to assume that this will be done by any good doctor without being asked. But you would be surprised how many times this simple precaution is overlooked.

3. When the doctor begins an examination of your child, ask to have ex-

plained to you precisely what is being done and why. This can be in simple terms. Don't be put off with medical jargon. It is important that communication of some kind be established.

4. If a doctor cannot make house calls, your telephone calls should at least be returned promptly. You can help if you won't unreasonably impose on the doctor's time by making unnecessary calls about problems for which there are ready explanations in Dr. Spock.

5. Ask if sample drugs are available when the doctor is writing a prescription. This can save you money. Otherwise, ask if the drug is really needed. Some doctors will write a prescription simply because the parent expects something to be prescribed. If the drug is needed, then ask the doctor to prescribe generically (by chemical rather than brand name). This saves up to 50 percent on the price.

6. What is fair as far as costs are concerned? The following figures are authenticated as of mid year 1974, and do not allow for subsequent escalation or inflation.

Hospital calls paid by the pediatrician on mother and new baby should be no more than $20 each. (Charges ranged, in our survey, from $15 to $30.)

Office calls should be from $12 to $15. Beyond $15, the patient is paying for the pediatrician's name value, which contributes little to a child's health.

House calls rate $20 to $25.

Yearly checkups, including blood and urine tests, should not exceed $25, though they can mount as high as $50. To this must be added, of course, shots and inoculations and vaccinations—tetanus, polio, measles, etc.—which should be no more than $5 each, but sometimes range to an out-of-line $10. X rays and special therapy are usually referred to specialized facilities, and can be costly. (Routine x rays range from $5 to $25, with neither rhyme nor reason for the variation, and laboratory blood tests from $5 to $30!) It is up to the pediatrician to refer you to modestly priced facilities rather than to those which overcharge for the identical services. Incidentally, this is one of the two areas in which there is a strong suspicion of fee-splitting. The other is the pediatrician-pharmacist relationship, particularly in clinics where the drugstore is on the premises and owned by the clinic itself, or when patients are referred to a particular drugstore to have prescriptions filled.

7. When you engage the services of a pediatrician, it is up to you to observe certain obligations. These include:

Schedule a check-up at regular intervals, and

   a. faithfully keep appointments. There is a reason, often an important one, for getting an injection at a specific time. There are also physical developments in the child, particularly from birth to the age of five, which must be observed closely.

b. Follow the pediatrician's instructions, particularly regarding medication. If an antibiotic is prescribed at "four-hour intervals four times a day," the medicine should be given until the prescription is used up. Too many mothers take it on themselves to stop medication as soon as junior shows improvement. This can be dangerous because a relapse, if it comes, is often more serious than the first onslaught of the ailment. And the prescribed antibiotic may not be able to combat it effectively the second time around.

One final warning: DO NOT use patent medicines. NONE is to be used without your pediatrician's permission.

Let us repeat that: *None is to be used without your pediatrician's permission.* Now write that out as a warning and paste it on your medicine cabinet!

THE ADVICE-GIVERS: "DOCTOR SPOCK SAYS YOU'RE WRONG!"

4

Every day millions of American parents open their newspaper or favorite magazine to consult a medical authority who, while charging them nothing, will give them the latest word on pregnancy and infant and child care.

Are you a recent mother who worries if regional anesthesia caused those pains in your lower back? Today's column is for you. It will inform you that new mothers experience low back pain as a result either of strains on the ligaments that support the enlarged abdomen during pregnancy or the constant bending and lifting involved in caring for a new baby.

Or perhaps you are not yet a mother but in an advanced state of pregnancy and you'd like to know how to distinguish false labor pains from real. You will read today that a mild sedative or a glass of sherry, or simply walking around, will often make false labor pains disappear, but when real labor begins nothing will stop it until the baby is born.

No one expects anything provocative, revolutionary or controversial to appear in these discreet columns. Women read them in search of some small valuable nugget of advice (if you use commercial baby food, listen for the popping sound as you open the jar; that's your assurance that the food is fresh), or for a reminder of some half-forgotten counsel (once labor pains have begun, do not eat or drink *anything;* your stomach should be empty in case you are given an anesthetic). But what they really want, as much or more than this kind of simplistic wisdom, is the soothing voice of authority.

Not long ago, an Army colonel was assigned to duty in South Korea. His wife became distraught because she was four months pregnant and accompanying her husband to the new assignment would mean being away from the daily comfort of her favorite doctor—a syndicated newspaper columnist who dispenses obstetrical advice to her and a legion of other readers.

The column appeared in fifty stateside newspapers but had no publishing outlet in Seoul, and the colonel's wife, who didn't mind changing domiciles or parting from friends, couldn't bear to be separated from her advice-giver.

It would have cost $150 a month to have the local newspaper airmailed to her in Seoul. The colonel, understandably, drew the line at that. The impasse was resolved when a close friend promised to clip and mail each day's column to her.

A successful businessman in Plainfield, New Jersey, recently offered his wife's "physician" (another well-known writer on the problems of bringing up baby) a free trip plus expenses and a generous fee if he would come to Plainfield for a few hours to talk over his wife's problems in person. When the offer was refused, he asked if he could install a tie-in phone, at a heavy monthly charge, so that his wife could call him directly for advice whenever she had a problem. That offer was also refused.

These are only two instances, striking but by no means rare, of how important advice-givers have become. Dispensing mental pablum in newspapers, magazines, and books—and via local radio and TV stations—is a multimillion-dollar industry. Advice-givers are not, however, substitutes for personal medical supervision, nor would they claim to be. The most frequent advice they give is: "When in doubt, consult your doctor."

We asked our interview panel of obstetricians and pediatricians how they feel about it.

From Boston, Massachusetts: "When you come right down to it, they save me time—explaining rudimentary things that might take me hours to put across. Women believe what they see in print, and most of what they see is true. Simple-minded but true."

A San Francisco colleague disagrees. "My job would be a lot easier if women didn't read the stuff. A magazine like *Redbook* or *Good Housekeeping* or *Woman's Day* or *Parent's* magazine publishes an article about crib death, and thousands of women go into a tizzy. I have to spend hours with my patients reassuring them. On the whole, these people are usually reputable doctors and give sound advice. But occasionally hell breaks loose."

From Los Angeles: "It's a racket. They've got women hypnotized. Parents come into my office and tell me what's wrong with their kids. They know because they read about it in a column in some women's magazine. If I disagree, they look at me as if I don't know what I'm talking about."

Variations in what advice-givers tell young parents are relatively slight. This leads some cynics to believe that unanimity of opinion exists because the thieves are stealing from each other. If so, this would not be a phenomenon wholly unheard of in the wider world of competitive enterprise.

The truth is that in medicine there is a more or less agreed-upon body of doctrine. Although each patient is treated individually, the physician regards a patient's symptoms as both common to humankind and singular to the individual. Advice-givers, on the other hand, since there is no "patient," must assume that all parents and their babies are blended into a homogenous mass which can be treated identically.

Even the smallest deviation from the norm is as frowned upon as if a priest were to attempt to change just a few words of High Mass. In *Redbook* magazine a few years ago, Dr. Elizabeth B. Connell challenged the accepted theory that a 15- to 20-pound gain is the ideal for the pregnant woman. She said new data indicated that some women who gain slightly more than 20 pounds actually may have stronger babies.

Dr. Connell's article was among the first to attack a premise that has always been more shibboleth than fact. But it provoked a storm of outraged protests from true believers of the original gospel. Their faith was shaken. Who was this pretender, Dr. Elizabeth Connell, to put forward such heresy? How dared she function as a new Lawgiver?

Then a deluge of magazine and newspaper articles supported the thesis that the kind of diet is far more important than the amount of weight gained. Most important was Dr. Janet Hardy, of St. John's University Medical School, who revealed that one conclusion of the gigantic study of 56,000 mothers and their children conducted by the National Institute of Neurological Diseases and Stroke was that heavier mothers mean heavier and healthier babies. "We have learned that 25 to 30 pounds is the optimal weight gain both in terms of perinatal mortality and birth weight which relates to intellectual and neurological outcome. In fact, the restrictions on weight gain placed on American women by their doctors may account in considerable part for the difference in neonatal and perinatal mortality between this country and Europe, where death rates are much lower. In Europe, the women customarily gain thirty to thirty-five pounds during pregnancy."

After that definitive statement, the controversy quieted down. God returned to His heaven, the snail to the thorn, and Dr. Connell to the pages of *Redbook*.

Advice-givers are quite as adept at soothing parents' fears as they are at arousing parental ire.

Take the problem of short children. Many parents are convinced they have a child who is "abnormally" short. Nine times out of ten the short child is a boy, although there are just as many girls shorter than the average. The reason for the parents' fear is the social premium that is placed on height for males. There is no equivalent of the flattering word "petite" for a male.

Most pediatricians are forced to deal with distraught parents who haul their "midget" into the office to get hormones or vitamins or "some special treatment"—presumably a modified form of the rack. The doctor knows the child is perfectly normal but has no way of convincing the parents. No use telling them that if the child were abnormal the rate growth would have fallen off over a period of months rather than continuing at a normal rate. Even less use in showing them the charts that reveal a child can be much shorter than other children of the same age and still be perfectly normal.

One harassed pediatrician finally solved the problem for himself when he attended a meeting of a Pediatric Society at which the guest lecturer was the widely read author of a syndicated advice column. Over drinks, the pediatrician asked the author to publish something in his column that would reassure parents about this problem. The next week an article appeared, in answer to a "query from a reader," setting forth the reasons why so many parents are afraid their children are short and explaining why they have little reason for alarm.

The complaints from parents stopped at once.

LYDIA BAILEY TO PHYLLIS DILLER

Advice-givers have proliferated mightily in the twentieth century, but they have been around for a long time—doubtless since Eve became a grandmother.

The first, naturally, were the midwife, the witch doctor, and the alchemist. Their advice was directed more toward insuring a safe birth, and so they were, strictly speaking, in the obstetrical line rather than in pediatrics, although of course the very coinage of those terms lay centuries in the future.

The first professional advice-giver was Lydia Bailey who, in the year 1853, wrote a short article recommending the "sipping of various teas, particularly those made of sassafras and juniper, to stimulate the blood and thus assist the health of mother and baby throughout pregnancy." This appeared in a handprinted London periodical titled *The Tatler,* and quickly became so popular among the learned women of the city that the issue went into five printings. From that time on, Lydia Bailey wrote an article for every issue dealing with aspects of pregnancy and child care. Other British newspapers and periodicals followed *The Tatler*'s lead, and by 1860 American newspapers began enlisting doctors and women of some degree of prominence to write similar articles for them.

It is amusing now to read these early articles and the accompanying advertisements. The two greatest problems seemed to be menstrual pain and baby's teething. Both forms of discomfort were treated by medicines or solutions containing so much alcohol that results undoubtedly were achieved—even if a woman stayed drunk throughout her period and her baby equally drunk during its teething. In 1919 *Good Housekeeping* recommended that a drop of whiskey be rubbed on baby's gums to relieve the torment of teething. Such daring caused the leaders of the temperance movement to arise in wrath and force the advocates of "whiskey for babies" to withdraw, leaving the field to patent medicines that were practically pure alcohol.

Early American magazines like *Godey's Ladies' Book, Delineator, Woman's World, The Saturday Evening Post,* and the weekly rural newsmagazine *Grit,* often combined articles slanted to the pregnant woman or the young mother with columns of more general medical advice. Question-and-answer features were extremely popular, and by 1910 a doctor with some degree of literary talent or a woman who could communicate with other women could make as much as $10,000 a year in an era when the dollar still merited the cognomen "Almighty."

These early pieces seem quaintly innocuous today. Sexual intercourse was not referred to, and the eliminatory functions of the body were discussed so vaguely that information had to be gathered between, rather than in, the lines.

It is interesting to read the sort of advice mothers were given as recently as 1938. Most mothers were giving birth at home, and the 1938 edition of a book on prenatal care sponsored by the U.S. government devotes an entire chapter to the preparations necessary for home delivery, including a list of twenty-eight items that should be close at hand. If any mothers were bottle feeding, it was certainly not with the encouragement of government experts. "It is the first duty of every mother to nurse her baby. Every doctor, nurse or other attendant should insist that mother nurse her baby . . ."

Birth was considered a much more traumatic physical event. The 1938 edition tells us, "Most women are allowed to sit up in a chair for an hour on the tenth day. Usually they may walk about the room after two weeks, and by the end of the month they will be allowed to go up and down stairs . . ."

PROGRESS AND PROSPERITY

Today, virtually all the women's magazines feature articles on baby care. *Redbook, Good Housekeeping, Woman's Day, McCall's, Family Circle,* and others pay over half a million dollars every year to doctors, psychologists, or free-lance medical writers to render advice for women that has progressed considerably in frankness and expertise. Add to these a handful of popular slick magazines devoted exclusively to the baby market, such as *Parent's, Baby & Child Care,* and *American Baby,* the syndicated newspaper writers whose advice appears in Sunday newspapers and supplements, and the locally sponsored "experts" on radio and TV, and the income to advice-givers runs into the millions.

Prominent among the "new wave" of advice-givers is Dr. Lee Salk, youngest brother of Jonas Salk, who developed the polio vaccine. Through his column in *McCall's* magazine, his books, and television appearances, Dr. Salk has acquired a large and loyal following.

A pleasant-looking, spectacled, balding man, Dr. Salk claims, with a smile, to be "the only non-sexist in child psychology." He explains that this is because he never had problems of sexual identity, that he had asked for, and got, a doll and carriage to play with when he was only three years old.

Dr. Salk, further establishing his credentials with the feminist movement, vigorously supports the option of couples not to have children. To the familiar argument that only selfish couples refuse to have children, he replies, "Negligent parents are more selfish. There are people who *should* choose not to have children. Among them are those who feel they can't be bothered, irritable people, those who have too little patience, and those who lead a highly organized life. However, I agree that society has not yet reached the point where it approves a decision not to have children. We have a way to go before people will feel liberated, and not guilty about making such a choice."

If fewer people had children, the doctor observes, couples who wanted to have children could have as many as they like without seriously affecting the rate of population growth.

Dr. Salk believes in the nuclear family as the best possible environment for having children and thinks that men's orientation toward business makes parenthood of second importance in their life. He says single parenthood is unwise because "experience tells me that raising children is very time-consuming." For such blandly non-controversial opinions, he is paid an estimated six-figure annual income.

With his own children he is not permissive, sets rules, and expects to be obeyed. "But you have to respect their feelings. You can't march in and turn off a television set. Instead you say, 'When that's over, would you mind turning it off?' "

More and more he finds himself confronted with parents' questions about the effect of TV viewing on their preschoolers. Studies show that the average preschool child spends thirty to forty hours a week in front of the television set. Parents are concerned that their childern will become robotized while watching Hong Kong Phooey or Sigismund and the Sea Monsters.

Dr. Salk declares this is a problem each parent must solve for himself. "A parent should help a child select programs that are emotionally and intellectually stimulating, and then be firm in limiting viewing to these. It is also far easier to divert a child with an interesting book or hobby than it is to turn off the TV and offer no alternative at all."

That question is pretty thoroughly begged. No definition of an "emotionally and intellectually stimulating" program is offered, and children are presumably left to a full working week of The Flintstones, Scooby Doo, and Yogi and His Gang.

Dr. Salk believes honesty is the best way of dealing with children. He even believes in being honest about such favorite child fantasies as Santa Claus. "Explaining that Santa Claus is a make-believe person does not take away the myth. It takes away the lie." He also thinks that precocious and difficult questions should be answered honestly. "If you try to leave gaps, the children will fill in the gaps with their own damaging ideas."

One day, after his daughter Pia had watched him on television, she told him, "I'm so glad you know so much about children. Everything you say is right!"

The most recent addition to the ranks of the advice-givers is Nancy Moore Thurmond, twenty-eight-year-old wife of South Carolina's Senator Strom Thurmond, seventy-two, and mother of his three children. She has been writing columns for her state's daily and weekly newspapers, not, as one might hope, to discuss such topics as the virility and fertility of the senescent male, but proffering the sort of wisdom usually found on weighing machine cards or Chinese fortune cookies. "Turn off the TV and tune in to your child," "Let the love shine through," "Communicate with children—treat them as little people," or, as one column even breathlessly inquired, "By the way, have you hugged your kid today?"

One popular advice column in *American Baby* magazine simply turns its readers into experts. The magazine invites readers to send in tips on baby care. In recent issues readers passed on such counsel as how to keep toddlers from being pests in the kitchen (get colorful kitchen magnets shaped like fruits and flowers, and toddler will stay out of mischief while arranging them on the refrigerator door), how to get a youngster to keep a thermometer in his mouth (set up a three-minute egg timer and he'll be entertained watching the sand run through the glass until you find out if he has a fever), or where to store baby food (an old spice rack) or pacifiers (empty baby food jars). To keep soap and water out of eyes during a shampoo, a reader recommended letting a child wear a snorkel mask, adding that it's great fun for the kid too.

Each year at least twenty hardcover books and a greater number of paperbacks are published that deal with pregnancy, birth, and baby care. Counting the endless reprints of books already established, a total of over $33 million worth of "baby books" are sold annually. Some even offer answers to things for which no one has questions. Pat Boone's star-spangled ode to fatherhood and Phyllis Diller's laugh-spangled takeoff on motherhood are very apt to share a store display beside the learned works of Drs. Bruno Bettelheim and Arnold Gesell. Joan Rivers' humorous book about how to have a baby will be found along with the zesty advice of Dr. Lendon Smith and the provocative tomes of Albert Ellis, Ph.D.

DR. SPOCK

Who are the most popular advice-givers?

There would be a dispute about any names that follow number one, but of his identity there is no doubt. He is Benjamin McLane Spock, whose *Baby and*

Child Care (known in the hardcover edition as *The Common Sense Book of Baby and Child Care*) has sold more than 26 million copies and has been translated into twenty-six languages. We are going to deal with him at some length. His career spans the growth of the advice-giving industry and, in effect, stands as a metaphor for all the others.

Dr. Spock's book has grossed between a quarter and a half million dollars annually since its first publication in 1946. The end is not yet.

He has earned a good deal less than rumor has it. In 1946, when his book retailed for 25¢, his royalties came to about $6,000. The book quickly became a standard item in every American home, and his royalties climbed steadily along with the price. He now earns $50,000 a year on the royalties of the 95¢ paperback edition.

Dr. Spock told us how he came to write it: "After my pediatric training I took a year's residency in psychiatry and then five years of part-time psychoanalytic training, because I wanted to be able to give parents sound psychological advice. I was fascinated by all the new concepts I learned, but it turned out that none of them had any direct, practical usefulness in advising parents of babies and small children. I realized I would have to find the answers for myself and that it would be a slow, painful process. All I could do was to experiment cautiously in the psychological advice I gave to parents and then, when they came back, ask them anxiously how it worked.

"Five years after I started pediatric practice a publisher (Doubleday) asked me to write a book on child care, and I said instantly, 'Oh, I don't know anywhere near enough yet!'

"After I had practiced for ten years, an editor of Pocket Books approached me about a book. He said jokingly that it wouldn't have to be a very good book because at 25¢ a copy they could sell it by the tens of thousands anyway. This both reassured me about my ability to satisfy them and also inspired me with the idea of how many families I could help. I said I was ready. I told him I could write it, in the evenings, in six months. Of course, it took three years. After my regular work was done, I wrote from nine P.M. to one A.M., seven nights a week.

"I worried that the large amount of advice I offered would offend many physicians, and that parental misunderstanding of the advice might lead to tragedies. As the months went by following publication, I was mightily relieved to find that most physicians welcomed the book and that no parents accused me of killing their child."

Most pediatricians, busy tending babies and small children, were pleased to have a handy guide for mothers who did not know even the plain commonsense things about raising a child.

As one doctor puts it, "I think that was a time in our contemporary history when the effects of the breakup of the multi-generation home—no grandmother on hand to give advice—and our rather nomadic moving habits had begun to take effect. The young mother lacked a point of reference. She no longer had close friends with children with whom she could compare notes, or an older in-law to pass on the results of her experience.

"I'd read other books on baby and child care, and there were some very good ones on the market, but they shared a common fault: they were over the head of the average reader. Dr. Spock kept his simple, using terms any parent could understand. No knowledge is really useful if it can't be communicated. I believe he helped every pediatrician in the country by providing mothers with the basic facts of baby and child care and behavior."

Criticisms of Dr. Spock's approach have varied widely, but most authorities in the field find themselves in basic agreement with his common-sense advice. A few caution against accepting what he says "as literally as the dictionary." There has also been criticism from those outside the medical field such as Norman Vincent Peale, a good friend of former President Nixon, who from the pulpit castigated Dr. Spock as "responsible for the most undisciplined age in history," and former Vice President Spiro Agnew, who condemned his "paralyzing permissive philosophy." There are clear political overtones in such commentary. So far Dr. Spock has not reproached either Dr. Peale for his permissiveness toward Richard M. Nixon, nor Mr. Agnew for his permissiveness toward his own peculations in a position of public trust.

Dr. Spock indignantly rejects the idea that he encourages anything beyond urging parents to be more relaxed about discipline, to understand and trust a child's own natural drive toward maturity and responsibility, and to give proper consideration to the child's legitimate needs.

In his latest book, *Raising Children in a Difficult Time,* he further clarifies his attitude: "Some people believe there are only two ways to raise children: with overpermissiveness which they think produces brats, or with sternness and punishment which they think makes good citizens. Neither of these extremes works well, I'm convinced, from knowing thousands of American families and from observing child rearing in other countries also."

He adds, "I am not inclined to give arbitrary or specific directions to parents. I explain children's feelings and the deeper meaning of their behavior. I sympathize with parents' exasperations. Then I leave the maximal leeway to the parents' judgment for their actual management.

"I believe my book is popular not just for its cheapness and its six hundred twenty pages of coverage. Its real secret is its friendliness. Many other child care books have dictated and scolded, in the general spirit of 'Look out, stupid. If you don't do just as I say, you may kill your child.'

"Perceptive parents have written me a thousand variations of the following message, which nearly reduces me to tears: 'I feel as if you are talking personally to me, and as if you think I am a sensible person.' "

As for the changes in his book over the years: "I have revised *Baby and Child Care* as customs and my own perspectives have changed. The first edition was written when pediatric advice was still extremely rigid—especially about infant feeding schedules, toilet training, and parental cuddling. I advised flexibility, respect for individual differences and plenty of affection. I never advocated 'self-demand' feeding schedules but suggested working toward a regular schedule as fast as the baby could tolerate the shift.

"Ten years later, the pendulum had swung so far in the direction of no schedule at all that the more timid parents were uncertain whether they were entitled to even set a baby's bedtime. So in the second edition, published in 1957, I put a lot more emphasis on children's need for firm parental guidance. An entirely new section called *Strictness or Permissiveness* came down flatly that firmness is one aspect of parental love. Firmness, by keeping children on the right track, keeps them lovable. And they love us for keeping them out of trouble. About punishment I said, 'It is never the main element in discipline —it's only a vigorous additional reminder that the parent feels strongly about what he says.' It's not punishment that builds character, but the parents' love of their child.

"The reason today's young people cannot be intimidated as much is that they were not intimidated by their parents when they were children. I admit that I was easily intimidated when I was a child, especially by my mother but also by my teachers, local bullies, policemen, and barking dogs.

"In the 1968 edition, having become convinced that there is much too much toleration of violence in America and that children are being harmed by it, I advised against war toys or letting children watch brutality on TV. I also suggested that, in this troubled country and world, parents bring up their children not just to seek fulfillment but to feel an obligation to work for the common good.

"I presented a broad, new explanation for such habits as thumb sucking, the stroking of a cuddly toy or blanket, head rolling and head banging, and for resistance to weaning from the bottle.

"For the 1976 edition I am removing the sexist bias: 'he' for the child is being changed to 'they' or 'she.' No longer will it be assumed that mothers necessarily take more care of children and home than fathers. The chapter now titled 'Working Mother' will be changed to 'Working Parents.'

"I deny that I was ever a 'permissivist.' I was not labeled as such until *twenty-two years* after *Baby and Child Care* was published. I dislike a bratty child as much as anyone. Some children *are* being brought up with an insufficiency of parent control. I'm not thinking just about interrupting adults' conversation and stepping on their toes, but saying 'I hate you' and sticking out their tongues.

"I believe that some parents unconsciously enjoy their children's misbehavior. They allow a child to act out the misbehavior that they themselves were not allowed to act out as children."

Reading the various editions of *Baby and Child Care* published over the years, we find Dr. Spock modifying his views on other subjects. In 1946 he says a child will toilet train himself sooner or later without parental interference. In 1957, his confidence ebbing, he suggests mothers might gently and gradually, and without struggle, encourage children to signal their need to use the bathroom. He says that by using this method, children will be toilet trained quickly. He was wrong, as mothers lost no time in letting him know.

By 1968, he is advising mothers to firmly begin toilet training the child by eighteen months and to persist until the job is done.

Queried about this, he replied quite reasonably that "all these methods were successful to a degree, but not enough. Why not change advice as experience shows that it was not good enough?"

Dr. Spock has now come to realize that people with less education—families he's known in clinics—do better at toilet training. "They don't worry about hurting their children's psyches because they've never read anything about psyches. They have no worries or guilt about neurosis, so they just go ahead and get the job done."

Events are trying to outstrip the good doctor. His estimate of the time required for toilet training, as an example, is now believed to be seriously off the mark. Two psychologists, Nathan H. Azrin, who heads the Behavior Research Laboratory at Anna State Hospital, Illinois, and Richard M. Foxx, who teaches child psychology at Southern Illinois University, claim that the average child of normal intelligence should require less than half a day of training. They have devised a training procedure that emphasizes "language ability, imagination, imitation, verbal rehearsal and verbal instructions in addition to learning by association and learning by reward."

Dr. Spock remains undismayed. "All pediatricians once assumed toilet training would take months, not just me," he told us. "And how do you know that the new method of Azrin and Foxx will prove effective and harmless in other hands? Proposals come and go."

Some say Dr. Spock does not lead but merely follows a trend. He himself interprets this differently. "I'm not trying to keep up with anyone, only with the truth as I perceive it." In his attempt to keep up with truth, Dr. Spock has altered his views on such topics as children's aggressiveness, sloppiness and fooling around at meals. He told us, "I think that many conscientious parents are still timidly permissive with their children. I see no signs of a swing back to authoritativeness."

Others do, however. "People are undoubtedly going back to the idea of role-authoritarian discipline," a noted psychiatrist says. "That is when you say to a child, 'Why should you listen to me? Because I am your mother, that's why!' There is definitely a return to discipline. And the emergence of the strong parent has brought back with it 'the model child.' "

Not every arbiter is happy with that. "Personally, I am much more worried about the quiet child than the rebellious child," says psychiatrist James Anthony. "The conformist child goes along for years, and then suddenly trouble comes in some big dramatic action."

Others are convinced that family income is what conditions child rearing and that neither parents nor children can be treated as homogenous groups.

"Dr. Spock has always been oriented toward the middle and upper classes," says a pediatrician whose practice is usually with clinic patients on the Lower East Side of Manhattan. "But that charge could also be leveled at the whole birth practice in the United States with its private doctor-and-patient, fee-for-services bias. It's perfectly true that most doctors practice on the poor until they learn how to take care of the rich. Poor children have more serious illnesses, die more frequently at all ages, have more personality disorders, and receive far less medical care and attention than those who are better able to pay."

"Dr. Spock might as well be writing science fiction," a Washington, D.C., pediatrician says. "It has no relation to what I see every day, no bearing on how poor people live. He talks about a family doctor and that's a joke to people who never saw a family doctor. The only doctor they know—when they get to see any—is the one who works at the clinic."

A black doctor in St. Louis: "Spock doesn't know where it's at with ghetto people. In his book the mother stays at home and looks after the children while the father works. With blacks, it's usually the mother who's working because she's the only one who can get a job. And most of the families on welfare have only one parent. What they have got is plenty of children—and no time to worry about raising them by Spock's rules."

"What makes me laugh is when he talks about how important it is for a child to have a room to itself," adds a Chicago pediatrician who treats mainly the children of welfare mothers. "He takes for granted that every child has his own bed. The kids I treat, they sleep anywhere from two to six in a room, and a lot of them sleep with their parents and not in a crib either. There's no room for a crib if they could afford one.

"And the parents don't worry about the psychological harm they can do to a child by forcing it to eat. They worry about putting food on the table and about the garbage piling up in the halls, the toilets that don't work, the lead poisoning from cheap peeling paint and the roaches and the rats. There's no such thing as preventive medicine for them. Doctors are for emergencies."

To give Dr. Spock credit, he is quite aware of the problems of the poor. "I used to assume that there has to be a certain amount of poverty, but now I realize that poverty simply isn't necessary in the world's richest nation. If the Scandinavian people can abolish it, why can't we?

"I used to hem and haw about the distribution of health care in America, saying I had been too busy with child development to study it. Now, it's easy for me to see that the unequal distribution of care here is absolutely unnecessary. We have the world's best researchers, plenty of money, and excellent training facilities. We could be first among nations instead of fifteenth.

"I am fully aware of the criticism that my books and articles for parents do not deal with poverty, inadequate living and recreational conditions, and the inevitable deprivation of children which results. But I write for parents who are seeking advice about the best ways to raise their children. That's why I discuss the value of good diets, nursery schools and day-care centers, educational and creative playthings, story reading, answering children's questions, having the company of loving fathers and mothers as much as possible. Books on child care are bought by people who have, or are striving for, middle-class values, not by people who are harassed and demoralized by poverty."

In 1947 Dr. Spock, who up to then had been in practice in New York City, was asked to join the staff of the Rochester (Minnesota) Child Health Institute which was financed by the Mayo Clinic, to work out an ideal physical and mental health program for the children of that city. In 1951 he went to the University of Pittsburgh to organize a department of child psychiatry and child development. In 1955 he moved on to Western Reserve Medical School to participate in a new curriculum in which medical students begin to care for a family from their first year in school instead of having to wait until the third year. He retired in 1967.

Beginning in 1954 he wrote a monthly column for *Ladies' Home Journal.* In 1963 he shifted to *Redbook.*

In 1957, while a revised edition of *Baby and Child Care* was being prepared, his paperback publisher, Pocket Books, decided to insert advertisements into it. Their reasoning: the book was so large (627 pages) and was then being sold for such an unusually low price (50¢), that the additional revenue was needed. Dr. Spock objected on the grounds that ads might "cheapen" his book, but the publishers had the legal right to disregard his wishes, and did so.

Dr. Spock insisted on a revised contract, which permitted advertising provided there was no connection between him and the products advertised, that the advertising claims were not to be exaggerated or undignified, and that he would have a veto over the products and the copy.

He carefully checked the copy for each ad that went into the twenty- to twenty-six-page supplement inserted into the middle of the book. We have seen a Johnson ad for a "unique, no tears formula" baby shampoo on which he scribbled, "Is this one really no tears?" and volunteered to try a drop in his own eye first. On another occasion he was seen sucking on a baby bottle nipple to check out an advertiser's claim.

However, the presence of advertising in his book continued to annoy him. Paperbacks had earlier included advertising, but eventually *Baby and Child Care* was the only one. He felt the publisher was trading on his good name to cash in on an advertising bonanza that exceeded a quarter of a million dollars annually.

When the publisher continued to ignore his complaints, he decided to sue. He claimed the publisher was hurting his good name, that his was the only book carrying ads, and that the very presence of the ads misled the public into believing he himself endorsed the products. The suit was finally settled out of court in December 1965. Pocket Books promised to remove the ads from *Baby and Child Care* after the 1971 printing, providing he agreed to another revision of the book that year and also promised to deliver by the following year a new book, *Facts of Life for Teenagers.*

Dr. Spock spent $40,000 of his own money in legal costs and ended up with a settlement most observers agree was heavily weighted in favor of the publisher. In his battle against the merchandizers of *Baby and Child Care,* he fared no better than the average consumer.

It may be impossible to estimate the full impact of Dr. Spock on our times, but one pediatrician puts it this way: "At least fifty million American women have raised their kids by his book. At this moment the bulk of children reared by Spock—eighty million or so—have reached or will reach shortly their majority. I think it's safe to say that no American in history has exerted as much influence on his nation."

We prepared a simple questionnaire and submitted it to a panel of one hundred mothers, almost all from middle-income families and ranging in age from twenty to forty-five. The questions and the answers we received follow:

1. Have you heard of Dr. Spock?
   Answers: 96 Yes, 1 No, 3 Don't know.
2. Have you read his book?
   Answers: 84 Yes, 10 No, 6 Don't know.
3. Do you believe in his approach to baby and child care?
   Answers: 60 Yes, 11 No, 29 Don't know.
4. Would you define his approach to childrearing as (a) too permissive (b) too strict?*
   Answers: 56 Too permissive, 22 Too strict, 22 Don't know.

Many interviewees volunteered further statements. Here is a sampling.

- "I couldn't have raised my kids without him. It was like having a doctor right in the house."
- "I think he helped ruin my kids. All this business about individuality may be good, but I've got three selfish, irresponsible teen-agers on my hands. It's because I followed his advice too much."
- "I think he's the most important man this country has ever produced."
- "If it wasn't for his book, I wouldn't have two well-adjusted children. I think the world of him."
- "He seems to think he's God or something. And lately he seems to be down on women."
- "He was a big help to us in raising our kids, but I wish he'd stay out of politics."

Another Dr. Spock book, *Decent and Indecent: Our Personal and Political Behavior* (1970), sailed full into the contrary winds of Women's Lib.

Dr. Spock admits, "I was skinned alive by the feminists on several scores.

*Dr. Spock's comment: "That's an insufficient variety of choices." (And he's quite right.)

In *Baby and Child Care,* the child is always 'he' and the parent is usually 'she.' I assumed that if both parents want careers, it is the mother who must make the career sacrifices, such as part-time work when the children are young, if no satisfactory sitter can be found. I said, and I blush to admit it now, that a father shows his appreciation of his daughter by praising her dress or the cookies she has baked. I was foolish enough to write an article years ago giving my ideas about inborn differences in temperament between men and women. Of course I was a sexist and a male chauvinist—as were one hundred percent of men and ninety-eight percent of women. The difference between the others and me was that I put my sexism into print where it could be singled out for scorn when the women's liberation movement arose."

Dr. Spock admits he has qualms about how far the movement toward rearing sons and daughters with minimal sex distinctions will go. "No country I know of has tried to bring them up to think of themselves as similar. Such an attempt would be the most unprecedented social experiment in the history of our species.

But I don't agree with the accusation that I have been 'a major oppressor of women.' I've always had deep respect for women, as readers of *Baby and Child Care* point out. And even in the 1946 edition, I urged fathers to participate in the care of their babies right from birth. I think that if the women who came down on me so hard had read the book, there wouldn't have been so much fuss."

It's now clear, however, that the "fuss" portends a significant trend in the making. The philosophy of the new feminism is at variance with the "togetherness" that is at the core of Dr. Spock's teachings. If the new philosophy continues to gain acceptance, his long reign may have reached its sere and yellow leaf.

Sales in this country of his famous book have dropped off, although they continue to climb in the rest of the world.* Perhaps the decline in America

---

*Pocket Book American sales averaged about 800,000 a year from 1946 to 1968. Since then about 500,000 a year. (Paperback publishers' figures vary a lot from year to year, representing not sales but shipments.)

From 1946 to about 1950	(sales 800,000 a year)
Price was 25 cents	gross $200,000
Royalty, ¾ cent	Spock income $6,000
From about 1950 to about 1957	(sales 800,000 a year)
Price was 35 cents	gross $280,000
Royalty 2.1 cents	Spock income $17,000
From about 1957 to 1968	(sales 800,000 a year)
Price was 50 cents	gross $400,000
Royalty 3 cents	Spock income $24,000
From 1968	(sales 500,000 a year)
Price was 95 cents	gross $475,000
Royalty 9.5 cents	Spock income $47,500

Foreign royalties averaged $7,000 ten years ago; have since climbed to $30,000 average.

is due to his involvement with the anti-war movement and the attacks on him by Norman Vincent Peale and former Vice President Spiro Agnew. (Dr. Spock comments humorously that he is very glad no one can say Spiro Agnew was raised by his book because everyone knows what happened to him!) The declining birth rate may also be an important reason for the decline in sales. But there are now several "generations" of pediatricians since Spock's book first was published, and many of them appear to modern parents as more "up to date."

That does not mean Dr. Spock's book will simply wither away. Nor will everyone stop reading Erich Fromm's *ABC of Child Care,* Lendon Smith's *The Baby Doctor,* or Albert Ellis's *How to Prevent Your Child from Becoming a Neurotic Adult.* It only means that new advice-givers are profiting from parents' anxieties.

Some doctors condemn parents' dependence on book and magazine and newspaper advice-givers, and recommend that they rely on their own common sense and intuition. But few have any real hope of changing a phenomenon that has acquired so much social momentum.

As one pediatrician told us, "The average American couple is as well equipped to raise a child as to fly by flapping their arms. If something they read helps them to do a better job, everyone will be better off for it.

"Especially the kids."

WHO'S SITTING WITH BABY?

5

"We'd go out a lot more often than we do, but we just can't afford it. By the time we get through buying tickets to a movie or a concert or a play, and something to eat afterward—and then add the price of a baby-sitter—forget it. It's better to stay home and watch TV than have to live on tuna fish and casseroles the rest of the week."

Robert Anderson of Eugene, Oregon, is one of 20 million young Americans with small children who finds the cost of baby-sitting more than he can handle. In an escalating economy the high price of the teen-ager or the adult woman "sitter" is a cruel blow to the family budget.

A New York theater manager complains, "It isn't enough that we have muggings and weird commuter schedules and high restaurant prices to contend with; now we've got a baby-sitting problem. Kids in their teens charging two fifty an hour—it's no wonder we've lost the parent audience."

Psychologists confirm the need for young parents to escape from the nest. In order to cope with duties and responsibilities, they need fun and games and recreation. That need is even more crucial for the young working woman who lives alone—widowed, divorced or unwed—and has preschool children to look after.

A young Detroit woman, who works as a filing clerk: "It costs me half of what I make to have my boy looked after, and sometimes he isn't looked after any too good. And I've lost two jobs just because sitters didn't show up and

I had to stay home with the baby. They don't much care whether they come or not because they can always get another job."

A Salt Lake City woman, divorced, who works as a cocktail waitress: "I've got a woman, finally, to take care of the kids. Two dollars an hour, plus—and it's those 'pluses' that add up. She demands a full dinner at night, a snack, and she always has a couple of drinks before she goes home. She won't lift a finger around the apartment; I'm surprised she even changes the kids."

Complaints about the cost of baby-sitting—and the care given small children—are endlessly repetitious. In several score interviews we heard only an occasional good word said for the practice. Most people who pay for baby-sitters think of them as a necessary evil, part of the price that must be paid for having and raising children.

We were not sure if we should include a survey of baby-sitting in this book, because the relationship between the producer (sitter) and the consumer (parent) is usually personal, informal, and non-exploitative. Parents are quite capable of judging the value to them of the service they are purchasing, and competition in the field keeps the hourly rate for sitters comparatively low.

It was, finally, the importance of baby-sitting within the average family's budget that convinced us it was a valid area for inquiry. The figures are surprising. In 1974, Americans spent a total of ten billion dollars on baby-sitters. Of this sum, three billion went to day-care centers, private or government-sponsored, and the remaining seven billion went to the "private" girl or woman who is paid, depending on area and demand, anywhere from $1.50 to $3.00 an hour.

According to a recent ruling of the Labor Department, baby-sitters who work less than twenty hours a week are exempt from the law covering domestic workers, which provides for a $1.90 an hour minimum wage. Baby-sitters are only covered if they sit on a regular or recurring basis for more than twenty hours a week or if they spend more than 20 percent of their time doing housework while baby-sitting. The question is academic, for in most areas the baby-sitter is paid more than the minimum wage.

SERVICE AND SUPPLY

Almost every city of 75,000 and over has one or more companies that offer baby-sitting services. The "company" has girls and/or women available for private home sitting.

Ruth Ashley, who founded Child Care in Atlanta, Georgia, in 1962, says, "Most of our sitters are older women—the grandmotherly type who want to pick up a little extra money without endangering their social security or welfare. We prefer that they have had children of their own and know the basics of child behavior.

"Occasionally a teen-ager applies who has helped raise younger brothers and sisters. We can send her out and be reasonably sure she'll do a good job. But most teen-ager applicants we turn down because they expect to be paid $2.00 an hour just to sit and neck with their boyfriends. They don't know the basic rudiments of child care and don't care to learn.

"Taking care of a preschool child is not the simplest thing in the world. An evening can be quite an ordeal if the child goes into a trauma about mother leaving and a stranger coming in to care for him. If an infant is teething, or feverish, or spitting up, the sitter can have a difficult few hours. Then there are the undisciplined kids who need spanking badly but can't be given one by the sitter.

"Our sitters have to know what to do in an emergency. We require that the parent leave not only the number where she can be reached in case of illness or accident, but show the baby-sitter exits in case of fire, the location of the fuse box, and a list of the appropriate emergency phone numbers. Parents are more careless about this than you would ever imagine.

"The rate we charge varies from two to three dollars an hour, depending on the hours involved, the experience of the sitter, the number of children, and any special problems. The fifteen percent we collect is worth it to the sitter because we can virtually assure all the employment she wants." (In New York City, and some other localities, the practice is for the agency to charge both parent *and* sitter.)

The major source of "labor supply" in the baby-sitting world is the teen-ager who wants or needs money beyond her allowance. Women commenting on the quality of care extended by the teen-age sitter split roughly 50-50 between pro and con.

Here are a few quotes:

- "Deborah is a gem. My children absolutely adore her. If we have to leave right after dinner and the dishes aren't done, she'll do them for me. She even straightens up the children's rooms."
- "I have yet to find a youngster who's worth the money they charge. I don't know how often we've tried to call home to see how things were going, only to get a busy signal hour after hour. Twice we've come home to see a boy sneaking out the back door. I plan a good snack for the sitter, but if I don't hide everything else that's edible, my grocery budget will be shot for a week. And most of them pay no attention to my kids. How often I've come home to find the pillows wet with tears, as though they'd cried for hours!"
- "We bought what was supposed to be a virtually indestructible hi-fi, a Magnovox console. It's been repaired three times in the last two years. Our baby-sitters busted the tone-arm and even kicked a hole in the speaker. The console is scratched and dented, and all our pop records are so badly scratched they're not playable. Kids today act like a wrecking gang when they go into somebody else's home."
- "We've had a few good teen-agers, but not many. Two years ago we had

problems with girls who had their friends in to smoke pot and do some heavy necking. Now we hide anything alcoholic because the kids seem to have taken up drinking. I shudder to think of what goes on sexually: we did learn that one sweet sixteen-year-old we hired made more money entertaining high school boys at five bucks a throw than she ever made baby-sitting."

· "We almost always have this nice girl, Marcia, who knows so much about little children because she has four younger sisters. She seems like one of the family."

THEY SIT AND WAIT

There's another side to this ten-billion-dollar coin.

Laura Rasmussen, a fifty-five-year-old Denver grandmother: "There are at least a dozen houses where I won't set foot no matter how much they offer to pay me. If a child is so spoiled he can't be controlled, the agitation is just too much to bear. And if a house is so dirty I'm afraid to eat anything in the refrigerator, I don't go back again. Thank God I can afford to be a little choosy."

Other grievances are cited by the fifteen-year-old daughter of a Larchmont, New York, family: "The people who really give me a pain are the ones who call at the last minute to ask if you can sit for them right *now*. Then they get annoyed if you tell them you have other plans for the evening. Other pests are the people who ask you to sit from seven thirty and then call up to ask if you can come half an hour earlier—just in time to miss having your dinner. And they don't leave anything for you to eat but cornflakes. I had one baby-sitting job that lasted from seven o'clock to two o'clock in the morning—and there wasn't any food in the house. All I had was a couple of sugar cubes with a cup of tea."

Marsha Stein, a Los Angeles high-school senior: "I've sat, usually four or five nights a week, since I was a freshman. It's the mothers that bug me. A lot of them will leave a sink stacked with dirty dishes, not even cleaned off, and say casually, 'Oh, if you get a chance could you tidy up the kitchen.' And they don't clean their diapers very well and I have to put diapers on the kids that smell like they were used. It makes you want to gag. Half the women I sit for are such pigs I don't even know how their husbands stand 'em."

A Madison, Wisconsin, college freshman who baby-sits to earn his spending money: "I always let people know I can't sit past midnight because I have to get up early for school. But there are always those who say that's okay and then stop off for drinks or go to a friend's house and don't get home until two or three in the morning. It just isn't fair!"

A Berkeley, California, teen-ager: "The main problems I've come across are **spoiled** kids and husbands who take me home and make a pass at me. You'd be surprised how many do that. It gets to be such a drag. It's safer on the street than it is in a car with some of those middle-aged husbands!"

Most informative was a talk with four teen-aged girls who formed a baby-sitting co-op in their home town, Seattle. The burden of their complaints was failure by parents to alert them to the small, overlooked problems.

"Parents know to tell you about the big things," says Lesley Schwarz, oldest of the group at seventeen. "You always get the doctor's phone number or how to get the police emergency squad. But that never has been a problem once for any of us. Why don't they tell us what rooms are off limits to the children? Are the kids the mischievous kind who turn on stoves or poke things into the electrical outlets? Is there a favorite doll or toy that they like to go to bed with—or that will persuade them to go to sleep when they don't want to? Do we just drop a diaper in the toilet when it's soiled? Do we put dirty plates and stuff in the sink—or in the dishwasher? Does the baby have to finish the whole bottle, or can a little milk be left over? Or suppose a baby gets hungry before mealtime? Do I feed it to keep it from crying or let it yowl?"

There is always the risk of tragedy due to a sitter's neglect.

Items:

· A one-and-a-half-year-old boy in Hartford, Connecticut, drowned in the bathtub because the baby-sitter left him alone while she went to answer the phone.
· A Milwaukee couple returned home unexpectedly early to find their sitter, a sweet "granny" type, holding their infant daughter over a gas jet, explaining that "she went to sleep so nice that way." It turned out, on investigation, she had been doing this to her charges for years.
· In Orlando, Florida, four youngsters burned to death when the sitter dashed out of the house after a greased pan caught fire in the kitchen.
· In Los Angeles, two small children were beaten to death by a sitter who "couldn't stand them crying."

The National Safety Council reports that upward of 7,500 children below the age of ten die annually through "improper care and attention . . . in the absence of a parent." What proportion of these deaths can be attributed directly to baby-sitters, the Council doesn't say, nor are there any other statistics available on the subject, but a common-sense verdict would have to place the percentage fairly high. And that makes baby-sitting a cause of death that ranks with better publicized medical killers of children!

LIVE-IN SITTERS

On December 30, 1971, a flash fire caused by a defective string of Christmas tree lights destroyed the home of William and Janet Martin in Santa Monica, California. The Martins were away in Palm Springs for the New Year holiday, but their resident sitter saved their three sons and three of their four dogs, bodily carrying the youngest child and the animals out into the yard and waking the older boys.

Pansy Storey, twenty-four, the heroine of the rescue, is an English girl the Martins hired in London and brought to the U.S. on a work permit.

"It isn't inexpensive," Janet Martin told us. "You have to pay their fare over and provide the additional fare for a home vacation every two years, but all things considered the monthly salary for a sitter who lives in isn't prohibitive. We go out a good deal and we love to travel, so think of what we'd spend by the hour or the day or the weekend if Pansy didn't live in.

"Pansy is finishing college while she's here so when she goes back to England she'll be equipped for a good job. In the meantime she's bringing up my boys with better manners than we'd have taught them ourselves, and she's so totally reliable we never have to worry when we're away from the house.

"What she did during that fire . . ." Mrs. Martin shuddered. "I wonder if I'd have had the good sense she had. No panicking at all, just very systematically getting the boys and the dogs out of the house. Her own life was endangered, but she never gave that a thought!"

Pansy Storey's behavior in crisis has, of course, more to do with her character than with the fact she was a "live-in" baby-sitter. But the chances of having such a reliable and resourceful person at home are much better if she is virtually a member of the family than a person unknown by the parents and a stranger to the children.

An increasing number of American families employ European girls, primarily of college student age, as live-in sitters. The permits are relatively easy to obtain if the girl comes to the U.S. with the returning vacationing parents and intends to study full or part time at a college or vocational school. Passport registrations indicate that over five thousand girls now work as live-in baby-sitters. Most are from Britain, Ireland, and the Scandinavian countries, though wealthy Italian and Greek couples are more inclined to import girls from their homelands.

Illana Papadakis, a Milwaukee wholesaler's wife, explains: "Stavros and I brought Melina back with us when we went to Greece three years ago. It is ideal for our household because at the same time she is studying in college, she is helping us teach the children Greek customs and the language. These things are very important to us."

In addition to transportation and (usually) tuition costs, the live-in sitter from abroad is paid from $150 to $350 a month, plus room and board. They are not expected to cook or clean, though most pitch in voluntarily to prepare snacks or meals for the children and to clean up after them. Most have Sundays off, plus their daytime or evening hours in class, and are free to date or have friends over on evenings when the parents are at home. It is difficult to estimate the hours they actually work, since the larger part of their time is spent simply "being there."

The question of why more American girls do not seek employment as "live-in" sitters, sometimes called mother's helpers or au pair girls, is probably answered by our attitude toward "domestics." In Europe there is no stigma to being a domestic, governess, nanny, or resident baby-sitter. Not so here, at least not since 1940 when the prewar surge in employment lured girls into factories and offices. For a century before that, millions of American girls, mostly from farms and small towns, had been working as live-in child tenders, maids or cooks. But with the shift in social attitude, domestic service of any kind came to be regarded as inferior to office or factory employment.

There are signs, however, that another shift in attitude might be occurring. It is being led by college students who want to earn money to help pay the ever-increasing tuition or living expenses. In 1964, few if any students advertised on college bulletin boards for live-in jobs. In 1974, a check at several colleges revealed dozens of such notices posted on the board at any given time. If this trend continues, it will undoubtedly influence social attitudes toward such labor, for it isn't likely that work college students find acceptable is going to be looked down on by those with less education.

How does a parent go about finding such a sitter? Usually via an agency. One of the better known is the Anne Andrews Employment Agency in New York City. This agency charges a fee both to employer and employee that amounts to eighteen percent of the first month's salary or ten percent of the total, whichever is less.

Mrs. Anne Andrews, who founded the agency, told us: "In most of these positions the major work involves the care of the children, which may include cooking for them (not for the whole family) and keeping their rooms picked up. Not the heavy cleaning. Time off is mostly one whole day a week, with evenings free when the mother is home, but almost never on weekends. The salary ranges up to $95 a week for experienced college girls, and teachers are paid $100 plus.

"I give an applicant one important tip about the interview: always ask the mother to outline a typical day, then definitely settle all the details of housework ahead of time. I urge, whenever possible, that a trial period for at least a weekend be tried before the job actually begins.

"I remember one young girl, pale, thin, with tired eyes who came back to my desk in September after a summer's employment.

" 'My mother is furious with you, Mrs. Andrews,' she said. 'I lost twenty pounds last summer taking care of those five children. It was so exhausting. Both the mother and the father spent all day, every day, in their studio on the top floor. They are both writers—they came downstairs only to eat the meals which I cooked. I had to do all the heavy cleaning, all the shopping. I got the baby up in the morning before getting breakfast for everybody. I did just plain *everything!* And you won't believe it, but I only had time off when they all went to church on Sunday mornings.'

"I said, 'Good heavens, why in the world did you *stay* there?' 'I'll tell you why,' she answered. 'Because of just one single thing. The children, the parents, the whole family were absolutely the most perfectly wonderful people I'll ever meet in my life. I've never been so happy. The summer was the most thrilling thing that ever happened to me. That's why I stayed!' "

We asked Mrs. Andrews to forecast the future in this field. "For the summer mother's helpers there will be fewer jobs if a lasting depression sets in. For others this may not be so, if more mothers find they *must* go to work. Because of inflation, the salaries will continue to rise—as they have done since the beginning. We may get fewer applications because more parents will try to save money by advertising in the newspapers, even though this can lead to a compromise about the quality of girls employed. Finally, more professional women will be applying for such jobs all the time!"

An interesting switch on the live-in baby-sitter is a new service that, in effect, offers to rent parents. For those who would like to go on a trip but don't know what to do with their children, an organization will provide a live-in couple. They will not only watch the kids but will clean the house, cook the meals, and do the shopping.

Ed Rockower, who directs University Home Services in Villanova, Pennsylvania, charges about $25 a day for this service. The average term of service is about ten days, and the longest so far is six weeks. About 150 couples, usually young and married, are available for home-and-children sitting through his organization.

University Home Services will also "sit" for plants and pets, or empty houses. If asked, the couples will perform such extra little chores as taking a regular turn in the car pool, forwarding mail, or even, as in one instance, showing a house to prospective buyers.

The very wealthy can, and do, go to great lengths to keep a good baby-sitter —even on the live-out basis. A Del Monte executive guarantees a high-school girl sitter a month in Europe each summer, all expenses paid, provided she is available when needed the other eleven months of the year. Other well-to-do couples take the sitter (of whatever age) along on vacations, just to make sure their services are retained.

"We spend the summer in Hawaii, and our sitter spends it with us," explains the wife of a C&H Sugar Company executive. "I know I can depend on her, and the children adore her, so why not?"

CO-OPS

Medium- and low-income couples cannot, of course, treat a sitter to such luxuries. The costs of baby-sitting are escalating along with almost everything else in the inflated seventies, and they have been forced to look for other solutions. Groups of suburban wives, married college students with children, and office women with youngsters at home have formed baby-sitting co-ops to eliminate baby-sitting expenses.

One such co-op is described by Ruth Taylor of Van Nuys, California. "When it got to the point that my husband's salary hardly matched our cost of living, we simply had to economize. I figured one way we could really cut down expenses was to eliminate the dollar fifty an hour [price is circa 1973] we paid for baby-sitters. With neighbors and friends, we worked out a system. We take the kids to each other's houses when we need a baby-sitter, or if both of them are home that evening, one of them will come over. We all feel better knowing we've got another parent sitting with our children and not just a teen-ager. And you know how youngsters love sleeping over at someone else's house!"

Sometimes the arrangement is on a couple-to-couple basis, an exchange of services on nights when social obligations do not conflict. More often, five to twelve couples are involved as a group, with at least two women sitting for the others' progeny on a night out.

In Park Forest, Illinois, where blocks of rental units are occupied by young couples with small children, the co-ops are casually organized on a block-by-block basis. Nonworking wives exchange daytime sitting for shopping or bridge as well as for nighttime social events.

"We could only afford to go out one night a week before we organized a co-op," one young wife explains, "and even at that, baby-sitters came to about eight to ten dollars a week. Now we go out two or three nights a week and don't pay a penny for sitters."

There are other advantages. The children involved in such a co-op arrangement have a built-in circle of friends, and their parents also come to know each other in a way that isn't easy to do these days in either suburb or city.

"I particularly like making friends with the other mothers," a twenty-two-year-old woman told us. "In our group, most of of us have only one baby so far. I learn a lot from listening to the others talk about their experiences. We compare notes and find out we're all living with the same problems and making the same kinds of mistakes. It's funny, but it can be a big help just to hear that all babies are cranky when teething and that they all wake up during the night and that you don't have to feel guilty because you hate being dragged up out of a sound sleep to look after them. I've got a lot more patience now with my own son because I understand that his problems aren't so peculiar—they're just a normal part of growing up."

Co-op sitting, however, has its own risks. In Marian, Indiana, five youngsters were left with a member of the co-op who was, unknown to the others, a secret tippler. She fell asleep on the couch and the lighted cigarette she dropped started a fire in which three of the children died of smoke inhalation. There is also the story of a Baltimore divorcee who left two children with a fellow co-op member. "Left" is the operative word—she returned two weeks later to claim her children after enjoying a tryst with her lover. And one sadder but wiser wife in a co-op in Park Forest, Illinois, learned why her husband, a college administrator, volunteered for nighttime sitting. It was not, as he said, that he could take a briefcase of reading material with him. He was meeting his girlfriend in each neighbor's apartment and saving the price of a motel room!

Because the convenience and economy far outweigh the risks, thousands of co-ops are springing up throughout the country. In the opinion of many mothers we interviewed, there would be a greater number of co-ops if more women knew how to go about organizing one.

"It isn't as hard as you'd think," says Mary Woodes of Orlando, Florida. "All it takes is a little effort. If you've met other mothers while taking your baby for an outing, then you've probably got a start right there. If you want to add others, put a notice on one of those supermarket bulletins or a small classified ad in a local paper—it only costs a few dollars. Once you're underway with a co-op, you don't have to worry about getting new members. Word of mouth is going to bring you all the mothers you need. You'll have to start limiting your group—maybe only accepting mothers with one or two children or those who live within a certain close-by area. Our group won't take anybody who lives more than ten blocks from the other members. Nobody likes to drive a big distance to get or drop off their kids."

Mary Woodes also suggests some rules that she has found worked well for her group. "The gadder [the mother who is going out] should always call for a sitter at least forty-eight hours in advance. And she should notify the secretary of points as soon as possible after the sit has taken place. Also, she shouldn't forget to leave a phone number where she can be reached, and there have to be definite rules about things like cancellations and penalties. In our group we've found it very helpful to supply each member with the names, addresses and telephone numbers of all the others. We have a mimeographed list that includes the name and number of the baby's pediatrician."

Although the purpose of baby co-ops is always the same, the organization varies. There has to be some way of keeping count of the hours each member spends in sitting for the others. In Mary Woodes' group, which consists of eighteen members, there is one who is assigned as full-time "secretary." She keeps the records and is "paid" in baby-sitting time by the others.

This is how it works: If Mary Woodes sits for another woman's baby for four hours, she then calls the secretary who adds four "points" to her score and subtracts them from the member she "sat" for. No one is allowed to be more than ten points in arrears, and if they fall behind, they are "assessed"

$2.00 for each hour owed, in addition to having to make up the owed time.

There are other variations to this arrangement. In some instances, coupons are issued to represent a sitter's time, and these coupons, usually simple index cards, are given out at the beginning of each month. Each member gets a certain number, and when these are used up, she must sit for another member to earn more. Or they can purchase coupons at an agreed-upon price—usually based on the cost of baby-sitting in the community.

In the majority of co-ops we investigated, there was no permanent secretary. The job was simply rotated on a monthly basis among the members.

To young white suburbanites involved in a co-op, the baby-sitting exchange seems an entirely new idea. But throughout American history, a similar arrangement has existed in rural communities, where farm wives expect a neighbor's children to be dropped off to be cared for in case of need. In the cities, this has also been a common practice in ghettos, slums, tenements and barrios. Among the poor, common needs are mutually acknowledged and taken care of.

"When I was growing up in Harlem," a black nurse comments, "I bet I shared my bed at one time or another with every little girl in the neighborhood, sometimes two or three of them at once. Their mothers would get sick, or have to go to work, and would bring the kids in. When my mother had to work or she and Dad took a trip somewhere, I'd simply be packed off down the street to a neighbor. It was fun most of the time."

"We have to do it," explains Maria Ortiz of East Los Angeles. "Life is hard enough as it is, and if we couldn't find somebody to take care of the kids we'd have a hard time keeping a job and we'd never get out to have any fun."

In northern Minnesota, the old and the new baby-sitting methods exist side by side. In the Scandinavian farm areas, the hired baby-sitter is virtually unknown. But there is another more prosperous community made up of couples who moved in during the middle 1940s. The area was then enjoying a boom based on a new discovery in processing the low-grade iron ore known as taconite. Companies recruited executive and technical help from outside the area, and these people still hire baby-sitters.

"You wouldn't believe the contrast in life-styles," says Marie Colman, a teacher in a Bemidji, Minnesota, grade school. "With the families native to this region, little girls didn't grow up playing with dolls—they tended their younger brothers and sisters. By the time they were eight or nine years old, their parents felt it was perfectly safe to leave them home to care for the younger kids. If there was no older sister, then there were grandparents who lived a farm or two away. If there were no grandparents, the kids were simply deposited with the neighbors, who would be paid back someday by being able to leave their kids.

"The contrast with the new people—we call them 'townies'—is incredible. There are only a handful of high-school girls to meet their demand for hired 'sitters,' and baby-sitting has become very lucrative. In fact, it pays better than working on the farm!"

The Minnesota example clearly illustrates that changing social patterns, which in turn are based on changing economic conditions, created the professional baby-sitter. The family of two short generations ago lived in a multi-generation residence with grandparents at hand only too eager to sit in for the mother. If grandparents did not actually share the house, they probably lived only a few blocks or a few miles away, thus making the "sitting" visit a happy excuse to visit their children and grandchildren.

"It was a lot better for the children," a young Evanston wife told us. "My family lived in Duluth, and both sets of grandparents loved to come to sit for us. They used to tell the kids stories about early life in Minnesota, and I guess it all gave the children a sense of continuity to life. I miss that now, and the kids miss it too."

USEFUL RULES

Despite an approaching zero population growth, a recession in business, soaring inflation, and an energy crisis, despite the co-ops and the ingenuity of parents in devising other means to solve their problem, the prodigious growth of the baby-sitting industry continues. It is here to stay—until the next revolution occurs in America's social patterns.

Since that is the fact, it would be wise for parents (the employers) and baby-sitters (the employees) to learn how best to get along with each other and to turn out the best possible product (care for children).

Interviews with a panel of mothers and baby-sitters, drawn from different age groups, income brackets, and geographical locations, distilled some basic rules that may help.

For parents:

1. Try to hire a sitter that you or a close friend knows well. If you must hire a stranger, do so through an agency or check with parents the sitter has worked for previously.
2. Don't hire subteens.
3. If you suspect a personality conflict between the sitter and your child— the best evidence is whether the child objects to having that sitter again —then by all means find another.
4. Return at the time you promised. If you are detained for over half an hour, for any reason, call home and let the baby-sitter know. You depend on her punctuality; there is no reason why she should not be able to depend on yours.
5. Let the sitter know, *clearly,* what your rules are about bedtime, pre-bed procedures, snacks, and acceptable TV programming. This should include snacks left for the sitter, and whether refrigerator raids are permissible.
6. If some small latitude in bedtime treats, such as TV watching, game

playing, storytelling, or a goody to eat, is required to placate your children, let the sitter decide. Keep the treats as small as possible, however.

7. If mealtime is within the sitting period, try to have an easy-to-prepare meal. Kids may enjoy TV dinners or Kentucky Chicken, but most teen-aged and adult sitters prefer larger, better-balanced meals.

8. Have very definite rules about visitors and use of the telephone. The same applies to the use of the hi-fi set. Most sitters, even teen-agers, will abide by the rules if they know what they are.

9. Be sure the rate of pay is agreed to initially, and both parties know what it is. But don't be afraid to tip the sitter if you feel she did an exceptionally good job.

10. Unless the sitter is a mature person or has received special instruction from the Red Cross or YMCA or a similar organization, don't expect more than two small children to be looked after for more than a few hours—especially if the job involves feeding, bathing, and bedding down.

11. Don't drive the sitter home if you've had too much to drink. Send her home by cab. (It goes without saying that letting a sitter walk home, under most circumstances, is *verboten*.)

12. Finally, the most important suggestion: Do everything you can to establish a sympathetic and friendly environment for both child and sitter. Some mothers we interviewed invited the sitter a paid hour in advance, thus helping the child and sitter to get to know each other better and aiding the illusion that the sitter is somehow associated with the family.

Most of the conclusions governing the conduct of the sitter are equally obvious and practical:

1. Follow all instructions given by the parents about bedtime, TV, snacks, etc.

2. Make sure the parents leave a convenient list of emergency numbers (including a physician, naturally). The parents should also leave a number where they can be reached.

3. Observe all instructions about the use (or non-use) of hi-fi equipment, household appliances, and the telephone.

4. Never allow visitors to enter the home unless you have gotten approval from the parents. This applies not only to your friends, but also to strangers who may drop in; unless you know their relationship with the family, serious trouble may result.

5. Remember that you do have the right to refuse a repeat sitting if an assignment turns out to be disagreeable. If you were hired through a service company, make this clear to them. You may help the service to identify "problem" or undesirable homes.

The billions of dollars spent each year on baby-sitting would, by almost anyone's standard, make it a major industry. Yet it does not resemble an

industry in anything except the amount of money involved. There is no defina-
ble marketplace, no reliable distribution system, no fixed charges, no executive
responsibilities, no ethical guidelines, and no union.

The social results certainly are not bad. Many teen-agers and college students earn their spending money by minding someone else's children. Many
older women supplement meager social security or welfare payments by moonlighting as temporary grandmothers. And many more couples get out of the
house to enjoy the rest and recreation so necessary to their psychological
well-being and to their ability to function well as parents. Any business that
has grown to such a huge annual volume has to be satisfying a real need.

Let's now take a look at the other part of the night-and-day job of minding
America's children.

DAY-CARE CENTERS: SOMEWHERE TO LEAVE THE KIDS

6

The problem of day care for children of working mothers has been with us at least since 1854. In that year, the first day-care nursery for children of poor working mothers began operation, admitting children from six weeks to six years of age. It was open from six o'clock in the morning to seven o'clock at night, coinciding with Mother's working hours.

Today, throughout most of the world, day care for children is well established. From China to England most such centers are government-subsidized either in part or in whole, and the mother is expected to pay only in accordance with her earnings.

Here in the United States a $2-billion day-care center program was passed by Congress in 1972. The program was endorsed by industrial firms, unions, educational organizations and health officials, who described the need as imperative.

The need is still imperative. Former President Nixon vetoed the bill passed by Congress.

In his veto message, the then President said, "I hold to the conviction that such far-reaching national legislation should not, must not, be enacted in the absence of a great national debate upon its merit, and broad public acceptance of its principles."

The furor caused by that veto led to exactly the kind of national debate the

President had deemed necessary. When the debate ended, both public and Congress had been educated to the existence of day care and its importance.

As a consequence, a new comprehensive bill for federally funded day-care services has been introduced in both the Senate and the House of Representatives. It provides money to plan, train a professional staff, and operate child-care centers for three years. The emphasis is on family services and child development and will cover prenatal nutritional advice to pregnant women, postpartum services immediately after birth, and preschool day care for working parents. It will also provide after-school recreation for teen-agers, and health and medical services within the centers.

Says Senator Walter Mondale of Minnesota, one of the bill's sponsors: "It is a major national challenge and necessity when you realize the number of families where both parents work, or the number of families with single parents. These children do not have a lobbyist and they do not vote, but millions of them are being damaged today because of improper care."

THE NEED

We interviewed families who might be affected by such a bill, and have chosen a typical sampling of the responses.

First, in the lower income bracket, a young black woman from Chicago Heights, Illinois, uneducated and unskilled, who hires out by the day as a cleaning woman. Her husband left her shortly after her youngest child was born.

"I make twelve dollars a day, plus carfare and lunch, cleaning houses. That comes to about seventy dollars a week, but I have to pay out thirty-five for having my two little kids looked after. For a while they had a day-care center in Chicago Heights, and it cost me twenty-two fifty a week to get the kids good care, lunches and naps. I guess somebody took away the money for that. Anyway, they don't have it anymore."

Middle-income mothers are also affected. Esther Radke, a Los Angeles legal secretary, is a divorcee whose ex-husband contributes only sporadic child support. Her twin girls, now three years old, are brought to a private day-care center each morning and picked up each afternoon by a neighbor, another working mother.

"My take-home pay is about one hundred sixty-five dollars a week, and the center charges me a total of seventy-five dollars for my children. That doesn't leave very much for rent and food and other necessities. But I can't complain —it would cost me more to have someone at the house every day to sit for the twins."

Occasionally a father has problems too. A Spokane accountant, a widower with daughters aged two and four, told us, "At first, after my wife died, I hired a sitter for the kids, but seventy dollars a week, sometimes more, took too big a bite out of my earnings. Now I take them to a private day-care center and it costs me fifty dollars. What else can I do?"

Social workers who administer to nonworking mothers of dependent children are inclined to become indignant at the lack of proper day-care facilities.

From Boston, a twenty-five-year-old woman who has been a caseworker on welfare cases for only two years: "There is no pride or dignity involved in being on relief, only guilt. Most of my women would rather work than wait for those monthly checks, but there's no way they can have their kids cared for at a reasonable price. So they stay home. They're bored and their pride has plain disappeared. Just give them a decent low-cost day-care center and two thirds of them will get off the relief rolls."

Vera M. Casey, who directs a high-school parent-child center in Berkeley, emphasizes the need for a program that will encourage teen-age mothers to keep on with their education. "When they can get day care for their children, they can stay in high school, prepare for jobs, and get off welfare. The cost of providing infant care and parent education for a high-school potential dropout is about twenty-six hundred dollars a year. If this same girl were on welfare, it would cost more than five thousand dollars a year."

An adequate number of day-care centers would not solve all the problems of working mothers, for the usual workday ends at five o'clock, and many day-care centers end with the school day at about three o'clock. Some arrangement has to be made to cover the intervening hours. Then there are the school holidays, when Mother may be working, and the inevitable children's illnesses when they can't go to the day-care center and someone must be at home to care for them.

But the number of day-care centers is far from adequate. According to the Women's Bureau of the U.S. Department of Labor, there is room for only 905,000 children in licensed day-care centers and family homes. Compare this with the 5.5 million working mothers who have children too young to go to school, and you begin to see the gap that exists between those who need day care and those who are getting it.

The gap is widening as more and more women enter the work force. Almost half the mothers in the United States work outside the home, including one in every three who have children under six years old. And the number of live-in relatives who could care for the children has drastically decreased.

Clearly, the need for care and supervision of children outside the home has become vital. But where is it to come from?

SPONSORS

Industry might provide part of the answer. A few employers currently provide day-care centers for their employees. The Women's Bureau estimates there are a dozen company-operated day centers in the U.S.—but in relation to the size of the problem this is like attacking Mount Whitney with a toothpick.

In Minneapolis, Control Data Corporation and eight adjacent industrial firms maintain a day-care center that looks after 110 children. Federal funding covers 75 percent of the cost and the companies pay the remaining 25 percent.

Why should the federal government pay any part of the cost? John Fruyn, a member of the center's board of directors, points out that your tax money is well spent. "Most of the mothers were previously on welfare, and our research team has found the savings in welfare payments to be averaging forty-eight hundred dollars a month, or about fifty-eight thousand dollars a year."

Nor are the benefits to industry unsubstantial. "We found a 21 percent reduction in absenteeism for each parent," Fruyn, who is also a Northern States Power Company executive, adds. "The turnover in employment among mothers using the center is 2.3 percent. For mothers not using the center, the turnover is nearly triple, or 6.2 percent. In general, job performance has also improved.

"You can *see* the happiness at the center," he concludes. "It's a benefit to everyone concerned."

Another successful day-care center is operated by Joshua Tree Manufacturing, Inc., a company that makes women's sportswear and dresses. The Joshua Tree center is licensed for forty-eight children, aged two to six, and employs a staff of ten, including two Spanish-speaking women. It's open every day from 1:00 A.M. to 5:30 P.M., and the children are served morning and afternoon snacks and lunch.

The largest corporation sponsoring day-care centers for its employees is American Telephone & Telegraph, but they pay only half the weekly $30 for each child.

During World War II, such industrial giants as General Electric, Westinghouse, Douglas, Boeing, and Martin all established day-care centers to induce young mothers to work for them. This was at a time when most able-bodied young men were off fighting Hitler and Hirohito. When the war ended and the young men came marching home again, industry's need for working mothers disappeared—and so did the day-care centers.

Short of another war, industry probably will never undertake the tremendous expenditure involved in setting up an adequate system of day-care centers. It would simply not be profitable, and altruism is not a word much in favor in cost control departments.

Some outspoken critics are against industry involvement in day care, anyway. Anne Kaufman, executive director of the Action Council for Comprehensive Child Care, adds that some corporate employers "offer child care as a carrot while denying other benefits." James Harrell, associate director of the Day-Care and Child Development Council of America, warns that day-care centers may be used by a corporation to achieve some less admirable purpose. For example, "several plants in the South use day-care as a kind of negative whammy to keep unions out."

A few centers are sponsored by labor unions. The cost of operating such centers, such as those paid for by the Amalgamated Clothing Workers, comes out of union dues.

We visited a model day-care center established almost four years ago for the children of workers in the Department of Health, Education and Welfare in Washington, D.C.

The center is situated on the roof of the HEW Building. On the day we visited more than sixty children, ranging from two to five years old, seemed to be having a wonderful time. They were supervised by several staff members while they played in the fenced-in roof area. There was lots of room for running around, lots of play equipment, tools and building material, and two groups were engaged in art projects. A smaller group of six children was enjoying a storytelling session with one of the staff members.

For this kind of supervisory care, the parents pay on a sliding scale according to their family income. The rate begins at $5.00 a week per child and escalates to a still quite reasonable $25.00. This covers not only the cost of supervised activities, but of hot lunches and snacks.

While this gives some indication of what can and should be done, there is little likelihood anything will be done.

Says a staff member of the Office of Child Development: "Despite all the fine-sounding talk about concern for the child from one to five years and the working mother, it's clear now that we just have to make the best possible use of existing facilities and hope we can get someone elected who is more sympathetic and understanding to the problem of day care for our nation's children."

Today, fewer than 200,000 children are enrolled in centers subsidized by government funds. With private centers and homes caring for 700,000 more, we come back to a hard fact: less than one out of six of America's working mothers enjoys the benefits of day care.

As more private day-care centers are established, the situation will slowly improve. There are mounting pressures from such groups as the National Organization for Women (NOW) who are promoting the concept of day-care centers in apartment houses, mobile home communities, and housing tracts.

Elizabeth Janeway, the outspoken writer, thinks day-care centers should be set up at every plant, factory, or office that employs more than a minimum number of persons. Parents would bring their children to work with them in the mornings, visit them during the day, and take them home at night. She believes older children could be brought to such centers after school.

"They could be offered informative courses on work being done at the plant," she suggests, "and perhaps offered an option of working there for fifteen hours a week, combined with fifteen hours of schooling. They could learn vocational skills which are realistic today . . . and you'd break the isolation of family life which really does worry a lot of child-care experts today."

Mrs. Janeway believes that the home has become little more than a "recuperation center and family dormitory," and its isolation from work makes it an unsuitable location for raising children. "Children who grow up without having seen anybody work seem to be very badly deprived." She proposes reuniting the family at a new site—the place of work.

Whatever the merits of Mrs. Janeway's proposal, there's no doubt that more and more of today's women are inclined to find life enrichment outside the home.

As one feminist puts it: "Mothers have exactly as much right as fathers to work outside the home, even if there are young children. The only way that is possible is if there are centers to provide for the all-day care of children until they're old enough to attend nursery school. The centers could be staffed by women who prefer to stay at home and care for children while others go out to work. Tenant fees can support it—just as they are doing in the places that have tried it. All that's needed is to bring builders, and the banks who finance the builders, to understand that women don't need frills—ceramic tiles, bathroom vanities with four-way mirrors and cultured marble," her voice tightened with scorn, "or bidets. What women need is day-care centers for their little children. We need an opportunity to use our intelligence in work we want to do, and not be so tied to the home we can't even be interesting companions to our husbands anymore!"

AS A BUSINESS

Private day-care centers, not subsidized by industry or government, tend to be expensive for parents. But the demand for them is so great that millions of dollars have popped up in a crash attempt to cash in on a new industry. The centers charge from $30 to $60 a week per child, and usually have cute names (Mary Moppet, Kay's Kiddie Kollege, Les Petites Académies) and brand-new equipment to amuse and distract Baby and to pacify nervous parents, and they are obviously geared to middle-class and upper-income families.

We talked at length with a former nurse who now runs a day-care center in North Hollywood, California. She has converted a large one-story building that once housed a dance studio into a two-room complex with a partitioned kitchen area and two extra bathrooms in the rear. She charges $35 a week per youngster, and they range from two to six years of age.

"Most of the children are beyond the formula or strained food stages and get a standard menu. I ask the mother to give the child a proper breakfast before he arrives at seven thirty, eight, or eight thirty. But it's amazing the number who go through a hungry morning because they weren't fed at home. At ten o'clock I serve cookies and milk—that helps revive children who weren't given adequate breakfasts. My standard lunch consists of a hot soup, a sandwich, some canned or fresh fruit, and milk. But no matter how many corners I cut, it is impossible to feed a child for less than a dollar fifty a day.

"Then there are the toys we furnish for their play. They're the most practical and imaginative we can find. No metal because there is always the possibility of injury through dismantling or cut edges. Glass and the sort of plastics that shatter are out of the question. We look for good toys made out of smoothed wood and solid plastics. Paints and crayons and the various papers we use are purchased in quantity.

"Then there's the staff. I am a registered nurse with a background in treating children's diseases and emotional problems, but I also employ two full-time ex-teachers with experience at the kindergarten or first-grade levels. I also employ home economics students from North Hollywood High School to prepare and serve lunch. And from three thirty to five o'clock I employ four more students to prepare the children for pick-up, and deliver them safely back to mother's care.

"At thirty-five dollars a week, I am barely breaking even. My rates have got to go up."

The mothers who can afford such privately operated day-care centers are usually enthusiastic. "Our two preschool children have gone to a day center since each was two years old," says a Kansas City, Missouri, mother. "They love it and are well adjusted to their playmates. It's so wonderful to pick them up after work and have them babble excitedly about what happened to them that day. I've noticed that most of the other children whose mothers stay home with them all day don't seem as alert and informed as mine are. It's been just marvelous for them."

The minority of parents who register complaints speak of high costs, a lack of discipline that leads to behavior problems at home, inadequate lunch and nap facilities, and improper medical supervision.

"I don't understand parents who try to sneak in kids who have an infectious illness, hoping no one will notice," said one indignant parent from Atlantic City, New Jersey. "No matter how minor the illness, even a common cold, it's bound to spread to the other children and cause more problems."

Dr. Virginia Pomerantz, a Manhattan baby doctor, told us that children in day-care centers are usually healthy. "I haven't noticed any ill effects whatever except for an increase in the number of colds they catch."

The advocates of day-care centers are heartened by the first carefully researched study of the problem. A team of University of Kentucky psychologists under the leadership of Dr. Richard Winett spent a year studying and evaluating more than one hundred primarily white and middle-income families. The project, which did not attempt to cover black families or those at the extremes of the economic spectrum, dealt with both parents and children in varied kinds of day-care situations.

Dr. Winett concluded that "children are not harmed by day care . . . and the family structure seems flexible enough to both accommodate and allow for these arrangements. The children did not differ either mentally or socially from the children who stay at home with their parents."

He did note, however, a marked difference between the parents. The at-home families were somewhat more conservative, had more children, and were "overwhelmingly middle class," whereas the families using day-care centers had more liberal backgrounds, fewer children, more varied income levels, and a mother working.

Dr. Mary Elizabeth Keister of the Child Development Center at the University of North Carolina, recommends that parents check out day centers before enrolling their infants or toddlers. "The parent should look for nutritious meals, clean rooms, and to see if children are supervised at play. There should be an attractive sick bay with adult supervision, and a written, agreed-upon plan for handling emergencies."

OTHER TRENDS

Standards for day-care centers differ from state to state and community to community. Some variations border on the quixotic. For example, Virginia requires 20 square feet of indoor space per child, while its neighboring state Maryland requires 30 square feet. If you have a two-year-old child, he or she will be welcome in day-care centers everywhere except the state of Pennsylvania, where children must be three years old to be enrolled. Twenty-four states require that the director of a center be licensed and qualified in early childhood education, child development, graduate pediatric nursing, and/or psychology. Other states require no permit or license at all. If there is a rational pattern behind all this, it escaped our notice.

One kind of building that should be a natural for housing a child-care center is frequently overlooked. Our churches can comfortably accommodate a sizable number of children in facilities that would meet the most stringent local regulations. They can also afford to graduate costs to income, charging low fees to the low-income mother and proportionately more to the mother who can pay more. The difficulty would be in keeping such centers free from religious indoctrination. Families that otherwise need the service badly might be unwilling to have their children looked after by day at such a price. This same objection would apply to any political or social organizations able to provide a needed service but also tempted to use the centers for the "brainwashing" of children.

Those few churches and charitable and youth organizations now operating in the day-care field do not charge much less than private centers. Their prices average about $140 a month.

Mrs. Doria Zavitkovsky, director of the Santa Monica, California, day-care centers, where eligibility is limited to those on welfare or with low incomes, says there is a real problem for the working parent who does not qualify for poverty care but has a borderline income. Fees are charged on a parent's ability to pay, and a single mother not poor enough to qualify on the basis of need faces a real dilemma. Should she remain working, barely eking out a living, or throw up her hands and go on welfare?

Mrs. Zavitkovsky adds: "There are very few openings for one-parent families . . . and they have a great need."

All public centers have been filled to capacity for more than thirty years and almost all have long waiting lists.

In some agricultural areas the growers, anxious to lure able-bodied adults into the field, have established day-care centers. One such center, at Bridge-hampton, Long Island, is sponsored cooperatively by farmers in the area. But this is still progress on a very small scale. Fruit and vegetable growers in California—a state where seven out of ten of the country's migrant workers are employed—have made no effort to relieve the plight of their working families. The workers unofficially (sometimes illegally) have improvised day-care centers of their own. These are rudimentary when judged by the usual standards, mere places "to be" rather than places in which the children are cared for.

In Chicano and Puerto Rican sections of American cities parents have for generations established their own co-op arrangements. These *de facto* day centers, observing no law or restriction, exist simply because it is vital to have children cared for while mothers work.

In black ghetto areas there has not been, until recently, a pronounced trend toward community action. The unemployed grandmother or the older daughter has usually assumed the responsibility of caring for the younger children. And with the current high rate of unemployment plaguing these areas, there is usually no lack of custodial care for the preschool child.

A few well-equipped and professionally run day-care centers have been established by militant black organizations. The Black Panthers operate four rapidly expanding centers, two in Oakland, accommodating up to two hundred children when fully opened, and two in Chicago which will care for four hundred preschoolers by the end of 1975. Again, low fees, proportionate to income and starting as low as $1.00 a day, make the centers invaluable to mothers who could not otherwise afford to go to work.

These centers provide certain peripheral benefits important to minority members. A nurse now teaching at the Oakland center puts it this way: "In just a few weeks' time the preschoolers learn to get along with each other. They're better fed and better rested than they were at home, so their behavior improves. We also give them a sense of identity—they begin to take pride in being black and in being individuals. They open up, almost like flowers, because they *want* to learn. It's incredible to watch."

In the Black Panther centers there are classes in which two- to six-year-olds chant, "I am black, and black is beautiful," for minutes at a time. Clearly, this is "brainwashing" of its own kind, even if most of us would agree with the objective of the Black Panther leader who says, "We want to take the black mother off relief and give her pride. We want to take the black child in and give him hope."

INDOCTRINATION CENTERS?

Opponents of child-care centers profess to see in them a turning away from the family unit and the "professionalization" of child rearing. They argue that as the role of the professional child worker grows, the authority and influence of the parent declines. And they foresee the transformation of our society into something resembling Mao's China.

"I can easily see child-care centers becoming indoctrination centers," one parent told us. "You let the government in on raising kids, and you open the door wide to whatever kind of thought control the government's leaders would like to exercise. What strikes me as peculiar is how easily our liberals can see this when it comes to something like prayer in schools. But how blind they get when it comes to something like herding children into places where their thinking processes can be controlled by adult teachers who work for the government and, in the end, have to do what the government tells them."

There does seem to be a practical alternative in Senator Mondale's bill, which would establish day-care centers that carefully avoid either ideological or specifically religious indoctrination.

The Senator agrees that we must be very careful about interfering with family life. "We want parental control," he told us. "The most important source of strength to the child is the family. Participation in the program would be entirely voluntary. Children would be eligible for these services only after a written request from the parents or guardians has been received.

"We are not going after a 'big brother' operation. The federal government, through what it does or does not do, affects family life intimately. We have economic policies that decide it is good for the economy to have five or six million people out of work. We have minimum wages that are too low and welfare laws that require a father's absence from home before his family is eligible for aid. We have limited tax deductions for working mothers—and no deductions for mothers who stay home, on the grounds that what they do at home is worthless.

"We have a Council of Economic Advisers for the economy, a consumer adviser for the plight of the consumer, a National Security Council for national security, and an energy consultant for the energy crisis. Why not an adviser on the family?

"Why not require a family-impact statement on any new legislation the same way we now require an environmental-impact statement?"

BIRTH IS BIG BUSINESS: THE GREAT CAMPAIGN

7

Mother-and-Baby is a voracious consumer. There is hardly an arena in which the "conspicuous consumption" defined by Thorstein Veblen is so much in evidence.

Middle-class people cheerfully sacrifice their own needs to supply frivolities for Mother-and-Baby. Daddy gets along without a new suit or a new pair of shoes to provide a luxurious carriage and layette. Lower-income people, striving upward, skimp on the less visible parts of the family budget in order to insure that baby gets nothing but the best. Where Mother-and-Baby are concerned, even people who have sufficient financial and social security not to care what other people think are seduced into caring.

A definitive answer would involve geographical, ethnic, and financial considerations. But it might be useful to compare the amount spent on mother-and-baby care and products with the amount spent in comparable areas.

A dozen years ago Jessica Mitford startled us with her brilliant exposé of the funeral industry, *The American Way of Death.* She pointed out that disposing of our dead was costing over $2 billion a year. In 1973, exactly a decade later, that figure had risen to $2½ billion.

The total funeral expense bill is not much in excess of the over $2 billion that will, according to the U.S. Department of Commerce, be spent in 1975 for Toys, Games, Dolls, and Children's Recreational Vehicles. It is less than the approximately $3 billion spent for children's outerwear, coats and suits, dresses and blouses.

And it should be remarked that funerals are a one-time affair, while the costs of providing for Mother-and-Baby go on and on—and on.

In the year 1975, just under $40 billion will be spent on women's and children's clothing, excepting footwear.

Let's compare that with what we spend in other areas. For example, with the $24 billion that in 1975 will be spent for physicians' services, or the more modest $6.5 billion that will be spent on dental care.

However, the cost of outfitting Mother-and-Baby is only a small part of the total birth bill. By any standard, the allied birth industries absorb a good deal of our national income.

But is there anything wrong with spending money for value received? Why shouldn't people choose how much of their money they want to spend on what? Surely that is a basic freedom in what we like to consider a free society.

Except: Are people choosing, or being chosen? Is conscious, independent decision-making at work, or merely brainwashing and exploitation? That is the real question.

LOCATING THE MOTHER-TO-BE

Before you can sell Mother-to-be the various products she will need, before you can persuade her that a need exists (even if it doesn't), there is one thing you have to know:

Which of those millions of married and unmarried women out there are about to become mothers?

Carol Johnson was only three months pregnant when the mail started coming. Very special mail, slanted to the wants and needs of the pregnant woman.

"I couldn't believe it," she recalls. "How did the whole world suddenly know? I asked my obstetrician if he'd given my name to these people, but he denied it. So how did it happen?"

It might be well to begin with a simple explanation of the mailing-list business for those who may not know much about it.

Four billion dollars was spent on direct mail advertising in 1974, and mailing lists are compiled with the thoroughness that such a volume of business deserves.

Any community of over ten thousand has one or more firms specializing in the preparation of these mailing lists. The lists are rented or sold to any company willing to pay the price, which currently (1974) averages about 10¢ a name on a "general" basis and up to 20¢ a name for specialized consumers. Pregnant women, who number over three million in any given year, are considered a specialized marketing group—not as specialized as *ornithologists* but far more restricted than *subscribers to the Reader's Digest.*

Carol Johnson's name appeared on such a list as soon as someone somewhere learned she was going to have a baby.

Whodunit?

"Her doctor didn't have to be lying to her," a mailing-list compiler says. He agreed to an interview only after being assured his name would not be used and that he could proofread this to be sure any and all clues to his identity were obscured. "I deal with a lot of people, and I don't want anyone saying I'm a bigmouth." His conditions were complied with, and the following is the version of his remarks as edited by him.

"It happens both ways; sometimes we get names from the doctor, sometimes we don't. Anyhow, no doctor is going to admit it. The American Medical Association doesn't come right out and say so, but it's not considered ethical to give out info like that. And who wants to get tagged unethical?

"Sometimes the information comes from somebody in the office who's not the doctor. A secretary or nurse who works for him knows the names, and she might want to pick up a little money on the side. Or suppose the doctor tried to get a credit check on a patient to find out if there's any risk in the pay department. The agency would have the doctor down as an obstetrician, right? You don't have to be a genius to add one and one together to make three.

"Or maybe a woman opens an account at a store that happens to sell a lot of maternity apparel. She goes automatically on their mailing list, and it's available for sale or exchange. Even if she ordered c.o.d., or just gave her name and address to a clerk writing up a sales slip, she goes on the list.

"Or suppose she subscribes to one of those baby magazines. That makes her a first-class prospect. You can get good results from other sources too. For example, the Motor Vehicle Department has an auto registration list that's usually free or only costs a little. I keep a watch out for people who register a new station wagon. People like that usually come through as buyers of baby products.

"It's a crazy business. One guy who was selling a gadget to clip nose hair got great results from a list of people who had subscribed to investment letters. How do you figure that? A pregnant woman could get herself listed not because anybody knows she's pregnant but because she bought a bathroom deodorizer and some smart operator took a chance buying a sample from that list to sell baby products.

"Look, it's impossible for anyone who owns a phone or drives a car or subscribes to a magazine to avoid ending up on a list. Bingo, everybody gets into the net! And you can always overlay on another list from some other source to find out what kind of consumer you've got. The Census Bureau is a big help. They just don't count heads, they make what they call 'tract' samplings [slices of the population taken by small geographic sections in cities and towns] and they've got all kinds of info on the people. Everything from sex, age, income of residents in the house, right on down to the kind of electrical appliances they use."

Is there a particular way in which he, personally, would go about acquiring a list of pregnant women?

"I'd get people working for me. Tipsters. Could be somebody in a church congregation who knows which one of the women in the church is about to add a little worshipper. I'd do it in a better-heeled community. After all, a person listed in a nice home-owning community like Wauwatosa [place name altered] is sure to be a better customer than someone living in downtown Milwaukee [ditto]."

One of the hazards of interviewing is in taking one person's word for anything. We talked with another mailing list compiler who assured us that "Some names may be obtained like that, but not many. And they wouldn't be too valuable. How could you know for sure she was going to be a mother because she drove a station wagon or took out a new subscription to *Parent's* magazine? In this business you play percentages. It's hard enough to get a good list together without adding questionable prospects. As it is, fifteen percent of the people on a list won't be living at that address any longer or there will be some other kind of mistake in the mailing that results in nondelivery. Just to hold those figures down, list owners try to 'clean' their lists from two to four times a year, crossing off 'nixies'—undeliverable addresses—and adding new potential customers.

"Some companies even cut names of anybody who doesn't buy anything within a certain period of time. And of course they drop anybody who gets mad at being a target for mailings. People send back brochures, samples of merchandise and coupons in the business-reply envelopes. That kind of thing costs the company postage. I've known people to actually send a package of manure. In one case, a reply card came back attached to a box of dead rats.

"Those people are dropped—pronto."

Businesses use direct mail because it is selective. Newspapers and magazines cannot be selective: obviously everyone who reads a newspaper or sees a TV commercial isn't likely to be pregnant or a mother. Via direct mail, most contacts are likely to be.

Contrary to the general impression, direct mail *is* expensive. Robert F. De Lay, president of the Direct-Mail Advertising Association, says: "Ten years ago the average direct mail piece cost seven cents to produce and mail. Today it's twenty cents, and the cost is going up. The new higher mail rates make it more urgent for direct mail marketers to be selective. You can't send to marginal people."

Mail order companies, however, run far less risk than consumers. When Bess Meyerson was New York City's Consumer Affairs Commissioner, she said fraud was one of the most widespread consumer complaints. True, the Postal Service does have power to deal with phony mail operators, and they are now required to provide the names, addresses, and telephone numbers of any box holders doing business with the public. But the frauds continue.

The most frequent complaint is nondelivery of merchandise that was ordered and paid for. This happens so frequently that Bess Meyerson remarked ruefully, "You would do better dropping your check down a well. At least then it wouldn't be deposited."

Back to Carol Johnson, whose name by whatever means got on a list of mothers-to-be. Let her relate what happened: "I can't even remember all the solicitations for products that I got in the mail. The ones I remember best came from a company that manufactures a salve for rubbing on my tummy to make me more comfortable as I got more and more pregnant. They even enclosed a sample.

"I got samples of baby power and ads for maternity girdles and support hose and special shoes. There were folders advertising vitamins and tranquilizers and calcium supplements. There were children's book club offers. My husband says I got over five hundred pieces of mail, including from insurance companies."

Carol Johnson had not yet entered her most profitable phase as a potential consumer. After her baby was born, her mail multiplied. Her name had appeared on more lists—including the hospital record and the local newspaper's vital statistics column. There were more products Mother-and-Baby might buy, and more businesses anxious to supply their needs. In fact, the infant half of the partnership was clearly the bigger draw. She was being offered everything from bronzed baby shoes to lotions that soothe gums or heal rashes on the little baby bottom.

In pursuit of the once Almighty Dollar, there is no one to match the agility, ingenuity, and perseverance of the American businessman. Norah and Clyde Baldridge of Chicago had an infant daughter who died three days after birth, but they were still receiving mail addressed to Angela, the deceased infant, three years later. Finally they had to ask the Direct-Mail Advertising Association to have their names removed from their mailing lists. The reputable firms that belong to the Association complied. Unfortunately, three out of four firms involved in direct mail selling do not belong to the Association, and Angela's mail continued to arrive.

Ada and Bill Duncan of Placentia, California, had their seventh child in 1972. During the next two years their little Jeffrey received over five thousand pieces of mail and his mother got over three thousand.

During the first three months of Jeffrey's existence as a consumer, hundreds of firms sent or offered to send free samples of baby food, baby oil, baby shampoo, discount-priced baby shoes. Eight foundries volunteered to bronze his shoes. Twelve photographic studios offered to immortalize little Jeffrey on film, and three talent agencies suggested he should be prepared for a lucrative future as a baby model. ("It has come to our attention that you may have a child with the necessary qualifications for the commercial advertising business.") Apparently the necessary qualification is to be born.

A deluge of congratulatory messages from strangers flooded the Duncan home, among them a letter to little Jeffrey's parents from their state assembly-man assuring them "I am interested in all my constituents, even little George [sic]," and another from the head of a pharmaceutical company selling contraceptive foams. This latter message did not amuse the Duncans, who are Catholics.

"What really appalls me," Bill Duncan says, "is that Jeff will be on mailing lists for the rest of his life. The mail will never stop."

He is right. The amount spent on direct mail advertising increases annually. At least $10 billion in merchandise is sold to mother and baby this way, and there is no likelihood of escape from the computerized lists. The only defense is a letter to the Direct-Mail Advertising Association (230 Park Avenue, New York, N.Y. 10017) and, as previously noted, that succeeds only in removing your name from the mailing lists of the most reputable advertisers.

It assures you of one thing: all your mail solicitations from then on will be from shadier promoters and fringe companies.

BIRTH IS BIG BUSINESS: DRESSING UP

8

Where does all the spending take place that makes Mother-and-Baby such a valuable customer?

Maternity clothes and accessories are a one-billion-dollar-a-year branch of the garment industry, representing 8 percent of the industry's annual volume.

"There is no reason why a pregnant woman cannot look and feel chic," said Lane Bryant in 1920.

Today, Lane Bryant stores in major American cities sell dresses, smocks, slacks, hose, shorts, and swimwear designed to fit the pregnant woman.

"We probably sell about thirty-five percent of the maternity clothes that are sold in the U.S. and Canada," a Lane Bryant executive told us. "We can fit any woman with what she wants."

We asked what the average Lane Bryant customer bought during the course of her pregnancy and were given this list. The prices were originally listed as of August 1973 and rechecked as of late autumn 1974—at which point they had increased an average of 11 percent. If double-digit inflation continues to publication time, the reader will have to make the proper adjustments.

- Three everyday dresses averaging $25 each: $ 75.00
- Two dresses for evenings or special occasions averaging $50
  each: 100.00
- Two jacket-and-pants outfits averaging $30 each: 60.00

- Three "separates" costumes (three pants @ $15 each and three tops @ $15 each):   90.00
- One pair of flat-heeled shoes at $30:   30.00
- One bathrobe at $20:   20.00
- Two nightgowns (especially for nursing mothers) or pajama outfits at $15 each: 30.00
- Three maternity bras at $7 each: 21.00
- Six maternity panties at $2.50 each: 15.00
- Two slips at $6 each: 12.00
- Three pairs support hosiery at $6 each and four pairs regular maternity hoisery at $2.50 each: 28.00
- Two girdles at $12 each: 24.00

A total of $500 is run up just for "essential" apparel. The word "essential" is, of course, subject to variation by income and customer's choice.

At the upper end of the scale, for the mother-to-be who shops at a prestige department store or in a maternity boutique, the cost can run well over a thousand dollars.

"Sometimes I'm actually ashamed of myself for selling my customers certain things," says Sylvia Peck, a clerk in the maternity wear department at Bullocks in Los Angeles. "A pregnant woman shouldn't buy a hundred-dollar dress. She'll wear it so seldom she'll never get proper use from it. At best all it will do for her is make her look like a prettier tent."

On the other hand, a saleswoman in one of the Motherhood Maternity Shops told us that splurging on an evening maternity dress is not as frivolous as it seems. Manufacturers today are making maternity dresses that only need slight alterations in order to be worn *after* the baby is born—and therefore serve a dual purpose.

Several years ago Princess Grace of Monaco had Balenciaga design her maternity wardrobe; it cost $25,000. A more "average" figure for the beautiful people is probably Natalie Wood's 1973 maternity wardrobe: a modest $10,000.

The operator of a Beverly Hills boutique, a quietly elegant place in which the word price never intrudes an ugly jarring sound, explains the philosophy of her wealthy customers. "They're not inclined to let pregnancy curtail their social lives. In fact, they want to look more fashionable than ever."

THE ECONOMICAL WAY

In the lower price range, Sears and Penney's and Montgomery Ward can outfit a woman with all the listed items for about $250.

Obviously, all of these items will not be purchased in exactly these quantities. Many a pregnant woman will probably have an adequate pair of flat shoes in her closet, and not all pregnant women will have swollen feet, nor do they all need new robes, housecoats, and nightgowns. They may be putting on weight, but they are not turning into elephants. This average is obtained by asking sales clerks and buyers at these stores to draw up lists, and reducing these to an overall comparable group of basic and "essential" items.

On lower income levels, a pregnant woman is likely to buy only the few things she absolutely cannot do without. This turns out, on examination, to be much less than appears on our list.

Dolores M. Martinez is a twenty-eight-year-old Chicano woman whose husband works as a clerk in a small grocery store. They have five children and live on the upper floor of a two-family house in East Los Angeles.

Mrs. Martinez told us some ways in which she economizes during a pregnancy. "I cut up a few old skirts and add stretch panels to them. I buy nursing bras a size larger than I normally wear and wear them for maternity bras— and after the baby is born, use them as intended. I buy some clothes at Good Will. Second-hand shops are good too, because you can usually get nice things for practically nothing. And we trade maternity clothes all around the neighborhood. Everything's gotten so expensive we have to trade and borrow nearly everything."

In most cities there exists a kind of maternity-and-baby clothing and baby equipment underground. Clothing is passed from mother to mother and baby to baby. Those who cannot afford all they need share what they have. "Pass it on, wear it out, make do, or do without," might serve as a rallying cry for the ingenious poor.

With clothing prices rising at over 10 percent a year, however, middle-class women are also looking to cut corners. For guidance in economy buying— "Depression dressing," if you prefer—they look back to the 1930s when women had to learn to get along on very little. The Hollywood movies of that era showed glamorous heroines in lamé and diamante jackets, although women watching the movies were wearing the one basic black dress which they varied with different scarves, hats and gloves. Today's outfit is more likely to be a good pair of jeans with corksoled sandals, worn with different tops. But the idea is the same.

There are savings to be made by thinking unconventionally about clothes. A pair of white drawstring pants recently displayed by a fashion model cost only 69¢ at a paint store, and she bought her T-shirt top for 39¢ in a boys department. Women who are veteran bargain hunters in clothing have long known about the advantages of shopping boys' departments for unisex clothes, or finding lingerie and loungewear that will get by quite acceptably as evening dresses.

There are other good ways to cut clothing costs. Catalog buying, for instance. Catalog prices are usually lower than store prices because of the reduced overhead. And the prices are frozen for the duration of the catalog— which can be as long as six months. Sometimes it pays to combine both ideas: e.g., Sears Roebuck & Company's latest catalog features a boy's rain slicker. The size 16 would fit a six-foot-tall woman. The price is only $3.49.

For the bargain hunter who lives in or near a large city, the best economy is to visit that section of the garment area where shops are run by jobbers. Here, everything is for sale at a marked-down price.

A jobber buys "distress" merchandise at a cheap price from the original manufacturer. "Distress" merchandise consists of garments that the manufacturer cannot sell through regular outlets, and also damaged goods. The jobber operates out of very low overhead establishments where no money is wasted on decor or service. He is able to resell his own bargains at a bargain price.

How well can the average buyer do in a jobber's store? "That depends on whether she has an eye for telling good merchandise from bad," a New York City jobber who specializes in women's clothes told us. "If she's got an eye for style or can spot defective goods, then she can save herself a small fortune. If not, she'll still do better than she would in a department store or a regular discount store. She'll learn how to buy smart through trial and error. Some women who come into my place can actually tell brand name merchandise even when the labels have been removed."

Manufacturers usually insist that their labels be removed from merchandise sold to jobbers. But jobbers cleverly evade the instruction by sewing the removed label into a side seam, or stamping it on the backs of belts, or leaving the label on hangtags. Some remove the labels but leave a small piece, enough for an experienced shopper to identify the manufacturer.

To manufacturers, the jobber is a necessary evil. One women's clothing manufacturer said, "Unlike doctors we can't just bury our mistakes. We've got to get rid of them. Some manufacturers send the stuff out of the country so the public won't know they had leftovers. But for the most part we dump the merchandise on jobbers at a fraction of its cost. I've sold merchandise as cheap as a dollar a hanger that cost me as much as thirty to fifty dollars. But when the jobber takes stuff, he can't pick and choose. He takes it all or nothing. The good with the bad.

"It's our loss, but I guess you could say it's the customer's gain. If she has the time and the patience to go through the lot and find what she wants, good luck to her!"

The second major clothing expense is Outfitting the Baby. Long before Mother-to-be enters the hospital, a part of her apartment or home has been turned into a nursery, and a dresser is crammed with the clothes baby will wear, some acquired at baby showers but most purchased by the proud parents-to-be.

Based on minimum needs, this is baby's wardrobe, again compiled from lists given to us by sales clerks and buyers, and carefully crosschecked to make an accurate composite list.

- 6 dozen diapers at $8.50 per dozen: $ 51.00
- 8 cotton undershirts at $1.25 each: 10.00
- 4 cotton kimonos at $3.00 each: 12.00

- 4 cotton gowns at $3.00 each: 12.00
- 4 sacque sets at $4.50 each: 18.00
- 4 waterproof panties at $1.75 each: 7.00
- 1 sweater set at $8.00:   8.00
- 3 stretch terry coveralls at $6.00 each: 18.00
- 5 receiving blankets at $2.00 each: 10.00
- 2 thermal sleepers at $5.00 each: 10.00
- 6 pairs of booties or bootie socks at $1.25 each: 7.50
- 3 crib blankets at $10.00 each: 30.00
- 6 knitted crib sheets at $4.00 each: 24.00
- 3 flannelette waterproof sheets at $4.00 each: 12.00
- 6 waterproof lap pads (3 for $1.50):   3.00
- 1 comforter or quilt at $12.00:   12.00
- 2 heavyweight outdoor or travel wraps at $15.00 each: 30.00
- Miscellaneous: 35.00

                                   TOTAL $ 309.50

Baby clothes, for infants from newborn to five years old, account for 18 percent of all business done by the garment industry. And baby shoes for children of the same age represent 22 percent of the business of the entire shoe industry. This does not include the fact that outfitting Baby includes buying some of the 1.5 million cribs, carriages, strollers, playpens, highchairs, and bassinettes that are sold yearly.

Their average retail prices as of this writing (autumn 1974):

- Stroller: $ 50.00
- Crib: 100.00
- Crib mattress: 30.00
- Crib bumpers: 10.00
- Infant Seat (to carry baby):   12.00
- Chest of drawers: 80.00
- Nursery lamp: 20.00
- Playpen: 50.00
- Highchair or Feeding Table: 50.00
- Bassinette: 50.00
- Diaper Pail   5.00
- Baby Swing (considered a luxury item)   25.00
- Car Seat: 35.00

These total $517, making a combined total of $826.50.*

*In those sections of the country where a baby carriage is used, that would cost an additional $100 or more. In rural areas or in cities where the automobile is the principal means of transportation, however, car seats are more popular and baby carriages are regarded as luxury items.

But what do couples actually spend of this total? How much is borrowed, bought at second hand, built at home, or otherwise improvised? One young San Francisco mother told us she bought almost all of her children's clothing at rummage sales. "The kids outgrow their clothes and you can pick them up for almost nothing, in nearly perfect condition. Just this week I bought half a dozen outfits for my children all at less than fifty cents apiece. That included two doubleknit nylon swimsuits and a hooded terry parka. I only spent a dollar for a harness for my youngest to wear when we're out driving in the car!"

Or listen to Patricia Reynhout of Worcester, Massachusetts, whose husband Jim recently got a teaching post at Holy Cross University. Her first three children arrived while her husband was a doctoral student earning only $8,000 a year, and there was simply no way to stretch the family budget to cover "extras" such as a new wardrobe.

Mrs. Reynhout gave us a rundown of some ways she used to cut corners. We print it verbatim since it doubtless represents the experience of many mothers who have no choice except to cope:

"Jim was paid once a month, usually on the last Friday of the month. So each month I bought one outfit for the layette—a cotton undershirt, a kimono, and a set of crawlers (terrycloth footed sleepers). I borrowed all the baby clothes I possibly could borrow. I knitted sweaters, booties and hat sets galore —up to age two. I also made the dressy, going-to-church outfits for the children.

"I made bibs from guest towels, and shopped at junk stores and the Salvation Army for nursery furniture. We ended up with a lovely nursery even though we papered the walls with cheap paper and bought a dresser for five dollars that Jim painted aqua and white. He attached a changing pad and belt to the top and that gave me a 'bathinette' with four drawers that held many more clothes than a commercial changing table.

"There were countless little ways we found to economize. We found two incomplete cribs at the Salvation Army and bought one half of each for $2.50 and combined them by drilling new holes. We were given a toddler-sized rocking chair that we painted white, along with an old end-table someone was throwing out. We painted the end-table white to hold my cotton, oil, diapers, pins, lotions and powder. I made the nursery curtains.

"We bought a plastic bathtub with green stamps. I made my own sheets from remnants and made crib bumpers to match. And I made Raggedy Ann and Andy dolls to dress up the room. We got some old rug-runners and pieced them into a wall-to-wall carpet for the nursery. It was a third-floor apartment so we needed the carpeting to absorb the sounds of baby crying and us walking with them at early morning hours.

"We always bought the cheapest make of clothes and I reinforced the seams on my sewing machine. I put two extra buttons on every pair of slacks to allow for some growth in the straps. The girls hardly ever wore dresses during the summer. They lived in diapers and undershirts.

"A carriage doubled as a car bed. The infant crib was a carriage and I could rock them to sleep easily.

"We stayed home just about all the time, though I tried hard not to let it bother me. After all, we did have a goal and I knew things would get better. We had a park across the street and that was our daily outing. I've *no* regrets!"

VERY SPECIAL THINGS

We asked a buyer at Bullock's in downtown Los Angeles, where the clientele is predominantly middle class, how much her customers trim these estimated expenditures on infant and toddler apparel.

"Not as much as you might think. In fact, I'd put the figure higher, because when it comes to anything beyond diapers and booties you're dealing with 'vanity shopping.' Every woman wants to dress up baby, no matter how much it costs. Most of our mothers get a little help where costs are concerned. First there's the baby shower—that's where the gifts are really inclined to be more expensive and beautiful, and second there's the gift-givers, grandmothers, aunts and cousins, friends and neighbors. I've been a sales clerk and buyer for thirty years, and I'd bet a mother does less than forty percent of the shopping for her infant from the time it's born to the time it's three years old.

"The shopping mothers do is less expensive and more practical. They spend about half for an item of what their relatives and friends do, and they have an eye for what might happen to the garment when it is washed and what kind of pressing will be required. They check a garment to see it's properly stitched. And they won't buy a spectacular-looking little dress or suit if there's going to be shrinkage.

"Of course, it makes a difference if the baby is a boy or a girl. We sell three times as many apparel items for little girls as for little boys. Boys get simple romper suits and knit shirts and sweaters, maybe one good little suit for special occasions. Baby girls are supposed to look frilly and adorable, and sometimes we hit the same levels of fashion and high fashion that we do in women's clothes."

A saleswoman at the May Company department store told us that buyers make a mistake by not ordering more for little boys. She says they could sell clothing at a ratio of 60-40 (little girls vs. little boys) if only buyers would order more.

A Beverly Hills boutique owner scoffed at our estimates for outfitting baby as being ridiculously low. "My customers aren't all rich people by any means. We get people who do a lot of their shopping at Sears or Penney's or from catalogues. No matter how they economize elsewhere—trading clothing or making garments themselves—they'll come to a relatively expensive store like ours for one or two very special things that are high style and have our label.

They can't afford those items, but every mother thinks her baby is special and this is how she proves how special it is. As for our regular customers, they spend close to fifteen hundred dollars per baby. *Well* over. I won't mention her name, but a movie star who just had a baby girl came to us this morning to arrange for a special showing of dresses and coats for the baby. I was glad to oblige, and we're staying open late tomorrow night to give her a private showing. If she spends anything less than three thousand dollars, I'm going to be furious!"

For many upper-class women, their infants are treated as "showcases" and the same attention and money is lavished on their wardrobe as on the mother's. "I can afford it, so why shouldn't I?" sums up their attitude.

MONEY'S WORTH?

An important question is whether people, at whatever income level, get their money's worth when they shop for infant's apparel.

Answers Bullock's buyer: "You've got to realize that when a woman spends thirty-five dollars instead of eight dollars for a baby dress or coat or suit, she's buying something other than just the material and design. She wants her child to look right for a special occasion—a christening or a baptism or a session with the photographer. Right now our best seller is a christening gown of embroidered polyester cotton that's trimmed with Swiss lace. With a matching bonnet, it goes for eighty dollars—and we can't keep it in stock!"

"Things just aren't made the way they used to be made," says an infants' wear manufacturer. "The stitching in baby clothes is sometimes so sloppy that I feel bad. A mother will buy—for thirty-five dollars to one-hundred dollars —an elaborate baptismal gown with ruffles and flounces and appliqués and synthetic lace fringing that will barely hold up through the ceremony. If they plan to keep the gown for other children to come, they'll find it's unravelled. And you'd be surprised what one washing can do to varying tensile strengths of fabric and thread. Our industry is like automakers—we're making a product with built-in obsolescence. We don't use any hems to speak of, so a little dress costing thirty-five dollars can't be let down to give a toddler six months' wear instead of three months. Even when there is a hem, the permapress definitions are so sharply implanted in the fabric the new hemline looks as if it *was* let down."

We spent an afternoon at the Broadway department store in Hollywood, interviewing customers on what they thought of the values they were getting in baby clothes, shoes, etc.

"They're wonderful," said a grandmotherly type who turned out to be a real grandmother. "I raised four children, and we never had permapress or stain-resistant fabrics. I had to spend hours washing and ironing and usually stains never did come out altogether. My daughters have it easy—they just throw everything into the washer. Yes, clothes cost a lot more. But they're worth it. And people save by buying fewer items."

"Look at this—twelve ninety-five—and it isn't even real linen," said an attractive girl examining a powder-blue "tent" dress that had kitten heads appliqued as pockets. "The pockets aren't even stitched on properly. My daughter would have them torn off in five minutes."

"I'm just looking at styles," admitted another young woman. "I make all my twin girls' dresses myself. Including patterns and material and ribbon and all that, I spend less than three dollars to make a dress they charge twelve or fifteen dollars here for."

"So many of these expensive little dresses aren't made as well as they should be," responded a mother of three who is about thirty five. "They're made pretty and ultra-stylish instead of made to wash easily. I think the tendency to overdress children is foolish. It's status seeking. The child isn't affected because other children don't care about how pretty she's dressed. It's just so a mother can say, 'My, but don't we look pretty!' "

A pediatrician comments: "Most babies and small children are properly dressed, although mothers do have a tendency to dress a child too warmly in cool weather. The child will perspire excessively with all those clothes on, then get slightly chilled when the clothes come off and possibly catch cold. Mothers should also pay more attention to fabrics involved in hot-weather wear. Cotton and wool and linen breathe, but synthetics don't. To put a child in synthetics is like hermetically sealing him up."

Is too much money spent on clothes that look pretty?

"I would think so, but largely because a mother then expects the child to stay neat and clean through a day's normal routine. Clothes ought to be adapted to a child's habits instead of the other way around. It's unfair to berate children for being 'careless' or untidy. It's even psychologically damaging. The little darlings weren't conceived immaculately, and they won't stay immaculate."

DRESSED TO KILL

Until July 29, 1973, loving parents could equip baby's crib with the softest, fluffiest blankets and the cuddliest sleep clothes—often costing twice as much as their spartan counterparts—only to learn they had unwittingly invited death into the nursery.

Of the five thousand infant deaths by fire that occurred annually, Ralph Nader estimates that at least three thousand were caused by the extreme flammability of those same fluffy and cuddly sleepsuits and blankets.

Nader's revelations, as usual, provoked a storm in Washington. Government agencies began an investigation, and when the facts bore out Nader's conclusions, new federal standards required all items of sleepwear and blankets for infants to be treated with flame-resistant chemicals. Leftover merchandise, manufactured before the deadline, had to be labeled with a warning that it was not flame retardant.

What were the results?

Sales of children's sleepwear manufacturers dropped 30 to 40 percent. Mothers refused to pay the higher price per garment—sometimes as much as double—so their children could go to sleep in clothes that matched federal safety standards.

What started as a laudable plan to safeguard children lit fires of protest not only from mothers but from the textile industry and children's wear manufacturers. Many manufacturers went out of business or entered related fields.

"Nobody has any argument with a law that saves children's lives," a children's lingerie manufacturer told us, "but we're being picked on unfairly. The government ought to look at its own statistics. Only one out of forty deaths at home is attributable to fires. Only a little better than a quarter of the five thousand, seven hundred deaths caused by fire are in age groups from one to fourteen.* There are more deaths caused by fire in age groups sixty-five and over. Why don't they make old people go to bed in flame-retardant pajamas?"

We asked the Consumer Products Safety Commission why children's wear manufacturers have to abide by the flame-retardant clothing regulations, while the manufacturers of adult clothes are free to continue making clothes from the usual fabrics.

"The total number of home-related deaths by fire is not the only test for whether there should be regulations about children's clothing," answered a spokesman. "If these protesters would study, as we have, the reports by the U.S. Department of Health, Education and Welfare, the Food and Drug Administration, and the Bureau of Product Safety, they'd find out that of three hundred thousand burn injuries reported in the last fourteen years—where the age of the victim is known—children-victims outnumber old people four to one."

Nevertheless, a little tag, "This fabric is not flame resistant, and care should be exercised when near heat or flame," is now attached to left-over children's sleepwear. It has the same incendiary effect on manufacturers in the field as a red flag reputedly has on a bull.

"The entire industry is being forced to switch over to flame-retardant fabrics," another businessman told us. "Most fabric mills don't make separate lines only for the children's wear market, so that means the entire textile industry will shift over. Whether anybody likes it or not. And I can tell you this. We're not the only ones who don't like it. The consumer doesn't either."

That seems to be true. Some mothers are putting their children to bed in

*Deaths from burn injuries are twenty-second on the list of all product-related deaths.

underwear because they can't afford the high prices of flame-retardant garments, some because they don't like the kind of fabrics available in the new process, and others are making their children's clothing out of nonflame-retardant fabrics.

"Most of the stuff I've seen is like a board," a housewife told us. "They can't be laundered with bleach or fabric softener. The only way I've found to wash them is with a phosphate detergent powder—and in double the recommended amount for other fabrics. After the same number of launderings I used to give other fabrics, this flame-retardant stuff either loses its flame retardancy or it just falls apart."

Another indignant woman says: "My kids always complain about scratchy pajamas. The whole kids' laundry pile is starting to look gray. No more! I'm not going to use that fabric. From now on my kids sleep in their underwear —or in the raw."

"It's not acceptable from either a standpoint of quality or price," adds a third mother. "The two fabrics my children like best—denim and corduroy—don't come in flame retardant versions. But I understand they're going to have a rule about those pretty soon. I don't know why we can't dress our children in the kind of clothes we've been putting them into for years."

There is opposition from experts also, although not as vehement. Henry Tovey, chief of the office of information and hazard analysis of the National Bureau of Standards, contends that the configuration and fit of a garment are more important in determining the extent of injuries from fire than either fabric construction or burn time. He says such items as free-flowing night-gowns and robes, wide, loose-hanging or billowing sleeves and other apparel items with certain kinds of flare designs, will someday be things of the past.

And Daniel Powderley, of Celanese Fibers Marketing Company, says: "Our industry has been rushed into unrealistic standards. But things are not as bleak as they were a few months ago. A number of new fabrics are being developed to meet flame retardant standards."

Many in the industry blame the medical profession for the new regulations.

A children's garment manufacturer: "Doctors were behind this and helped persuade the government to put the new rules into effect. With a deadline! Suppose we gave doctors a deadline for curing heart disease, could they do it? The problem is overkill. Flame-retarding fabrics are getting better and time could be a big help, but we didn't get time. Now we have to worry about even staying in business!"

A small manufacturer complains that the regulations play into the hands of big business. "I can't find the fabrics. A mill shows me a fabric, I like it, I try to buy it. Then they tell me it isn't available. I know what's happened. It was bought up by the big guys like Sears and Penney's. And I'm left standing with my ____ in my hands."

Most industry leaders share the view of Bill Roen, president of Hollywood Needlecraft, who told a feature writer from the Los Angeles *Times,* "Socially, the law is good. It protects a child at an age when he or she is most vulnerable. On the moral side, I'm one hundred percent in favor of flame-retardant children's wear. The trouble is, the customer is not yet receiving a quality product. Fabrics are generally inferior. Returns to stores are astronomical. Because the manufacturer must pay for all the research and development that goes into the product, many of the small manufacturers simply can't compete.

"The legal profession will profit from all the product liability cases. And the small manufacturer who is not in a position to fight the long legal battles will be forced to go into another business. At this point, it would seem that the customer is paying a lot of money for a small bit of protection."

"A small bit of protection?" counters a young lawyer who has worked with Nader's Raiders. "If it saves even one child's life, who'll stand up and say it wasn't worth it? And it saves *hundreds* of children's lives every year. I can't accept the morality of businessmen. Profits before everything, that's their motto.

"In nineteen seventy-two, when I was with Ralph Nader, we shocked the public and the FDA with the story of lead-based paints and the crippling effect they were having on infants. The killer qualities of lead-based paint had been recognized since nineteen twenty, but somehow nobody ever bothered to ban its use in cribs, playpens, baby furniture, toys, or the walls and ceilings in nursery areas. The U.S. Department of Health, Education, and Welfare estimated that between one hundred ten thousand and two hundred twenty thousand tots chewed off paint peeling from handrails and windowsills, particularly in the older tenements where old-fashioned paints were still being used instead of the new latex-based products. They also estimated five percent died of it. Add up those fatality figures if you want a shocker. And consider how many kids are alive today because of Ralph Nader, and how many haven't suffered terrible injury to their bone structure and kidneys, suffered blindness, deafness or mental deprivation. Thank God there's somebody around like Ralph Nader who cares more about human life than dollars and cents!"

BIRTH IS BIG BUSINESS: FRINGE BUSINESS

9

The clothing and outfitting of Baby represents only a small part of the overall expenditure for Mother and Baby.

Let's take a look at other products and services that must be reckoned into the cost.

We'll begin at the periphery. "While I was still in the hospital," a young mother relates, "I received several phone calls and at least half a dozen mail solicitations from different photographers who wanted to photograph my baby."

Lest casual readers think we have defined the periphery as being too far out of their orbit to really matter ("After all, what's the cost of a few photographs?"), we will supply the kind of relevance that impresses the statistically minded. According to the latest Department of Commerce figures, the volume of business done by the photographic industry will rise in 1975 to nearly $7 billion. Of this sum, almost $1 billion, 700 million will be done by photographic studios.

And Baby is the star at most photographic studios.

Professional photographers, who derive a considerable portion of their revenues from the new-baby market, have noted with alarm the recent growth of a do-it-yourself tendency. This is, in turn, part of the wider trend toward less formal portraiture, which has existed for some years. The use of movie cameras and of outdoor settings is steadily increasing.

To counter these threats to their business, professional photographers now try to get to the client quickly, at the hospital, before the movie cameras, the Polaroids, and the amateurs close in. There is hardly a family that does not have at least one enthusiastic amateur camera addict who will volunteer to save the cost of a professional photographer.

Not too long ago it was a reasonable assumption that half the new-baby crop had its portrait taken, at an average cost to the parents of about twelve dollars and fifty cents. An insignificant little item that in itself amounts to about twenty million dollars a year!

Considering photography in a wider sense, how much would you say Polaroid and Eastman Kodak and their lesser rivals owe to the baby market? We checked with the processing plant division of Eastman Kodak, the largest company in the field, and a spokesman told us he had no way of estimating the figure. "How do you know whether a given photograph would have been taken if baby wasn't in it? Or whether an Instamatic or a movie camera was bought mainly to show baby growing up on film? We know there are fourteen million cameras grinding and snapping away out there, and of all the photographic subjects it's obvious that baby is a chief favorite. Every day millions of snapshots and hundreds of thousands of feet of silent or sound film are being taken of babies—and shown to people who would probably fall asleep during the chariot race in *Ben Hur*. But they'll stay in there and look, or how will they get people to look at *their* baby pictures?"

The processing division sees film on a bulk basis, and therefore has some experience with what proportion is devoted to recording baby's first gurgles or first steps or to showing baby with Papa and Mama and relatives. Our spokesman ventured a "guesstimate" that baby is the subject of 20 percent of the film he sees. That would mean the "baby market" generates an estimated annual volume of $1.4 billion!

The florist supplying bouquets for Mother does not have to contend with that forbidding "Please Omit" that so often blights their funerary trade. No parent will prohibit lovely roses, chrysanthemums and daisies, the delicate blooms of spring, summer, and fall from gracing the joyful occasion of a birth.

We inquired of several Southern California florists and were informed that "appropriate" floral bouquets for a new mother were available from $10 to $40. When baby is born, floral tributes pour in from father, family, and friends. One Manhattan florist, who grosses more than $200,000 a year, told our interviewer that he estimates any birth at a nearby west side hospital is worth an average $55 to him in sales. A florist trade journal editor estimates that flowers delivered to a new mother, either in person, by telegraph, or ordered over the telephone, represent a quarter of the industry's total revenue. Since the total expenditure for flowers is just under $2 billion, that would add another half billion dollars to the birth bill. On a per capita (infant) basis, this would come to $165 yearly, a figure that struck us as unreasonably high, until a check with the *Florists' Review* indicated that "it was somewhere in that ballpark."

There are other "peripheral" areas. "Within a week after I got home from the hospital," another young mother told us, "my husband and I were visited by two encyclopedia salesmen who tried to convince us that without a set of their encyclopedias at hand, we'd probably raise a congenital idiot."

Children's encyclopedias—usually featuring a free or nominally priced Volume One as a come-on—are burgeoning. At prices ranging to $200 a set, they can be a real item of expense for culture-conscious parents and are guaranteed to make any child's mind ache with the burden of all there is to learn.

Magazine and direct-mail advertising can be used to measure their sales success. No fewer than four double-page ads, inducing parents to start building a collection of children's books at age zero, are to be found in a representative issue of *Parent's* magazine.

According to Octave Stevenson, chief of the literature division, District of Columbia Public Library, parents do not need an encyclopedia for their children. The nearest public library has immense resources in books and periodicals that provide a more up-to-date view of things and a wider perspective than an encyclopedia. All that children need is a reliable, inexpensive reference book shelf for the home. Stevenson recommends a one-volume encyclopedia, such as the Columbia edition. The *Guinness Book of World Records* is also informative and entertaining reading, and will encourage children to look up things. A good atlas and an almanac, such as *World Almanac* or *Information Please Almanac,* will round off a home reference shelf at a cost hardly to be compared with the prices charged for children's encyclopedias that are advertised as a complete home education unit.

Nor should we overlook how much is spent on children's books and book clubs. Combined, they account for $300 million of business a year. That averages out to over $100 for every baby being born in the United States.

What are the best sellers in the children's book field? According to the authoritative trade magazine, *Publishers Weekly,* the answer is preschool picture books. *PW*'s survey of bookstores and publishing companies reported "a brisk trade in dinosaurs and reptiles." Despite escalating prices, customers are apparently still willing to pay $7 or more for a high quality illustrated child's book.

A gauge of the widespread interest in children's books is that several television programs and a column in *Ladies' Home Journal* regularly make pre-Christmas recommendations. Several bookstores have now begun specializing only in children's books, and there are growing numbers of lower-priced paperback reprints available.

Fringe business it may be, but the fringe is pure silk.

ELEGANCE AND WAHOO

The greeting-card industry, according to Department of Commerce figures, does a $766-million annual business—hailing with nonpartisan zeal birth, birthdays, sickness, death, and any other occasion worth memorializing. Hallmark's public relations department estimated for us that approximately 16 percent of their greeting-card business is a birth announcement or a congratulation. Applying this percentage to the business as a whole, we come up with the interesting figure of $127 million plus—an investment of approximately $42 per baby!

This omits the more extravagant examples of the genre. Those who do not reckon tawdry costs often employ the services of a calligrapher who will individually address a birth announcement in fancy script more suitable to the birth of a prince to the royal family of England. That kind of elegance is precisely the effect being striven for. The cost—$3 and up, depending on the length of the announcement and the number of them being ordered.

We hate to single out Texas as the home of the flamboyant spender, for the *nouveau riche* oilmen do not represent a significant part of the state's population. But they are responsible for the national attitude toward that expansive region, an attitude that might be summarized as, "What is the United States doing in a place like Texas?" At times, one is inclined to believe that these larger-than-life Texans are characters out of a fairy tale—everyone knows they don't really exist even if we like to read about them.

A Houston oil baron sent out nearly eight thousand birth announcements on the arrival of his six-pound, five-ounce son. All eight thousand announcements were done with the elegant flourish provided by a small battalion of calligraphers.

A resident of Dallas tossed a "Meet the Baby" gala on the occasion of his son's birth, inviting guests with customary indiscriminate Lone Star State hospitality. Over six hundred guests showed up for a Wahoo barbecue served at the "Meet the Baby" gala. Over ten thousand yellow roses decorated tables on the spacious lawn, and five hundred magnums of champagne were consumed in toasts to the host's son and heir. Said son and heir, blissfully asleep, was displayed to the assembled multitude from a safe distance and welcomed with a rousing rendition of "Deep in the Heart of Texas."

In the Lone Star State—at least among the wealthier citizenry—birth is really BIG business.

BABIES NEED PROTECTION

Let's return to problems that are scaled to a more human dimension. The question of life insurance, for example.

There is nothing like starting a family to turn father's and mother's thoughts toward ways of attaining financial stability. Insurance is a subject about which the average man and woman are woefully uninformed. Half of the new parents in the country do not have any life insurance in force at the time the baby is born. With the arrival of the baby, this situation is likely to be remedied at once.

A young couple that has any other form of insurance—homeowner's, fire and casualty, auto, health care, you name it—will soon hear from their present insurance agent or from an agent associated with his firm.

The approach is along these lines: "Congratulations on the birth of your son [daughter]. I have a small present for him [her] [a framed copy of the birth certificate, an offer to bronze the first pair of baby shoes, or an engraved insurance portfolio] and I was wondering when you'll have time to consider his [her] insurance needs."

There follows an appointment at home, usually at night when both parents can be confronted. The sales pitch is based on the advantages of a compulsory forced-savings insurance program that provides the new baby with a sizable amount of income when it's time for college (and can, of course, always be borrowed against at minimal interest rates). Also on the fact that the premiums for such insurance are so low almost anyone can afford to pay them. Unspoken is the appeal to the "protective" instinct of the parents, and to the almost universal anxiety among "responsible" family men about being "underinsured."

Those who do not have an insurance agent will not be overlooked. Agents have access to hospital records listing new births. They also get leads from the vital statistics section of the local newspaper, from "contacts" who let them know of any likely prospect in their neighborhood, among their circle of acquaintances, or even among acquaintances of acquaintances. In addition, most agents spend from $15 to $20 monthly, depending on locality and the extensiveness of the lists, for the new births carefully documented by the mailing list companies.

How well do these aggressive selling tactics work? The results are astonishing. "It's my bread and butter," one Prudential insurance salesman told us. "Every year sales to new parents supply the income I actually need to live on. Anything beyond that is gravy."

We asked what was the biggest insurance policy he had ever sold on an infant. "I sold a New York industrialist one hundred thousand dollars in term policy on his newborn son. Since I moved to L.A. a few years ago, the closest I've come to that is a fifty-thousand-dollar policy—on a movie producer's daughter. But I've heard of two-hundred-fifty-thousand-dollar policies being sold out here. I understand the Kennedy children start off with a hundred thousand dollars in term insurance, paid by the estate. Considering the size of that family, that's a pretty lucky insurance agent involved."

Most agents we interviewed estimate as high as one in three "sales" made for every valid new contact. Statistics bear out the estimate. Fully 65 percent of newborn infants are covered by "average" $5,000 policies before they are six years old. The premiums on these policies average $4.50 a month, or $54 a year—which puts the annual gross volume of insurance for baby at something in excess of $150 million a year.

Insuring Baby, however, is the least lucrative of the possibilities, even though the agent can plan on increasing the coverage as the child reaches age five, ten, twelve, etc., and as family fortunes improve. Far more important is the increased insurance taken out by Father. (Women, who constitute 43 percent of the U.S. labor force, own only 15 percent of the total life insurance.)

In 1975, over $280 billion of new life insurance will be bought. A new study, conducted by the Life Insurance Marketing and Research Organization, reports that most people who purchase life insurance are between the ages of twenty and thirty-five, and most is purchased by brides and bridegrooms starting new households and by expectant fathers. That means a considerable percentage of this new insurance business can be directly or indirectly attributed to Baby. In dollar terms, that makes insurance the biggest "baby business" of all.

Is it worth the cost? We discussed this with independent agents who represent all the major insurance companies, and with the vice president of one large company that sells millions of dollars of insurance to young families. What follows is distilled from these conversations.

Insurance policies usually offer "protection" and "savings." Some, such as term policies, offer only "protection" at a smaller premium cost, while endowment policies are weighted heavily toward the "savings" feature. Most fall somewhere between.

The disadvantage of a term insurance policy is that, like homeowner's and automobile insurance, nothing is provided except protection, usually against the death of the major breadwinner in the family. And unlike homeowner's and auto insurance, the premiums do not remain at the same level, but increase whenever a new term period is entered. That is, provided there is a renewable feature which allows the holder to continue the policy. This renewable feature itself usually expires when the holder reaches the age of sixty-five.

There are also term policies with convertible provisions, which allow the holder to change his coverage to a cash-value insurance, generally at any time before he is sixty-five.

The popular straight or "whole" life-insurance policy is a combination of protection and savings. Cash value builds up over the years. The premium doesn't change as it does with term insurance, and can be paid all your life, or for twenty years, or just until age sixty-five.

The catch? The premium is initially about three times as high as term insurance premiums.

Endowment policies, popular at one time, now constitute only 5 percent of the policies being sold. They pay off a certain sum of money at a certain time or upon prior death. The accent is on savings, not protection, and the premiums are high. With inflation soaring as it is, the money you pay in is worth a lot more than the money you or your family is going to get. To an extent, this is true of all insurance but it is particularly true of the endowment policy.

As a "savings" plan, any insurance policy is just this side of ridiculous. Whatever portion is "savings" is being paid the lowest rate of interest anywhere available. Your neighborhood savings bank offers a much better rate.

How can parents decide how much insurance they really need? An insurance salesman will tell you that the "rule of thumb" is five times your annual income.

Don't panic. It ain't necessarily so. Most families have much less insurance than this.

Here is a common-sense formula, based on today's realities.

1. Figure out how much your family requires as an annual income if the major breadwinner should die.
2. Estimate how many years it will be until the children are out of college.
3. Multiply number one by number two.
4. Estimate the probable net income of the surviving spouse, and the income from social security, interest on savings, mutual fund or other investment dividends.
5. Subtract this from the total in number three.

This isn't as hard as it sounds. Simple addition, multiplication, and subtraction provide an answer.

For example:

1. My family will need $15,000 a year.
2. They will need this sum for ten years.
3. The total is $15,000 × 10—or $150,000.
4. My surviving spouse will earn a net income of $8,000 a year for ten years —a total of $80,000. Social security income will be $3,000 a year for ten years—a total of $30,000. Interest and dividends at $500 a year will provide another $5,000 in ten years. All together, this amounts to $115,000.
5. $150,000 minus $115,000 equals $35,000.

Okay, you need $35,000 insurance.

The figures have many variables, so this can be only an approximate reckoning. We have not included any allowance for an "inflation factor," since we do not claim any ability to forecast the future. But this is a better guide than an eager insurance salesman's "rule of thumb." And you can make the needed adjustments upward or downward as your own circumstances (not his commissions) dictate.

What kind of insurance? A young couple with an unstretchable budget should probably buy a term policy, which will give them the most protection at the lowest cost during the children's growing-up years. Insist on a conversion provision, so you can switch to a cash value policy when you have the extra money.

How much will it cost? A term policy providing $35,000 in coverage for five years on a parent aged twenty-seven will cost approximately $200 a year. For an additional $35 you can probably add a provision that doubles the coverage in the event of accidental death. And since accidents are the chief cause of deaths under age forty, this is a pretty good buy.

Major insurance companies seeking to increase their income in this market are offering eighteen-year endowment plans for the newborn that can be converted to cash at college time, and prepaid life policies that will return interest dividends as the years go on. The new father is also being urged to add to his health insurance.

Savings bank life insurance is probably your cheapest buy, since some "middleman's" costs are avoided. But contrary to popular belief, the cost of the same insurance policy will vary, often considerably, from one company to another.

The American Institute for Economic Research rated seventy insurance companies and found that the twenty-year net cost per $1,000 straight life insurance for a thirty-five-year-old man varied from $81.34 to $152.36. That comparison is certainly odious, for the same product is being sold.

As for the risk of deception or fraud, you are probably in good hands if you take a policy with one of the major insurance firms. When buying from a relatively unknown firm, be sure to read the fine print. We have seen policies that do not cover the insured in case of death from chronic or contagious disease, auto or travel accident, or epidemic. An unsuspecting buyer may only learn of such loopholes after tragedy strikes.

Usually these policies are offered at deceptive bargain rates. "After all," as one insurance executive told us, "any company can sell a cheap policy that will insure someone only if he happens to be killed by a falling tree limb while driving a motorcycle through a typhoon."

The mutual fund industry has long recognized that trust funds for new babies represent a most promising market. And the liberalized deductions of the 1969 tax reform bill gave their salesmen a new selling point: Baby as a tax shelter.

It appears that while death is inevitable, taxes are not—at least not for the well-to-do investor who wants to create a temporary trust for his children or grandchildren. By putting money into the trust, which could be for the stated purpose of, say, paying future tuition bills, he diverts money that would ordinarily be paid out in taxes. That saving, especially in the upper income brackets, increases the dollars-and-cents value of baby tremendously.

An even simpler method being offered to well-to-do parents is the custodian account. What this amounts to is putting money aside that will belong to the minor when he or she turns twenty-one. All you have to do is register securities thus: John Doe as custodian for Richard Doe under the (home state's) Uniform Gifts to Minors Act.

As adult custodian, you retain a good deal of power over the "donated" securities. You can collect income, hold, manage, sell, invest and re-invest, or use the income and/or principal to support, maintain, and benefit the minor. Catch 21 is that when the minor reaches that age, the securities must be turned over to him or her.

There's a way around that too.

First, though, let's look at what you, as the parents, gain. Husband and wife can contribute $3,000 each into a custodian account without incurring a gift tax or any other kind of tax. If grandparents are living, they can also contribute $3,000 each without being taxed. That's $12,000 in a year (or $24,000 over the two months of December–January), and it's money that's free of taxes. The parents and grandparents can keep adding to the custodian account each year for as long as they choose.

Doesn't this represent an unfair tax advantage for the rich?

"Sure it does," replied a well-known tax attorney. "But the rich have to be clever these days, or they could never survive, outnumbered as they are."

This same tax attorney set up a custodian account for each of twelve grandchildren and four nephews, giving him a potential tax shelter of $288,000 over the next ten years. That's not merely a savings in income taxes, for the eventual estate taxes are also lowered correspondingly.

Mutual fund salesmen point out what a fine vehicle their funds make for custodian accounts. The funds have accumulation plans to automatically re-invest all dividends, capital gains inducements, and the advantage of holding record-keeping to a minimum.

Now, what about that Catch 21?

According to attorney Eugene Bogan, a tax specialist, "The law clearly states that the money in a custodian account belongs to a minor when he turns twenty-one. But if the kid becomes a bad apple or refuses to spend it on his education, a custodian has a practical solution. Tell the brat to sue you." Often there's not much he can do. The legal process is lengthy and expensive, and verdicts are highly unpredictable.

SUCCESS STORIES

Many American corporate enterprises are partly dependent on the baby market, selling products that range from greeting cards to sterling silver. Estimates of how much this represents of their total business volume are hard to come by and would not be wholly reliable.

It might be more rewarding to take a closer look at a corporate giant, Johnson & Johnson, whose annual sales volume exceeds $1.5 billion, of which 90 percent is to the baby market.

Their advertising budget exceeds $8 million annually, $5 million of it devoted to television, the rest to print ads that usually appear in color in all women-oriented magazines. It is hard to fault the corporation advertising on grounds of taste; the soft-sell messages appear to be steeped in love and concern. As a result, many consumers seem to think the corporation's major concern is not profits but mother's aid.

"I don't think of Johnson and Johnson as a company," a mother of four remarks. "They simply make things that you have to have for babies. They're *there*, that's all."

Indeed they are. The leading sellers across the nation are Johnson & Johnson's baby powder, baby oil, and baby shampoo, and this in a field in which the smallest drug store stocks twenty separate items for children and the largest drugstore stocks eighty. Johnson & Johnson's Big Three outrank such vastly popular products as Mennen's Baby Magic, Chesebrough-Pond's Vaseline and Q-tips, Curity's gauze pads, all the brands of disposable diapers, Bayer's and St. Joseph's children's aspirin, and all the teething lotions.

Each year, in drugstores or via mail, $6.5 billion are spent on products like these or for newer products like Diaparene Peri-Anal Creme, an antibacterial for cleaning Baby's behind, and Vaseline Wipe 'n' Dipe, a soft treated tissue designed for the same purpose, or Wet Ones Towelettes in a pop-up carton, to clean Baby's face as well as his sitting place. Each year more convenience products appear on the drugstore shelves.

One pediatrician told us, "All that junk isn't really necessary. But if mothers are willing to spend money to buy their way out of work, who am I to say they shouldn't? What I do wonder about is how much big business is feeding off people, not in dollars and cents, but in terms of the old values. Are we really going to be better off if we completely merchandize motherhood? The whole process is getting so cushioned by products that the only step left is not to be a mother at all. Maybe that's the end result that women in our country are aiming at.

"We already use more birth control than any other nation, and if a baby does get born it is over-valued, mis-valued, spoiled. I blame business methods for a lot of that. They not only make a mother's lot easier—which is fine, providing she ends up doing something more useful with her time—but they also sell the wrong idea about mothers and babies. The image is taking over the reality.

"Take those people at Johnson and Johnson: one of the things they have done for years is to make their ads feature pictures of lovely models with charming beautiful babies gurgling happily. If only it were like that. But it isn't. All mothers and babies aren't beautiful. Mothers get cross and irritable, and babies cry, and it's tough. Maybe more mothers and fathers should know how hard babying is, and then they could make intelligent decisions and not just buy and buy—trying to ease their way closer to all those phony mother-and-baby pictures that have conditioned their thinking too long.

"And·if people didn't spend so much trying to look like perfect parents, it might make them easier to live with when the kids grow up and don't show enough appreciation. We might get parents who didn't go around begging for recognition and saying, 'Look what we did for you, you ungrateful so and so's.' "

A remarkable success story in baby products began in 1965 when the Mennen Company presented Baby Magic.

Baby Magic was first formulated in 1964. After it passed initial lab tests, Mennen executives were sure they had a winner. They backed the product with a total of two million dollars for an all-out eighteen-month campaign to introduce it to America's mothers.

Lillian Smith, the J. Walter Thompson advertising agency account executive in charge, explains the philosophy that governed the presentation.

"All of us felt that the time was right. Products that were obviously oily, in the general cosmetics field as well as the baby market, were giving way to lotions and creams—formulas which left little or no oily residue. From the medicinal standpoint we could do the same thing as oily products without staining clothing and towels and diapers with a film, or making hand washing such a chore. The new cream came off without soaping, for example, whereas with oils soaping is necessary.

"We named the product 'Baby Magic' because we felt that had the most appeal to the consumer. Then we did an extensive test market in fourteen cities, mailing free samples, making sure the product was well distributed and stocked. The results were fabulous. Then we turned, naturally, to the women's magazines and network television. Wooing mothers away from the 'other product' was not nearly as difficult as we anticipated. More free samples, more instant sales. It simply took off.

"Mennen did everything right. The color, a soft pink, is a tone naturally associated with babies, and the scent is a slight but hygienic perfume. Since it was a lotion, mother felt she was taking care of her hands at the same time she was pampering and protecting her baby. We were scrupulously accurate —you have to be, as far as the FDA is concerned if you bring out anything that involves infants—but we didn't mind glamorizing things a bit. We felt we had a valid and important product, and time has proven us right."

Another hugely successful product that owes much to the power of big business advertising is one that has been received with mixed feelings in the medical profession: the disposable diaper. The American mother, trained from childhood to accept the quick 'n' easy, was psychologically preconditioned to receive the new miracle product. Even at two years old a child wets or soils himself seven or eight times a day, and each change of diaper requires approximately ten minutes from detection to completion. This comes to about nine hours a week. Add the time spent washing or drying diapers, and the mother of a two-year-old is spending more than one fourth of a full-time work week simply changing diapers.

Mother may love baby, but cleaning diapers is an unattractive and malodorous chore. Soaking and washing involves repeated exposure to the smells of urine and feces, the diaper pail is a constant annoying presence in bathroom or laundry room, and the wringing out process before the diapers can be put into the washer is enough to make delicate sensibilities reel and lotioned hands pucker.

The problem is age old. Queen Marie Antoinette refused to watch her children eat because she knew what would follow. Andrew Jackson's mother told her son ". . . don't get uppity with me, Mr. President, because I used to clean the shit out of your drawers." Even Eleanor Roosevelt remarked that ". . . although I have never wished that my children could have been conceived by immaculate conception I do wish there had been a way of immaculate elimination."

In the year 1947 a long forward step was taken to help mother in the battle of the dirty diapers. Diaper services offered relief that the American mother of 1930 had only yearned for. She no longer had to buy diapers, nor wash or dry them. In that first year the diaper service industry grossed $5 million. Ten years later that figure had grown to over $100 million.

The millennium was not at hand. Mother still had to clean off the diapers, soak them in a diaper pail, and wring them out before the service man came by to collect them and leave a fresh supply. Meanwhile, the diaper pail itself was an unwelcome tenant in the house. "I'd love to know what Jackie Kennedy or Grace Kelly did about that!" one exasperated mother exclaimed. "That stinking pail had to live with the Beautiful People too, didn't it? Or did they have a special diaper pail room where nobody ever went but the maids?"

A further disadvantage was that laundering and hygienic standards varied widely from one company to another and one area to another. The diapers delivered each week might contain chemicals in amounts equivalent to a mild toxicity, a discoloration might make the diapers appear more yellow than white, or because of a less-than-thorough washing they might even carry the possibility of infection or disease.

In 1966 three major paper manufacturing companies test-marketed the disposable diaper. In 1967 a brand labeled Chux, manufactured by Chicopee Mills, appeared on the national scene.

During the introductory ad campaigns for Chux, the emphasis was placed on convenience. Price was never mentioned, nor economy, for the simple reason that any mother who could add would quickly find out disposable diapers cost her considerably more than she was paying to the store for cloth diapers or even to her diaper service.

"When you and baby are out . . . on the town or out of town . . ." was the theme of the first Chux ads. The first TV commercials implied that disposable diapers were to be used only for emergencies and not on a regular everyday basis.

However, to the surprise of marketing experts, women in the test areas began buying disposable diapers in quantity. Obviously, what the manufacturers intended to sell as a luxury item was being treated by mothers as a necessity.

Pediatricians were not uniformly enthusiastic, but most accepted the dictates of the marketplace. "Disposable diapers," wrote Dr. Spock, "were as inevitable as man's reaching the moon. Whether they were good for baby is beside the point; mothers immediately welcomed their convenience."

By 1972 Kimberly-Clark Corporation had made their Kimbies brand a staple, as had the Scott Paper Company with their Baby Scott and Procter & Gamble with Pampers. Disposables were also manufactured and sold by chain stores such as Sears, Ward's, and Penney's.

The success of the new product can be easily told in sales figures. In 1967 $500,000 worth of disposable diapers were sold. In 1968 sales were fifty times higher—$25 million. By 1972 this figure increased to $320 million, and in 1975 a further gain is projected to $485 million.

Seldom has any product met with such spectacular sales response. Only an acute petroleum shortage and a consequent shortage of plastic sheeting can prevent the figure from passing the half-billion-dollar mark.

The structure of the disposable diaper is simple and logical. Most consist of three layers. The outer layer is a waterproof plastic film. The inner, next-to-the-skin layer is a web-type nonabsorbent (hydrophobic) fabric. Between these two layers is a highly absorbent cellulose-based filler. Urine passes through the inner layer to be blotted by the filler. Even when not totally absorbed it is supposedly prevented from leaking through by the outer plastic film. In principle, it is similar to the leak-proofing offered by a heavy diaper and plastic pants snapped over the diaper.

Some deficiencies have begun to be noted. Three out of ten infants suffer mild to extreme allergic reactions to either the hydrophobic fabric or cellulose filler. (The incidence of babies allergic to cotton is so small as to be virtually nonexistent.) The filler also varies in absorbency from brand to brand, and the outer layer varies in thickness and therefore in heat retention. Sore bottoms and private parts are caused by continued exposure to the acid and heat of urine and there is a tendency to "fleece," leaving particles of synthetic material in the anus and the vagina or tender head of the infant penis. If not carefully cleaned, infection can result.

Another complaint is the high cost. The disposable variety ranges in price from $6.50 to $10.25 per 100. The best grade of cotton diapers cost less than $6 a dozen. Even the cost of a diaper service is less. (One hundred diapers delivered each week cost from $5.50 to $6.00.)

In addition to mothers and pediatricians, the chorus of complainers is augmented from an unlikely source: municipal sewage workers. Purchasers are warned not to flush the diaper down the toilet, but the majority still flush, and the resultant tidal wave of nonsoluble plastic and synthetic fibers creates havoc at treatment plants. An occasional small but expensive havoc is created at home too. One plumber gleefully remarked after getting an emergency call that "the plunger ain't the plumber's best friend; it's the disposable diaper."

It's safe to say by now that the disposable diaper is a fixture on the American birth scene. Hospitals are buying them at reduced quantity prices, and almost every new mother is being introduced to them via generous samples of Baby Scott, Kimbies, or Pampers in the mail. Further research will undoubtedly enable technology to triumph over the complaints.

Science will eventually find a way for the disposable diaper to be disposed of.

BIRTH IS BIG BUSINESS: KEEPING BABY FED 10

Half a century ago most babies dined at mother's breast, or else from commercially prepared infant food that consisted mostly of cow's milk to which various mineral substances and other compounds were added.

Of the two choices, it was better to nuzzle than guzzle. Mother's milk was more digestible and less likely to upset baby's tummy than formulas that came in bottles. Its temperature was right and it was free from harmful bacteria.

Both human milk and cow's milk have about the same number of calories per ounce, but human milk is higher in polyunsaturates and also contains more lactose, or milk sugar. Its two-to-one rate of calcium to phosphorus is ideal for the maximum calcium absorption that a baby's developing bones and teeth need. Human milk has twice the amount of vitamin A and niacin, twice as much vitamin C and iron as cow's milk. Iron is especially important, because during the first months of life a baby's red blood cells increase by millions. In breast feeding, the iron in the mother's milk along with the supply stored up in the fetal liver make the giving of extra iron unnecessary during the first six months of life.

Breast feeding—the ancient and ideal form of infant nutrition—is perfectly capable of meeting most babies' needs for the first four to six months of life. During this particularly vulnerable period, human milk supplies immunological aid and a good quality protein that contains all the essential amino acids.

The old saying that breast feeding is the best feeding is not far from the truth. In fact, even after the introduction of supplemental foods to the baby's diet, human milk can continue to serve as a significant source of the infant's nutritional well-being. From the sixth to the twelfth month it can supply up to three quarters of a child's nutritional needs, and a significant portion for some months afterward. Mother's milk is literally saturated with antibodies which are transferred to the newborn baby, helping to protect against many contagious diseases to which it would otherwise be vulnerable.

In the past quarter century, since breast feeding yielded to bottle feeding, cases of severe malnutrition are being reported in babies at an earlier age—an average of eight months instead of a year and a half. Even doctors do not yet fully understand the remarkable health-giving properties of breast milk. It is often the only food which can be assimilated by some sick or premature infants.

Recently, a newborn baby in a Manhattan hospital was literally starving to death. The infant could not digest any prepared formula, and continued to lose weight and strength. After six weeks he weighed less than five pounds. Then one of the staff physicians prescribed a diet of breast milk.

The baby's mother had died of a heart ailment only two days after he was born, but the Mother's Milk Bank supplied pasteurized breast milk. The malnourished infant immediately began to improve on the new diet. At seven months old, he was thriving and happy.

It now appears that mothers who don't breast feed their babies are missing an opportunity to lose the weight they've added during pregnancy. A renowned University of London nutritionist, Donald Naismith, writing in *World Medicine Journal,* reports that mothers often continue to have serious overweight problems if they are bottle-feeding their infants. In addition, bottle-fed babies tend to get obese more easily, perhaps because cow's milk contains far more protein than the baby needs.

Babies, however, can be put on a controlled diet a great deal more easily than Mother can. They have not yet been introduced to the delights of other foods or snacking between meals and are wholly incapable of opening a refrigerator door "just to see" what's inside.

Breast feeding eliminates the necessity for making a formula, sterilizing bottles, or waiting for the milk to get warm. Human milk is exactly the right temperature, and nature designed it as a formula for an infant's nutrition. The container is clean and a rinse of the nipples with water is all that is required after nursing.

Finally, we should not overlook the cost factor. An infant nursed through the first two years receives an average of almost 400 quarts of breast milk, nutritionally equal to about 15 percent more of cow's milk. At today's prices this represents a not inconsiderable saving—about $185.

On the other teat, cow's milk, incorrectly referred to as nature's most perfect food, is far from that. Cow's milk is deficient in vitamin D, vitamin C, vitamin

E, thiamine, and iron. It is high in phosphates, which an infant's kidney can't handle. Cow's milk—and most formulas—contains three to four times as much salt as human milk. A baby *can* handle that much sodium, but should it? Baby rats given large amounts of sodium, even for a short while, have been shown to develop high blood pressure in middle age. There is no proof that this will apply to human babies but it seems an unnecessary risk.

Lest anyone think we are only, because of some anti-bovine prejudice, kicking cow's milk around, let us state the argument for the bottle. Commercial infant formulas can be modified to supply more nutrients, and even be made to a formula that closely approximates human milk. Formulas, based on cow's milk, can also be adapted to special dietary needs. Premature infants need a higher concentration of calories—and commercial formulas can be enriched from the usual 67 calories to as high as 100 calories per 100 milliliters. Babies whose problem is gaining weight too fast can be put on a less-rich formula. And special formulas can be prescribed for babies who have food allergies. If the baby is allergic to ordinary milk protein, soy protein can be substituted, or even, as has been shown, liquid puree of lamb meat.

But the battle of human milk versus cow's milk is no contest—unless, of course, you happen to be raising a calf.

The process of lactation developed through long eras of evolution, and it is specifically adapted for the use of various mammalian species. Whale milk contains high calorie fat which helps to provide suitable protection for mammals that live in cold water; rabbit milk is very rich in protein, which aids the very rapid growth of their young. Human milk, too, is uniquely suited to the human child. Within the last few years the biochemistry of mother's milk has been shown to exactly match that of the infant and to possess still unidentified factors which protect against infections. Cow's milk may do a lot for calves but does not possess the best qualities for human babies.

Why, if this human milk is so important to health and so economical, has it fallen out of favor? A nationwide survey found that in the last twenty years the number of mothers breast feeding at the time they left the maternity hospital had declined by over 50 percent.

"It's all women's vanity," says a professor of public health at a leading university. "Ever since the female breast became a sex symbol, we have been treating it like some secret treasure. There's been a mystique built up about it—and it's so powerful that hardly any American woman will nurse her baby in public. That's changing a little now, with this back-to-nature movement among the young people. But it's going to have to change a lot before we all get back to regarding the female breast as something other than an overswollen, erotic sweat gland. The female breast was put there to feed kids, and we shouldn't forget that natural function.

"Most women's fears that the shape of their breasts will change if they feed their babies are silly. All that's needed is a good bra to keep the skin from being stretched while baby's nuzzling. After weaning, the breasts will return to normal size."

"It's the pediatricians' fault," says a spokeswoman for La Leche League, a voluntary women's group that promotes breast feeding. "They've always devoted themselves to pleasing the middle- and upper-class woman who either has a good job she doesn't want to give up, or simply doesn't want the bother of breast feeding. Most mothers don't realize what an essential part of motherhood breast feeding is. It's almost as important as nurturing a baby in the womb and giving birth to it. But the pediatrician encourages a mother to use the bottle."

"No doubt the pediatrician has been a willing ally, but I'd put the blame squarely on the food industry," replies a nutritionist who is also a qualified pediatrician. "Their multimillion-dollar campaigns encourage mothers to believe bottle feeding is as nutritional as breast feeding. It just isn't so. But with all that money behind them and expert marketing techniques, they can sell mothers baby foods that are not as nourishing as human milk and are much more expensive."

A professor of public health at the University of California, Los Angeles, Derrick B. Jelliffe, speaks of "commerciogenic malnutrition," and refers to the "well-financed steam-roller marketing techniques of the food industry" as the real culprit. Professor Jelliffe is particularly angry at "food industry representatives who mouth sanctimonious platitudes" about their role in improving child nutrition. He believes that the Department of Health, Education and Welfare should inform parents of the advantages and techniques of breast feeding and that infant formula cans and literature should not be permitted to carry such statements as "nearly identical to mother's milk," because such labeling and advertising is deceptive.

Recently, the Protein Advisory Group of the United Nations has been conferring with baby food company executives to try to persuade them to change their methods of promotion. According to Max Milner, director of the U.N. group, the food company executives react with surprise and indignation to the suggestion that they are not performing a public service. Milner says the usual reply is that they never lift a finger until they have the complete concurrence of the medical profession. Milner adds: "I think they are fudging because they know the medical profession is easily manipulated."

The dispute between pediatricians and the baby food industry as to who is most to blame seems a question of which is the devil and which is the Faust who summoned him up. But there is no question of who is the victim in the four-sided relationship that includes Mother, pediatrician, baby food company, and Baby. It is Baby.

Ironically, the decline in breast feeding is most apparent among the poor. In a poverty area of Chicago, less than 6 percent of infants under one month old were being breast fed. Other surveys show that only 8 percent of grade-school-educated mothers now breast feed.

But there has been a recent increase in breast feeding among college-trained and well-to-do mothers. Their average is now up to 32 percent. This may signal a change for the better. Artificial feeding began among mothers of higher income and took many years to become the practice among lower-income families. Now that the bottle is no longer a status symbol, lower-income families may follow the trend back to mother's breast.

If that happens, we will have stopped wasting one of nature's superior foods.

FOODS FOR SALE

Daniel Gerber, who died in 1974, was associated with his father in what was then called the Fremont Canning Company. When his infant daughter Sally became ill, the doctor suggested that Mr. Gerber strain some peas for her to eat. At the time, 1928, strained baby foods were available in some areas of the country, but were sold only in pharmacies on doctors' prescriptions. Daniel set about remedying that situation, and within six months he had put baby foods on grocery shelves across the nation. As the line of baby foods expanded, he introduced such related items as powder, plastic pants, and dishware for infants.

In 1931, Beech-Nut entered the baby food field, and since then infant foods have become much more sophisticated. Today Beech-Nut (Beech-Nut, Inc., 460 Park Avenue, New York, N.Y. 10022) and Gerber (Gerber Products Co., 445 State Street, Fremont, Michigan 49412) offer pamphlets that give the nutritive values of their various baby foods: juices, packaged cereals, cereals in jars, fruits, vegetables, meat and egg yolks, dinners, and desserts. The values are shown for seventeen food elements including proteins, carbohydrates, crude fiber, etc., and for five or six minerals and five vitamins. Both companies were pioneers in hiring dieticians and nutritionists to supervise production.

As the variety of infant foods has increased, so has the cost. There are now more than 115 varieties of baby food sold, and every food label is required by law to state the quantity in the jar or tin, so it's easy for the purchaser to do a price comparison on the different brands and quantities. But not many do. The companies are far too clever about their merchandising to allow buyers to become fixed on comparison shopping. All those rows of delightful-looking little jars, so attractively lined up on the shelves, are packaged not to price but to entice. Any parent moving down the aisle will want to fill up the shopping basket with all those multitudinous treats for baby—either to delight or to perk up a picky appetite. How can baby not be given a "treat" when the shopping cart is loaded with "treats" for other members of the family? Little frankfurters, darling-sounding combinations of foods (strained bacon and eggs, or green beans, potatoes, and ham casserole) will appeal to the feeling so many parents have that their babies are really "miniature" adults. A gourmet label such as "peach cobbler" to describe mashed cooked peaches has no meaning to baby, but helps to persuade the mother that she is feeding her offspring elegantly.

Of course, there is no reason not to prepare the same food at home and freeze little amounts in ice trays, which many good cookbooks will tell you preserves it better than in jars in stores.

Most pediatricians go along with the practice of giving an infant solid food as soon as possible. It is common to introduce cereal and applesauce when the infant is only two weeks old. This is helpful to the baby food industry, but is not the most healthful diet for Baby.

A recent study by Johns Hopkins researchers shows that mothers who start infants on baby food too soon are unwittingly contributing to obesity and degenerative diseases later in life. The researchers said that "the premature introduction of infant foods appears to be a critical factor in excessive nutrient intake." At the age of two months, the study demonstrated, "the nutrition needs of the infant are adequately met through formula, breast milk or milk." But at that age, 97 percent of the infants in the study were being fed dry cereal and 70 percent were eating strained fruit.

"It is important," the Johns Hopkins report concludes, "that mothers do not yield to the strong commercial and peer pressures to introduce baby foods too soon. Milk foods alone provide adequate nutrition for most babies for the first six months of life."

As Professor Jelliffe says, "There are no good reasons medically for the earlier and earlier introduction of semisolids into the infant's diet. There is no doubt that the major influence here has been commercial firms who, not unnaturally, welcome an increase in their market."

Some far-sighted leaders in the baby food industry are worried about their dependence on medical trends. In an informal, off-the-record conversation, a vice president of one of the Big Five companies in the field expressed this concern. "There are fashions in medicine like in any other field, and sometimes doctors latch on to a new idea and practically create a whole new industry. That's all fine, but the time span from novelty to obsolete is getting shorter. The same doctors who practically gave birth to this baby food business can abort it. Just let them start hollering for cow's milk or mother's milk or something else that doesn't come in jars, and we're in big trouble."

It reminds us of the remark by Max Beerbohm: "How I wish I could keep up with all the latest fashions as they go rushing by me into oblivion." The feeding of baby, an enterprise which, if any, was handed down to us from our earliest ancestors, has by the miracle of modern merchandising and the vagaries of modern medicine, been transformed into a fad!

Like most fads or fashions, it can be expensive. *Family Health* points out that no matter how carefully a mother shops, food in jars is a costly way to get protein for her child. A jar of strained baby food costs about 15¢, and by the time baby has graduated to a jar of "baby meats" the price will more than double.

Preparing baby's food at home is clearly the most economical method. A mother can get ten grams of protein for under 3¢ in high-protein dry cereals. But the same ten grams from jars of strained rice cereal with fruit would require 19 jars and a total cost of $2.80. Nearly 100 times as much.

"I have three children, all under five years old, and I simply can't afford to buy all that commercial baby food," one mother says. "It isn't hard to prepare cereal, applesauce, and bananas. I take a banana—especially one that's a little ripe, peel it and scrape off a little of the fruit with a spoon. What I get is very soft, and my baby loves the taste. For cereal, I buy a regular Cream of Wheat, cook it with a little water, and after cooking I mix it with milk. I use a little plastic inexpensive grinder and prepare small portions of cooked vegetables and meats right at the table. It grinds food to a consistency that's suitable for the one who's six months, and I feed the others right from the table with food prepared for the rest of the family. I even take the grinder along when we bring the baby with us to a restaurant. It'll take our food and make baby food out of it!"

By feeding Baby on little bits of food that were already prepared for adults in the family, a mother can save not only money but some of that valuable refrigerator space that would otherwise be taken up with half-consumed jars of baby food.

Is there a reason that most mothers continue to buy the expensive strained baby food? There is.

It's convenient.

Period.

Infant food manufacturers would like everyone to believe infants need their products for really adequate nutrition. The difficulty with this is that it happens not to be true. Babies do just as well on the milk, cereal, and liquid and vitamin supplements that most pediatricians recommend. In fact, a Consumer Report test showed that most jars of baby food contain a relatively low percentage of an infant's daily nutritional needs. The test also showed that some baby food analyzed contains too much salt, sugar, and starch.

Confronted with this, a nutritionist employed by Gerber Products Company, the largest baby food manufacturer, simply laughed. "Who says what is too much? By their own test figures the salt content averaged only 0.31 percent. A dash of salt makes the food taste better to mother and she's the one who decides. The baby can't because his sense of taste isn't developed and he has no experience in judging what tastes good or bad. You have to put things in perspective. A quart of milk supplies nearly 500 milligrams of sodium in its salt and your average jar of baby food supplies around 100 milligrams. If you stand that kind of argument on its head, then you ought to avoid milk. And how silly can you get?"

Not silly enough, hopefully, to be unaware that a jar of baby food contains less than a fifth of a quart, so the concentration of sodium is much greater.

The giants in the infant food field, Gerber, Beech-Nut, Libby, Heinz, and Swift, cater to a national market that has a potential buying power in excess of $15 million a week. Gerber alone sold $278-million worth of its products last year.

Unlike other big businesses, the baby food industry has remained remarkably free of serious scandals. A near-exception occurred in the early 1970s when monosodium glutamate (MSG), a flavor enhancer that had swept the market a few years earlier, was suspected of causing cancer and inducing hypertension and heart disease. Manufacturers reacted promptly. They ceased adding MSG to their products.

Later, after extensive testing, the National Research Council concluded that there was no evidence MSG was harmful, but manufacturers continued to omit it since it served no purpose other than to enhance flavor for the mother's benefit.

The Food and Agriculture Organization, an official agency of the U.N., has warned that most food additives in baby foods present a danger because infants do not have fully developed systems to eliminate poisons from the body. They recommend that "synthetic or even natural products should not be added to baby foods unless absolutely necessary, and in only very limited quantities." They also say that even adding starch and egg powder can pose toxic hazards owing to the possibility of their carrying bacteria or fungi. The Consumer's Union tests, however, showed baby foods to be virtually free of harmful microorganisms.

Our own survey of mothers who buy baby food products turned up comparatively few complaints.

A Detroit housewife and mother says her husband became upset because the jars of strained vegetables and fruits listed only the ingredients and not the amounts of each. " 'That means,' he said, 'we have to guess how much of it is really nourishing food and how much is water.' Then somebody who's a health food nut told us that tests proved nearly eighty-eight percent of all baby food in jars is water. That includes the strained meats and puddings. Well, we were pretty upset for a while until another chemist friend told us that even the fresh ingredients that go into the food have that much water content. All foods practically have, and some are as high as ninety percent. When you don't know too much about it, you surely can get excited about nothing."

"I wanted to know if the baby food jars used only fresh fruits and vegetables," said a Phoenix, Arizona, mother. "I didn't want any frozen or canned stuff for my baby. There was no way to tell from the labels, so I wrote away to the manufacturer. I finally got back a letter that told me it was not the company's policy to reveal anything about that to the general public. Well, I didn't like that at all. There ought to be a law that makes any company tell a mother anything she wants to know about the kind of food she's feeding her baby."

The Food and Drug Administration has the authority to compel infant food manufacturers to list percentage ingredient labeling on foods. But the companies are fighting such a regulation. "Our mixture of raw ingredients is a secret formula," says a spokeswoman for Beech-Nut, "that keeps our food from tasting the same as Gerber's or Heinz. I don't think any of the companies would go along."

John Whitlock, speaking for Gerber Products Company, forcefully agreed. "The formulation of products in a highly competitive business is privileged information, and I think this is true in the food industry as in any other industry. Chrysler doesn't tell General Motors what it's doing. We do not feel that the formulation is a valid request. Did you know that an apple is eighty-seven percent water? God never labeled an apple."

Predictably, another complaint of parents has to do with costs. Several mothers in interviews repeated much of what a Syracuse, New York, mother told us: "I sat down to figure out what it cost me for baby foods and it runs six to eight dollars a week, including the cost of milk. That adds up to a lot in a month's time. I tried doing it myself to save money, but cooking and preparing, mashing and straining fruits and vegetables and meats by hand is just too much. I have an electric blender to help, but I don't have that many extra hours in a day. For a baby, eating is practically a continuous all-day operation, and my pediatrician likes it that way. He says a lot of small feedings are better than the three-meals-a-day schedule. Maybe it's better for my baby, but it made a nervous wreck out of me! So I'm back on the jars, even if I can't afford them!"

The Food and Drug Administration currently takes the attitude that there is no need to differentiate between additives for adults and infants. In this regard, they lag behind the British Ministry of Agriculture, which has banned several preservatives that are used simply to keep baby foods tasting fresh and delay rancidity or loss of flavor.

The FDA is also lax in dealing with the problem of contamination. *The New York Times* reports the case of a Princeton, New Jersey, housewife who on opening a jar of baby food found a worm on top of the contents. According to a federal agency, there was no "per se" violation of the law in the presence of the worm! But the report led to the disclosure of a previously unknown source of contamination. A representative of one manufacturer admitted that, in the processing of baby food, foreign material could be sucked under the flange of the lid. Such foreign material could include dust, filth, insect eggs—and, obviously, worms. Over 85 percent of jar caps are of the type in which this can occur, and approximately 2½ billion of these caps are put onto baby food jars.

Some contamination also occurs in the supermarket, where mothers sometimes open a jar, taste the food, and then return the jar to the shelf, bacterially contaminated. Anyone who finds a jar of baby food not tightly sealed should take it at once to the store manager. Bacterially contaminated food can lead to a serious intestinal upset in babies, and even to sudden "unexplainable" death.

If you're worried, there's a simple test. The central circle on the lid of the jar should be depressed, indicating there is a vacuum and that the contents have not been contaminated by someone removing and then replacing the lid. Also, when the jar is opened, a definite pop or hissing should be heard.

As for feeding a child who is beyond the infant food stage, here are several common-sense rules that will help you to save money.

Avoid cold cereals. They are less nutritious and cost more than the ones you cook yourself. The new so-called natural cereals are the most expensive of all and don't provide any extra nutritional value. In fact, they contain as much sugar as the presweetened cereals, except it appears in the form of sucrose because honey and corn syrup are used in the processing. Rice, preferably brown, is better for your child.

Stock up on frozen food specials as they are offered at your local supermarket. If you have freezer space, you are sure to get some excellent bargains.

You will occasionally find an excellent buy on local, store brand items. Look for these. Some stores will place the more expensive brands at eye level. You may have to rummage around on lower or higher shelves to find the cheaper store brands or off brands, but these offer quality comparable to the better known, more heavily advertised products. Why pay for the label—or the cost of the manufacturer's advertising?

Nonfat dried milk, fortified, is a best buy. You can pick it up in large economy boxes and it can be stored for months in any large metal container with a tight lid. Powdered milk is highly nutritious, gives plenty of protein for the money, and can be mixed with peanut butter and used with cereal to provide even greater food value.

Buy day-old whole grain or enriched bread. It will provide protein, iron, calcium, and B vitamins, and the fact that it is a day old does not detract from its nutritious qualities. Day-old bread sells for a fraction of fresh bread prices. Never buy any loaf by its size. Those clever food merchandisers know how to fluff up bread to make less look like more. Buy by weight only (it should be indicated on the package).

For more nutrition and money-saving food tips, get the booklets offered by your local or county cooperative extension service. Look them up under county government listings in the telephone book.

THE SALES PITCH

Until very recently, you could have tuned in to almost any TV show with a large audience of preschool children and heard an outspoken directive to "Go tell your mommy to buy Crunchies . . . in the specially marked package that has a Spaceman's whistle inside."

Children who watch television thirty hours a week, which is the average, are subjected to about five thousand food commercials a year. The kind of food commercials aimed at children have now come under fire from parents and leading government figures.

"At the same time that the medium is subjecting the minds of our children to hundreds of hours of nutrition miseducation," Senator George McGovern said at a Senate hearing on children's TV advertising, "it is doing virtually nothing to provide them with the fundamentals of good nutrition and good health. The good foods, milk, meat, vegetables, and fruits, seem not to exist at all in the land of children's television advertising."

The dominant sales pitch on the food commercials might be described as sugar and sweetness, because the principal fare being offered are candies, cookies, snacks, soft drinks, fake fruit drinks, chewing gum, and sugared cereals.

"We should ban the advertising of sugar-sweetened products on television," says Dr. Abraham E. Nizel of Tufts School of Medicine. Most of the nation's 104,000 dentists agree. They recommend a diet that avoids sugar and emphasizes proteins reinforced with fluorides, vitamin D, and calcium to combat tooth decay.

Yet the continuing barrage of TV advertising for sugar-sweetened products has nearly leveled the defenses of America's parents and children.

"On a Saturday morning show I counted fifteen commercials," one indignant mother told us, "and more than half were for presweetened cereals and expensive snack foods. That's during a thirty-minute program! After the show ended and before the next one began, there was a short commercial showing a boy holding up a box of Sun-Maid raisins and saying it was the only candy his parents let him eat. That kind of double-dealing propaganda message is downright sneaky!"

A group called Action for Children's Television, of Newtonville, Massachusetts, has tried to persuade the Federal Trade Commission to outlaw sales pitches to children on television for all cereals and snack foods that contain sugar. The FTC declined.

There is considerable pessimism among advertising men as to whether there exists the desire or ability within the industry to police itself. A survey by the Gallagher Report, a media newsletter, shows that two out of five advertising men do not think the industry will do anything to correct abuses.

However, some progress is being made on limiting the number of commercials. A few years ago there were sixteen minutes of commercials on every hour of children's television. In 1973, that was cut to twelve minutes. In January 1975, this was cut to ten minutes, and in 1976 it will be cut to nine and a half minutes.

"Even more important is what goes on during those ten minutes," observes Peggy Charren, president of Action for Children's Television, promising renewed efforts to get advertising for presweetened cereals and snack foods off the air.

Dr. Alan Pearce, a Federal Communications Commission economist, suggests that children's shows should charge sponsors higher prices for fewer commercials—thereby enabling television networks to be more selective about the kind of sponsors they accept.

Predictably, the executives of the three networks, NBC, CBS, and ABC, disagree.

"We're getting pretty close to the point of no return already," says George Newi, a sales vice president at ABC. "Children's television is profitable, but not very."

Among network executives, Newi is the only one willing to admit that children's television is profitable.

Don Carswell, NBC's vice president for business affairs, says that gross revenues declined 10.5 percent, or more than $7 million, from 1973 to 1974. And he is not optimistic about results in the recession year of 1975.

A similar answer is given by Frank Smith, a CBS sales vice president. "We are getting to the point of great concern with the future of children's television shows. That programming is not inexpensive. It's getting much more expensive."

During a recession, the task of persuading television networks to turn away advertisers, even of non-nutritious food products, approaches the Herculean.

Nevertheless, the reality remains that an audience of children is impressionable and does not have sufficient information or expertise to counter what they are being sold. They have what in legal terms would be called a "diminished capacity" to resist.

GOODY-YUM-YUM

Sally Gibson was a copy supervisor and group supervisor at the Minneapolis-based Knox Reeves advertising agency for twenty-three years. She has been closely involved with many of the sales campaigns for General Mills products. General Mills is one of the world's largest manufacturers of cereal products. Their net sales are in excess of $1½ billion annually, and the largest portion is in sales to the children's market.

"Our appeal was directly to the kids," Sally Gibson admits. "We relied from the start on their ability to convince their mothers. As soon as they were old enough to respond to what they saw on television or packages, we went after them.

"I never thought there was anything wrong with what we did, and that's why I was shocked when the FDA lambasted the cereal manufacturers so badly in 1972. We were always careful not to claim that a cereal would give a child 'all the energy he needed' or that it would completely replace protein or carbohydrates or vitamins or even minerals. We merely urged children—and, yes, mothers—to 'start the day right.'

"The big market—and it will always be there—is in the two to eight crowd. The cereal manufacturers know it, and they'll be doing their darndest to sell to the kiddies things that are—to quote—quick 'n' easy and nice 'n' tasty and goody-yum-yum."

Sally Gibson regrets the introduction of sugar-coated and presweetened cereals, for she feels these have put the manufacturers more into competition with candy makers, "and I've never felt that candy should be served for breakfast." Dentists and pediatricians agree. Sugar added to unsweetened cereals dissolves in the liquid milk; that portion which does not dissolve collects at the bottom of the bowl. In sugar-coating or presweetening, however, the sugar is deposited almost as a gum, a sticky substance which readily adheres to the teeth and is difficult to dissolve through normal salivary action or brushing, and this encourages tooth decay.

Robert Choate, head of On Second Thought, a group sponsored by the Consumer's Federation of America, the Society for Nutrition Education, the National Council of Negro Women and other consumer oriented groups, sent to seventy television stations three professionally produced public service announcements aimed at improving children's eating habits. He asked that the announcements be aired during the heavy TV viewing hours for children, Saturday and Sunday mornings and early evening hours. The announcements were each thirty seconds long and depicted the results of overeating snack foods, the relationship of sugar to dental problems, and the hidden volume of sugar in many foods. Cartoon, puppet, and live action were used to get the message to the kiddies.

After several months, twenty-nine of the seventy stations had agreed to air at least one of the messages, twenty-eight refused to broadcast any, and thirteen stations still had not replied one way or the other. The three national networks refused to have anything to do with the announcements. NBC's reply was typical: "While we have examined some of the statements submitted during the recent Senate hearings . . . we are not equipped to make a scientific judgment with respect to this controversy."

Apparently they are able to resolve the controversy with no trouble when the message is commercially sponsored.

Last year, the first positive step was taken to restrain the ability of TV to dictate the eating habits of America's children. Industry rules were revised so that advertising of candies, snacks, gum, and soft drinks to children cannot suggest or recommend "indiscriminate or immoderate use." Each commercial for a breakfast-type product must include at least one audio reference and one video depiction of the role of the product in a balanced diet.

The National Association of Broadcasters also agreed that TV commercials would no longer direct children to buy or to ask a parent or other adult to buy the product for them. There are also rules that curb cholesterol claims and the significance of vegetable oils and margarines high in polyunsaturated fats, as well as ban other specific health claims.

Some leading nutritionists worry about the attitudes children are acquiring toward certain foods simply because they are not being advertised extensively on TV. Says one: "If they don't see commercials that emphasize the good qualities of fruits and vegetables, won't they get the idea these are inferior foods, that they aren't really worth anything? You can do harm simply by not letting people know what is good. In fact, that kind of miseducation can be more dangerous, because its effects are subtler and harder to combat."

We may be raising a TV-bred generation that is even less informed about real nutritional values than the preceding one.

In a question-and-answer session, Dr. Theodore P. Labuza, professor of nutrition at the University of Minnesota, said the biggest nutrition problem today is not lack of vitamins, but overweight. Dr. Labuza thinks the kinds of foods promoted on television contribute directly to aggravating this problem, and so does the encouragement of snack eating and "getting food fast."

"I'm teaching at college level what should be taught at elementary level," Dr. Labuza said. "It's a real educational mixup when students are learning in college, for the first time, what foods are, what vitamins are, what calories, diets, chemicals and digestion are, the difference between natural and processed foods, and why foods are processed."

The "educational mixup" is easier to understand when one considers that for the preceding fifteen years or so of their learning lives these young men and women have been getting five thousand messages a year that retail exactly the wrong advice about foods and eating habits—a considerable and prolonged "miseducation" by any standards.

Apparently, television networks believe that deceiving children and possibly risking their health comes under the heading of normal business procedures. If that indictment sounds harsh, remember that all "public service" is reckoned under the loss column, while a profit is never without honor.

BIRTH IS BIG BUSINESS: KRIS KRINGLE LAND

11

The toy business is big even by the standards of modern corporate America.

Take for example Elliot and Ruth Handler, the Mr. and Mrs. Horatio Alger of an extraordinary rags-to-riches saga. In 1945 Elliot and Ruth were making picture frames of scrap wood and plastic. Then Elliot had the bright idea that some of the leftover plastic could be used to make doll furniture. So they got into the toy business and began to grow moderately. They moved out of the garage that had been their manufacturing plant and office, and with Elliot handling the manufacturing and Ruth handling sales, they expanded into lines such as plastic ukuleles and automatic burp guns.

By the mid 1950s they were prosperous enough to undertake an advertising campaign for the toy products, and they chose for their medium a TV program, the Mickey Mouse Club. They aimed their commercials more at kids than at parents, and a year's experiment in advertising proved worthwhile.

Then Ruth remembered that her daughter as a child had always preferred to play with paper dolls because "real dolls have such distorted, grotesque figures." She made a doll that would look older than the "flat-chested, malformed, child figure" dolls then on the market, and christened it Barbie after her daughter Barbara.

"We settled on the shape of the Barbie doll body fairly quickly," she remembers. "In some ways the doll even resembled my daughter. But that was just coincidental."

When the Handlers first sent Barbie to market she was not successful.

Mrs. Handler says, "There'd been miniature dolls with separate costumes that were a glut on the market. And they would look at our doll with breasts and a narrow waist and slender ankles and say, 'How do you give a child a woman's body to play with?'" Then there were buyers who said they didn't know how to handle such a broad line as that offered by Barbie and her many costume changes. They didn't believe they could sell that many items.

Most store buyers were also certain the doll would not sell to parents, which contributed to their lack of enthusiasm about Barbie's prospects. During the first year Mrs. Handler estimates that only about 20 percent of the buyers saw the possibilities, only 5 to 10 percent were enthusiastic.

But when Barbie reached the sales counters in volume, she quickly persuaded all doubters. True, Barbie never did become a favorite with parents, but she caught on with the kids. In fact, she became, in all her variations, the best-selling item in toy-making history. To date Barbie has sold eighty million dolls, plus warehouses full of clothes and accessories. She became that fantasy wish of every toymaker: a staple, an item that continues to sell year after year after year. Despite the recent woes of her parent company, Mattel, Inc., Barbie's future continues to look bright. In 1975 she is expected to sell about seven million dolls. As Mrs. Handler observes, "We're really on our second generation of Barbie children. Today's young mothers can't wait to get their daughters turned on to Barbie the way they were turned on to her."

Barbie, with a Raquel Welch body and the features of a young nun, has become the progenitor of a family that threatens to extend somewhere beyond infinity. There is a Barbie with a real hair dryer that runs by batteries and sells for $15. There are Barbies with different hairdos and even with different faces. Only the body never changes. Pluperfect, her body is attired in endless costumes. In deference to the women's liberation movement, she even has a doctor's uniform to add to the registered nurse's outfit she had for many years.

Now sixteen going on seventeen, Barbie has made her parents Elliot and Ruth Handler wealthy, and transformed little Mattel Creations into Mattel, Inc., the biggest toy company in the United States.

Barbie has a chief wardrobe mistress who oversees a manufacturing setup in Korea, Japan, and Taiwan that turns out the endlessly increasing Barbie wardrobe. Something like 20 million Barbie costumes are sold every year— which clearly makes Mattel the largest manufacturer of women's garments in the world.

But one item that you'll never see Barbie wearing is a chemise. During the period when the chemise was in fashion in the 1960s, there was consternation in the Mattel, Inc. designing offices, and no one was sorry to see the fashion pass out of style.

Why?

"Barbie looks pregnant in a chemise," says the chief wardrobe mistress. "Her bosom is out a good deal farther than the natural bosom."

Someone has estimated that if Barbie were magnified to a normal 5 feet 6 inches, she would have an 18-inch waist and size 46 breasts—*Playboy* magazine's version of a dream girl.

BARBIE'S FRIENDS

Mrs. Handler is aware of some sex-oriented criticism, and has responded to suggestions that she create a doll that will not drive young women to silicone implants in an attempt to look more like Barbie.

Barbie has also been pounced upon by those who think she exploits and stimulates a desire for possessions, and emphasizes sex appeal to the exclusion of other values. Harriet Alpern, who heads the media committee of NOW, says, "There's nothing wrong with being sexy, but Barbie's total emphasis is very commercial. There is no balance."

In 1966 Ruth Handler introduced a flatter-chested companion for Barbie, a doll called Francie whose breasts are smaller and curves not as pronounced. Barbie also acquired a little sister named Skipper—who has the configuration of a small child—strictly for children who are role-playing their own age.

As for Ken, the male doll (named after Elliot and Ruth Handler's son) whose relationship with Barbie has been the subject of a good deal of comment on the Johnny Carson show, there were also physical problems to contend with. Ken finally appeared in 1961 with his underwear on. Molded on, so no one could take an unfair peek. In the end, Mattel's designers simply couldn't risk giving him genitals.

"We had a very controversial problem there," Mrs. Handler admits. "We just didn't know how to solve it. We didn't know if it was our role in society to tackle that problem. I have no objection to dolls with genitals, but it wasn't appropriate at that time. We decided to give him underpants with a slight bulge, and I think that was the right decision."

So it is likely that Ken's fourteen-year courtship with Barbie will remain unfulfilled—unless he can figure out a way to get his underpants off.

Less than seventeen years after Barbie's first arrival on a toy counter, Elliot and Ruth Handler's personal worth was estimated at $250 million. Their company owned many youth-oriented businesses, ranging from aquariums to magnetic tapes, and including at one time the Greatest Show of All: The Ringling Brothers, Barnum and Bailey Circus.

Nineteen seventy-one was the company's high water mark. Then came financial reverses, with multimillion-dollar losses over the next three years. Elliot and Ruth Handler lost control of the company they founded; Barbie and Ken became orphans and Mattel, Inc., plagued by stockholder suits and charges of fiscal corruption, was described by a Wall Street newspaper as "the world's biggest broken toy." However, outfacing calamity, Mattel, Inc. continues to dominate the toy industry.

JUVENILE PRODUCTS

That industry is made up of over nine hundred manufacturers of toys, games, and craft kits who divide up a $2-billion a year kitty. Competition is cutthroat and individual pickings slim.

Of the four hundred products that the Food and Drug Administration recalled from the market last year as too dangerous, few were from the top seven manufacturers, who gross a minimum of $50 million a year each. Most were the faulty dream children of a toymaker such as the man we will call Winston William. He is a tall, colorful Dutchman with shaggy black hair that clusters thickly on his head and neck, and he dresses in a flamboyant fashion —suede jacket, scarlet scarf, and well-shined leather boots. "You gotta make an impression in this racket. You gotta make 'em remember you."

Winston William cannot be accused of making excessive profits. He says himself, "The people who make toys for the kids of this country are probably the poorest paid businessmen in the whole damn world."

Winston William blames the low profit margins (an industry average of about 3 percent) chiefly on the industry's cruel vulnerability to unpredictable and sometimes dizzying shifts in fashion.

"What makes this business really rough is that your profit for the whole year probably depends on the success of one new item, or in the case of the giants, on the success of one season's line. February is go-for-broke. That's when the New York toy fair is held, and after fifteen years in this business I still come up to that with giant butterflies in my stomach. I've gone in with everything from musical potty chairs to folding strollers, and with no idea of whether I'll be a rich man or have to gumshoe it around the trade trying to slap my new baby product on the bottom to get it to let out a noise that can even be heard."

At the time we interviewed Winston William, he was pinning his hopes on an item we'll call the "baby gym." His line usually falls somewhere between "toys" and what are labeled "juvenile products." In the trade, a "juvenile product" is apparently anything not strictly a toy or clothing. Winston William's line included a special car seat for baby, a night light shaped like a reindeer for the baby's nursery, an "improved walker," and a swing. The nearest item on his list to a "staple" was the musical potty—in which a music box played when the baby performed as intended. It sells every year in a not too exciting fashion.

Winston William was not anxious to discuss the product that had carried his hopes the previous year. This was the "school crib," fitted out with "learning modules" that were supposed to help baby develop its intellectual capacities more quickly by "learning through play." Unfortunately, a child psychologist denounced the claims as "pure bilge" and suggested that parents would be better off to give a baby a pan and a spoon. Then the government decided that some of the sharp-cornered "learning modules" were dangerous. The "school crib" was withdrawn and Winston William's hopes for a marketing blitz went glimmering. All his baby-blue dreams of empire sank without a trace in a sea of red ink.

"It was a real shocker. Nobody ever proved that even one kid got hurt on those learning modules. Just that they could've got hurt. But I don't look back. The 'baby gym' is a winner. I'm setting up deals to promote it, and I've got a hunch this time my luck is gonna change . . ."

Then Winston William was up and off to a meeting of free-lance sales representatives he hoped to persuade to sell his baby gym in stores all across the country.

"It's gonna revolutionize the whole idea of baby care and baby exercisers," was his parting word. "What you've got to have is imagination, foresight. Then turn it over to hustlers. Salesmen who aren't dead from the lips up. Personalities with impact who know how to eyeball store buyers."

Hope springs eternal in a field where not even the most astute or experienced can pretend to know what the public will buy. In a sense, toymakers are high rollers, and everything rides on the next toss of the dice.

THE LEADERS

Five years ago *Fortune* magazine decided to ask the seven largest toy companies to name their two best sellers over the preceding decade. The answers proved once and for all that there is simply no way to predict success in this field. *Fortune* came up with a composite list of ten all-time top sellers that no one over the age of twenty-one could possibly have chosen in advance.

Here they are, in order of descent:

- The Easy Bake Oven (General Mills toy division)
- The Crissy Doll (whose hair "grows" at the turn of a knob) (Ideal Toy Company)
- Chatter Telephone (Fisher Price Toys)
- Tyke Bike (Milton Bradley Company)
- Mouse Trap Game (Ideal Toy Corporation)
- Johnny Lightning Car and Tracks (Topper Corporation)
- The Barbie Doll (only one of the family) (Mattel, Inc.)
- Play Family School (Fisher Price Toys)
- Big Wheel (Louis Marx & Company)
- Hot Wheels (Mattel, Inc.)

Those last items deserve special mention because they provide a fine illustration of the risks and rewards involved in the highly competitive field of toy-making.

Most parents remember fondly the beloved tricycle they once pedaled as a kid. Well, the tricycle is rolling down an accelerating slope toward extinction, and what gave it the fatal push was a sleek, racy, brightly colored, low-slung "ride 'em" (the toy industry's word for anything with wheels). The Big Wheel can whiz, spin, skid, slide, race, and even roar.

"The Big Wheel is the hottest-selling toy in the country," says Joe Karalla, a Detroit toy seller for eighteen years. "If you can walk, they'll get you in one. They really move, you can't break 'em, and you can't hurt yourself. Kids throw 'em everywhere, ride 'em in all kinds of weather. They're fantastic."

The original Big Wheel was introduced by the Louis Marx Company in 1969, and the firm has added three smaller models. Children from eighteen months to seven years old can ride in one or another model, costing from $11 to $18.

The reward for Louis Marx Company has been eyepopping. More than 8 million have been sold to date, for a total gross sales revenue on this one toy approximating $100 million. What's more, the Big Wheel has not only become a "staple" in the trade, selling year in and year out to each new generation of youngsters, but it will eventually climb higher on that all-time list of best-selling toys.

When Mattel, Inc., introduced Hot Wheels, toy racing cars, they were so popular that for two years the company could not keep up with the demand. Retailers were caught short and orders couldn't be filled.

Then Mattel, Inc., decided to bring out an addition to the line, called Sizzler Cars. These miniature cars were "improved" versions, juiced up with battery power. Retailers rushed to buy early in order to avoid being shut out again. Sizzler failed to sizzle. Hot Wheels continued to sell, but Sizzler sat neglected on retailers' shelves.

Why? No one really knows, although with the wisdom of hindsight, some toy buyers inform you that the Sizzler sets were lacking in play value, didn't involve the child, and didn't allow for competition since the track only accommodated one car and children could not stage races. It is also possible that the batteries gave too much trouble or encountered resistance from parents. Mattel, Inc., spokesmen are inclined to put the blame on the glut that year in miniature car sets.

Whatever the reason, Sizzler was a fiasco. Partly as a result, Mattel, Inc., suffered its first deficit in over twenty years, and the value of its shares on the stock market was sliced nearly in half.

You risks your money and you takes your financial bath.

DOG EAT DOG

Overall, the formidable competition in the field has kept profits low despite manufacturers' sales that register more than $2 billion a year. Even Mattel, Inc., the number-one company, had only 10 percent of the total sales last year, and its nearest competitor had only 5 percent. After-tax earnings amount to only half the average for U.S. corporations. There is no joy in Toyville.

In the dog-eat-dog competition, big toy companies spend more and more heavily on advertising, particularly television. In fact, their ad expenditures, which run between 7 percent and 10 percent of sales, are higher than their profits. The sales pitch, in these Ralph Nader days, emphasizes not only that toys are fun but that they are educational, safe, and designed to last. This advertising pitch runs in the teeth of a rising gale of criticism that says while toys may be fun, they certainly don't teach, aren't safe, and aren't designed to last.

Only a few years ago the complaints reached such a level that Congress passed the Child Protection and Safety Act. Under the provisions of the act, the Food and Drug Administration was given the power to outlaw toys that did not meet its safety standards. In succeeding years that list has been steadily expanded to cover, in minute detail, the characteristics considered hazardous.

The toymakers haven't taken this lying down. A television show, sponsored in prime time, gave, in slightly veiled symbolic terms, their idea of what kind of people are attacking them. The program, "Santa Claus Is Comin' to Town," tells in song and story of a place called Sombertown in which a killjoy mayor named Meisterburger becomes incensed because one day he trips over a small toy. Infuriated, he pronounces a ban on all toys. One member of a family of toymakers named Kringle is forced to flee for his life. This fellow's name is Kris, and when he gets to the North Pole he grows a beard and changes his name to Claus. And in a happy ending the good people of Sombertown at last come to realize "how silly the Meisterburger laws were."

The critics of the toy industry have not faded away as conveniently as Mayor Meisterburger. If anything, they've gotten tougher. Both the Federal Communications Commission and the Federal Trade Commission are now studying restrictions, or even a complete ban, on television advertising aimed at children. The organization, Action for Children's Television, has been responsible for thousands of indignant letters from parents to advertisers and TV stations warning them to stop the pressure on their children to buy. What their kids want, parents often don't want them to have—and think they are qualified to judge. Partly as a result of parental protests, Santa Claus doesn't appear on toy commercials on TV.

Jerome Lansner, assistant director of the National Association of Broadcasters Code Authority, confirms that Santa has been scourged off the tube. "The ruling goes back about five years. The ban on fantasy figures like Santa Claus came about because they have a tendency to overglamorize the product. We didn't want Santa Claus saying 'Go out and buy this toy.' "

However, the toymakers' paranoia is heightened by the fact that this ruling applies *only* to toys. Santa can be used in other commercials aimed at children.

Another source of friction between toymakers and parents is the kind of misleading advertising that promises much more than it can possibly deliver. The problem is familiar to almost all parents of small children.

"Christmas Day in our house," one young father says, "usually turns into a nightmare of disappointments. My kids have seen all those fabulous toys on television, and they look at the real thing in bewilderment. And who do they blame? Not the television advertiser. Me. Somehow or other I just didn't buy the right thing. They way they see it, television wouldn't lie. So *I* must be stupid."

From Labor Day to December 24, tots are literally bombarded with TV ads. Seventy percent of the money spent on toy advertising is spent during these months. Ads show dolls that appear to walk and talk by themselves, or eat and wet, or even go to parties and have boyfriends. There is one called Baby Alive who eats gel, which then comes out to soil its diaper. TV advertises war game sets that appear so luridly realistic they make the Battle of the Bulge look like a skirmish. Scale model electric trains and racing cars guarantee an orgy of thrills and spills that could not be matched at the Indianapolis Speedway. A youngster is depicted becoming an instant genius by creating masterpieces with paint sets, putties, make-it-yourself jewelry kits, and all sorts of arts and crafts (last year's hit was a candlemaking outfit). Model planes perform miraculous maneuvers in the air, and a new tricycle with balloon tires makes junior the fastest thing on wheels. There's even an Evel Knievel stunt and crash car which "performs an exciting crash finale."

The kids see the ads and are conquered. Indeed, they are overwhelmed. And they make their parents buy the toys—or arrange for Santa Claus to deliver them.

Comes Christmas morning and not even a child's vivid imagination can discover any relationship between the toys he finds beneath the Christmas tree and their dramatic TV counterparts.

DON'T HARDLY MAKE THEM LIKE THAT NO MORE

In some instances the misrepresentation is so clear that angry parents go to the law to punish manufacturers. Recently a complaint by the father of a little girl who found only seven gum balls in her new toy gum ball bank led to a civil suit by the state attorney general for deceptive packaging. According to the suit, the gum ball banks advertised were between half and completely filled with hundreds of gum balls when in truth and in fact said packages contained seven small gum balls. Unfortunately for the company, nine-year-old Susan Carol Genard was the daughter of an attorney. He filed the original complaint, and the offending company was forced to pay fines of $1,750 in civil penalties and $750 in costs to state prosecutors, and to promise from then on to clearly indicate the number of gum balls in its toy machines.

The fragility and increasing complexity of toys also cause parental complaints. Letters tell of toys that break down or fall apart under ordinary usage, of toys that only a qualified building contractor could put together ("Insert prong A into slot B, coupling C with H, and attaching R to T with bolt and nut 3 and 4. Longitudinal wires should be fed through apertures D and E, connecting with the battery electrodes at point F").

Most large manufacturers will make refunds when their toys break down prematurely ("that means right after you get them out of the wrapping," says a bitter parent), and will make repairs and exchanges on defective toys returned by customers. But too many parents feel that the effort of making returns isn't worth the bother. The head of the toy department at Sears reports that toy returns run lower than the rest of the store's merchandise.

"You also have to keep in mind," says the sales manager of a company that sells walking dolls, "that different people have different ideas about how long a toy should last. I could show you letters we've received complaining that our dolls stopped walking after one or two years of regular use. We never claimed to make toys that would last a lifetime!

"What we're up against is the grandmother who still remembers the kind of toys that were around when she was a baby. Sure, during the Depression years families used to make rag dolls out of old scraps of material. Almost any mother or doting relative could simply draw an outline on a folded piece of flour sack, cut it, stuff it with cotton batting, sew the edges, and paint a smiling face on one side and a crying face on the other. The cost was practically zero, and the damn thing lasted as long as the Sphinx."

Competing against nostalgic memories makes the task of today's manufacturer of plastic gadgets more difficult. Those sterile store counters all aglitter with breakable, crushable, bright toys destined in a few months for the trash can appear to people over forty as a swindler's collection. Older people are not impressed by the argument that the type of toys available today simply reflect the values of a modern world in which nothing seems to be worth preserving or cherishing. Instead, they pour forth complaints to stores who refer them in ever-increasing volume to toymakers.

The toymakers are beleaguered from other areas as well. An increasing number of parents who grew up during the tragic Vietnam era now protest strenuously against the "harmful" psychological effects of war toys and games. Actually, there is conflicting evidence on this point: some psychologists believe that allowing children to play-act their aggressive impulses gives them a useful outlet for what might otherwise become socially directed violence.

As one such psychologist remarked, "You take away the toy soldiers and cannons and war games and what have you got? Kids pointing their fingers at each other and crying bang-bang you're dead, then graduating to throwing snowballs with rocks or bashing each other with sticks."

But most young parents continue to believe that giving sanction to violence in toys and games raises the line of aggression in their children, and they want such toys removed from store shelves where they may be a temptation.

"Those Evel Knievel toys are just one example of what I call exploitation of children," says one parent who is also a teacher. "He's supposed to be some sort of folk hero or a superman because he risks his neck on meaningless stunts like a rocket-powered motorcycle jump across a canyon. The big attraction was really that he might get himself killed. It's death worship. People pay to see a man kill himself. Is that a healthy example to set up for children?"

The ignominious failure of Evel Knievel's well-publicized jump—the chute opened before he cleared the ramp, and he floated down to the river—gave a momentary check to the toys capitalizing on his name. But he recovered in time for the Christmas season. Stan Ostrowsky, assistant manager of Cincinnati's largest toy store, reports: "He's bigger than GI Joe, Big Jim, Kung Fu, and the rest of them. Even Johnny Bench [Cincinnati's baseball hero] is striking out against him. Johnny doesn't stand a chance against Evel. We've even had kids come in and ask for a cane just like Evel Knievel's. I told 'em, 'Okay, but it'll cost you $22,000.' "

In the coming year, no one knows what our hero may do to catapult himself back into the limelight and into another surge of popularity on toy store counters. What knext, Knievel, the toy industry asks.

With a knut like Knievel you never kno.

Toymakers are also being assaulted by women's groups who object to "sexism" in toys. These women see no reason why there should be boy toys and girl toys, and they are hard at work trying to expunge "sexist" stereotypes from the impressionable world of infants and children.

The National Organization for Women awarded PANS (Protests of Advertising Nonsense) to Mattel's Barbie and Ken dolls, Hasbro's GI Joe doll—because he focuses on war, killing and violence—and Skicraft geology, chemistry, mineralogy, and electronic kits—because they only show boys playing with them.

They gave PATS (Praise for Advertising Truth) to Playskool's building block sets for three- to five-year-olds, Kenner's Dusty doll, who is a champion girl athlete, and Gilbert's Chemcraft sets. These were cited as good examples of nonsexist playthings because they appealed to children of both sexes or showed boys or girls in nonstereotyped, multidimensional roles.

"Why should baseball games all show young boys in the illustrations?" asks a NOW activist. "Or feature male plastic figures? Girls now play Little League baseball. And they play football too. What's going on in toyland is just an extension of what's been going on for years in books. Girls are always cookers and sewers, and boys are do-ers and achievers. In animal books, lions and tigers are male and the hippopotami are female. Sometimes girls don't even make it as animals at all. Dr. Seuss shows all his animals—even the hens—as male. The only woman in all his books who even has an occupation is the royal laundress in *Bartholomew and the Oobleck*. But that's got to change. If there are going to be dolls, let them be Big Jack and Big Jim dolls instead of Barbies, and let's have train sets and chemistry sets for girls. Dr. Spock is changing the pronouns in his *Baby and Child Care* book, and the toymakers can do something about the sexist patterns in their industry.

"Have toymakers given any thought to why the teddy bear is one of the most popular toys of this century? It's sexless. It can be given to a boy or a girl, it can represent a mama or a papa, a baby brother or a baby sister. All those generations of macho toys and ultra-feminine frilly dolls have come and gone, and the teddy bear is still with us. That's the direction the toy industry has got to take. If it doesn't adapt to the changes in social attitudes, it'll go the way of the harness maker."

Add such antagonists to the regular battering that toymakers get from parents about durability, and throw in the attacks on toys that are difficult to assemble or are too dependent on lost parts or only run on batteries, and it's no wonder these harried businessmen think the whole world is inhabited by Meisterburgers.

SAFETY FIRST

Or by Ralph Naders.

For we now come to the chief front on which the toy industry is embattled: safety. Here they are against that formidable people's champion, Ralph Nader, whose unceasing campaign for safer toys has already had results in modifying their basic design. Celluloid and other casein plastics have virtually disappeared from the market. The once-standard rattle, easily punctured by baby's first tooth or banged into jagged openness against the playpen bars, is rarely seen anymore. Jagged edges of surplus plastic left from the molding process must be filed off at the factory. Wooden toys cannot be painted with lead-containing pigments. Toys for infants under two years old are no longer vulnerable to a dismantling which would produce parts small enough for the baby to swallow.

Despite these changes, violations of safety are still reported. Typical recent "accidents": in Glendora, California, a five-year-old got hold of a spring-type dart shooter, inserted a pencil, and put out his eye; in Chicago, a two-year-old choked to death on a plastic ball he somehow extracted from a presumably sealed pinball game. And in Prospect Park, Pennsylvania, Mr. and Mrs. Aubrey Clark sued WTAF-TV, Ideal Toys, and their ad agency for a total of $24 million. The reason? They claimed their ten-year-old son was "goaded, inspired and urged" by the Evel Knievel Stunt Cycle toy commercial into trying his own daredevil stunt—jumping a bicycle over some piles at a construction site using makeshift plank ramps. The boy missed the jump and ended up in the hospital with multiple injuries.

Edward Swartz, a lawyer who specializes in product liability, is a crusader for toy safety. He appeared before the Consumer Product Safety Commission with a group of dangerous toys that he said had been bought during a half-hour shopping trip, and his testimony is credited with having given the safety movement a fresh impetus. In a book he wrote, *Toys That Don't Care,* he lists a multitude of toys dangerous to children either physically or psychologically.

"Don't talk to me about that man," declares a spokesman for a leading toy company. "As far as I'm concerned, he lives on the lunatic fringe. Who the hell is he to judge what toys are psychologically dangerous? Is he a psychiatrist? No, he's just a lawyer. And when he talks about unsafe he includes anything that possibly *could* be dangerous. If you want to use that standard, you could never eat dinner because the food might get stuck in your throat. I mean, he's opposed to practically all toys that plug into wall sockets because of the danger of shocks. Okay! So what goes next? Lamps?"

According to A. B. Castle, Jr., director of the Consumer Product Safety Commission, however, more than 1,500 toys have been banned as unsafe. Unfortunately, toy manufacturers are not required to have their toys tested by the CPSC before marketing, so the dangerous toys are discovered only after they reach the children.

Mr. Castle lists toys he considers most dangerous for children. They include:

- Toy rattles and noisemakers with sharp edges or protruding loose small objects which a child can swallow or aspirate. Aspiration (inhaling into the lungs) presents the greater risk. When swallowed, an object will normally pass through the body and be eliminated, but an object caught in the lungs must be removed surgically.
- Dolls or stuffed animals that have eyes attached with sharp pins. Curious toddlers often pull out the eyes, exposing the pins projecting from the back of the eye.
- Lawn darts. These are supposed to be for adult use only, but thousands of sets are sold for children.
- Baby walkers that have sharp points or a construction that causes severe pinching of fingers or legs.
- Clacker balls (solid plastic balls on either end of a string). These present a fragmentation danger because of the force with which the balls strike each other, and a child can also get a good knock from them—or give one to an unfortunate bystander.
- Toys made of brittle plastic or glass.
- Toys involving electrical or heat hazards. Most American-made motorized toys are safe, but those imported from Europe or Japan don't meet our safety standards.

Ralph Nader is encouraged by the diligence of the CPSC but he has some reservations.

"The fact that they've banned fifteen hundred toys since nineteen seventy-two is a big step in the right direction. But controls won't be fully effective until the toy manufacturers are required to have their toys tested *before* they reach the market. Even one injury or death caused by a newly introduced toy is too many."

Charles Collins, who manages one of the largest toy stores in the country, Toys 'R' Us in Los Angeles, discusses his twenty-year experience with toys and consumers.

"I won't handle what I call high-risk toys because I'm afraid for the child who will play with them. Nobody can take away all the risk because kids will hit each other with toys or throw them at each other; that way a perfectly harmless plastic boomerang can become a lethal weapon. I've sent back as many as one hundred thousand dollars' worth of toys, retail, to the manufacturer because they came either badly made or with risk factors I hadn't realized.

"Frankly, I miss the good old days when things like Erector Sets, the model planes that had to be assembled from scratch, and the elaborate sets of wooden building blocks were our chief sellers. Now everything is plastic or fully assembled and unimaginative. Oddly enough, the exceptions seem to involve the kind of toys that cost big money. People come to me to find out where they can get really elaborately scaled dollhouses. One couple from Beverly Hills spent forty-five hundred dollars last Christmas on a dollhouse that took a year to build. And a man from Orange County special-ordered a fifty-five-hundred-dollar electric train, a model that when fully assembled would be big enough for kids to ride in, with about a mile of steel track.

"One encouraging thing is the increasing number of people who come in and ask for an educational toy. *They're* thinking in the right direction."

On the subject of educational toys, Dr. Joyce Brothers, the well-known psychologist and television personality, says: "Such a toy is of no value unless the child is interested in it and it's fun, because obviously a child won't learn if he doesn't play with it. By the same token, you shouldn't pick a toy that is too sophisticated for a child's age. That can only lead to harmful frustrations. On the other hand, don't pick something that is too easy because then there's no stretching of a child's ability. The toys that a child simply watches perform, such as some of the mechanical toys where they do everything for him, leave him as a mere audience, a spectator.

"We need ways that children can be encouraged to develop their creativity."

Dr. Brothers is opposed to giving a coloring book which a child only has to color between the lines. Instead, she suggests giving crayons or fingerpaints. She also urges parents to buy toys that can be played with in many ways—a set of blocks that can become a house, a store, a truck, a train, an airplane. "The more opportunities in play for a child, the better and longer lasting the toy. Every parent has had the experience of buying an expensive toy, only to see the child play with the box it came in. Why? Because the box could take on many shapes and forms in the child's imagination, while what came in it was too specific and one-dimensional. The more uses and the more things that can be made up with a toy, the better, and the more ingenuity required of a child, the better."

Other authorities echo Dr. Brothers' advice. It is better to let children play with boxes and balls and string than with store-bought replicas of what the child can fashion out of its imagination. Literal embodiments of things have a stifling effect on a child's creative ability.

What about the problem of a parent whose child has been given some creatively stimulating but cheap toys, while the kid next door gets the shiny new gadgets that are being advertised on TV?

A well-known child psychologist told us, "The main issue here is to be certain your child does not feel deprived. If a child has been brought up in the right way, he won't be. He will have learned to share the family's values, and to recognize that money is not the best way of measuring achievment. The price of a toy is not a proper measure of its value or of the affection with which it was given. If it's a question of financial limitations or competing needs within the family, then the child must be made to accept the realities. In any case, the situation and the reasons for the parent's action should be carefully explained."

A toy buyer, an attractive woman of thirty-six who has a Ph.D. in psychology and three children, aged two to six, at home says, "By all means, get children the inexpensive things that will spark their imagination. Above all, avoid giving presents with an ulterior motive, for your own reasons rather than the child's. For example, giving boxing gloves to a boy who doesn't seem aggressive or 'masculine' enough, or a chemistry set to a boy or girl who isn't 'intelligent' enough, or any of those obnoxious children's books that are trying to point a moral. Believe me, there's a reason why kids are still reading Nancy Drew and the Oz books.

"As for the competition between kids and also, let's face it, between their respective parents, my suggestion is to compromise. If your kid is going to feel left out without some nice big bright shiny plastic toys, then buy them. When Santa unloads his pack, the last thing you want in the house is a disappointed child. Let them have the fun of opening the presents. After a few days, or a couple of weeks at most, put those expensive toys back into the closet or the attic. The child will probably be tired of them by then, anyhow. Then you can bring them out later, and they'll be like new again."

Perhaps the basic answer is expressed by Dr. Walter Alvarez, the well-known syndicated columnist who has lived through many revolutions in American buying patterns:

"We live in an age where we are apt to start off our children with more than they need. But the important thing isn't the money spent. It's whether or not we still give our children the attention and love they need, things far more important than material goods. Every parent must ask him or herself if this is truly being offered. If it is, the family is still in good shape."

Amen.

It is time to turn from our survey of the direct costs of having and raising Baby, those personal expenditures all too visible to parents, and venture into an area where the costs are less directly observed although fully as real.

We are considering birth not only in the narrow commercial sense, as something which creates a consumer and therefore affects the production, distribution, and sale of products.

Birth is also, we think unarguably, a phenomenon that can be examined in terms of its social costs and rewards. In both the private sector and the government sector, huge sums of money are spent on problems involving birth and babies, and that money has to come from someone. The someone is you. Directly or indirectly, you pay for—purchase if you prefer—these various services.

And you are entitled therefore to be given some clue as to whether your money is well spent. In effect, you must judge if you are making a "profit" on what is being done in your behalf or whether your money, and the energies of those being paid with your money, should be directed elsewhere.

ADOPTION: OUR CHANGING VIEWS

12

A childless couple wants a child. A parentless child needs a home. If ever a twain was destined to meet, this should be it.

But.

Because of stringent rules and codes surrounding the whole process of adoption, millions of Americans grow up in foundling homes, orphanages, and foster homes. And the parents who would like to take them in remain childless.

The absurdities of the adoption rules, the grotesque price paid in human misery, have led to the growth of gray and black markets in babies. In the gray market the procedure is simple: a doctor or a minister or a priest knows of a woman pregnant with a child she does not wish to keep. The infant, when released from the hospital, is taken directly into the home of the adoptive parents. An attorney then legalizes the procedure. The natural mother has, of course, waived her rights to the child either before or at birth.

Gray market fees have always been steep. Today, where the practice still thrives, a doctor receives $500 to $1,000 for his services, and the natural mother is given an equal amount. There are also attorney fees to be considered.

Despite the expense of private adoption, however, until very recently more children were adopted this way than through agencies.

Why is such a practice necessary in these modern, enlightened times? Consider the case of Linda and James Hurley of Shaker Heights, Ohio. Linda could not become pregnant, so they decided to adopt. Everything seemed in their favor. They were both in their late thirties, an ideal age for adoptive parenting in the view of most agencies, Hurley's income had reached $25,000 a year, and both Hurleys were church-going Lutherans. One could not deliver better parents from a computer profile.

What happened?

"We started working with five different agencies in the Cleveland area," Linda Hurley says. "If we had a dollar for every form we filled out and every worker we talked to, we'd be wealthy. It was endless, an exercise in frustration. The agony of it was knowing that children were available, children that needed homes and love.

"Finally, a friend told us about an obstetrician in Toledo who could probably find us a baby almost immediately—most likely one from an unwed mother. We went to see the doctor. As it turned out, he had a patient due to deliver in a few weeks. The baby would be white, of Scandinavian descent, and he described the mother as an intelligent seventeen-year-old girl who did not wish to keep the baby. We paid the doctor five hundred dollars, half his total fee, and three weeks later we had our baby."

Linda frowns. "We hadn't wanted to go to the gray market, but they forced us to. The same doctor will have another baby for us next month."

The Hurleys' case is in no way exceptional.

"There just aren't any adoptable white babies coming in," an adoption agency official told us. "The shortage is really unbelievable. It started to get really acute when the Pill got into widespread use, and it became critical with the liberalized abortion laws."

The Spence-Chapin agency in New York reports that only 97 children were placed in new homes in 1974, compared to 472 in 1966. Their waiting list of approximately 150 couples can look forward to an average delay of three years before getting a baby.

"The waiting list was three hundred a few years ago," says a spokesman, "but was shortened because the agency sees no point in keeping people waiting so long when the prospects are so dim."

This situation has led not only to the gray market, in which babies are legally adopted outside regular channels, but to a thriving black market.

In the United States a black market transaction begins after an unwed mother has given birth. She is contacted by a lawyer who makes a financially attractive offer for the surrender of her baby. Lawyers get the names of such women from hospital employees who are suitably rewarded. Because these approaches are often embarrassing to the young mothers, some hospitals are now making active efforts to track down these lawyers and force them to abandon the practice. But so far counter measures have proved ineffective.

Babies are easy to obtain from outside the United States. According to Leslie

Tisdall, head of obstetrics and gynecology at the Catholic Medical Center in Brooklyn: "In the backward countries of South America and Southern Europe, families with too many children routinely sell their babies. Spain, Portugal and some parts of Turkey are also likely sources of supply."

What is the going rate in the United States? Since the entire transaction is illegal, there are no quoted figures. But an indication can be gathered from the results of a year-long investigation conducted into one alleged ring of black marketeers in Los Angeles. According to evidence gathered by the district attorney and presented to the grand jury, an unlicensed organization known as the "Save A Life Adopting Agency" developed contacts with pregnant women, paid them varying sums of money, and arranged for the falsification of court documents. The black marketeers made contacts by advertising in Mexico and Canada, and even sent pregnant women on holiday to the Caribbean to have their babies.

The price tag for a black-market baby: from $10,000 to $15,000.

"Some people get tired of waiting for the baby they want," said an investigator at the district attorney's office. "A lot of them are older people who don't feel they have the years left any more. Through a black market operation they get what they want in no time—and I guess price doesn't matter. Time is money, like they say, and these people have got more money than time."

Almost 170,000 children are adopted legally each year, and at the present time almost 2.5 million American children under eighteen are legally adopted.

On the other side of the ledger, there are right this moment more than 60,000 children available for adoption. This number includes 40,000 non-whites. These are official government figures. The Child Welfare League sets the total considerably higher, saying there are 80,000 non-white children available for adoption, plus 110,000 that have been placed in foster homes where no adoption is intended. Senator Alan Cranston of California, co-author of a proposed federal adoption act, puts the figure of hard-to-place children either in foster homes or in institutions at a still higher 150,000.

Accepting these various estimates (for they are no more than that) as setting the parameters, it is obvious that somewhere between 60,000 and 230,000 adoptable children cannot be placed with legal parents.

There are times when only flexing our imaginative muscles can give a true sense of dimension. Even the lowest of these figures is still considerably higher than the total number of U.S. servicemen lost in action in ten years of Vietnam war.

Nor does this include the anguish of thousands of couples whose homes and lives are deprived of children they might have loved and helped to raise. We interviewed twenty such couples. These excerpts will have to suffice:

"We waited five years for a child from the Cradle in Chicago. I suppose the fact that I'm a Catholic and my wife a Presbyterian aggravated the problem, but we kept at them until they finally gave us a baby girl. Now we want another baby, but because of our age (I'm fifty-two, my wife is forty-seven) the agencies won't even take our applications."

Another: "We're of Russian descent, and we wanted a Russian baby. Even though we worked through six different agencies, it took us seven years to come up with our boy."

A third: "We waited four years, and I don't know how much longer it would have taken, but we decided to take a baby with a physical defect. Our little boy came to us with a club foot. We paid for surgery to take care of that."

Fourth: "We wanted a baby that was white because we are white. We didn't care about nationality or religion or the sex of the child. Well, four years went by and nothing happened, so we indicated we were willing to take a child of mixed blood, preferably white and Oriental or white and Chicano. Three weeks later we got our baby, a healthy beautiful boy who is half Mexican and half Swedish. The trouble with couples trying to adopt is they're just too fussy."

Fifth: "We're black, and we had a minimum waiting period—twenty-four hours. The trouble was choosing. It was heartbreaking to see all those babies, knowing most of them would grow up in orphanages or be farmed out in foster homes. But we could only take one. It's a real pity more blacks don't know how to go about adopting, or can't afford to."

To set the record straight, the ratio of black families that adopt is equal to white families. But the number of black children available for adoption is so much greater than the available homes that nine out of ten black babies will never find new parents.

The third side to the triangular human problem in adoption is that of the natural mother who gives up her newborn baby. Through the good offices of a Chicago adoption agency and of an obstetrician who is active in the gray market for babies, we were able to interview several such women. For obvious reasons, none wanted their last names publicized.

Janice P., a public relations counselor, was a sophomore in college when she became pregnant by a young man who would not accept responsibility as the father. "I couldn't afford the eight hundred dollars it would have cost for an abortion," she told us, "so I just kept on with my studies, pretending that I'd been married. I got through until June, and had my baby six weeks after school was over. When I held that gorgeous baby boy in my arms, I wondered if I'd have the courage to give him up. I finally did because I had to go back to school and graduate. And there was no way I could be a mother to him. But giving him up was a thousand times harder than I imagined. I know I'm going to think about him and wonder about him the rest of my life."

Donna K., a waitress, says she had gotten married a week before the baby was born so "I could have kept her, but my husband didn't want her. I think what we did was wrong. Nobody has a right to do that to another human being. But I had to put my husband's wishes first. We've got enough problems in our marriage without adding a baby to it. What's done is done, but I don't know if I'll ever have another baby now."

"What does it feel like? Like a lost part of my own life," says Betty S., now a housewife, who relinquished her baby boy six years ago. Although married, she has not told her husband about the baby. "I kept it to myself, and for the first two years it was really rough. Then we had a baby boy of our own and I started to feel better about it. But I still catch myself daydreaming about him. He's in school now. I keep imagining him at home with his new family, what he looks like, how they're treating him. I go past boys about his age on the street and I wonder: is it him? It's possible I've even seen him and we didn't know each other. I'm so curious. I've got all kinds of questions that are never going to get any answers now."

Among the very poor, and within minority groups not fully assimilated into American society, adoption is an informal procedure. Each year thirty thousand black and Latino children are "taken in" by friends and neighbors—people who are usually, but not always, related to the child. It is a form of adoption that is practiced quietly and without legal sanction. Seventy-five percent of the children are illegitimate, passed on to a mother or sister or grandmother by a girl who cannot keep them. The other 25 percent consists of children whose parents die or cannot care for their offspring.

Becky Lincoln is a seventy-eight-year-old black woman who has lived all her life on Chicago's South Side. She has totally reared twenty-three children.

"Eight of them was mine, but the rest—they just naturally came to me. Three of my daughters had babies before they got married and I took them in. One of my sons, his wife left him after they had six kids, and I took them in. I never did mess with no lawyers. All they do is take your money and probably take the kids, too."

D. C. Taggart, of Homes for Children in Chicago, says: "The real solution is to help the black community to be economically secure, so more black families may be enlisted. We do have a good many black children in foster families who are adoptable. We're going to have to expand our effort to get them adopted."

"We've always had more applicants for white children than we can possibly process," says a spokeswoman for the Illinois Children's Home & Aid Society. "It's the black and the bi-racial babies who are in the greatest supply."

In Detroit, a group called Homes for Black Children has placed over three hundred children in the five years it has been open. "There are plenty of qualified black families who'd like to adopt a child," says co-director Sydney Duncan. "But the black person says to himself, 'If I adopt a child, I'll have to go to court. Man, I can't do that. That's the cops.' At the Home we try to show the would-be parents that they don't have to be afraid of court procedure. We help to process their applications and cut through the red tape."

Some of the difficulties have their origin in the ignorance and prejudice of the past. Not many years ago, blacks in the South were not given birth certificates because the authorities in their communities refused to regard them as people. So when these people wish to become adoptive parents they must go back to their birthplace and find witnesses willing to swear that they actually did enter the world at a given place and time.

It isn't hard to see why many black families prefer the less troublesome method of simply "taking a child in." But this makeshift form of adoption can only be a temporary response to a genuine social need of much larger scope. Of the more than 200,000 non-white babies born out of wedlock in 1974, almost 90 percent will be "taken in" rather than given legal status as an adopted child.

What happens to the remaining 20,000 who are placed in agencies or homes? A check with agencies revealed that their adoptability is "minimal."

We talked with three obstetricians who engage actively in supplying babies to the gray market.

"In the first place, at twelve hundred dollars a case, it's a lucrative income, and I've arranged over a hundred adoptions," said a San Francisco doctor. "Another reason is I know a baby is going to get a good home. I screen the applicants very carefully. I also try to convince the girl who's giving up her baby that she shouldn't feel guilty for providing a good home for her child. You don't believe what it does for them psychologically to get rid of that guilt."

"I'm in it because of the way the agencies screw things up," a Dallas-based obstetrician said. "I've seen too many childless couples in their twenties wait until they were in their forties before they could adopt a child through an agency. That's not right. A child should grow up with parents the right age, not a couple who are closer to being grandparents as far as age is concerned. The way I look at it, I'm doing a job the agency just isn't willing to do."

"It's an alternative to abortion," a New York obstetrician told us during a staunch defense of the practice. "Girls know their pregnancy costs will be subsidized. And it saves the taxpayer money, too. The cost of the average adoption handled in the regular way comes to just over nine thousand eight hundred dollars!"

After World War II, the gray market slackened because American couples discovered it was easier to adopt babies—fathered by American soldiers or orphaned through war action—in England, France, Germany, and Italy. By 1950 over 200,000 American couples had brought back children from a sojourn in Europe. This particular boom lasted until more states began to examine their adoption rules closely.

Elizabeth Taylor, the film star, helped to bring the problem prominently to public notice. She was married to Eddie Fisher and the mother of three children of her own when she adopted an infant in France.

We asked Miss Taylor what happened, and this is her reply:

"Well, I guess you could say it happened simply because I love babies, children. I was at a point where my boys were almost grown up and Liza (Todd) was ten and so precocious she wasn't really a child any more. I couldn't adopt a child in the United States because I'd been divorced and I wasn't precisely regarded as a woman of impeccable character, and I couldn't have any more babies of my own because of my hysterectomy. But something seemed terribly missing from my life because I didn't have a small child around.

"I didn't actually start out to adopt when I went to that foundling home outside Paris. I simply asked if I could take a baby to care for over a weekend. They were very kind and said yes, and they showed me—oh, there must have been a hundred babies, all cute and cuddly and just plain dreamy. But then I saw this one child—she was three months old, and she was literally covered with a terrible, scaly type of eczema, and she had a deformed hip, but she had the most beautiful big eyes and a smile that melted me. The sisters said, 'Oh, no, she isn't a healthy baby, you don't want her,' but she was the one I really wanted, and finally they let me take her home with me.

"I was to bring Maria—that was the baby's name—back to the home on Tuesday, but over that weekend I fell in love with Maria and she seemed to fall in love with me. Just in those few days her eczema started improving, as though attention and affection were better than that horrible-smelling salve they were using. Anyway, Tuesday morning I went to the home without Maria —I'd left her back at the suite with a nurse—and told them I wanted to adopt her. The sisters were horrified; they couldn't understand my wanting a child that was not absolutely perfect. They tried to get me to take another baby, any other baby, but I only wanted Maria, and finally they seemed to understand and actually helped me prepare my case for the French government, which had to approve the adoption. I'll admit that I paid some money here and there, mostly to speed things up, but I got Maria.

"It must have been a matter of love, reciprocal love, because the eczema cleared up almost immediately, virtually without medication. A few months later, when Maria was old enough, we started the series of operations that cured her hip deformity. By the time Maria was ready to walk, nine operations later—I didn't let the press know anything about this, by the way, nor let them come near Maria—the deformity was simply nonexistent.

"They wouldn't have let this happen in the United States. They seem to try to keep you from adopting a child rather than getting one, which is a cruel thing to do to people who want children and the children need homes."

In 1972, having turned forty, still married to Richard Burton, Miss Taylor tried again to adopt a child. ("I would give up everything I have—I would live in a shack—if I could give Richard a baby.") While in Yugoslavia with Mr. Burton, who was starring in a film, she asked Marshal Tito's wife if there was a baby she could adopt, but nothing came of that. Finally she turned to agencies that were placing hundreds of children born in Vietnam of American fathers and Vietnamese mothers. She was refused.

Another well-known film actress, Julie Andrews, had better luck. Miss Andrews says, "Two different couples we know had successfully adopted babies from an agency in Saigon (South Vietnam), and on their recommendation we wrote to that agency.

"It snowballed from there. I had to prepare a large dossier which they went through in a very detailed way, and then they finally sent us photographs. We decided on one little girl. The agency told us she was sweet, lovely—and sick. She might not survive. If she does, they said, they would let us know."

Everything worked out for Miss Andrews and her husband Blake Edwards, the well-known film producer and director, in the most supercalifragilisticexpialidocious way. After anxious months of waiting, a jet brought the orphaned baby girl to London airport.

"Suddenly, there she was," Miss Andrews says. "One tired little baby accompanied by one tired little nurse. They had had frightful connections out of Paris and the flight had been delayed. The baby simply smiled at me on first sight, and my heart melted.

"She hasn't stopped smiling since. She's more than a year old now, with a kind of radiant, quicksilver personality which is just lovely. If we had gone to a nursery and said, 'We want that one,' we could not have been more lucky. We're terribly grateful."

People who are neither famous nor rich have a much thornier time coping with the rigid requirements, understaffing of federal bureaus, complicated processing of applications, and the ever-multiplying paperwork that is the trademark of most governmental operations.

After the Korean War, the legacy of orphans and illegitimate offspring of American servicemen became adoptable through an arrangement with the South Korean government. An effective publicity campaign—coupled with the fact that the babies were so pretty—eventually placed 2,300 in American homes, most of them white. But many thousands of Korean orphans never did find homes. Their hopes were strangled by years of bureaucratic dawdling and red tape.

The tragedy is now being repeated with the homeless orphans of the Vietnam War. The average waiting time for adoptions is more than two years.

And while would-be parents wait, children die.

"We used to quote figures that six out of ten children died during the paperwork," says Jeanne Thieneman, director of adoptions for Friends of Children of Vietnam, a nonprofit organization authorized by the Republic of Vietnam to place children in American homes. "But we just don't know now."

Other authorities place the death rate of infants in Vietnamese orphanages at about eight out of ten, a figure that far exceeds the percentage of deaths in any intensive care unit in any United States hospital.

"There's anguish in waiting while children are dying over there," says Mrs. Barbara Brown of Woodland Hills, California, who has been waiting more than a year and a half for a Vietnamese child.

"It's really one of the most agonizing times a family can experience," adds Mrs. Lee Krupp of Studio City. "We had to wait almost six months for our first meeting with the Department of Health, where they explained all about adoption. And we already knew everything about interracial adoption. After all, we've lived with and loved our adopted racially mixed daughter for three years."

The total number of children awaiting adoption is unknown. But parents wishing to adopt a child from overseas must run the gauntlet of the state Department of Health, an international agency that works within the child's country, the U.S. Department of State, and the government of the foreign country.

"The process requires thirty to forty steps," says Jeanne Thieneman.

Ray Leber, assistant chief of the adoption services section of the California Department of Health, agrees that the adoption procedures are too cumbersome.

"Since 1969–1970, the availability of local children for adoption has plummeted and the interest in intercountry adoptions has become great," Mr. Leber says. "Suddenly we had an avalanche of applications. I don't think anybody keeps nationwide statistics, but I suppose that at any time more children are waiting for homes than there are parents—although some parents are waiting for special type youngsters."

United States adoption agencies have not been asked to find homes for children from other countries. But some agencies are active. The Holt Adoption Program of Eugene, Oregon, expects to place nearly three thousand Korean and Vietnamese children in 1974. The agency is receiving about two hundred inquiries a week from prospective parents.

Ray Leber points out that most of the children available for adoption in Vietnam are full-blooded Vietnamese.

"Most of the kids left behind by our servicemen have already been placed," he said. "Or they're dead. Whenever you have a war, you know what happens."

IN THE BEGINNING

Children available for adoption have, from the beginning, been (a) the offspring of a deceased parental couple, (b) born out of wedlock, and (c) passed on, voluntarily or otherwise, to a presumably "better" environment.

In primitive societies, the child of deceased parents was usually adopted by a grandparent or by another couple within the tribe. The practice was encouraged, and even today it persists throughout large areas of the undeveloped world—in rural India, Africa, New Guinea, South and Central American hinterlands, among the Lapp and the Eskimo, and with the American Indian.

The first elaboration of this simple and serviceable method of adoption occurred in China around 800 B.C. Emperors, high court officials, military leaders, and prominent tradesmen were allowed to "adopt" a concubine's child. This usually happened when the gentleman in question was dissatisfied with his legal offspring and wanted someone worthier of his inheritance, or perhaps easier to train.

The human desire to perpetuate a superior lineage soon was supplemented by political and social considerations, and the practice was followed by the powerful to gain more power. If a talented nephew or cousin became a potential threat to the dynastic head, the alternatives were either to lop off his head or to welcome him into the bosom of the family as an "adopted" child. This latter course did not wholly eliminate the danger—the impulse to power being what it is—but it did have a neutralizing effect. The adopted son was conveniently provided with another possible route to power.

The Greeks, by 220 B.C., had legalized adoption to the degree that there were no restrictions on the adoptee's full rights of action and inheritance. The adoptee was fully recognized as a natural and legal child, whether or not there existed any affiliation of blood.

The Romans carried the Greek practice over into their celebrated laws. Under the Empire even the offspring of Christian martyrs could be legally adopted into noble Roman homes. Doubtless, a few pagan Romans hoped this might have a neutralizing effect on the wrath of heaven, if the Christians turned out to be right. Under any regime there are those who like to hedge their bets.

The corruption of Roman society spread to its adoption procedures. Nobles, even emperors, started to adopt young boys and girls for purposes which had more to do with sex than with family or politics. These practices increased in ratio to the decline and fall, until by the year A.D. 200 the institution of adoption had already fallen into disrepute. Only the less distinguished Roman families, who remained the guardians of an ever-corroding morality, continued to adopt children (usually orphaned by their relatives) for conventional reasons.

Most legal processes and social customs of Rome survived the end of the Empire. Not so adoption, which languished through the Dark Ages. In most European countries a youngster could be taken into the home as a "ward" or foster child but could not be legally adopted or acquire rights of inheritance.

Even when the Renaissance and then the Industrial Revolution prefaced a change for the better, the evolution was circular—back to the ancient Roman concept, whose chief fault was that adoption was considered to be solely for the benefit of the adoptor.

It was not until as recently as the period following World War I, when millions of youngsters were left parentless and millions of illegitimate children crowded foundling homes and orphanages, that modern "civilized" nations began to accept the view that the process should be focused on remedying the plight of the adoptee.

Today this view, initially accepted in the United States in the middle nineteenth century, is the one that generally prevails.

In our own country, adoption was first legalized in 1851 in the state of Massachusetts. Until that time we followed the practice of the rest of the western world: children were placed in homes as wards of the state and were denied the right of inheritance. The Massachusetts Adoption Act provided, in a dramatic precedent, that a child legally adopted would share fully in the rights of inheritance regardless of blood affiliation. Other states followed the Massachusetts example. Yet as late as 1974, two states—Texas and Louisiana —still hedged on inheritance rights.

Much of the good intentions of the Massachusetts law strangled to death in snarls of swaddling tape. Adoption agencies tried to insure the welfare of the child by placing him in a "proper" home, and their Victorian interpretation of the word became so unrealistically haughty that most foundlings and orphans found no home at all.

In most states, adoptive parents had to be childless and of a certain age (from forty to fifty for the male, thirty-six to forty-five for the female). They had to provide proof of infertility, to live within a specified area, to have secure employment and an adequate income. If the wife was employed, she was asked to give up work. The adoptive parents also had to be in perfect health, church members, and devoid of any possible suspicion of alcoholism or other "undesirable" weaknesses. "All I have to do," one woman remarked bitterly in 1930, after a six-year bout with the St. Vincent home in Chicago, "is prove I'm so pure I wouldn't know how a child is conceived."

Twenty years ago, Mrs. Sophie Kennan, head of the famous Cradle adoption agency in Chicago, explained her view of selective placement for children.

"There isn't enough we can do," she said, "to make certain that all of our children are placed in proper homes. The moral character of the couples who apply to us must be unimpeachable. They must be able to provide for the child. Matters of religious faith and political affiliation and the level of education must be approved. This does take time, and many applicants are turned down, naturally, but we believe it is better for a child not to be placed in a home than to be placed in the wrong one."

A glance at the educational standards and the living conditions that prevailed in most orphanages at the time Mrs. Kennan was speaking makes one wonder why she insisted that the adoptive parents be so "perfect."

Legal restrictions were not the only barriers. There were also religious boobytraps sown throughout the no-man's land between would-be parents and the children who needed them. In 1900, 60 percent of the children available for adoption were in homes operated by Catholic, Protestant, or Jewish agencies. Catholic homes insisted on a "nice Catholic home" for their adoptables, Jewish homes insisted on a "nice Jewish home." The Protestants went a step further, and required a "nice Lutheran" or a "nice Methodist" home.

Somehow, despite all this, the United States led the world for over a century in the number of children adopted annually, and in adoptions per population ratio. This reveals something about the state of things in the rest of the world. Not until 1926 did England pass an adoption law similar to the Massachusetts statute that had then been in effect for almost seventy-five years. France had done the same exactly three years earlier!

In New York, Chicago, Boston, and the other industrial cities of the East, adoption rates continued to run far behind our national average. The new tide of immigrants had beached in these cities, and most adoptable white children were the illegitimate offspring of poor immigrant girls who "got in trouble." They were usually Irish or Polish or Slavic. And Catholic. Families who might have adopted these children, and who qualified on religious grounds, were also immigrants and therefore usually too far down on the economic ladder to meet the other requirements. Since a foundling home would not release a Catholic child to a non-Catholic family, stalemate resulted. Millions of children grew up in orphanages.

LATEST TRENDS

Even today forty-six of our fifty states cling to archaic adoption procedures.

But there has been progress, occasionally by edict, often through spontaneous actions from many sources.

- The New Jersey Supreme Court reviewed a county court's refusal to grant an adoption to a couple who declared they did not believe in a Supreme Being. The Court decided that the disqualification of parents on religious grounds violated the rights guaranteed by the First Amendment.
- In the Chicago and Minneapolis-St. Paul areas, the dominating Roman Catholic and Lutheran adoption agencies began to waive the requirement that adoptive parents be of their faiths. New York's old-guard Catholic Foundling Hospital went a step further: the babies received there for placement were no longer baptized, thus removing any religious "label" to be carried by the baby into its adoptive home.
- Equally significant, judges are now occasionally ruling against biological parents in cases where they are for one reason or another "unfit" to raise their own children. These reasons have broadened beyond child abuse, alcoholism, perversion and the like. In October 1972, the Iowa Supreme Court ordered seven children taken away from their families and placed for adoption on the grounds that their parents weren't intelligent enough to look after them. The parents had IQ's of forty-seven and seventy-four respectively, compared to the 100 national average. Their sickly and unresponsive children, the court ruled, needed more stimulation, love, and affection to grow up and develop into normal healthy adults.

· There is increasing support for federal legislation that would provide financial incentives for the states to pass uniform adoption regulations and to promote the adoption of hard-to-place children. In California, which has had a subsidized adoption program since 1968, the cost of caring for children in foster homes has been cut by 75 percent. The subsidy is temporary, usually lasting from two to five years, and helps the adopting family pay for special costs, such as medical expenses, and contributes toward the child's support.

Senator Alan Cranston, who has prepared a federal adoption bill, says: "We already know that costs are much higher if a child remains in either an institution or a foster home. Under most state laws, the state has to maintain guardianship until the child reaches eighteen, and a caseworker has to provide supervision. And in human terms for the child, the benefits of a permanent home and the identification with his own Mom and Dad are inestimable."

ADOPTION: IT TAKES ALL KINDS OF PARENTS

13

The sharp decline in birth rate among whites of all classes has made the adoptable white baby extremely rare—in zoological terms the species would be near extinction. The predictable result is that many white families are considering for the first time the prospect of adopting a nonwhite infant.

The mere prospect of such an event would have seemed farfetched a few years ago, but social mores are changing and the change is being embodied in the law. The Supreme Court has struck down the remaining state prohibitions on interracial adoption. There is now no legal barrier.

In Connecticut, Wisconsin, California, Michigan, Missouri, and Massachusetts, a broad appeal was made by public and private adoption agencies to encourage multi-racial adoption. Though there has been resistance, seven thousand black, Oriental or Chicano-Latino children have been placed in white homes. In Michigan, judges may no longer use race, culture, or other environmental factors in deciding a child's adoption, and may consider religion only if the child is over seven years old.

But social customs linger on, something like the spasmodic jerkings of a chicken after its head has been cut off. Interracial adoption runs counter to two traditional motives for seeking an adoption—the desires to continue a family line and to secure rights of inheritance. Even those who believe they are not blinkered by racial prejudice sometimes object to having their name and lineage and estate inherited by a child of another color.

In addition, middle-class families in white neighborhoods confront genuine difficulties and real embarrassments when presenting a black or Oriental child to neighbors, schools, and church groups. A racially different child has its own problems growing up within a predominantly white community.

Among white couples who had completed interracial adoptions, we found widely varying opinions on how it has worked out.

"We adopted Steven, who is black, when he was three years old and as cute as a baby could be," say Betty and Allen Charles of Pasadena, California. "Now he's six and the problems we've had are outweighed by the love that exists between us and the way he just doesn't let any negatives get to him. He seems to understand, almost instinctively, that certain children won't accept him and that he's something of a curiosity in the neighborhood. He's been called 'nigger' and he's come home crying, but a little reassurance, just letting him know we love him and that he has as much right to be in school and play as any other child does, makes everything okay again. Even those friends of ours who were shocked when we adopted him have come around to accept our decision."

On the other hand, Alice and Adolph Schroeder of Milwaukee say: "We'd never do it again. At least, not in the neighborhood we live in. People are more bigoted than we ever imagined. Our Laura is seven now, and she hates to go to school, hates to go outside, has no real friends, and it's all we can do to prevent a serious feeling of rejection that can lead to neurosis. We're actually considering selling the house, so that we can move to a biracial neighborhood. Maybe that would help the situation. As things stand now, it isn't fair to her to live here."

Allen Coates, a spokesman for the National Association of Black Social Workers, agrees with the Schroeders. "It's a cruel trick to play on a child," he says. Dr. Alvin Poussaint, a black psychiatrist, believes that black case-workers should screen "conscious and unconscious attitudes in white applicants. I'm skeptical of those who keep telling the child that color doesn't matter when it most certainly does." Other objections by blacks include the argument that the adoption is not for the benefit of the child but for the parents, who think this will establish their credentials as liberal and unprejudiced, or who have the attitude that since there are no white babies available, they'll take what they can get.

The increasing numbers of black, Chicano and Latino babies in foundling homes has, however, redirected the efforts of social workers. Three quarters of the adoption agencies in New York have stopped taking applications for white babies—they have too few to offer—and instead are urging couples to adopt beyond racial lines. In a parallel effort, they are trying to encourage more black families to adopt.

In the new campaign to win homes for these unwanted children, agencies have enlisted the aid of traditional advertising methods. One of the most effective was sponsored by the Illinois Children's Home & Aid Society. A large billboard, dominated by an appealing black baby with the message: "Will Black Be Beautiful? Only if this baby finds a family," appeared for nine consecutive months at eight locations on Chicago's South Side. The telephone number of the adoption agency was prominently printed at the bottom.

The campaign resulted in a 20 percent increase in the number of adoptions of previously "unwanted" children.

Says Emma Golden, who heads a Chicago home: "I think that within ten years we will increase the number of black adoptions by at least five hundred percent. If we do that, we will have begun to lick the big problem remaining on the adoption scene: the proper handling of non-white children."

The projected increase of 500 percent appears to be incautiously optimistic. In the U.S., we blitz a problem and then move on to a new one, and there is evidence that the problem of transracial adoption is sliding into the background of our national consciousness. Overall, the number of black children adopted by white families doubled in the years 1968 to 1972. But since 1972 there has been a 39 percent *decrease* in the adoption rate. Some attribute the decline in part to the resistance to transracial adoption by the black community, although other black spokesmen contend that to deny black children homes because of the color of adoptive parents is merely to continue the old forms of discrimination.

Another reason for the decline, according to some observers, is an inherent dislike of applying merchandising techniques to the "selling" of children. "It's too much like the old slave auction blocks," one black critic told us. "You can't peddle human beings that way, not in this day and age."

Perhaps not. But the problem remains. It may be glimpsed in a startling statistic: since 1949, in Los Angeles, only one half of one percent of the children placed for adoption have been blacks placed with white families.

Transracial adoption is still making snail's progress in our race-conscious society.

A MOTHER AND A FATHER?

New York, Michigan, Illinois, and California are where the reforms in adoption procedures are happening. Since 1965, the California State Department of Social Welfare has been allowing some children for whom two-parent homes could not be found to be placed with single adults.

"If we can find couples, let's do it," Walter A. Heath, then executive director of the Los Angeles County Department of Adoptions, told his staff. "If not, let's get off the dime and get some single parents. The stability and security offered by one parent is better than the insecurity of an institution or a series of foster homes."

During the ten years in which single-parent adoption has been permitted, Los Angeles social workers have placed 224 children with single parents.

"When you stop to consider our divorce rate and the number of 'natural' children that end up in the care of one parent," Walter Heath says, "it's hard to fault one-parent adoption."

Lenore R. Campbell, who succeeded Walter Heath on his retirement in 1974, adds, "Ten years ago, when single-parent adoption first became possible, such arrangements were made only when two parents were not available for a child. Today, single parents are sometimes *preferred* as adoptive parents because of the emotional needs of the individual child."

Other authorities in the field are promoting the idea. As one declared: "More than one out of four of all children are presently living with one parent because of death or divorce or separation. That's double the number of ten years ago. So why shouldn't children also be *adopted* by one parent?

"Most states allow the adoption of adults by single adults. In fact, they don't even require an age difference between the adopter and the person to be adopted. If one adult can adopt another adult, why can't an adult adopt a child? Whose need is greater? Does it make any sense to discriminate against children?"

In metropolitan New York, Chicago, and Detroit, single-parent adoption programs are moving ahead. "The legal restraints are just plain foolish," a young woman social worker told us. "There are almost one million families in this country headed by women who have never been married. And there are seven million mothers—unmarried, separated, widowed, or divorced—who are living alone with their children. That whole idea of a typical American family being made up of a mommy, a daddy, and two cute kiddies is straight out of Norman Rockwell and it never was typical except on a *Saturday Evening Post* cover. But the idea lives on even when it doesn't correspond to reality any more. TV and movies and books and even toys all preserve the image by showing images of mom and daddy, with daddy coming home from work to mommy in the kitchen. There's nothing better than a family when it works, but there's nothing worse than a family where the parents fight all day and the children suffer."

In a growing number of divorce cases, neither parent is willing to take custody of the child. Obviously, if these couples had stayed together, they would have been unsatisfactory parents and their children would be much happier if adopted by someone else.

According to the U. S. Census Bureau, more than 836,000 children under the age of eighteen are living with their fathers only. This is less than ten percent of the 9.6 million children living with their mothers only. But it represents a sharp increase in the last few years, and Arthur Norton, a Census Bureau demographer, believes the increase can be attributed to "the really startling rate at which marriages have been disrupted."

Does the absence of a mother produce bad psychological reactions in the child?

Not at all, says Dr. Lee Salk, who in addition to being a famous columnist on parent-child problems is the director of pediatric psychology at the New York Hospital-Cornell Medical Center. "Males clearly have the same instincts, the same protective feelings that females have. There is no scientific basis whatsoever to indicate that the female is superior to the male in this. The only condition under which the female is perhaps better suited for child-rearing is the process of breast feeding."

Paul D., a forty-one-year-old tax accountant from Cambridge, adopted a mulatto boy who suffered from crossed eyes. "He wasn't very appealing, and maybe that's why I took to him. He so obviously needed someone, and if it wasn't me I didn't know who it was going to be." Shortly after Paul D. took the boy into his home and before the final adoption papers were signed, the boy, Michael, had a corrective eye operation. "He's much better-looking now, more normal, and that's had a good effect on his behavior problems. Having Michael has curtailed a lot of my outside activities. I am not able to keep up with my church activities, and I don't date as much as I did. Recently, I met a woman I liked very much and made a date. But when the night came, Michael had a bad throat infection and ran a fever, and I had to stay home with him. When I called to break the date, she was understanding, or seemed to be, but she didn't accept any further invitations. There are always problems. Michael is allergic to milk, and he likes to play with matches, and when he's in a mood he tries to punish me by not eating. Anybody who says raising a young kid isn't rough doesn't know what he's talking about. But the real answer is, I would do it again. He's worth all the trouble many times over. And it keeps getting better, the older he gets."

Mary Sibley, of Los Angeles, adopted an older child, Nancy Ann. She was nine years old at the time. Mary Sibley, too, admits that there are special problems for the single parent. But: "When I come home from a hard day's work, it's very rewarding to come home to my child. She's happy, we're happy, and we can do things together. For the single parent, working parent, who thinks it's impossible for single adoption to work, I'm here to say it can be done. It isn't easy, but it can be done."

The agency and social worker requirements for single-parent adoption are fairly stringent. They try to determine the financial responsibility of the parent, the job stability, and personal habits that might be detrimental to the rearing of the child. These criteria are used in any form of adoption, but a more careful scrutiny is given to the single parent, and in addition the agency or social worker tries to make sure the child will be exposed through the single parent's friends or relatives to adult members of both sexes who will provide a psychological and social balance.

Some would-be single parents think the agency rules are far too stringent. Reva Rose, an actress, says: "Being single, I couldn't even get a home study [in which a county representative comes to the residence of a prospective parent to check on emotional background, environment, and financial situation]. There was no way for me to get a baby unless it had some terrible psychological damage. I'm considering private adoption through an agency in India. I'm flying to New Delhi to pick out a baby."

A problem for the agency in checking a would-be single parent is homosexuality. "We always look for the possibility," says Dr. I. M. Luezy, a consulting psychiatrist for the Los Angeles County Department of Adoptions. "We can't take a chance of having a child abused sexually."

A number of children have been adopted by homosexual couples, but social workers try to avoid such placements because of the inherent sexual imbalance. It's even difficult to find anyone who will admit to knowing such an adoption took place. A discussion with an agency head about the problem proved less than illuminating.

Q. Is it possible for a homosexual couple to qualify as adoptive parents?

A. I don't know that I would answer yes or not to that. It would all depend on the situation. It's very hard to theorize about a situation when you don't know if the situation exists.

Q. What would you do, personally, if a homosexual couple who qualified in every other respect, as to income, stability, church attendance and the rest, came to you and asked to adopt a child?

A. I've never had that happen. I would be giving you an answer to a situation that is simply outside of my experience.

Q. Can you give us any general rule that would apply? For example, if a homosexual couple qualifies in every other regard, would their homosexuality in itself disqualify them?

A. I don't know of anyone who fits that description. In one regard they certainly wouldn't qualify.

Q. What is that?

A. If they're homosexuals, then they're both the same sex, you understand, and that wouldn't provide the kind of balance we're looking for. There might be other objections too, but there would certainly be that one.

Q. Then you'd say a homosexual couple could not meet the requirements for your agency?

A. Well . . . I . . . no, I wouldn't go that far. I just said I've never come up against it. Quite frankly, I'm not sure whether it would be in the child's interest and that's how we're directing our efforts at the present time. That's our position.

Q. May I quote you?

A. I'd prefer this to be off the record.

Other sources indicated that while there may be a few "regular" adoptions through public or private agencies by homosexual couples, the vast majority take place in the black market. No one seemed to have any idea of how many such adoptions occur. One woman added firmly: "The whole idea is abhorrent to me. We don't encourage perversion of any kind."

Clearly, the admitted homosexual, male or female, living alone or in company with a member of the same sex, has virtually no chance of legally adopting a child. Authorities are too concerned with the child's being brought up in a home where the influence of both sexes is "normal."

For male homosexuals this does not appear to be a serious problem, since they don't have a strong urge to adopt. "Gays just don't have strong paternal or maternal instincts," says a spokesman for the New York Gay Liberation Movement. "A child is an encumbrance, hardly fitting into our business or social lives."

The situation among female homosexuals is, however, precisely the reverse.

"I think it's ridiculous that we aren't allowed to adopt," a lesbian acquaintance told us indignantly. "A stable relationship between two female lesbians is a great deal more permanent than among heterosexuals. A child adopted by a lesbian couple will get a good home, warmth, and a degree of security he will never know in a foster home or an orphanage."

We interviewed a lesbian couple who live in an expensive, security-guarded highrise in Westwood, California. They spoke freely after we assured them their names would not be revealed.

Ruth, the executive secretary to a bank president, admitted, "I want a child very badly, and I don't feel our home is complete without one. Our combined incomes are such that a child would never want for anything material. We've tried to adopt, but it's impossible. And it's so unfair—my marriage is permanent, and you can't say that for too many legal marriages anymore."

"I've told Ruth," said Ellie, her roommate, "that the best thing is for her to have a baby that she can keep." Noting confusion on the part of our interviewer, she explained: "We've gone down the list of men Ruth used to date and picked out a prospect. If he agrees, he'll be under no obligation whatever, and we'll have our baby. You'd be surprised how many couples like me and Ruth are doing exactly that."

P.S. The man agreed.

OVERAGED AND HANDICAPPED CHILDREN

At kindergarten age a child is "over the hill," a geriatric loser as far as his adoptive potential is concerned. The cuteness and special appeal of a baby only a few weeks old is what melts the heart of would-be adopters, and that appeal diminishes in almost a directly proportionate ratio as the child grows up out of infancy to form his or her own personality.

The problem of the "aging child" has drawn more and more attention in recent years from social workers and adoption agencies. Since 1970, they have markedly increased their effort to find homes for "aging" children who are otherwise condemned to grow up in the impersonal realm of an institution, with all the consequent problems of inferior education, incomplete psychological development, and unstable social position.

Although the situation is clearly improving, the agencies have not yet done more than tap an almost bottomless well of need. At kindergarten age, a child is still virtually condemned to grow up in an institution, and the consequences are sad to contemplate.

More difficult to place than the "geriatric child" is the youngster who suffers from a mental or physical handicap. The odds are great that they will never find a family to take them in. Many are simply abandoned at birth by parents who cannot face living with a handicapped child. These children must then live out their lives in institutions, without experiencing the joy or closeness of a family or the meaning of parental love.

As early as 1967, the Ben Hunter Show in Los Angeles worked with the County Department of Adoptions in placing "special needs" children—infants and preschoolers with physical and even mental defects. Often accused of flesh peddling, playing on sympathies, etc., the Ben Hunter Show nonetheless placed over six hundred children in homes, including a two-year-old with acute anemia, a four-year-old hemophiliac, and an infant girl born so deformed she would never be able to walk.

Simultaneously, the *Detroit Sunday News* adoption column placed over five hundred supposed "defective" children in parental homes. The ages range from two months to six years, and the defects from heart ailments requiring open heart surgery to uncorrectable limb maladjustments.

Robert and Dorothy De Bolt founded AASK—Aid to Adoption of Special Kids—in May of 1974. Since then, they have found over 150 families willing to take in these children.

Mrs. De Bolt says they now receive up to one hundred letters a day expressing an interest in the organization's work. From donations they receive, the De Bolts are able to help adopting families with expenses not covered by public agencies, such as legal fees and transportation costs.

The AASK offices are in the basement of the De Bolts' Spanish-style home in Oakland, California. Dorothy De Bolt and her husband, a civil engineer, devote every evening to the affairs of their organization. Their work is literally never done.

"We are extremely organized," Dorothy says. "That is the only way we can make anything function."

The De Bolts believe in practicing what they preach. They have seven children, but have adopted eleven others—almost all handicapped in some way.

Many children are in a kind of legal limbo because their parents cannot or will not take care of them, yet won't voluntarily relinquish their rights. As a result, the children are condemned to life in a series of foster homes or in an institution.

Terry, a lovely two-year-old girl in Boise, Idaho, was taken from her parents by a court order. Both parents were alcoholics who neglected and beat her. Terry has been living with foster parents who love her, take good care of her, and would like to adopt her. But Terry's natural parents refuse, and they retain legal guardianship.

According to government estimates, there are 120,000 such children in this country.

In many instances, says Beatrice L. Garrett, a specialist in foster family services at the Department of Health, Education, and Welfare, these children have little chance of ever finding a home. The state can appeal to the courts to terminate the parents' legal claim, but it takes time, energy, and money to do this, and most agencies are too far behind on their workloads, understaffed and under financed.

Nor are the courts always cooperative if a case does reach them.

Victor A. Pike, director of a HEW-funded project in Oregon to free foster care children for adoption, thinks most juvenile court judges find that terminating parents' rights is a traumatic decision. Judges will usually act if there is a clear case of desertion by parents, but they are reluctant to declare parents unfit to care for their own children.

Meanwhile, the children grow up with foster care or in institutions.

Which brings us to the question: are children better cared for in an adopted home or an institution?

Abraham Loewe, a Minneapolis child psychologist, replies: "The adopted child is usually happy, responsive, and advanced for his age, probably because the adoptive parents wanted him so badly they lavished him with extra care and attention. On the other hand, the child left in the institution is inclined to be emotionally undeveloped, withdrawn, and so shy in his relationship with adults he actually may seem retarded."

"NATURAL" PARENTS

Many adopted children want to know who their natural parents were, but it isn't easy for them to find out. All too often the information is permanently beyond recall, for records are sealed and birth certificates have been legally altered.

To some these precautions seem logical. Dr. Spock, for example, believes that an adoption agency should "stand like an impenetrable wall between the two sets of parents." And an adoption agency social worker told us, "If you start opening the records, you wreck the whole idea of adoption. What about the woman who gave up her child when she was sixteen or seventeen and then remarried and never told her husband? What kind of pain would this cause mothers who reluctantly gave up babies they've never forgotten in their hearts?

Women who've been trying for years to make a new life, to forget? Not to mention the possibility of blackmail—of a parent who might be forced to pay up to keep a secret."

On completion of an adoption, most agencies supply to the adoptive parent on request the basic background information on the child's natural parents, omitting names but including age, family descent, education, physical description, and interests. Along with the final decree of adoption, the new parents also receive a revised birth certificate, and the original birth certificate is permanently "sealed."

Recent evidence indicates that secrecy leads to an identity problem for the adopted child. Not knowing his "real" mother and father can become a source of frustration and anxiety. It sets him apart from other children.

Dr. Arthur D. Sorosky, an Encino, California, psychiatrist who has been studying the problem, suggests it may even be detrimental to the child's psychological health. Dr. Sorosky believes this is reason enough to break the anonymity contract, even though it may have been agreed upon by both natural parents and adoptive parents prior to the child's birth.

Dr. Cynthia Martin, a San Diego psychologist, has adopted three children, the third by a so-called open adoption in which the natural parents got to know the adoptive parents.

"We picked up the baby from the natural parents, both the mother and the father, and had quite a bit of contact with them. They visited us, and so did the natural grandparents. It worked out beautifully." Although there was "trauma connected with it," Dr. Martin preferred this to the secrecy and intrigue of the adoption agency about the first two of her adopted children.

The question of whether the records should be opened was first brought to public consciousness twenty-five years ago by Jean Paton, an adopted child who found her natural mother and wrote a book about it called *The Adopted Break Silence.* She started an organization, Orphan Voyage, to help others who were in a similar situation.

In 1971, Florence Fisher, an adoptee, placed the following ad in *The New York Times:* "Adult who was an adopted child desires contact with other adoptees to exchange views on adoptive situation and for mutual assistance in search for natural parents."

More than eight thousand people wrote to her, and more than eighteen hundred became members of her organization, ALMA. Of these, almost six hundred were mothers looking for the babies they gave away.

Mrs. Fisher claims to know of more than two hundred reunions. She says natural mothers have rejected their children in only three or four cases. One of them, as she relates in her book *The Search for Anna Fisher,* was her own mother, who even denied she was her mother at their first meeting. Since then her mother has remained unwilling to tell her husband and her two other children about Florence.

ALMA—an acronym for the Adoptees Liberty Movement Association—is now fighting the legality of sealed records in the courts. The organization also instructs adoptees and natural parents in how to find each other.

"The big question is what are they really searching for," says Mrs. Barbara Miller, a social worker in Manhattan. "What is there to go back to? . . . They're searching for something that never was."

Although at most agencies the amount of information given to those searching for their real parents is still limited, many adoption agencies are re-evaluating their positions in the controversy. There are still those strongly opposed to any change, however.

"What good could it possibly do?" asks Mrs. Florence Kreech, executive director of the Lois Wyse agency. "Psychologically, humanely, do we have a right to interfere with the adjustments these people have made? Do we have a right to disrupt commitments made twenty-five years ago?" Mrs. Kreech concedes, however, that most agencies are more candid than they were in former days when the standard answer to queries was "that all the fathers were killed in the war and all mothers died in childbirth . . ."

Adoptive parents fear that the opening of records would reduce them to mere caretakers until the child becomes old enough to search out his or her real parents. They react belligerently to the possibility that the child whom they have seen through infancy and adolescence would someday desert them for its "natural" parents.

Florence Fisher has no sympathy for these people. She says, "They never should have adopted in the first place. They never saw their children as people. They saw them as possessions. If the relationship was good, it will remain good. A third person can't break it up."

The issue of confidentiality sharpened recently when a case was disclosed in which an eighty-year-old adoptive father had to give his permission before an agency could release any information to a fifty-year-old woman adoptee!

"I used to think that when grown people came here looking for information about their natural parents they were suffering from some kind of obsession," an agency official told us. "I couldn't understand or sympathize with their agonizing need to know. It now seems terribly wrong that I should have sat there in full knowledge of these people's backgrounds and refused them the information they wanted. Those records didn't belong to me—they belonged to them. And they should have been able to see them. Certainly they had more right to see them than I did."

"Sealed records," says a young woman social worker, "are just invitations to frustration for all concerned, I wouldn't be surprised if some day an adoptee breaks in here and steals his records. I don't believe the law could even punish him. As far as I'm concerned, he's only stealing back what belongs to him in the first place."

Action is pending in the courts to get a definitive ruling on whether adoption records should be opened, but by the time the ruling is handed down, the controversy may be over. Along with the change in attitude there have already come the first signs of a change in procedure. A few agencies have decided that the right of secrecy has to be breached when the child becomes an adult and demands the information.

Says an agency head: "We're advising adoptive parents that they simply have to stop thinking of their sons and daughters as children after they have grown up. We understand their feelings of fear, of being threatened, but they have to confront and conquer their feelings."

Some objections to full disclosure are based on the possibility that the natural parents may not wish to have their identity revealed. The Adoption Research Project's poll on this question reported that an overwhelming majority of natural parents would want to see their natural children if they knew the children were looking for them.

Florence Fisher adds with more than a touch of ire: "Where does the natural mother get this right to privacy? My mother does not have a right to privacy from me. I want a face-to-face confrontation, not answers from a social worker. My mother is obligated to tell me: who is my father? What is my hereditary background? Do I have any brothers and sisters?"

The trend is clearly toward Mrs. Fisher's position. If anyone in the adoptive triangle is going to be favored, the adoptee is destined to be the one.

A CONSUMING NEED?

The New York *Daily News* published a series some years ago about adopted children who felt compelled when they became adults to search out their natural parents.

We conducted our own survey among adults who had been adopted as children and found only a minority were consumed with a need to discover their natural parents. Most said they had no interest in finding out ("Why dig up the past, it's too painful," was a response that summed up the general attitude), a few admitted to having some curiosity, and only three actually had gone to trouble to locate one or more of their parents.

A young doctor in Rochester, New York, told us about finding his father. "He was a handsome man in his sixties, the kind who had a way with women. But I've never met anyone more shallow and self-centered. I don't blame my mother for not marrying him. She tried for a while to look after me alone, then had to turn me over for adoption. Luckily, I was adopted by a wonderful couple who will always be my real parents. I'm sorry now that I ever bothered to find out about the other two. My natural mother is dead, and my natural father is an eighteen-carat phony. He's written to me several times since we met, always trying to get me to invest in one of his get-rich-quick schemes. I made a silly emotional trip."

A clinical social worker in Little Rock, Arkansas, told us how she had been looking forward to a meeting with her natural mother. "I remember thinking of her as some kind of a goddess in a long white flowing gown—although if anyone should have known better, I should have. When I discovered she was as human as other people, my heart broke. I didn't want her to be real. Not really real. But at least finding her helped to satisfy my need to know who I really was. And I think that's what I was looking for."

A young woman in Tucson, Arizona, three times married at twenty-eight, thinks her search for her mother was prompted by the desire to find some excuse in heredity for "my own instability. I was looking to blame it on my mother, and that was ridiculous. When I found her in New York, working in a garment manufacturing firm and having a dead-end affair with her married boss, we were complete strangers. I didn't even know what to call her. I couldn't call her Mom, and it seemed too informal to call her Marie. I ended up calling her Aunt Marie—which is probably even sillier. I flew home and went out to the cemetery where my adopted mother is buried. I brought a corsage of flowers and stayed at the gravesite for a whole afternoon. I never cried so much in my whole life. I really loved her, and I wish I had been able to be the right kind of daughter to her. God knows, she was the right kind of mother to me."

ADOPTIVE PARENTS

There are other problems for adoptive parents and adopted children.

First there is the question: How do you tell a child he is adopted? Most professionals in the field agree that a child should be told.

"Too many friends and members of the family know about the adoption for the child not to find out sometime," says Mrs. Evelyn Nerlove. "And people who don't tell their children are in for a disaster when they do find out. It's pretty hard to explain to a youngster why you didn't trust him enough to tell him."

"It's all in the way you present it," says Mrs. Shirley Mintz, a clinical social worker who leads discussion groups for adoptive parents. "If the parent shows a lot of anxiety and fear about discussing it, the child will pick up on it. But if the parent is positive and confident, the youngster accepts it like any other form of learning."

One method recommended by several social workers was for the adoptive parent to stress that the youngster was chosen to be their child, while other parents had no choice in the matter.

A recurring question: should a child be told that his natural parents were not married?

"Yes," says Reuben Pannor, supervisor of an adoption and foster home at Vista Del Mar, California. "All a kid has to do is go to the library to find out that ninety percent of adopted children come from unwed parents. You start making up stories about the parents having died in an accident, and you end up embroiling yourself in lies which you can't substantiate."

Most of the people we interviewed confirm Mr. Pannor's assessment.

What do you do when an adopted child, in the midst of a teen-age rebellion against parental authority, uses his or her ultimate weapon: "You're not my real parents!"

For the adoptive parent, struggling with problems of infertility, competing against a youngster's idealized version of his or her biological parents, and trying to cope with the problems that all parents face in trying to rear children in today's world, this presents an exasperating additional challenge.

"The way to deal with it," says a psychologist to whom we presented the problem, "is to treat it like any other challenge from a youngster. The first thing is to find out what is really being said, and almost surely you'll discover it is not a rejection of the adoptive parent, or even a threat that the child will leave to seek out his natural parents. It is only another weapon by which the youngster is trying to assert what he or she believes to be a right. So you have to deal with whether that assertion is worthy of being acknowledged. If it is, say so, and at the same time make clear that the youngster had no right to use the weapon of biological parentage to get his or her way. If the assertion of rights has no validity, carefully explain why—and add that same caution about trying to prevail by force.

"Look, this is a hard time for *all* parents to raise children. Young people are questioning the supposedly sacrosanct values. It can be a devastating experience for a parent to be confronted by a rebellious youngster, and the fact that the youngster of adoptive parents has an additional weapon only makes it a little harder to cope. But the adoptive parents are still the authority figures, and if they use their authority wisely—counseling rather than commanding— they won't have anything to really worry about."

A HOUSE IS NOT A HOME

An alternative to adoption is the foster home. Foster parents are paid a specified fee, ranging from $35 to $65 a month, and until the child is eighteen he can be kept in foster homes unless adoption procedures are instigated. The cost to the American taxpayer for the foster home programs exceeds $900 million a year.

Two of the most progressive states, Illinois and California, have made adoption more feasible and attractive by paying some adoptive parents a monthly fee almost equal to that paid the foster parents.

In the first few years this procedure was employed, adoptions rose 22 percent while the caseload carried by the foster home programs dropped 22 percent.

"We couldn't afford to adopt the two kids we were caring for," admits

George Martinson of Champaign, Illinois, "until this new law came along. Now we've adopted them, and they're legally ours, and it's kind of a great feeling all the way around."

In many instances foster parents end up by adopting the children in their care. This usually occurs when the child is about to be taken from them, and the imminence of separation compels a decision to make the arrangement permanent.

Foster parents are screened as carefully as possible to make sure they can provide the proper environment, and social workers check the home frequently to make sure things are going right.

"We want to place the children, not just put them somewhere," says one social worker. "Essentially what a child needs is a loving home with people who will be supportive."

We asked to interview "ideal" foster parents and were directed to John and Joan Lohnes of Westwood, California. They were chosen because they have six children of their own ranging in age from fifteen to twenty-four, have adopted a black girl, Frances, who is now six years old, and in addition have taken in sixteen foster children during the past four years.

Joan Lohnes, a very attractive, vivacious blonde who looks at least ten years younger than her forty-five years, was interviewed in her spacious, lovely home adjacent to the UCLA campus. She told us: "Most foster parents certainly don't do it for the money. You couldn't do it just for the money. It's like nursing [Mrs. Lohnes is a registered nurse]—you need some sort of motivation, some altruism.

"We really care about the children. I try to follow up on what happens to them after adoption. I make a special effort to stay in touch. I send pictures, make up an album of photos taken when they were with us, and send Christmas cards every year.

"People think of foster parents in terms of stereotypes—the foster mother who does it just for the money, the foster father who's a child molester—like with Marilyn Monroe, everyone always brings *that* up about her. Adoptive parents regard foster parents as transition people who don't count. If they aren't thought to be ogres, they're thought to be nothing. It's unfair.

"One foster mother I know has started going around with a group of other foster mothers to the White Memorial or wherever unwed mothers are staying, just to talk to them and show them that they are really nice, dependable people who love children. A lot of natural mothers particularly have the idea that their babies are going to be neglected in a foster home. They *want* to feel nobody can take as good care of their children.

"I don't blame them for that. But as a mother and an adoptive mother, I wish someone would speak up for foster parents. I know many, and they are all fine, down-to-earth, giving people. Foster fathers too—they're fabulous. Most men just wouldn't do it, or let their wives take all that time away from them."

Louella Johnson, a San Francisco social worker, has a caseload of seventy-seven children in foster homes in the Bay area.

"I would say that sixty percent of the time the child is happy with his environment, is well fed and clothed, and regards his foster parents as his own parents. And it does satisfy a need for people who love to have children around. Those same children, in an institution, would not develop nearly so well.

"The less fortunate cases are difficult to explain, but I know, almost intuitively, when something is wrong. The most obvious are those where foster parents merely want the money paid them to care for foster children without giving them any love or attention. A child who feels he's unwanted may be better off in an institution than with people who are unresponsive to his needs.

"There is another inherent problem the foster child faces which psychologists have never explained satisfactorily, at least to my knowledge. This is the fact that any child who's been in an institutional environment for his first two years has emotional and psychological problems that are not easy to cope with —not for the child and not for the foster parents. My theory is that at the age of two they somehow come to believe they weren't wanted by their natural parents, and feel rejected or abandoned. As they reach the ages of five and eight and ten, this feeling will grow in proportion to the lack of a favorable home atmosphere.

"If their situations are agreeable, they will suffer a minimum of the sort of trauma that leads to rebelliousness, hatred for authority, and the lone-wolf tendency. But if the situations are untenable, the trauma will more or less command the child. There is nothing more pitiful, no person more difficult to reach, than a child who's burdened himself with the guilt of rejection."

Crime statistics bear this out. Forty percent of children below eighteen who are arrested for crimes ranging from misdemeanors to felonies to murders come from foster homes or institutions. One of the most notorious is Charles Manson, who spent most of his childhood in a series of foster homes.

A major disadvantage of foster home placement is the transiency.

"The child who's sort of bounced around from home to home has a terrible time adjusting," says Lois Anderson, a social worker in Evanston, Illinois. "He never feels he belongs, and consequently any behavior problems he has are magnified because he feels he's in another temporary environment and that he cannot allow himself to become emotionally attached to his foster parents or the home. It's a vicious circle, because if he's given up by foster parents who can't control him, he's apt to be more uncontrollable in the next home."

Sometimes, of course, the transfer from one home to another is desirable. Sometimes, too, as in the case of job transfers, they are inevitable.

"I've had kids come in here who have been in as many as seven foster homes," says Kay Donley, director of Michigan's Spaulding Home for Children.

A serious need is for foster parents who will care for infants. Many unwed teen-agers try to keep their babies, then find it is too difficult and want to place their children temporarily in foster homes until they can get their own lives in order.

All agencies bless women like Mrs. Deborah Mara of Staten Island, New York. Since 1939, Mrs. Mara has cared for eighty-three foster children, usually two at a time, from shortly after birth to five or six months, simply out of a desire to give them the loving care they need. In the meantime, she has raised four children of her own. "I can't picture myself without a baby. They come and they go, but when they go, me and my husband and the kids sort of feel there's been a death in the family. With the first few I took it so to heart that I hated to give them back."

As costly and impermanent and fraught as it is with problems, the foster home program seems an essential adjunct to adoption. So is a new program called Good Neighbor homes, in which people accept children at any hour of the day or night when a crisis occurs. When a parent becomes ill, for example, or is injured in an accident, the Good Neighbor home will take a child in and provide not only shelter but consolation during the time of stress. Not long ago, an infant was abandoned on the center dividing strip of the Ventura Freeway in Los Angeles. She was picked up, miraculously unharmed, and taken immediately to a Good Neighbor home. This type of crisis intervention is suitable for those couples who would like to help but do not want the longer commitment of traditional foster care.

For every size and shape of human problem, there is usually someone somewhere who has compassion to fit.

PROBLEMS REMAIN

We have come a long way in the past ten years toward making adoption practicable and relatively painless. Some social attitudes have softened, and multi-racial adoptions and "single adoptions" are more accepted. But a few problems are still unresolved.

Among them:

· At least 25,000 babies are born each year to unwed teen-agers who refuse to give them up at birth, believing they can care for them themselves. Five or six months later these mothers abandon their babies or place them in a home for adoption. The infants at that age have become geriatric casualties, and the chances for adoption are slim.

The reason for abandonment is often the fact that the unwed mother discovers she cannot support her child on welfare payments and cannot find day-care facilities that will enable her to work. More thorough instruction by a caseworker on what she will face economically after the baby is born might reduce the number of these delayed abandonments. And a more intense program of educating adoptive parents to the plight of these pre- and post-kindergarten "geriatrics" will help to ease the situation further.

· Although some of the bureaucratic red tape has been eliminated and the waiting periods reduced, too many parents are still being forced into the gray or black market to adopt babies. Obstetricians involved in such placements earn high fees for placing babies in homes, and there are far too many instances where the profit motive speaks louder than more human motivations. The result: too many babies placed in unsuitable homes.

The bellwether states of California, Michigan, Illinois, and New York are pressing toward legislation that will eliminate the baby black market. But their efforts have not yet resulted in any enforceable new law. And the efforts elsewhere are sporadic and ineffective.

· One major step toward helping connect would-be parents with available children would be to find out exactly how many children are available. No one knows for certain, and the statistics are no better than informed guesses. In a nation where computers keep accurate and highly detailed records of credit backgrounds, of criminal histories, where airline seats are matched precisely to the needs of passengers who wish to fly, where tax statements are finecombed by the IRS, and political affiliations known to the FBI, where everyone has been profiled on computers to determine buying habits for the benefit of merchandisers, it hardly seems too much to ask that computers keep some comprehensive account of children who need permanent homes and parents.

· Twenty-three of the United States have a law which entitles a mother to reclaim her child within six months after giving it up. A few states contend that a child is not legally abandoned as long as the natural parent remains in some kind of communication. This has been interpreted by tolerant judges to mean that as little as a birthday card and a Christmas card every year is "communication." Naturally, the law, and this attitude, is a deterrent to many couples in these states who wish to adopt.

THE DE MARTINO CASE

The most celebrated and publicized case involving "change of mind" occurred in 1972, when Jean and Nick De Martino of Brooklyn adopted a baby given up by Olga Scarpetta, a native of Colombia. Olga declared that she had made a mistake and wanted her daughter Lenore back.

Seven months of unbelievable legal hassle occurred. After three costly trials, the New York Supreme Court ruled that Miss Scarpetta had the right to custody of her child. The De Martinos refused to give Lenore back to her natural mother. Before the injunction papers could be served, they moved to Florida with Lenore.

A New York judge sentenced the De Martinos to thirty days in jail for refusing to obey the legal order to return the baby. They filed an appeal with the U.S. Supreme Court while the mother, Olga Scarpetta, had her attorney file a kidnapping charge against the De Martinos.

"It may not be," Jean De Martino told *Time* magazine, "as obvious an example of man's inhumanity to man as a killing or a war, but it's a horrible thing to have to go through. We adopted Lenore in all good faith just five days after she was born, and she became ours. We loved her intensely—we have another adopted child, now seven, but Lenore immediately became the most important thing in our lives.

"To be told, a few months later, that we had to give her up was impossible to bear. We wouldn't give her up, even if we had to move out of the country to keep her. The law in New York is absurd, giving the natural mother the right to change her mind six months after someone else has reared her child and come to love it and built a home and life around it.

"With the millions of children who need homes and the millions of childless couples who want to raise and love a child, why does everyone try to make adoption difficult? They'd be doing humanity a favor, a great favor, by making it easy."

In January 1974, the Florida Supreme Court finally ruled that the De Martinos could keep their adopted daughter. By then, they had been compelled to sell their home at a loss and their life savings had gone to pay the legal fees.

The De Martino case lies very close to the heart of the basic problem: what is a parent and what is the essence of parental love?

We are in the process of redefining our attitudes toward adoption, beginning to question whether blood ties are, after all, the most important. We are searching out other possible definitions for such familiar words as father, mother, parent, and family. There are 3 to 5 million adopted persons in the United States, half of whom are adults—and for them the usual definitions simply will not suffice.

When the process of social change is complete, we may confront a world in which the family unit is regarded only as a convenient grouping within which the needs of a developing child are met along with the needs of other family members. Within such "families," the link of blood, the kinship created by biological reproduction, may not be the most important bond. After all, many natural fathers and mothers are unfit to raise their child, and many adoptive parents have been marvelous fathers and mothers in the best and truest sense.

The next generation may regard our attitudes as having been too rigid and narrow. They may understand better than we do that parenthood, apart from producing a child, means nurturing him, raising him to adulthood, and letting him go.

ILLEGITIMACY: IF YOU DON'T KNOW WHO YOUR FATHER IS, WHAT'S YOUR MOTHER'S NAME?

14

In 1975 more than half a million illegitimate babies will be born in the United States.

And the total has been increasing sharply every year.

1946:	125,200 recorded illegitimate births.
1964:	240,000
1966:	302,400
1968:	339,000
1973	473,000
1975:	520,000 (projected)

What's the reason?

Says a leading Protestant spokesman, "The blame for the startling growth of illegitimacy can be put squarely at the door of the new permissiveness among young people, the lack of an abiding morality."

This belief that young people, especially teen-agers, are responsible for the bumper crop of illegitimate babies is mistaken. Among women aged fifteen to nineteen, only about 2.3 out of 100 give birth to illegitimate children. Despite the recent increase in teen-age illegitimacy, the majority of unwed mothers are women above the age of consent. The average age of unwed mothers fluctuates between twenty-one and twenty-three years. And the greatest rate of increase in illegitimate births is among women between twenty-five and twenty-nine years.

Some authorities believe the blame for the teen-age pregnancies that do occur rests with the parents.

Says a psychiatrist, "The chief problem for these girls is social pressure from parents who want them to reach earlier maturity. We are steadily moving up the date of 'adolescence.' There's a lot of parental anxiety about their children being 'popular' and 'accepted' in their peer groups. Naturally, this communicates itself to the child, who then adopts a code of behavior that will maintain a busy social life and 'popularity.' Their opinions are formed by osmosis—seeping through to a child's mind from every conceivable source. Newspaper advice columns now answer questions on the propriety of combining a bridal and baby shower, or of a pregnant bride wearing white. Nor can we rule out factors like TV, movies, and books, advertising messages, even clothing styles—all pursuing a line of erotic stimulation in the name of increasing profits."

A professor of sociology who works with the national board of the Young Women's Christian Association maintains: "Parental permissiveness is to blame. No child has to wait anymore to get anything he wants, including things that once were the exclusive privilege of adults. They get trips to Europe and drive their own cars. They get plenty of spending money. They're allowed to drink. And if they get into trouble they don't have to worry. Papa and Mama will understand. Whether it's an auto accident, or vandalism, a shoplifting arrest, or marijuana, good old Papa and Mama will be standing by.

"What they do eventually is to send a child into a world that it thinks will be just as indulgent. Then parents pretend to be shocked when something bad happens, like an unwanted pregnancy. It's so hypocritical. These parents are shocked by their children getting caught, not by what they've been doing. And I don't blame the children for becoming cynical. They know their parents condone exactly the same attitudes and behavior among themselves. 'Don't do as I do—do as I say!' And who has a right to throw that first stone?"

The fact remains that teen-agers are not the principal cause of the steep rise in illegitimacy. Those who try to make us think so are merely "moralizing" the problem and building a convenient if rickety platform from which to decry the sexual permissiveness in our society.

ARE ATTITUDES CHANGING?

Ten years ago the New York *Herald Tribune,* now defunct, interviewed 105 students from 16 colleges on the subject of premarital sex. They reported that 42 percent of the students approved of premarital sex, whether or not the relationship was permanent, and an additional 13 percent approved if the couple was engaged. This clear majority in favor of "illicit sex" doubtless contributed to public alarm that a sexual revolution was taking place among our young and the old standards were collapsing into an unrecognizable rubble.

To find out whether attitudes on the subject have changed during the intervening decade, we submitted a questionnaire—permitting the respondents to remain anonymous—to a group of one hundred college students across the nation. The students ranged from sophomores to seniors, and in actual numbers conformed to the statistical validity of the New York *Herald Tribune*'s sample. The only change we made was to add the question about actions as well as attitudes. We felt this more in keeping with today's social mores.

The results show a remarkable agreement with the survey made ten years ago. Slightly more than half of the ninety-one replies we received (forty-seven) admitted to having sexual intercourse, and all but three on more than a single occasion. Regarding approval of premarital sex, the figures were in rough correspondence with the *Herald Tribune*'s, with only five more (fifty-two) condoning premarital sex than actually engaged in it. An additional twelve said they would approve if the couple were engaged or "pinned."

Two further questions received overwhelmingly one-sided replies. On the question of whether pregnant students should be allowed to stay in school, there were only two dissenters. And to our query, "Do you believe the causes of illegitimacy are due to abnormal psychological factors or to social and economic factors?" Eighty-six out of ninety-one favored the socio-economic explanation.

One student wrote: "It seems peculiar that we are always trying to weigh economic factors in studying the sexual behavior of Negro women, but with the middle-class or upper-class women the answer is that they are some sort of sexual deviates just acting out some really deep psychological problems."

Some other comments added voluntarily to our questionnaire are worth recording.

"A lot of what they call sexual promiscuity happens in small towns where there isn't much to do."

"I'm too young to get tied down to responsibility but that doesn't mean I want to give up sex."

"I'm going to be a farmer, but before I can get married and start raising a family I need to get some money behind me. If the crops fail or prices are shot to hell, I'll have something to fall back on. Meanwhile we have to be practical.

We're waiting for marriage but we don't want to wait for anything else."

"My parents tell me that in their day girls were terrified because if they didn't get married by the time they were twenty-six, they were old maids. I may not marry at all unless I want children."

"We find out a lot about sex before we feel any real need for it. At fourteen I knew a lot more about sex from reading than older people know. We don't have hangups or guilt about it. We see it as a natural thing."

"I don't see any point in jumping into bed with the first fellow who asks me. The trouble with having sex is you have to handle the emotions that go along with it. I don't think I know enough about myself yet. I don't want to rush growing up."

"Everybody tells me I'm missing out because sex is fun. But right now I'm scared of going to bed with someone who'll just get up and say, 'That was cool, baby,' and walk out. When I make love the first time I want it to be with someone I love."

The consensus is against casual sex, and many students emphasize the desirability of fidelity. "If you care about somebody, you don't have to make it on the side." The sexual experimentation that seemed in vogue during the sixties—although actually confined to a minority of young people—is now generally regarded as ridiculous. "That group sex is for the birds," a University of Wisconsin student summed up. "It's hard enough for two people to get along. With eight people you've got just that many more problems. If I sleep with somebody, I'd at least like to remember her name."

In view of evidence to the contrary, why do so many people cling to the belief that today's youth are responsible for the "new permissiveness"?

Says a Chicago executive who also serves as a college trustee, "The public attitude has become so narrowed and rigid that not even publishing the facts can change it. Older people *want* it to be so, as another proof of the moral rot in society."

In fact, sexual permissiveness appears more prevalent among adults. A recent poll conducted by the Elmo Roper organization reported that nearly one third of all women polled saw no reason why single women should not give birth and raise their own children if they want to. The belief that premarital sex is immoral had dropped from 65 percent in 1970 to 53 percent in 1974. Almost half of those interviewed would accept a daughter's living with a man outside of marriage. Even interracial marriage, taboo a decade ago, is acceptable to 52 percent of the women.

Jerome D. Pauker, Ph.D., a professor of medical psychology at the University of Missouri Medical School, may offer a better insight into the reason for the rise in illegitimacy than either the simplistic "blame it on the young" or the hue and cry about "moral rot" in our society.

Dr. Pauker thinks the reason may be the increasing frequency of sexual intercourse. (See page 250 for further evidence on this.)

"There are bound to be slip-ups in planning, errors of judgment, oversights, impulsive acts, and mistakes based on lack of knowledge," Dr. Pauker concludes. "How many married women in this country have had unexpected and often unwanted little blessings as the result of an oversight or of a mistake in counting, or of taking a calculated (or uncalculated) risk?"

THE PAST AS PROLOGUE

Recently in New Jersey, a judge turned the clock back to the year 1796. Charles Saunders, twenty, was convicted of "committing fornication" under a statute that makes it illegal for single persons to have sexual relations. He was fined a maximum $50, although he argued that the statute had been established "in the prevailing religious notions of the latter eighteenth century." The judge rejected the argument, deciding that New Jersey had compelling secular reasons to enforce the law—such as preventing the birth of illegitimate children and the spread of venereal disease.

The judge was not merely turning back the clock—he was moving the law back to an era when people used sundials. If all the single people "committing fornication" in New Jersey today were fined $50, the revenue obtained would balance the entire federal budget.

The judge's decision would have appeared equally outrageous in the year 1796, but for a different reason. It would have been considered far too lenient. In early Massachusetts a girl who conceived a child out of wedlock was driven from the colony—usually after her parents had already driven her from her home. Only in Pennsylvania, where Quaker concepts of tolerance held sway, was an unwed mother considered anything more than a pariah. Even there she was consigned to a life of servitude. The one route of escape was to move west. Horace Greeley's advice to "Go West, young man, go West," applied with more pertinency to the unmarried young mother.

"Betsy left us today," a farmer near Philadelphia wrote of his unwed daughter in a 1799 diary. "A man who stopped briefly convinced her to join him and bring her child to move with him to the glorious country that is supposed to be near Fort Pitt."

Betsy was lucky. About the same time, Massachusetts journals included more harrowing notations:

"It was discovered [we are modernizing the spelling] that Abigail Davies was with child, perhaps three months along, and though she claimed to have been assaulted by an unknown man she was promptly and properly banished. On her way to Rhode Island, she fell ill with a fever and mercifully died."

Ann Ross was not so fortunate. Neither "she nor her unborn survived the dousings fairly given any girl engaging in carnal witchery."

A few girls seem to have lucked out, transforming grave sin into blessed matrimony. A mother wrote: "To my astonishment and disgust, my son Peter insists upon marrying Jane Clarke, the wanton slut who allowed him such detestable liberties that she conceived his child."

Sex wasn't altogether approved of even within the realm of wedlock. Women were taught to consider sex a duty, an indispensable preliminary to procreation. And the whole subject of sex was considered to be, like other necessary but odious bodily functions, in very bad taste.

For a man to perform the sex act outside of matrimony, unless with a prostitute, Indian, or Negro, marked the depth of personal and legal degradation. It was in the heart of Puritan New England that the British legal phrase "Fornication & Unlawful Carnal Knowledge" was abbreviated to the four-letter word known today.

To deal with youthful sexual ardor, our colonists had one solution: marry young.

In the South—at first in the settled areas of Maryland, Virginia, the Carolinas and Georgia, and then in all slave states—our early sexual history, and consequently attitudes toward illegitimacy, followed a somewhat different trend. To begin with, the influential settlers of these states were not subscribers to the Puritan ethic. They were often castoffs of Britain's royal, semi-royal, or landed gentry, and brought with them more free-wheeling attitudes toward sex. Their double standard was complete: a daughter must remain virginally pure until marriage, but a son was under no sexual restraint except lack of opportunity.

The hot-blooded white male, particularly if "landed," always had, according to Thomas Jefferson, ". . . a place in which to insert his member." Female slaves, whether assigned to the house or the field, were required not to resist the demands of their white masters. Most slaves were, of course, black, though a few were indentured women sent from England to endure slavery rather than imprisonment. Many mulattos showed up as generations passed, and the early Southern morality in the sexual treatment of the Negro may very well have some bearing on the illegitimacy quotient among blacks today.

It was not until the mid-nineteenth century in America that the white male involved in getting a girl "in trouble" was encouraged to marry her in order to "legitimize" the child. Until then the unhappy girl was considered unworthy of marriage. In most instances her lot was tragic. If she kept her baby and stayed in the community, she was considered fit only for the most menial employment. Her bastard child was someone with whom "nice" children did not associate, and in fact was usually subject to verbal and even physical abuse. If an unwed mother moved away from her home community, she might pretend to be a widow or work as a seamstress, governess, waitress, or teacher, and "pass" as respectable. "Have baby, will travel," quickly became the watchword for the unwed mother.

Along the ever-moving frontier, illegitimacy was of less account. Couples lived together, sometimes for years, until a preacher happened by to conduct a marriage ceremony. The legitimacy of the children produced during that time was retroactively assured: the minister predated the marriage certificate.

In the rest of the country, however, the growing number of orphanages and nursery homes was more than matched by an increasing number of unwed mothers willing to give up their babies. The burden of caring for the illegitimate child was often too much to bear, no matter how much a mother loved and wanted her child.

"There may be no true substitute for a mother's love," Ada Strom, a matron at the Minneapolis Lutheran Home for Unwed Mothers, commented in 1920, "but I think it is usually better for her to let her child out for adoption than to raise it with the deprivations and stigma both would bear."

By the late 1840s, unwed fathers were encouraged—often at the business end of a shotgun—to marry the girls they'd gotten in the family way. Oddly enough, the "backward" hill people of Kentucky, Tennessee, and West Virginia were the first to regard their pregnant daughters as salvageable souls rather than as irretrievable sinners. German and Scandinavian immigrants just beginning to make their presence felt in America shared this enlightened attitude. Within a few decades, American society as a whole had adapted to the point of accepting the child born within less than nine months of the wedding. "The second child takes nine months," a hill woman remarked laconically. "The first can come out in a week."

Relaxing social attitudes encouraged more liberal premarital sexual conduct among the young. The Reverend Luther Ludlow, a Lutheran pastor in Milwaukee, remarked in 1900 that "of the seventy-five marriages I performed this year, fully thirty-five of the brides were already with child." In rural areas the percentage was higher; a Presbyterian minister whose pastorate embraced a large rural area near Wilmette, Oregon, claimed that "only my intervention saves seventy-five percent of the women for whom I perform the marriage ceremony from producing bastards."

Still, if a pregnant white woman did not marry before her child was born, the stigma of immorality and bastardy was so great that she and her parents would go to any lengths to avoid admitting her pregnancy and the birth of a child out of wedlock.

The ruses were many and varied, and performed at all class levels, from the tenement girl to the Park Avenue heiress. If a husband was not in the offing, the unfortunate young woman was sent—as soon as she began to "show"— for a prolonged stay with relatives or friends in a distant city. There she could wait out the full term of pregnancy and have the baby, which she was then encouraged to turn over to a foundling home. If a girl refused to give up her baby, she almost invariably made her home in the new city, claiming widowhood; as time went on, the increasing frequency of divorce also became a satisfactory explanation for the lack of a husband.

An alternative—one which became more popular as the Salvation Army and various Christian and Jewish charitable organizations began to open more facilities—was to send the girl to an orphanage or foundling home in another part of the country where she could spend her confinement and where, after birth, the child could be put up for adoption.

A Hollywood actress, now in her fifties, recalls the birth of her illegitimate child in the Texas foundling home somewhat immortalized by Greer Garson in the movie *Blossoms in the Dust.*

"I was sixteen, and simply didn't want to marry the boy who'd gotten me pregnant. I had to quit school, and my parents sent me off to Fort Worth, Texas, when I was four months along. About all I did there for five hot months was wait—I wasn't given any sort of instructions on caring for a baby because I'd already signed an agreement to surrender the baby for adoption. They had a rule I didn't understand then, but which makes sense now—we weren't allowed to hold, or even see, our babies. My baby was just sort of spirited away —probably to the big foundling home across town that was run by the Salvation Army. A few days after giving birth I was hustled off as if nothing had happened. In a way nothing had, because there was nothing to show for my labor pains. I had a terrible hollow feeling inside, but that wasn't visible, not like my flat tummy was."

More unusual is the story related by Victoria Lincoln (now living in a Los Angeles rest home) that begins in Terre Haute, Indiana, in 1918.

"I was seventeen when I found out I was with child. My parents were horrified, naturally, and it really was a traumatic situation. I had to quit high school a week before graduation and I would have been valedictorian.

"I couldn't marry the child's father because he'd moved on somewhere, and I didn't really know his last name. It was a one-night stand, but he was irresistibly handsome and obviously persuasive. My parents knew they'd have to send me away and that I would have to give up the child, but my mother decided she wanted to raise another baby. So she sent me to visit my aunt in Indianapolis, and while I was gone she kept stuffing pillows and things over her stomach to make people believe *she* was pregnant. When it came time for me to deliver, she came to Indianapolis. I had the baby and she went back home without all the pillows and raised my son as her own."

One of the side tragedies of illegitimate birth at the time was that a girl had to quit school as soon as she "showed." She could return to school after her mysterious "illness" or "breakdown" was over, but few did, and so they entered an increasingly competitive world without training or skills.

Only in the lower economic strata, or in immigrant families, did the young white girl keep her baby. The best she could hope for, in such an event, was a man who would come along to marry her and adopt her child. Otherwise both were ostracized by the community. No public assistance was provided for the unwed mother or her child, and the financial stress added to her other burdens. Unheralded by birth announcements or festive reception, the bastard began his unpromising life.

IF THOSE PEOPLE CAN DO IT, WHY CAN'T I?

Today, illegitimacy is so much in fashion that it is about to become boring.
In fact, among the Beautiful People it is always that season in which, as
Ogden Nash says,

> Ladies grow loony and gentlemen loonier,
> This year's June is next year's Junior.

A unique opportunity was afforded recently to British author Anthony West
when he was asked to review a book about the long love affair between H. G.
Wells and Dame Rebecca West. A consequence of that affair was the birth of
Anthony West.

The author of the book, Gordon N. Ray, claims that Anthony was born
because one night H. G. Wells "in an angry moment, when he feared that
Rebecca might leave him, intentionally omitted to take precautions."

In his review, Anthony West observed that this would appear to make him
the product of "what I can only describe as a dirty trick." He inquired
plaintively, "How can Gordon possibly know that?"

One way Gordon N. Ray might have known is from Dame Rebecca herself,
now eighty-one, who assisted him in editing his book.

Whatever the merits of the argument, the circumstances are clearly another
sign of how à la mode illegitimacy has become among the rich and famous.

Certainly no one seems to be concerned—dare we say interested?—that
Marlon Brando is not married to the mother of his Tahitian children. Nor that
lovely Catherine Deneuve has had children out of wedlock with both Roger
Vadim and Marcello Mastroianni. Nor that Mastroianni also fathered Faye
Dunaway's illegitimate child. Nor that Liv Ullmann lived with director Ing-
mar Bergman and bore him a child.

The Beautiful People have been breeding out of wedlock so cheerfully and
publicly that it now takes something unusual to waken a glimmer of interest.
A movie star like Mia Farrow can announce that she has conceived a baby by
André Previn (before benefit of marriage) and neither press nor public appears
to take much notice. Geraldine Chaplin can let it be known she is joining the
Unwed Mother's Club, and the yawns come up like thunder.

Those over forty can remember that medieval era when Ingrid Bergman had
Roberto Rossellini's baby (before benefit of marriage) and the resulting furor
made it appear that the end of western civilization was at hand. It must come
as a shock to these old-timers to read about Connie Stevens who was starring
on Broadway in *Star Spangled Girl* when she became pregnant by Eddie
Fisher. Miss Stevens, who was not married, said frankly, "I probably would
have had an abortion, but I was told that I might never have another shot at
a child because I'd had three miscarriages. I wanted that child."

It's all become so commonplace. Little newcomers arrive at the homes of the Beautiful People every day without benefit of church or state's blessings, and certainly with no attempt to conceal the fact. Peggy Lipton, popular star of TV's "Mod Squad" series, didn't bother to deny she had black composer Quincy Jones's baby before they were married. Chad Everett, known for his role as a crusading doctor on a TV series, did deny paternity of a woman's child, then decided to contribute liberally to the child's support. The general response appeared to be, "Why bother to deny it?" Movie stars like Dominique Sanda and political firebrands like Bernadette Devlin openly had their so-called love babies.

Katharine Ross, a mother, still hasn't wed. Elliott Gould only married Jennie Bogart following the birth of their second child—and they divorced not long afterward. Mick Jagger of the Rolling Stones is the proud parent of a five-year-old illegitimate daughter. Sylvester (Sly) Stewart of the rock group Sly and the Family Stone probably set some sort of record for public acknowledgment of paternity. He married the mother of his eight-month-old son at a wedding party in Madison Square Garden to which 23,000 guests were invited.

When rumor spread that Lou Adler, the multi-media mogul, planned to marry the mother of his baby, actress Britt Ekland, in Switzerland, quick denials ensued. It was pointed out rather severely that Mr. Adler was still married to actress Shelley Fabares, although they'd been separated for six years. Miss Fabares is Catholic (and Old School) and they've never divorced. Soon afterward the speculation about marriage ended. Mr. Adler and Miss Ekland broke up.

Omar Sharif, Roger Moore, and Anthony Quinn once made the news head-lines with stories about their illegitimate children. Such stories, unless they involve a lawsuit, no longer rate coverage except in movie magazines.

Occasionally a fresh angle will make an illegitimacy newsworthy. Most newspapers carried the story about Helen Morgan, the twenty-one-year-old beauty who was chosen Miss United Kingdom in 1974. She promptly an-nounced that she was an unwed mother. "I'm not married, but I'm not ashamed. I'm proud of my baby," said the hazel-eyed brunette. Her baby was fifteen months old when Miss Morgan won the title of Miss United Kingdom. She went on to compete for—and win—the Miss World title. It appears that the Miss World contest rules ban married women but not unwed mothers. A disappointed rival claimed the judges had been prejudiced in favor of Miss Morgan *because* she was an unwed mother!

When Desi Arnaz, Jr., then eighteen, became the unwed father of twenty-four-year old actress Patty Duke's baby boy, the chief focus of interest was not on the parents. Newspaper stories featured Desi's glamorous mother, superstar Lucille Ball, who at the age of sixty became the world's best-known illegitimate grandmother! She lost her title a few years later to Elizabeth Taylor, whose son Michael Wilding, Jr., became an illegitimate father.

Newspaper gossip columnists now mention infants conceived in liberty only as parenthetical items. For example, Joyce Haber's syndicated column on

September 1, 1974, offered the following two items:

"I asked one star at the party the name of Donald Sutherland's girl. 'She's Jeanine something,' he replied. 'I can't remember. She had Don's baby.' "

A bit further in the same column Miss Haber, discussing Paul Getty 3rd, grandson of the multibillionaire, asks, "Won't Getty, who's a mere seventeen, soon marry divorcée Martine Zacher-Winkelmann, twenty-four? She's his constant companion, now three months pregnant." (They did marry soon afterward.)

It is hard to find a celebrity unwilling to discuss the subject. Talk to Lainie Kazan, who had a daughter by conductor-arranger Peter Daniels: "We wanted to be together our way. You have to work harder at a relationship when you're stuck with it. I'm not into the sensationalism of it. I'm into the happiness. I have a loving, free, very open child."

Or Barbara Seagull, who says she did not consider marrying David Carradine, "Kung Fu" television star, although she bore his son: "I don't want to get married. Parents should be together because they want to be together, not because of a silly piece of paper." At last report, Mr. Carradine was planning to get married, but not to Miss Seagull. At press time, however, he again changed his mind and wanted to go back to live with Miss Seagull and their child.

A new first in frankness was recorded when Steve Allen, the TV comedian and emcee, revealed in the December 1974 issue of *Ladies' Home Journal* that his mother gave birth to an illegitimate son. The boy, Steve's older brother, was fathered by the scion of a wealthy family and given up for adoption a few years before his mother, Belle Montrose, met and married Steve Allen's father.

"How had I heard about my brother?" he asks. "I'd overhear things late at night in the apartment. Or during a family drinking bout. I'd pieced together things I heard as a kid. What my mother did was highly scandalous at the time. She had a very strong overt guilt about the matter."

Mr. Allen went through his mother's papers after her death and found a photograph of his older brother as a golden-haired young boy. He's written letters to relatives and friends in an attempt to find him. "I know who I am," he says. "I'm anxious to know who he is."

The identity of another "lost" extrajudicial bantling has become one of Hollywood's favorite guessing games. Milton Berle, in his recent autobiography, started the guessers going when he referred to his love affair with a pseudonymous "Linda Smith," one of eight children from Nebraska who married the head of a movie studio. According to Mr. Berle, "Linda" bore him a son, who is today a leading Hollywood TV producer. Suspense is heightened because Mr. Berle's reticence on this point is the only discretion he committed in his book. He cheerfully acknowledges liaisons with everyone from Marilyn Monroe to evangelist Aimee Semple McPherson.

Vanessa Redgrave, mother of an illegitimate child fathered by Italian actor Franco Nero, had no trouble reaching her decision to have the child. "I wanted very much to have Franco's baby," she tells us. Vanessa, one of the most articulate and intelligent movie stars, thinks however that such decisions may have an unfortunate influence on those less able to cope with the problems.

"People can be very nasty about unwed mothers," Vanessa admitted during an interview. "The people who give jobs, and the people who have rooms and won't rent them to unmarried mothers . . ." She pointed out that these were not problems for her because she had money and a nice place to live and no trouble obtaining work, but they can be real problems for those who have to make more difficult adjustments.

What effect, if any, does the "celebrity sanction" of illegitimacy really have on the public? Martha Greene, a Chicago social worker who deals with unwed mothers, says: "I think it's helped ease the guilt feelings single girls have when they get pregnant—particularly among the teen-agers, who tend to be star-struck. It may even be having some effect on conservative older people who used to automatically condemn a girl who got into trouble. These are positive things.

"The negative effect is obvious—it has tended to encourage promiscuity among the very young and to make them careless or even heedless as far as contraception is concerned. They don't stop to think that a movie star's baby will never be on welfare and that she won't have to raise it in a ghetto."

Our interviews with pregnant teen-agers supported Ms. Greene's theory. Some sample comments:

"It can't really be so bad to be having a baby like that when someone really super like Katharine Ross has one."

"Joanna Shimkus had Sidney Poitier's baby—and they're not only not married but they're not even the same color. Having an illegitimate baby didn't hurt them, so why should it wreck my life?"

"Look, I'm not proud of myself, but I don't think I'm any worse than some of those movie people, and nobody's putting them down."

What seems to be consistently overlooked is that the rich and famous unwed mother has one further advantage. Married or not, a man is still around to give her the stability and emotional support she needs—at least for the crucial first years of the baby's life.

"There's no denying that the unwed mother is becoming a romantic symbol in our day," says a doctor who does volunteer work for a Chicago maternity home. "Young girls see these older women as persons to admire—because they are single mothers leading their own lives above convention. So when she makes the same decision, that shows *she's* responsible and entitled to the respect and dignity of a fully grown woman. It may seem an odd contradiction but it's a fact."

REALITY INTRUDES

Few unwed mothers who do not have independent means can cope with the reality of dentist and doctor bills, additional rent, the costs of baby-sitters, the difficulty of obtaining and holding a job, getting credit or insurance, filling out embarrassing forms and questionnaires, buying children's clothing and food, or the severe emotional conflicts brought on by financial deprivation.

"They don't give a dime's worth of thought to what's going to happen to the child," observes a therapist who works in a hospital that's connected with a maternity home. "A bastard child definitely has the cards stacked against it. The kid starts out right away with only a single female parent and no man to act as a guide or a model for future relationships. Sure, that happens in other cases—divorce, widowhood, single parent adoption—but that doesn't change the fact that most young children need a surrogate father. They are going to be badly influenced by the mother's feelings of inadequacy and depression, which are inevitable once she discovers what a stupid decision she made. I've seen kids whose whole personalities are warped by the fact that they were told they were bastards.

"Then there's the other pressures. Usually the mother ends up pretending she's divorced or widowed just so she and her kid won't be looked down on by the neighbors. But in most cases the truth leaks out, and there's nobody crueler than other children. They're the *first* to start calling names. The poor mother and her child are going to spend years trying to deal with the intolerance of other people, and before they're through they could write a whole book on discrimination."

Most social workers agree that a woman would be better off having an abortion or giving up a baby for adoption than going the route of out-of-wedlock motherhood. And most psychologists believe that the woman who becomes pregnant out of wedlock and decides to keep the baby is trying to solve some emotional need of her own at the expense of the child.

"There's simply no reason for her to get pregnant in the first place," a Miami Beach analyst told us. "Forty years ago, maybe. Women were more ignorant then, more likely to get tricked by casual lust. But today, with contraceptives so readily available, including the Pill, the reason for an unwanted pregnancy can't be that simple. It usually represents a very complicated personality problem. Maybe she knows she isn't having a really loving, sharing or meaningful relationship with the man, so she decides to use him as a sperm bank. Maybe she wants a baby as a replacement for him, because she knows the relationship won't last. More and more I come across women who don't even tell the man about it. You usually find out she's pretty hostile to him—and this is one way of expressing her hostility. She punishes him by not even letting him find out he was potent enough to have a child. It all gets pretty woolly, but one thing I can tell you. A woman, any woman, who has a child outside of marriage today and then decides to raise it herself is one of the walking wounded, emotionally speaking."

PERSONAL STORY

Florence L. is thirty-four years old and the mother of a three-year-old boy. She works as an executive secretary for a labor union, although she once was a magazine editor and earned more money than she makes now. On a July Fourth weekend we went to her home, a small rented duplex in Thousand Oaks, California. She pays $198 a month rent for one bedroom and den (now used as a baby room) which is scantily furnished with the things she had in her previous smaller "bachelor girl" apartment.

"Holidays are something I used to look forward to," she told us. We were interviewing her in the living room while her son Donald was asleep in the den. "Not anymore. During the week Donald is looked after by a neighbor, a woman who takes in about six kids by day to help her husband make ends meet. Donald's there from eight to six, five days a week. I get off work around five thirty and by the time I pick him up, it's usually just before six. Then it's home, do the morning dishes, make dinner, and put him to bed. It's nine o'clock by the time I sit down to television and I'm usually too tired to care what I'm looking at.

"That's my usual routine, but holidays are the worst. Three whole days in which Donald and I have nobody but ourselves for company. And he isn't good company for a woman my age. I don't really enjoy going to the park or the zoo or the aquarium, especially when I've been there a dozen times. And the conversation is limited to what he can understand. I really expect one day I'm going to be out on a date with a man, and we'll be walking along the street and I'll grab his arm when a fire engine goes by and say, 'Look at the pretty choo-choo!'

"I knew from the first his father couldn't ever marry me. He was married, a very successful executive in a publishing company. In fact, he was my boss. But I didn't want to go through my whole life without knowing what it was like to have a baby. I couldn't face that. I sat myself down for a good talk, and finally decided to go ahead and have the baby.

"Of course, I had to quit my job. The father offered to help out with money, but I didn't feel that was right. Then everything started to go wrong. My life had changed radically, but I hadn't changed inside.

"I'm sure Donald would be happier if there were a father around the house. Why not? It's a better existence. I do what I can to make it up to him, and when he's old enough for school, he'll have playmates. But it just isn't the same. And I don't want to start living with a whole succession of men that he'll have to start calling 'Uncle.' That's just sucking him into my troubles, having him grow up with contempt for me.

"I look back, and I know it was a risky decision. I didn't know all the risks, but I'm not sure whether I'd decide differently or not if I had it to do again. I've found out it's tough to challenge the way everybody else lives, and do it on your own.

"I don't have any friends. Not one close woman friend. My closest friend got married to a man who doesn't approve of me or what I did, so that's that. Other women see me as a kind of threat to their marriages. Either because I'm going to steal their man or give him the wrong ideas about whether it's so important to be married.

"I wish the day would come when we would accept single mothers the way I hear they do in some Scandinavian countries. I'd like to write words like illegitimate and bastard and out-of-wedlock and all the rest right out of the language. Why shouldn't having a child be a possible choice for an unmarried woman? *Why shouldn't it?*"

ILLEGITIMACY: THE HIGH COST OF LOVING

15

Until recently in most maternity homes the telephone was answered only with the telephone number or the address. That was so accidental callers would not be enlightened as to the true nature of the place they were calling. Maternity homes were not even listed in the telephone book. The very name "maternity home" conjured up images of secrecy and shame, a place for wayward girls to reflect on their sin and to bring forth in guilt and humiliation their "tainted" child.

But in the past few years the changing attitudes of society have caused changes in the way maternity homes are run.

Jackie Pattison, maternity social worker at St. Vincent's Home in New Orleans, says, "What has happened has been a transformation. Before, homes had tunnel vision. Now, we are becoming open to all alternatives. The number of girls who hush-hush their pregnancies has dropped so drastically that we sometimes wonder about the girl who wants to keep it a secret. We're thinking of changing our name to St. Vincent's Residential Treatment Center for Pregnant Women."

Another indication of the change taking place is how many maternity homes are going out of business. In New Orleans alone, the Protestant and Methodist maternity homes have closed their doors. Of three remaining, only St. Vincent's is filled and has a waiting list. The Volunteers of America home is averaging less than half its capacity of thirty-five women, and Sellers Baptist Home is doing only slightly better, with twenty to twenty-three in residence and a capacity of thirty-five.

The well-known Dana House in New York was forced to close, and the Florence Crittenden Association of America, the largest chain (148) of maternity homes for unwed mothers, has shut down eighteen homes. The House of Mercy in Washington, D.C., which operated at full capacity as recently as 1970, is down to half its occupancy rate. Kansas City, Missouri, which had a total of eight maternity homes, now has only three, and the number will probably be smaller by the time you read this.

"It isn't hard to figure out why," says the director of a Florence Crittenden home. "Most homes get their operating funds from the United Way. When we operate at capacity, it costs about two hundred to two hundred fifty dollars a month to keep a girl here. The difference between what we get from United Way and the real cost is made up either by the girls or their parents or other social agencies. We're suffering from a shortage of funds because we're suffering from a shortage of clients."

Some homes are changing their policy—a few Crittenden establishments, for example, have initiated programs for nonpregnant delinquent teen-age girls—or are shedding the former aura of confidentiality and aggressively seeking out new clients.

Other homes have tried promoting new business in various ways. St. Anthony's home in Kansas City distributes brochures to ministers, priests, and social workers, while the House of Mercy offers services such as helping its "graduates" to find jobs and apartments and offering day care for the children ranging from three months to two and one half years. Some maternity homes offer vocational work programs and classes for unwed mothers, and a few provide pediatric services.

Across the nation other maternity homes are being converted into refuges for runaways, alcoholic females, and single parents. A few have been made into day-care centers. Everywhere, those that remain maternity homes are opting for increased "visibility."

"We no longer strive to preserve the anonymity of the girls; we try to publicize our other services," says the resident manager of a midwestern home. "We've even opened a gift shop in town that sells things made by our girls. They get fifty percent of every dollar and it's a moneymaking project."

MORE THAN ROOM AND MEALS

Betsy T. was sixteen years old when she entered a Salvation Army Booth Memorial Hospital. She was four months pregnant at the time. "I had all the wrong ideas about what a maternity home would be like," she told us. "I guess

I thought of it as just a place where bad girls went to have their babies—a sort of reform school. But I met a lot of really nice girls who were there just because the guy has walked out on them and they had no family to turn to.

"We all got good care, a nice room and board and group counseling and even individual advice when we needed it. The girls got together and we talked about our problems and worries and how come we had messed up our lives. That was the best thing of all, just being able to talk to girls who were in the same fix I was.

"I'd like to tell other young girls not to worry about going into a maternity home. They'll give you a lot more than room and meals. It's the other help that really counts. Every unwed mother needs somebody who cares about her —even the ones who say they don't."

Most professionals people in the field agree with Betsy T.'s evaluation. "We're convinced that if we can reach the unmarried mother as soon as possible—during her first pregnancy—we can reduce the chances of it happening again," says a Detroit social worker. "We have programs that are designed to cope with specific medical and social problems. We even have discussion groups that include other members of the girl's family. What we've found most girls to be suffering from is a poor image of themselves and a lack of motivation. Apathy's also a problem—the 'what's the difference whether I do or not?' attitude. The majority are definitely not promiscuous. They don't do it for the sex alone. Many have been involved with one guy for a long time and simply never used a contraceptive. That's usually because they have an unconscious desire to be pregnant—to tie the fellow more closely to them or to test the sincerity of his feeling. There are so many underlying causes that you can't deal with just the symptom."

Another social worker in Chicago told us, "The average teen-age girl who finds herself pregnant comes from a broken home, a 'cold' home, or a home where both parents work and consequently give little time to their children. She usually isn't the most attractive girl in her class, nor the brightest, and she tries to win popularity by 'putting out.' Her availability as a sexual partner becomes her real identity.

"She usually has no recourse to the Pill or any other effective birth control method, so she relies on the boy to take contraceptive measures or trusts to luck. Then she finds out after the first or tenth or fiftieth sexual encounter that luck isn't enough."

The director of a St. Louis maternity home believes, "The only solution to the problem is education. I really don't understand why there's such parental opposition to sex education in schools. Most teen-age pregnancies simply wouldn't occur if girls and boys knew what the score was. It's impossible to eliminate sexual activity—in a society where students start 'going steady' in grammar school and where parents encourage socials and dances for ten-year-olds. But we *can* prevent conception. These girls don't really want to have a child out of wedlock."

Many homes report an increasing number of girls who elect to keep their babies. At St. Anne's Hospital and Home for Unwed Mothers in Los Angeles, an overall 60 percent of the girls do not surrender their infants for adoption. Adoption fees pay part of a maternity home's operating cost, and some homes don't like to accept girls who don't intend to give up their babies for adoption. "There's a national craze among adolescent mothers to try to raise their babies by themselves," says the director of a Children's Bureau which offers counseling to unwed mothers. "In most such cases, the mother finds it too hard to do and gives up the child for adoption after it is two or three years old and not only harder to place, but psychologically damaged by the rejection."

FOR MOTHERS AND BABIES

Gateway House in Pomona, California, is a rather unique home, for it accepts only teen-agers who are already mothers.

Gateway is a white clapboard house on an older residential street, divided into apartments. At the time of our visit, there were six young women living there with their children. The young women, averaging seventeen years of age, were receiving the standard $212 welfare allotment for a mother and one child. Out of that sum, $95 is spent for Gateway's rent, and approximately $62 a month purchases $92 worth of food stamps. The remaining $55 a month must purchase all other essentials. One of the lessons that Gateway's mothers must learn quickly is "money management."

Gateway has a paid resident manager, but everyone else does volunteer work. That includes professional nurses, teachers, psychologists, and social workers. Several community agencies make their workers available.

"Years ago, agency people didn't realize the strong feelings girls have about wanting to keep their babies," says Sallie Foster, a Children's Services social worker who is one of the founders of Gateway. "At that time, workers insisted on the unacceptable solution of relinquishing the child. The result was an almost inevitable second pregnancy. We have proven that the more service and information given during a first pregnancy when a girl keeps her baby, the less likely it will be that she will get pregnant again."

Some believe maternity homes are headed for eventual extinction, but Rochelle Trigg, who directs St. Anthony's residential services, disagrees. "There is a new morality," she concedes, "but when the pendulum swings, it can swing too far. There will always be a need for the old-fashioned maternity home which protects the confidentiality of its girls."

And John Rush, associate director of the Kansas City Regional Health and Welfare Council, says, "Abortion is still an emotion-laden issue for some girls, and others who want an abortion can't afford one. We will always need some residential beds. The question is—how many?"

THE SOCIAL COST

Nineteen seventy-five will add over $1 billion to the taxpayer's already astronomical burden of providing shelter and hospital services, visiting nurse and other medical help to unwed mothers.

According to studies provided by the National Council on Illegitimacy, 80 percent of these babies are going to live in substandard housing and receive substandard education.

Also:

- 70 percent of these babies will be born to women of subnormal intelligence.
- Venereal disease, syphilis in particular, will show up in almost three times as many unmarried pregnant women as married women.
- The death rate through illegal abortion will be eight times as high among unmarried women.
- Twice as many unmarried women will have premature births as women in wedlock.
- Twice as many infants born to unwed mothers will die within the first year of life, compared to infant deaths among married mothers.

The social cost is obviously tremendous. What can be done about it?

Birth control would be the best answer. But it isn't clear exactly how to accomplish that. And many wonder why the legalization of abortion hasn't been more effective. Shouldn't it be apparent to the mother-to-be that she would be better off if the child was not born?

National Council of Illegitimacy researchers and social workers in all major cities recognize and deplore the lack of progress made so far in applying the remedy of abortion to the problem of illegitimacy. Less than 10 percent of prospective mothers who are receiving, or will receive, help from Aid to Dependent Children will submit to abortion.

Members of the National Council of Illegitimacy, social workers, and psychiatrists seem to agree on the reasons.

- Abortion is a sophisticated procedure, and fully 80 percent of unmarried pregnant women are extremely unsophisticated.
- Adequate information about abortion procedures only just now being made available through clinics and birth control centers and via case workers.
- Among lower-income groups a dislike and distrust of surgery prevails. Abortion is often confused with sterilization.
- Having an illegitimate baby no longer results in condemnation by the mother's peer group. Sandra Haggerty, the syndicated newspaper columnist, reports this reaction from a pregnant girl in an Oakland, California, high school: "It's not really that big a deal. You can go to class and everything. Everyone knows. Some of the goody-goody teachers act like their children

were immaculate conceptions, but the kids couldn't care less. Oh, they tease you, but it's not a putdown."

Nancy Myrhe, who has taught in Wisconsin high schools for three decades, says, "When I started teaching we could expect to have thirty percent of our girls quit school because they were pregnant. Today the pregnancy rate is the same but less than ten percent of the girls fail to get their diploma." In Compton High School, Los Angeles, twenty pregnant girls were in the 1974 fall term—all taking a class in infant care. One fifteen-year-old student will have a three-year-old baby when she receives her diploma.

· At least sixty percent of illegitimacies that will receive ADC (Aid to Dependent Children) were "repeaters"—i.e., women producing a second, third, or even fourth child destined for welfare support. Many of these women refuse abortion because it would interfere with their "livelihood."

"You wouldn't dare quote me," one cynical Chicago social worker remarked, "but I'm afraid the ADC program has become a racket."

ADC is a sociopolitical football that nobody wants to catch. Politicians who depend on minority votes won't speak out for abortion or against welfare; black leaders, whether speaking politically or socially, are too quick to come up with the word "genocide." Yet privately—*not* for quotation— all readily admit that welfare programs have gotten completely out of hand, and that restrictions should be placed on ADC programs, particularly on the repeaters.

REPEATERS

The "repeater" is a woman who has more than one child out of wedlock, either purposefully or because of extreme carelessness. Ninety-five percent of multiple illegitimate births occur among women who live at or near the poverty level, and the mother and children are on welfare.

That means, to put it bluntly, that somewhere along the line the American taxpayer is being screwed.

No one is more outraged by this than social workers who deal at first hand with the problem.

We offer a sampling of representative opinion.

From South Boston: "I am not against aid to illegitimate children per se. You can't let kids starve. But I don't think we should let unwed mothers make a career out of having illegitimate children either. A mistake can be made once, even twice—she may be a rape victim, or not know about birth control methods, or be overtaken by a so-called romantic impulse. But to pay steadily increasing sums to a woman who has three, four, or five illegitimate children is ridiculous."

From inner-city Detroit: "I visit mothers with dependent children who tear your heart out because they'd much rather be working, supporting themselves and their children than taking welfare payments. But they can't work because there are no day-care facilities to take care of their children while they work. Then I visit others who run around hiding the empty beer bottles and eliminating the evidence of a cohabited bed and shooing the guy out the back door. That kind doesn't give a damn for the children as long as the money keeps coming in."

From Chicago's Near North Side: "If I feel any resentment at all, it's against the repeaters. So many of them are cold, mercenary women who don't love their children, don't attempt to care for them properly, and have one after another to get their welfare checks raised."

Even more alarming is the fact, noted in a report by the California Social Welfare Board, that "a definite relationship exists between illegitimacy and the problems of abuse, abandonment, and neglect of children. It appears that in situations of multiple illegitimacy, these factors increase with each successive illegitimate child."

A supervisor in the Denver, Colorado, Department of Welfare adds: "No one realizes just how incompetent these women are. They live in unsanitary, dangerous conditions and expect nothing from their landlords. They cannot understand contracts and sign them without realizing the consequences. They have no money for transportation so they don't get to stores where they could buy bargains. And they wouldn't know how to comparison shop anyway. When a child is sick, the mother must either take all her children with her to the clinic, or leave them home alone, or not go at all. Many of them can't read or write, so they can't read the clinic doctor's instructions but they're too ashamed to admit it. They have no friends. Their lives are lived in a complete human vacuum."

THE "OTHER" PARENT

"The father of the baby has been neglected," says Katherine Daly, executive director of the Crittenden Association in Chicago. "There has been a punitive attitude toward the man, but he may be just as troubled as the girl. Sometimes, in fact, he is the one who wants to get married."

No doubt the problems of the unwed mother are a good deal more visible than those of the unwed father. Studies of unwed mothers outnumber those of unwed fathers by about 30 to 1.

"It isn't surprising," says a sociologist who has written on the subject. "After all, the unmarried father can't become a problem to be studied unless he's known. Too often he isn't. By staying unknown he doesn't get called to account, doesn't have to shell out money for child support. As for the girl, she frequently helps him stay unknown, either because she wants to 'protect' him from her parents or social workers who might try to 'make him do the right thing,' or because she doesn't want to be forced to marry him—or because she simply doesn't know for sure who the father really is."

An interesting variation on this occurred in late 1974 in Oakland, California, when Leslie Ann Bacon, twenty-two, the antiwar activist who was accused in the bombings of a New York bank and the U.S. Capitol, tried to qualify her baby daughter for aid under county welfare regulations. The law required her to name either the father or the possible fathers.

Miss Bacon gave the names of three men, but refused to name Stephen Schulberg, with whom the county alleged she was living in a Berkeley apartment. Under the law, if Miss Bacon named a man living with her, the county could then demand that he support the child.

That, of course, may not seem an unreasonable requirement to the county residents who otherwise have to chip in for the living expenses of Miss Bacon's infant.

Apparently, imminent fatherhood is a staggering emotional experience to some young men. In their book, *Teenage Pregnancy,* J.P. Semmers and W.H. Lammers describe the suicide attempts of boyfriends of pregnant teen-age girls. They attribute this either to neurotic atonement for "guilt," a desperate unwillingness to be married, or to a symbolic gesture of revenge against some individual.

The unwed father probably did not become a parent because of a casual or one-time sexual encounter.

John J., twenty-two, is a clerk in an I. Miller shoe store in New York City. He had been going with his girlfriend, whom we will call Liza T., for almost three years.

"We met at a barbecue in Jones Beach. Everyone had a little too much to drink, and we ended up under blankets on the beach. No protection, no anything. And nothing happened. I really liked Liza, and I guess she liked me because we began seeing each other regularly, once, twice a week. I didn't see anybody else, and she didn't either. We made plenty sure nothing happened. Then, one night, she got a last-minute offer to be a baby-sitter for a cousin who was married and had two kids. We always had trouble finding a good place —I've got parents and a couple of brothers and sisters at home, and her parents are always on the lookout. So this was a natural. Because it was last minute, she didn't have a chance to bring along her diaphragm. We risked it, and this time it happened she got caught.

"Liza would like to get married, but no dice. I can't see myself getting trapped at my age, with a lousy job, a kid, and no future. I'm willing to pay for an abortion—I told her that—but she's got her mind made up. She wants the baby. If she wants it, she can have it. That's *her* bag."

On the other hand, Paul H. would like to get married and his girlfriend doesn't want to. "She says having a baby is the most important thing that can happen to a woman, and that's why she's going ahead. But she wants the baby to have the right kind of father, too, and I'm not it. Can you beat it? My own kid, and she tells me I'm not the right kind of father! I'm still hoping to change her mind."

The unwed father is not usually a boy of a higher social class who takes advantage of a poorer or less educated girl. Typically he is of the same social class as the mother, has had the same education, and is of the same general age. The pregnancy usually results from a "dating situation" of some length and not from anything that could properly be called a seduction, or from taking advantage of a girl whose ability to resist is limited by an inferior education, income, or intelligence.

Mrs. Beatrice Liebenberg, in a paper presented in 1967 to the American Orthopsychiatric Association, told of interviewing sixty-four unwed couples undergoing a first pregnancy. The majority of her subjects were under twenty-six years old.

Mrs. Liebenberg affirms that most young fathers are "scared" at the prospect of becoming a father, worried about their readiness to take on the responsibility, and anxious about whether they can afford the costs of raising a baby. She found this response so common among her interview group that she classified it as "normal." In addition to this, Mrs. Liebenberg found a recurring psychological pattern: during the girl's pregnancy, the young father also is in need of emotional support and consolation because he is about to abandon his previous roles as "son" and "lover" and assume a new graver responsibility as "father." His reaction is usually resentment and anger, and a flight from the new role in which he has unwillingly been cast.

We found sufficient evidence that this attitude exists, even though the psychological reasons for it may be deeply repressed.

A sampling of quotes from our interviews will prove the point:

"She was old enough to know what she was doing. I don't see where it's my fault. To tell you the truth, I think she set me up for it. Everybody has to look out for themselves. That's how I feel about it."

"I saw what happened to my own father. Five kids before he was thirty. The poor bastard never had a chance! It isn't going to happen to me. Easier to live something like this down than wreck your life over it."

"It was all just a mistake, a damned silly mistake, but we both made it. She isn't ready to be a mother, and God knows I'm not ready to be a father. I'm a junior in college. I intend to graduate. The way things are, there isn't any future for anyone without a college diploma. How happy will I be able to make her if I'm miserable?"

"Even if I wanted a kid, which I don't, I couldn't afford one. I can't afford to look after myself. I give ten bucks a week to my family. Dad and Mom had too many kids, and now they're old and sick and broke. If I don't watch my step, I could end up just like them."

"She hasn't acted like I'm the father. In fact, she's paid less attention to me since she got pregnant than before. That'd be a fine way to start out a marriage, wouldn't it?"

"I asked my folks about it, and they set me straight. It's her doing, not mine. Women arrange these things. Nobody's going to make a sucker out of me."

Before passing judgment on these apparently callous remarks, bear in mind that they are in most cases merely surface reflections of a deep psychic disturbance.

"Young unmarried fathers go through the same sort of trauma as young unmarried women," a psychologist says. "The only difference is that their emotions are more deeply repressed. Actually, they envy women and the whole ritual of childbirth and motherhood, the passive and protected status women have, and the mother's total physical identification with the baby-to-come. In some primitive societies men go through a 'male childbirth,' complete with psychosomatic complaints, odd cravings, and weight gain from overeating. Something of the sort happens to all fathers, but especially to those who feel guilt because they have caused all this without marrying the mother.

"There is also a hidden hostility to the fetus, which shows itself as anxiety that something bad will happen to it—the classic 'hope masked as concern.' He's also likely to resent the way the girl is neglecting him, and even the fact that she has established a relationship with a doctor that practically or entirely excludes him. He'd like to compete with her for the affections of 'his' child. In some cases, after childbirth, when he pushes the girl to take an outside job, he is acting out an unconscious desire to separate mother and child and provide himself with a useful role in the whole procedure."

Much of this cannot be changed. It is a biological truth that an unwed father cannot become pregnant, and needs no prenatal care. Whether he drinks, smokes, or eats the wrong foods is a matter of total indifference to the developing fetus. But that does not in any way diminish his genuine, all-too-real psychological problems.

Among blacks and minority groups, unwed fathers have additional economic and social problems to contend with, and they inevitably interact with the parental role. If a young man admits fatherhood, he might be solicited for child support. He and his family are probably poor, so how can he pay? If he marries the girl, his situation is worsened by being compelled to support a family.

Most young men in minority groups are keenly aware that their only hope of escape from poverty is through education or job training. There are fewer and fewer jobs for unskilled labor. A young man who cannot achieve a reasonably satisfactory living standard for himself is unwilling to take on the further responsibilities of a father. To become a father and support a family may exclude him from a practical opportunity to get further training and education.

Black and other minority fathers often feel semi-castrated. The woman becomes responsible for the well-being of her children, and the male role is usurped. The only useful function left for the man, *the assumption of responsi-*

bility, is forbidden to him. No wonder his position becomes ambiguous and he chooses anonymity and rejection, taking out his inner conflicts on the woman. "She knew what she was doing." "All she had to say was no, but that word isn't in her dictionary." "I ain't stupid enough to think it's mine. It could be anybody's."

A FATHER'S RIGHTS

We won't dwell any longer on the psychological aspects of unwed fatherhood, for there are other problems that fall more clearly within the scope of this book. There is the question of legal status, for example.

Julian Brantley, California executive director of the Children's Home Society, says: "Under the present law there is no way a father can assert his rights if he has not legitimated the child."

Legitimating does not necessarily mean marriage, but it does mean acknowledgment of paternity. Many groups favor legislation in order to require an unwed father to register before or soon after the birth of the child if he is interested in the child's future. This would take place at a state registry office.

Then, if the mother decided to give up the child for adoption and the father wished to take custody, a court hearing would be held. If he was found to be a fit parent, the child would be turned over to him.

At present an unwed father's rights to his child trace back to a United States Supreme Court decision known as Stanley vs. Illinois. In that case, a man had fathered five children by a common-law wife who had steadfastly refused to marry him. When she died unexpectedly, Illinois welfare officials took the children away without a hearing. The Supreme Court ordered a lower court to give Stanley a hearing on his own fitness, and eventually custody of the children was awarded to him.

Stanley's rights would never have been questioned under the laws of many other states. In California, for example, the children would have been considered his legitimate offspring because he lived with the mother. In California a father may also legitimate a child by taking it into his family—even in the absence of a mother—and by publicly acknowledging it.

Most problems with unwed fathers arise when the question of adoption has to be decided. Mrs. Geri Humphrey, Los Angeles district director of the Children's Home Society, says that although most unwed fathers express no interest in the future of their illegitimate children, many also refuse to sign relinquishment papers. This makes a long and expensive court procedure necessary.

She cites one instance in which a man living in a midwestern state managed to hold up his baby's adoption for months because he wanted to force the mother to keep the child and raise it. In another instance, a sixteen-year-old high school student tried to force his girlfriend, also sixteen, to keep their baby. If she did not, he warned that he would block any adoption until she agreed to let his parents raise the child.

Under the procedure followed by most adoptive agencies, a missing natural father has to be tracked down at his last known address. Neighbors are questioned, and the records of the Registrar of Voters and the Motor Vehicle Department are checked. If he was a serviceman, records of all the armed services must be searched. If there is still no trace of him, legal advertisements must be placed.

"This whole process takes months," says Sister Bertille Prus, director of the Holy Family Agency, who said that the agency had ten-month-old and year-old babies still in foster care because their natural fathers had not been located. "It is not in the best interest of the child. Those first weeks are vital, and moving from one place to another is not good for emotional development. It can very definitely cause a basic insecurity."

"What's really happening is that mothers are being forced to keep illegitimate babies against their will," says the head of a Chicago adoption agency.

Even if the identity of the unwed father is known and he is located, it is very often difficult to persuade him to relinquish the child.

"We have always tried to involve young fathers in counseling," Mrs. Geri Humphrey says. "We are trying to help them but they run a hundred miles an hour in the other direction. They don't realize how they are tying up the baby. . . . Where the known father is interested in the future of the child, there is no way we would place the baby without his consent."

Not everyone agrees that unwed fathers are entitled to so much consideration. David Keene Leavitt, an attorney for adoptive parents in a pending court case, put it strongly: "A man can have seven minutes of pleasure with a girl, and then come back later and ruin her life and that of the child. This is the rankest kind of injustice. There are legitimate legal differences between boys and girls, and one of them is in the area of having babies. If there is no affection and cooperation between the two, someone has got to have the rights and it has got to be her."

Suppose the father wants the baby, and the mother doesn't? Leavitt believes that if the mother thinks adoption is the best solution, she should have the right to make that decision.

"The girl says, 'If I wouldn't marry him myself, how can I marry my baby to him?' It's not that the mother wants to discard the baby, but that she wants to make a decision for the baby she can live with. In most cases, it is a permanent home through adoption. . . . The baby deserves a secure, happy family. The court should consider the child's interest."

The consensus, however, favors some guarantee of rights for an unwed father. Several states have pending bills that would allow a father to block the adoption of his child—at least until a court hearing on his own fitness as a parent can be held. None of these bills affects a woman who wants to keep her child born out of wedlock.

"We need some legislation of this kind," says a child welfare official, "simply to end the chaos and confusion now running rampant in this field. All the trouble started when unwed fathers began getting court decisions saying they had rights, in some cases, to the custody of their illegitimate child. Before that, only the mother's consent was necessary."

An adoption agency official concurs: "Right now, some judges are insisting we have to get a father's consent to adoption, although it isn't required by law. We haven't been able to find some of the fathers. And that's causing a delay of up to a year in placing an infant in a new home."

IS THERE AN ANSWER?

Illegitimacy is not a sin to be stamped out, but a problem to be solved. We have only partly transcended the smug moral stance that condemns the unwed mother as a fallen woman and her child as a bastard. The solutions must be looked for on a wider social level.

Several methods of approach to the problem are being discussed. One is to make an unwed father assume his share of the responsibility. The difficulty is that when the woman has several children, there is usually more than one father, and rarely does a stable protective relationship exist between the father and the mother.

However, where fathers do ask for visitation rights, or the right to prevent an abortion of an expected child, or a voice in deciding its religious upbringing or education, they should be asked to contribute to the child's support.

Another suggestion is to provide sufficient day-care centers and baby-sitting co-op arrangements so the mothers can go to work, or so they can receive vocational training that will equip them to hold jobs. Until adequate facilities are provided, there is no real answer to the unwed mother's plaintive question, "How can I work when there's nobody to take care of my kids?"

A suggestion that seems to have merit is to insure wide distribution of birth-control information and equipment, ranging from the Pill to intrauterine devices, to any woman who produces a child being supported by an ADC agency. Despite the opposition of the Catholic Church and various minority organizations, this program is now meeting with a fair degree of success. Programs are underway in Chicago, New York, Atlanta, and Miami.

Among the less humane suggestions under consideration are:

· Voluntary or involuntary sterilization of females proven to be mentally subnormal, abnormal or deficient, and who produce more than one child who must receive any form of ADC care.

Opposition to this from civil rights groups, who contend it is a clear violation of constitutional rights, and from the Catholic Church on religious grounds makes the acceptance of such an admittedly harsh procedure unlikely. There is also considerable opposition from minority groups, who claim the idea is backed by a white majority bent upon racial genocide.

· Withdrawal of aid from a dependent mother who has a third child produced at ADC expense. This measure would not deny aid to the first two children supported by an ADC agency, but would deny aid to any beyond that number. It met with vociferous opposition when proposed and has not progressed far beyond the mere proposal.

Illegitimacy is definitely not a racial problem. During the past fifteen years the white illegitimacy rate has sharply increased, while the illegitimacy rate among blacks has shown a small decline. It is hardly a coincidence that this happened at a time when blacks were making proportionately great economic strides. The illegitimacy rate among blacks remains higher than among whites, but as the above trend demonstrates, the root cause is not color but poverty. As income rises, illegitimacy declines.

ALL CHILDREN ARE *NOT* BORN EQUAL

16

The common wisdom of psychologists and doctors says that what happens during the first two years of an infant's life will have a profound effect on the quality of his intelligence for years to come.

However, recent scientific evidence indicates that this may be wrong. For example: infants born to middle-class mothers in eastern Holland are customarily placed in an isolated room with no toys and little contact with adults for the most of the first year. This is thought to promote healthy development. In fact, it does quite the reverse. Yet, tests show that at five years of age, these children have overcome their initial handicap and are intellectually normal. This, and other similar studies, establishes that lack of stimulation as an infant is not the major cause of the difference in later school achievement between poor and economically privileged children.

A dozen years ago welfare officials asked Mrs. Marianne Thach if she would care for an unwanted two-year-old in her home until a place could be found for him in a mental institution. He had been classified as mentally retarded.

"I noticed that he seemed pretty adept at looking after himself and he made his needs known to me even though he never uttered a sound," Mrs. Thach said.

She took the child to an ear specialist who diagnosed deafness and operated to partially restore hearing.

"The operation changed his life," Mrs. Thach says. "By the age of four he could read, and when he was six I taught him simple arithmetic."

Authorities still insisted that he should go to a school for the mentally retarded. Mrs. Thach, who by then had adopted him, refused. For six more years she battled with school authorities. Finally, in 1973, at the age of thirteen, her son was admitted to a local school. He's already caught up with the other children and is a B+ student.

"It's hard to believe that anyone ever labeled this boy as mentally retarded," says Ralph McInnes, his science teacher at the Livermore, California, junior high school. "He's a credit to himself and an example to others."

Jerome Kagan, a professor in the Department of Psychology and Social Relations at Harvard University, says, "We must distinguish between natural mental abilities that all children develop and culturally arbitrary skills whose acquisition depends on opportunity and motivation. Very few children will know how to compute a square root or parse a sentence into its grammatical components unless they are taught, even if they have the basic intellectual ability."

Equally, no child will learn the meaning of dollar devaluation, the Declaration of Independence, or the distance from Minneapolis to San Francisco without having been exposed to that information.

Yet, says Kagan, intelligence tests used in the United States to classify children as intellectually retarded assess both natural skills and this kind of acquired knowledge. The tests may require a child to remember a string of numbers, but will also ask him to define the meaning of unfamiliar words. The first is a "natural" skill and the second an "acquired" one. It is obviously ridiculous to assume that a child who does not know certain arbitrary facts, such as words, is less capable than a child who by reason of circumstance has already learned them.

As a consequence of such unreliable and biased evaluations, children are classified as "absolutely" retarded when they are only "relatively" retarded in terms of the level of knowledge so far obtained. The greatest difference between the IQ scores of privileged and those of poor children continues to occur on exactly that portion of the test one would expect: the vocabulary test.

Even the term "relatively" retarded has to be put into context.

"Consider a Mexican-American nine-year-old from Los Angeles," Professor Kagan says, "whose score on the vocabulary test is eleven. If we compare him with a white middle-class Los Angeles child with a score of fourteen he is, by definition, retarded. But if we compare him with a rural Indian child in Arizona with a score of seven, the Mexican-American is advanced."

Will Rogers put it more succinctly: "We are all ignorant, but on different subjects."

Poor children seem to be one to three years behind privileged children in the emergence of those mental abilities necessary to survive and prosper in our industrialized world. The danger is in our assumption that to be behind is equivalent to being qualitatively inferior. The usual standard sets seven years of age as the point at which children must be classified as competent or incompetent. This confuses the difference in rate of progress between poor and privileged children with a difference in their basic intelligence. This is precisely as logical as classifying girls as more or less fertile depending on how early they have their first menstrual period.

The implications for our programs of health care and education are far-reaching. We may be condemning children of the poor not only to shorter lives through inadequate health care, but condemning them unnecessarily to a "twilight life" of diminished intellectual capacity.

A recent television documentary on ABC called "Children: A Case of Neglect" offered evidence to support a depressing statistic: the average child of poor parents born in the United States has much less chance of surviving than children of similar parents born in Japan, Sweden, and eight other countries. The verdict of guilt came down hard on the Nixon administration for deliberately not enforcing laws passed by Congress to help children.

AN INTENSIVE SURVEY

Some help is now on the way. Not specifically directed to children of the poor, it deals with the 300,000 newborn babies a year who emerge from the womb mentally or physically retarded.

During the next five years over $10 million will be spent on the branch of medical science known as teratology. (If you draw a blank on the word teratology, don't worry. The word was coined only a decade ago and refers to the study of birth defects.) As a result of research now underway, some doctors predict that the number of birth defects will drop substantially.

A chief reason for their confidence is the increasing availability of the electronic fetal monitor. This impressive device was first made available for general use in 1969. It is a large oblong box with two extending wires, both of which are inserted into the birth canal when contractions begin. One wire is attached to the scalp of the baby and conveys the baby's pulse to the monitor. This appears as an electrocardiogram on a screen and also registers continuously on moving graph paper. The second wire, capped with a plastic tube, is placed inside the womb to measure the frequency and strength of contractions. A doctor observing the relationship between the contractions and the fetal heartbeat is given a constant running record of the unborn baby's condition.

Recently, a forty-year-old woman who was giving birth to her first child was hooked up to an electronic fetal monitor. She was overdue for delivery, and at her age the birth was classified as "high risk." She was given oxytocin, a powerful birth stimulant, and labor began in earnest.

Two hours later the technician at the monitor noted that the baby's heartbeat was fluctuating rapidly after each contraction, then resuming its normal beat. He called the doctor. The pattern grew worse until an hour later the baby's heartbeat was dropping rapidly from a normal 120–160 beats per minute to as low as 50. Recovery was becoming slower, indicating that the flow of satisfactorily oxygen-rich blood to the baby was being pinched off.

It was the classic "cord compression pattern." The baby was slowly strangling for lack of oxygen.

The doctor ordered the mother to be given oxygen, hoping it would get through to the baby. It didn't. The mother was rushed to the operating room where her baby was delivered by Caesarean section, slightly blue, but healthy. The doctor found the reason for the compression—two knots in the umbilical cord.

Without the electronic fetal monitor that baby would have been born dead, or with severe brain damage. He might have joined the half million victims of cerebral palsy—an infant suffering from this disease is born every hour. Or he might have been one of the six million other mentally retarded in the United States—a victim is being born every five minutes.

Tests show that cases of cerebral palsy and mental retardation in just-born monkeys can be created simply by cutting their oxygen intake. "In addition to causing severe brain damage or death," says Dr. Harry Shifrin of Harvard Medical School, "we think lack of oxygen may result in the minimal brain damage that may later show up as clumsiness or as behavior or reading problems. Roughly 10 percent of our school children have some degree of this."

Dr. Abraham Towbin, also of Harvard, adds that many seemingly normal individuals might have a touch of mental retardation as a result of a slight brain damage suffered as an embryo.

Further refinements of the electronic fetal monitoring technique are on the way.

At the University of Southern California's Medical Center, computers will soon be used to help in fetal monitoring. A mini-computer at a central point will oversee all the monitors in the hospital. If a patient gets in trouble, her name will start flashing on and off. The doctor will then punch a button and get a printout of the patient's clinical history. By punching another button he will get a data sheet summarizing everything that has happened during the course of labor with the patient, recorded at ten-minute intervals.

This kind of fetal monitoring will also enable consultants to give advice in an emergency. Fetal monitoring patterns can even be transmitted by telephone.

At the present time, only one in six of the 5,200 maternity wards in the United States employs the basic fetal monitoring device. The principal reason is that each unit costs about $5,000. But this works out to only a few dollars per patient on an annual basis, and disposable supplies add about $10 to the cost. Some hospitals now add $25 to the patient's bill for monitoring. In some instances, the extra charge is paid for by Blue Cross and health insurance policies.

No statistics are available on how many clinic patients or patients not covered by Blue Cross and health insurance policies are being given access to the device.

A marked advance in prenatal diagnosis was made possible in 1972. It is called "amniocentesis" and consists of obtaining a small sample of amniotic fluid through a transabdominal needle. This helps to determine the condition of the fetus. If the fetus is abnormal, the mother can then obtain a therapuetic abortion if she so desires.

Amniocentesis can also indicate the sex of a fetus. Dr. Amitai Etzioni, a professor of sociology at Columbia University and director of the Center for Policy Research, is apprehensive about that. "Before, it was nature's decision if a family had a boy or a girl. This minute, right now, any pregnant woman can in effect decide whether to abort a child if it isn't the sex she chooses."

Dr. Etzioni concedes that amniocentesis has valuable uses as well. "Amniocentesis can tell whether or not a child will be mongoloid, and that is a problem for many pregnant women over thirty-five. . . . And we must consider that it costs the nation one point seven billion dollars a year for institutional care of mongoloid children. But who is going to make these decisions?"

As amniocentesis becomes a standard procedure, the incidence of "abnormal births" is certain to drop. Fewer "monsters" will be carried to full term, and a tragedy such as that which occurred in the epidemic of German measles in 1964–1965, when 50,000 fetuses died in the womb or were eventually born deaf, blind, and/or mentally retarded, will not be repeated.

Teratologists are not able either to divine or to cure all causes of imperfect births, but they now suspect many are caused by drugs or by the pollutants released in the air and water and on land.

"All drugs are suspect," says Dr. Virginia Apgar of the March of Dimes, an organization now devoted mostly to the study and cure of birth defects. Today's pregnant woman is advised against consuming laxatives, pep pills, tranquilizers, pain suppressants, reducing pills, sleeping pills, or even vitamin supplements.

Another method of reducing the number of children born with birth defects is genetic counseling. According to one estimate, 25 percent of all handicapped people now in institutions are there because they inherited some genetic disease. Many of the causes are unknown, but at least two thousand genetic defects in human beings have been identified, and with the aid of genetic counseling a couple can find out whether they run a prohibitively high risk of having abnormal children.

This presents another problem: whether a couple wishes to enter into a marriage that has no reasonable prospect of producing normal children. But whether they opt for a childless marriage, or no marriage at all, that is surely a more humane decision than allowing a baby to be born with a serious genetically caused disease.

At present, the only genetic counseling services are in the larger medical centers and are supported by grants from the federal government and such organizations as the March of Dimes. Genetic analysis is lengthy and expensive, and as yet not always definite. But progress is being made, and the day is not far off when genetic counseling may be as routine as the premarital physical examination for people about to get married.

Some help may also be looked for as a byproduct of the fight to protect our environment. No one knows how many birth defects—or for that matter, adult diseases—are caused by the incredible amount of pollutants being poured into our environment. But the statistics on just one—lead poisoning—are frightening. Lead poisoning has been recognized as a danger to infants and small children since the early 1930s. We have already discussed Ralph Nader's successful battle to ban lead-based paints, which caused 25,000 to 50,000 children a year to suffer brain damage or death. But a less determinable effect of lead poisoning is now being investigated. This is the 200,000 tons of lead being added to the atmosphere every year. Ninety-five percent of this comes from automobile exhausts. Per capita, it breaks down to about two pounds of lead a year being ingested by each and every person in the United States.

No doubt a clearer relationship needs to be established between air pollution and infant mortality and retardation. When and if that relationship does become clear, the public may become aroused enough to do something about it.

"We simply haven't begun to understand the toxic effects of our chemical age," a chemical engineer told us, "but we're pouring stuff into the environment that simply hasn't been there before. We found out the horrible effects of DDT on birds and fish and animals. But nobody knows yet how many of our children are growing up with a toxic residue in their bones, their lymph nodes, and their blood."

In 1973, two prominent physicians frankly disclosed that they had withheld vital treatment from forty-three infants and allowed them to die. Dr. Raymond S. Duff, a Yale University pediatrician, and Dr. A. G. M. Campbell of the University of Aberdeen, Scotland, told their story in a paper published by *The New England Journal of Medicine.*

In every case the child was hopelessly ill, congenitally deformed, or both. Every effort was made to spare the babies from experiencing any pain, and the decision regarding their fate was made only after consultation with the parents.

"What else is there to do with a hopelessly afflicted monster except to let it die?" a sympathetic obstetrician said when the newspapers published the story. "It saves the poor thing a painful, useless existence. And it spares the parents the grief and the expense of trying to keep the creature alive."

One baby permitted to die had an incurable lung disease. He had to labor constantly for each breath, had a weak heart, and already, at the age of five months, needed 40 percent oxygen to survive. His parents had spent $15,000 on hospital care, the other children in their family were emotionally disturbed, and their marriage was at a breaking point. When the decision was made to take the baby off oxygen, he died within three hours.

The report by the two doctors surprised few of their colleagues. Most, without being willing to admit it, had made similar decisions regarding newborn "hopeless" infants.

More surprising was the public reaction. People rallied to the support of the doctors and of the argument that it is sometimes more humane to decide that children should not live.

As a nurse remarked about one doomed baby, "We lost him weeks ago. Isn't it time to quit trying to save him?"

COLOSSAL UNDERTAKING

The National Institute of Child Care and Human Development is funding a project that, by the time you read this, will have in operation a nationwide computerized system capable of detecting outbreaks of birth defects.

The program will monitor about 2 million of the 3 million births expected in the United States next year. The data will come from about 1,500 hospitals cooperating in the program. It is the first nationwide attempt to determine whether the incidence of birth defects is affected by the thousands of new drugs and environmental chemicals to which pregnant women are exposed.

According to the most recent atlas of birth defects published by the National Foundation, there are 842 separate defects, and they range from an aberrant lobe of the lung to yellow-blue color blindness.

If a specific defect occurs in only one of every thousand births, the doctors and nurses at a particular hospital that may deliver five hundred babies a year are not likely to notice an increase in the incidence, for there will be only one such case in two years. Even if the ratio doubled or tripled, it would quite likely be written off to mere coincidence.

However, if a number of hospitals are submitting records of defects to a nationwide surveillance program, the computers will quickly pick up the increase, and medical researchers can go to work to try to determine the cause.

A $100-million, fourteen-year colossal undertaking sponsored by the National Institute of Neurological Diseases and Stroke may also bring about significant changes in pediatric practice in America. The study of mothers and their children is being conducted by fourteen hospitals and twelve medical schools across the country. Since the first mother was registered in January 1969, hundreds of doctors have completed more than 1 million comprehensive medical examinations and more than 6 million pieces of information are recorded on computer tapes.

Doctors expect that the data will yield clues to the prevention and cure of many diseases, including cerebral palsy and mental retardation. But the mills of medical research grind slowly, especially on a project conceived on such a vast scale.

"Before we can get a handle on the relationship between prenatal factors and the neurological condition of the child," says Dr. Leo Fox, chief of collaborative research at one of the government's National Institutes of Health, "we've got to complete the study and go through the seventh and eighth year examinations of forty thousand children we've been following through the first eight years of life. At present, about ninety percent of the children have reached the eight-year-old cut-off point. The first child studied is now thirteen years old."

"Just what we've got in frozen blood samples taken from mothers in different stages of pregnancy and from the umbilical cord of the newborn is a unique reference library," says Dr. Janet Hardy, of St. John's University Medical School, who has been associated with the study from its inception. "There are more than one point five million vials of frozen blood serum stored at a laboratory in Bethesda. The serum really represents a unique resource that we are guarding very carefully."

As a result of the close watch kept on thousands of mothers and their children over an extended period of time, there is sure to be general improvement in patient care throughout the country. The information will start coming out this year, and the investigation will end in 1976.

THE DANGEROUS WORLD OUR CHILDREN LIVE IN

17

"Child abuse occurs in all walks of life," says Dr. Roy Horowitz. "Doctors and lawyers, too, batter their kids. Ten percent of children under five years of age who come in with trauma are cases of child abuse."

Dr. Horowitz is chairman of the subcommittee on child abuse of the Nassau County Pediatrics Society, a group of pediatricians trying to help local doctors to handle child abuse cases so that children are not mistreated again. Studies show that the problem is real and critical. Fifty percent of the children brought in to hospital emergency wards suffering from "battering" return again "dead on arrival."

What is shocking, in view of these statistics, is that in almost every case of child abuse that came to the attention of the police and juvenile authorities, the judge at the court hearing later returned the child to the home where he was almost certain to receive more abuse. Often there are several abused children in a family, with scars of repeated injuries which have never been reported.

Peter DeCourcy, a clinical psychologist who worked with child abuse cases, did exhaustive research into the problem. He and his wife Judith talked with social workers, judges, policemen, parents, and abused children in two middle-class communities. One was the affluent suburb of a large city and the other a prosperous medium-sized city. The families involved in these child abuse cases were respected in the community and lived in their own homes. The neighborhood schools were better than average, and the Parent-Teacher Associations were strong. Almost all of the parents had at least ten years of education, and several had college degrees. They were white, Christians, churchgoers. Yet within their fine large homes there occurred appalling abuses of children.

The result of the DeCourcys' investigations was a book: *A Silent Tragedy, Child Abuse in the Community,* which details dozens of cases in which one or more children in a family were badly beaten, sexually abused, neglected or badly cared for, psychologically damaged, or killed by a parent or step-parent.

Very little was done to protect the children from further danger, and the DeCourcys put the blame for this on juvenile court judges who are not properly trained in psychology or sociology, and sometimes do not even have law degrees. Cases are heard without a jury and decided by the judge alone. The child has no one to speak in his behalf because he is considered to be represented in court by the parents' attorney!

The DeCourcys discovered that judges often discount psychiatrists' reports because they "don't trust headshrinkers," or because "psychiatric gobbledygook is too hard to understand." When parents are "sentenced" to consult a psychiatrist, they usually don't benefit from the therapy because they don't feel they need it in the first place. It isn't surprising that abusive parents quickly return to their old ways.

Obviously, say the DeCourcys, the child abuse laws are inadequate to protect children. And the other steps so far taken are a good deal like trying to stop Niagara with a spoon. There is a small Parents Anonymous organization made up of abusive parents who try to counsel each other on ways to keep from harming children. And in Santa Barbara, California, an organization called CALM was founded in 1970 by a nurse who will talk on the telephone to people who are afraid they will harm their children or know of child abuse cases in their families or neighborhoods. Similar services are now being established in other states, and there are a number of organizations that are concerned with the problem as part of their overall effort. One of these is the American Humane Association in Denver, Colorado.

In New York State a promising system for reporting child abuse or neglect began in the fall of 1974. You can call a toll-free telephone number to report a suspected case (the number is 800–342–3720), and local welfare agencies are set up to receive reports at any time of the day or night and to investigate them within twenty-four hours. To put further bite into the law, anyone who knows of a case of child abuse and does not report it is guilty of a misdemeanor.

Dr. Roy Horowitz's subcommittee is alerting other doctors to suspect child abuse more often and to keep the victims in hospitals rather than return them to their homes. "The parent may say that a child slipped when it was really thrown down the stairs. Physicians and nurses tend to buy the story, either because they don't want to believe the parents did it or they don't want to think about it. The reporting of child abuse cases has increased enormously with our new system, but what we're looking at is still the tip of the iceberg."

For doctors who suspect a case of child abuse, the committee recommends a course of procedure. The first step is to get an immediate history from the parents so that their reports can be compared later with subsequent accounts of how the "accidents" occurred. The child's story should also be obtained, if possible, at this time. Dr. Horowitz says it is particularly important for the doctor to keep the confidence of parents so they will respond favorably to any recommendation that they receive psychiatric help after the investigation is concluded.

The next step is to have the child admitted to the hospital, on a pretext if necessary. The abused child can also be kept in the hospital for legitimate medical reasons—for example, to discover if bruises have been caused by abnormal bleeding or bone fractures by a metabolic disorder resulting in bone fragility. While in the hospital x rays can be taken of other parts of the child's body to see if there are healed fractures unreported from previous incidents. A nurse, or preferably, two nurses should be present to hear what the child has to say about it.

Dr. Horowitz and members of his committee are giving lectures on child abuse to emergency room personnel at hospitals, and designate one or two persons on the hospital staff to funnel any suspected cases to the County Children's Bureau. They also arrange lectures for other medical and paramedical personnel who might possibly encounter cases of child abuse without being aware of it, such as orthopedic surgeons, dentists, and school nurses.

The campaign is not without some risk. "Many times the parents resent what you do," Dr. Horowitz says. "I had a friend who reported a case of child abuse, and the father, from jail, vowed he was going to come back and kill the doctor."

In view of the 50 percent fatality figure for children brought back a second time after suffering from battering, Dr. Horowitz and his fellow pediatricians feel their efforts, and the risks, are worthwhile.

Much harder to combat is the abuse dealt by a parent who would never think of striking or using any kind of "real" physical violence against a child.

These parents limit their corporal punishment to spanking or merely grabbing a child by the shoulders and shaking vigorously. However, this kind of rough treatment may also cause severe physical trauma. According to Dr. John Caffey of the University of Pittsburgh, it is the cause of "mild" mental retardation or "mild" cerebral palsy in thousands of otherwise normal children. Unlike the "battered baby" who shows clear external signs of its beating, the trauma of "shaken babies" often goes unnoticed.

Writing in the journal *Pediatrics,* published by the American Academy of Pediatrics, Caffey points out that an infant's head is relatively heavier than the rest of its body and the neck muscles are weaker. An infant's unsupported head therefore bobs freely under stress, creating hemorrhages in the brain. **Dr.**

Caffey believes that many slow learning and physically clumsy children might well have been intelligent and normal today if they had not been shaken as infants. And he concludes that, "The hands of an angry parent or a jealous older sibling can be deadly weapons."

MYSTERIOUS KILLER

Each year almost 200,000 children under twelve die from disease or organic malfunction. Cancer (bone and leukemia in particular), heart disease, and the still-resistant staphylococcus infections, ranging from pneumonia to fatal blood conditions, will account for most of these deaths.

Doctors are fighting to save children by new medical techniques, intensive care nurseries, baby ambulance services, and continual research into the illnesses that kill so many children each year.

It may be instructive to examine how medical researchers in the pediatrics field are grappling with one cause of infant death—the most mysterious and therefore most frightening of all.

In 1975, between fifteen and twenty thousand apparently healthy infants between the ages of one week and one year will die suddenly and quietly in their sleep. They will be victims of the silent, invisible killer known as "crib death." These babies will be put to bed via the established routine, will not have colds, or be fussy, and will not have temperatures. Yet within a matter of hours they will be dead.

The traumatic shock to the parents is enormous, and most will accuse themselves of negligence, mishandling, or carelessness. "I smothered her by letting her sleep face down." "I put too many covers on him." "I should have taken his temperature; he *did* feel a little warm when I put him to bed." "I had a feeling at midnight that I should go into the nursery. If I had, my baby would still be alive." "I just didn't pay enough attention to him." These are common parental reactions.

One couple, Arthur and Marie Noe, of Philadelphia, lost nine children in infancy, suddenly and with no apparent cause of death. Except for one baby who died at birth, each death followed an insidious pattern. The baby was placed in its crib, Mrs. Noe later heard a thrashing or gasping, and the frantic rush to the hospital proved to be of no avail. Investigators invariably found no sign of violence, and no trace of poison or any other type of lethal substance. Dr. Joseph Spelman, the city medical examiner, was fully as mystified as the grief-stricken parents.

A Seattle pediatrician, Dr. Abraham B. Bergman, declares: "The management of SIDS [Sudden Infant Death Syndrome] in the United States is a disgrace." According to Dr. Bergman, SIDS "constitutes a real disease entity which warrants being listed on the death certificate as a cause of death."

However, a survey of 148 counties and towns in 48 states—consisting of interviews with the coroner or medical examiner, with a sampling of local physicians and bereaved parents—showed that autopsies were routinely performed in only 25 percent of the communities. Fifty percent of death certificates listed SIDS as the cause of death. Other causes listed: pneumonia, respiratory infection, acute necrotizing laryngitis, suffocation under bedclothes, and lack of oxygen due to undetermined causes.

Bergman states that "many doctors insist on putting pneumonia or other diseases down as the cause of death because it sounds more 'scientific.' The net effect is to make the parent feel guilty for not having taken the infant to the doctor. In reality, SIDS itself cannot be predicted or prevented. Parents are being made to feel guilty about something they could not prevent."

Margaret Sigley, herself a pediatrician, lost her baby while vacationing in California. "One morning I went to awaken my two-and-one-half-month-old boy, Danny, and found him lifeless in his crib. He had been dead for several hours. I work at Children's Orthopedic Hospital and Medical Center in Seattle, which has the largest SIDS research project in the world. The fact that I am a pediatrician and intellectually aware that SIDS is neither predictable nor preventable did not protect me from painful guilt feelings and depression."

Theories that the infants are smothered in their bedclothes have been discredited. No known bacteria or enteroviruses are to blame. Doctors once speculated that crib death babies produced abnormally large amounts of antibodies against cow's milk and died from shock because of hypersensitivity. But studies by Dr. Marie Valdes-Dapena of Philadelphia's St. Christopher's Hospital for Children showed that crib death babies often had fewer cow's milk antibodies than other children.

Equally puzzling to scientific researchers who are trying to grapple with the baffling mystery is that most crib deaths take place between two and four months of age, seldom before three weeks and after six months, that most victims are males, underweight at birth, and that the majority of deaths occur during the winter.

There are some clues. Dr. Fredric Rieders, a toxicologist, discovered an abnormal metabolic product, which he named the "red substance" because it turns alcohol red in certain chemical tests. This substance was present in about 80 percent of the brains of a group of crib death babies studied in Philadelphia. Only about 20 percent of infants dying from identifiable causes had produced this substance. But no one has yet discovered how and why the body produces this strange substance, nor what direct connection it has with the infant deaths.

The most promising investigation has been conducted by two researchers at Brown University. Dr. Judy F. Rosenblith and Rebecca B. Anderson-Huntington ran a series of tests on more than 1,500 infants. Among the tests was a "tactile" stimulation, in which pieces of cotton and cellophane were placed on the baby's face, blocking nostrils and mouth. The two researchers then observed how the infant tried to get rid of the obstruction—by opening its mouth to breathe, batting away the hand holding the cotton, or turning its body or head.

Later, checking on the infants in follow-up studies, Rosenblith and Anderson-Huntington discovered that a dozen had died, apparent victims of SIDS. All of the dead babies had shown coldlike symptoms, and many had received oxygen therapy after birth. Most important: all had scored low on the tactile stimulation test. This suggested that a respiratory problem had been present at the outset.

On the basis of their discovery, the two researchers theorize that some subtle neurologic damage involving the respiratory system takes place during fetal life or very shortly after birth. In sleep, while respiration is at a low level, a stuffy nose would require that a baby open its mouth to breathe. But with the neurological impairment, the normal reflex response fails, and instead the baby clamps its mouth shut. The oxygen level in the blood continues to fall until the child goes into a seizure. One confirming symptom would be the light bloody froth that is so often found on the lips of SIDS victims.

Even if this theory does not prove to be the answer, it may suggest ways in which pediatricians can prevent SIDS. Children of low birth weight or who require oxygen therapy should be given tactile stimulation tests. If they score poorly, they should be closely watched and hospitalized when they catch colds, so their breathing can be monitored around the clock. If respiration should stop in a hospital, it is comparatively easy for a nurse to resuscitate the infant.

Of course, this suggestion not only adds to the present burden of hospitals, but will be expensive for parents. SIDS may join the long list of diseases for which only the rich can afford adequate therapy on an individual basis.

Many pediatricians suspect the real root causes of SIDS are socio-economic. This theory gained support when a map pinpointing crib deaths was superimposed on maps showing the slum areas in Manhattan and Philadelphia. The areas coincided almost exactly.

Crib death may be a killer that afflicts mainly the children of poor and minority parents..

NOT SO MYSTERIOUS KILLERS

Sometimes the cause of children's death is a manmade product. This was true of the recent shocking tragedies involving the use of Pertussin, an aerosol decongestant spray that has been directly linked to the deaths of eighteen children. Manufactured by Chesebrough-Pond's, Inc., the spray can—first marketed in 1961—is an enticing soft blue in color, illustrated with a sleeping baby blessed with an angelic smile. "Build a roomful of relief " from colds and hay fever is a further enticement. Directions suggest spraying the contents of the can around the room, on bedsheets and pillows, and on handkerchiefs to be held to the face. No limit was placed on the dosage. In fact, the can states, "Repeat as often as desired," and compounds its promise with "Safe even in the nursery." FDA approval had been obtained, and the valuable endorsement of *Parent's* magazine. Over 30 million cans were sold.

On April 12, 1973, Marcia Overfield, a five-year-old Cleveland girl, went to bed with a light cold that was being treated with a Pertussin-sprayed handkerchief. Three hours later her parents found her unconscious with the handkerchief lying beside her face. The little girl remained in a coma for five days before she died. As far as the Cleveland coroner and the FDA could determine, Pertussin Medicated Vaporizer had been used as directed. But it killed her.

Pertussin was recalled from the market by the FDA, whose official statement read that "seventeen of the deaths clearly are associated with abuse or gross misuse of the vaporizer product." That was all the FDA would say; the names, dates, and places of death were withheld.

According to the *Los Angeles Times,* however, further investigation shows at least two more Pertussin deaths. Teresa May Cummings, twelve, from Richmond, Virginia, sprayed her pillow with Pertussin before retiring and was found dead a few hours later. The medical examiner's report states that the cause of death was "the inhalation of decongestant spray." And in July 1972, Tammy Braswell, fourteen, from Euless, Texas, died almost instantly after inhaling Pertussin.

All three of these cases have been launched into the lengthy litigation process which accompanies any suit against a pharmaceutical house.

A San Francisco pediatrician was asked for his opinion on the Pertussin tragedy: "As far as I'm concerned, it falls into that very disturbing area of many FDA-approved products that simply aren't tested thoroughly enough before they're placed on the market and heavily advertised. A worried, anxious parent will grab at something which promises relief or cure. I think any doctor should make it very plain to a patient that no patent medicine is to be used unless he is consulted first. But I'm afraid many of us are slack in laying down this rule."

A DANGEROUS PRODUCT

What follows is the step-by-step story of what led to the eventual recall of one well-known product.

The story begins on July 27, 1973, when Dr. J. Rodman Seely, a pediatrician at the University of Oklahoma Health Sciences Center, was called in as a consultant to examine two infants born with similar birth defects. Examination revealed that the infants had deformed joints, missing discs in the spinal column, softening of the larynx, bone abnormalities and considerable damage to the central nervous system.

In questioning the parents, Dr. Seely learned that a link between them was their heavy use of a spray adhesive—the kind used primarily in arts and crafts hobbies. He asked if friends of theirs, who had also used the sprays, would submit to chromosome analysis. They would, and Dr. Seely's examination of this group revealed a much higher percentage of chromosome damage than in a second control group. He submitted his report to the Consumer Product Safety Commission in Washington, D.C., and a week afterward a team of investigators was sent to Oklahoma City to continue the investigation.

They subjected Dr. Seely to a grilling, and after several lengthy sessions concluded that there might be some validity to his findings.

During the week of August 6, 1973, two weeks after Dr. Seely first got in touch with the Commission, Borden Company and 3-M Company, the manufacturers of the sprays, were alerted.

The manufacturers' response was that Dr. Seely's evidence was limited and inconclusive. They engaged an independent outside laboratory to conduct testing on the products, and promised to cooperate with the Commission's research program.

The Commission's researchers had to find the cause, and they knew it would not be easy. It was a complex problem. The spray adhesive had a three-component system: an adhesive base, a common solvent system, and a propellant. But it would not be enough to merely examine the three parts of the product's makeup. There were numerous other factors. The cause might be a minor ingredient, or a material formed in the atmosphere of the aerosol, or even something in the environment inhaled by the individual. Or it might be in the metabolism, breathed in as one thing and broken down by the body mechanism into something else.

One basic fear in everyone's mind was that the problem might be in the propellants. If so, hundreds of other products with similar systems would be affected.

Barbara H. Franklin, one of the agency's four commissioners, says: "We didn't want to start a scare and alarm people, but it might have meant danger with deodorants, hair sprays—you name it. It might have opened a whole new thing."

The Commission issued a preliminary set of guidelines for those who might have been exposed to the spray adhesive. Individuals were urged to consult medical authorities and genetic counselors in their communities. This was not particularly helpful advice, since chromosome analysis is not readily available in many areas and will not always provide a definitive answer about an expected child.

Couples where one or both had been exposed, and the wife was not yet pregnant, were asked to delay any pregnancy until further information was available. Recalling the epic proportions of the thalidomide scare a decade earlier, the Commission tried to keep the lid on. They refused to recommend that pregnant women who had been exposed to the spray terminate their pregnancies. "Don't ask me about abortion," one commissioner said. "I don't know how to counsel anybody. There's just no pat answer for what can be done."

On August 17, the Commission issued a statement warning the public not to buy or use the sprays manufactured by the Borden and 3-M companies. Three days later the Commission acted under the Hazardous Substances Act to remove the sprays from the market.

Borden sent the following telegram to its four thousand distributors: "Due to allegations of the Consumer Product Safety Commission, Borden Chemical is withdrawing Krylon Spray Adhesive #8010 from the market. Discontinue sale and shipment of the product at once. Further information will follow."

"I'm sure the companies would have preferred we didn't issue the ban," said Richard O. Simpson, the Commission chairman. "One always prefers to study things a little more. But how can you take a chance with something like this? We certainly want to be prudent—but in this case being prudent meant moving fast."

Dangerous products do remain on the market for years, causing genetic damage, deformities and death without anyone's taking official action.

A typical instance is reported by Ellen Stern Harris, who writes a consumer advocate column for the *Los Angeles Times*. She became concerned about the proliferating use of aerosol sprays, and asked her readers to write in and tell their experiences with aerosols. "In the two years that I've been writing the column I have never received a volume of mail to equal it. It was so overwhelming that I wrote to Consumer Product Safety Commissioner Barbara H Franklin and told her I would like to bring the letters to Washington for her and her fellow commissioners to examine." A hearing was set for November 16, 1973.

On that day Ellen Stern Harris entered a small room filled with representatives of such organizations as the Cosmetic, Toiletry and Fragrance Association, Bristol Meyers Company, 3-M Company, American Can Company, and an industry group called the Aerosol Education Bureau. The only person on hand, besides her, to present the consumer's case was a friend, Meredith Brokaw, who was then living in Washington.

Ms. Harris read excerpts from the letters she had received, and presented the entire collection to the Commission for its files. She also left with the Commission a sample aerosol can filled with a plastic material that was designed to be sold for use by children.

The result: she was told by Commissioner Franklin that "these data will be factored into our considerations."

That same day the respected *Medical World News* came out with a cover story saying aerosols had become suspect and concern was mounting that they posed "significant cardiac, cancer and accident dangers."

There the matter still rests.

SHORT LIVES

In previous generations, infant mortality was considered an inevitable part of the birth process for which every father and mother had to be prepared. Today, the death of an infant is a tragedy compounded by its comparative rarity. With the statistical decline of infant deaths has come a heightened psychological fear, a feeling among parents that capricious fate will choose *them*. They can no longer escape guilt, as their forebears did, by ascribing it to the workings of inscrutable providence. Somehow it must be their fault, or the fault of their doctor.

When death does occur, they try to expiate guilt and assuage grief by that sovereign remedy: spending money. In the United States, infants are buried with costly pomp and ceremony. That includes those whose entire life span can be measured in hours or days.

Most hospitals maintained by religious orders or denominations will baptize a baby at birth if it seems likely not to survive. The baby then becomes a "soul," even if it has breathed for only a moment outside its mother's womb. And it must be accorded a Christian burial.

The burial rite is an emotionally disturbing event for parents and all too often a financial burden. Between $500 and $1,000 may be spent to bury the baby that "almost was," although according to medical authorities $50 would be a reasonable charge.

A century ago, Mark Twain remarked on this discrepancy when the child of one of his acquaintances died. The father—who earned less than $400 a year —was charged $26 for the plain wooden coffin. "It would have cost less than $4," Twain remarked, "if it had been built to put something useful into."

The funeral industry has somehow managed to equate a lavish burial with the amount of grief that parents feel for the loss of a newborn. All too frequently parents are persuaded to make a financial sacrifice, even taking away some necessities from their living children, to give the dead infant a "fitting" sendoff.

Recently in Cincinnati, an undertaker promised a grieving young couple that he would "look after everything" when their two-day-old infant died of hyaline membrane disease. He more than kept his promise. The funeral was an impressive affair, a tiny casket lined in pink satin and velvet, a "resting room" full of flowers, an organ and soloist, limousine transportation to the cemetery plot, and a $600 concrete sheath to protect the casket. The total bill came to $3,000, and the young couple had to refinance the mortgage on their home, at a much higher rate of interest, simply to pay the funeral bill.

Psychiatrists and physicians, on the whole, are opposed to the way infant deaths and funerals are handled.

"I deplore the way a dead infant is interred," said the late Dr. Claude Bundesen. "It is natural to feel grief, but it is not natural to have this grief extended through an unnecessarily lengthy and costly funeral service. It becomes an orgy of grief without good reason. If a baby lives long enough to become a person in the hearts and minds of its parents, a simple burial is deserved. But if it has been stillborn, or dies before it meets any of the normal responses between parents and child, the burial service should be dispensed with."

Jessica Mitford, whose *The American Way of Death* has become one of the celebrated crusading books of modern times, told us: "I find baby funerals possibly the worst of all—that pitiful little box advertised by Casket and Sunnyside probably cost the parents $350 at least, and it cost all of $50 to make. The plot, unless it's on a family reservation, probably cost another $200. The mortician charges a minimum of $150. If people can afford it, the costs don't mean that much—I understand Jacqueline Kennedy spent $2,500 to bury her baby boy—but it is the emotional cost that bothers me. It's a drain and a waste!"

A Forest Lawn funeral director, who requests anonymity, surprisingly concurs: "You would think that a man in my profession would become immune to reacting to death, and to a great degree we do because we have to. But I still become rather upset about the way so many baby funerals are handled. The really pitiful ones are the deaths that occur either through stillbirth or that come shortly after birth.

"God only knows what the poor mother goes through. She's not only lost a baby, but now she's obliged to choose a casket, consult with her minister, and give the lost baby a name if it hadn't been baptized. And then attend a funeral for a baby that she never really knew as her own."

An obstetrician states his view: "A baby who dies before its mother has left the hospital should be given to science for medical research. Even a thorough autopsy would be valuable, but sixty percent of my patients refuse to allow an autopsy. I hate to sound inhumane, but if we had full access to these tiny bodies we could probably reduce infant mortality drastically."

TO BE—
AND NOT TO BE:
FERTILITY
DRUGS OR

18 # CONTRACEPTIVES

In the last decade multiple births have become increasingly familiar through-out the world. Quintuplets and even sextuplets are being reported in the U.S., Australia, Brazil, England, Poland, and South Africa.

Multiple births, four or more, have always fascinated people. Back on May 28, 1934, when the Dionne quintuplets were born near Callander, Ontario, the world was so enthralled that the quints became a huge commercial venture, lending their endorsement to baby foods, sleepwear, toys, et al, and bringing hordes of curious tourists to Ontario. They were instant celebrities. Everyone heard that the chance of naturally conceiving quintuplets was 1 in 3.5 billion, so the Dionne quints were accorded the treatment given only to the unique. They were made wards of the King and lived in a nursery built by the government. At age of one, they even appeared in a movie based on the life of their doctor, Allan Roy Dafoe.

Today everything is different. Triplets hardly rate a paragraph in the local newspaper, and the once rare quadruplets don't attract much more attention.

The reason is simple—fertility drugs.

Fertility drugs—those in most common use are labeled Clomid and Per-gonal—were not compounded and marketed with the idea of producing hu-man litters.

These drugs are given to women to wish to conceive, are in sound health, and have no basic physical or mental malfunction to render childbirth dangerous. Their success has been remarkable. But "remarkable" may not be the correct operative word, for we are witnessing the near epidemic of quintuplets and sextuplets that has resulted.

Most physicians do not look kindly on multiple births. The infants are almost certain to be born premature, weigh from one to three pounds, with organs such as lungs, heart, and liver not developed enough to cope with life outside the womb.

"The human woman simply wasn't born to have litters," one obstetrician says. "There's a certain amount of heartbreak when the babies die, and hardly ever do the majority survive. It's virtually impossible to have six babies that are physically—and mentally—sound."

Until the arrival of the Dionne quintuplets, not one member of any quintuplet set had survived more than a few days. Nearly unknown is the fact that there was a sixth child in the Dionne set, but it aborted during the third month of the mother's pregnancy. What made the Dionne quintuplets even more remarkable is that they all originated from one fertilized egg, which through repeated twinning of the early single embryo became five children. Believers in astrology may also draw significance from the fact that the quints were born under Gemini—the sign of the Twins.

The most notable multiple birth in the United States occurred in 1973 in Lakewood, Colorado, when a thirty-four-year-old woman named Edna Stanek gave birth to sextuplets, five of which, despite heavy odds, survived.

Five years prior to the birth of the sextuplets, Edna Stanek had borne a son. After that she failed to conceive and wanted another child badly. So she turned to the fertility drugs—first to Clomid, which did nothing to induce a pregnancy, then to Pergonal. After daily injections for two weeks, she became pregnant.

In her twenty-fourth week doctors pronounced she was carrying at least four fetuses, and ordered her to bed because the danger of miscarriage outweighs the chances of carrying through when more than triplets are involved. X rays proved the presence of sextuplets, and the doctors then had to face a real challenge.

She went into labor some three weeks before the birth of the sextuplets and was rushed to Rose Memorial Hospital where ethyl alcohol was injected intravenously to halt labor. The ethyl alcohol acted as a muscle relaxant and suppressed uterine contractions. She was also given three ounces of vodka daily. When she finally went into labor she was in her seventh month. Her weight had gone up from her normal 130 pounds to 190 during her pregnancy.

The delivery was as complex as her pregnancy. The first baby was born naturally, the other five by Caesarean section. Two pediatricians and a nurse attended each baby at the moment of its birth.

The babies' weight—exceptionally high for this number of babies—ranged from just under 3 pounds to 3 pounds, 10 ounces. They were placed in incubators, and four of them were given extra oxygen. Despite this, their under-developed lungs almost immediately became afflicted with the respiratory problems that account for half of all deaths among premature babies. Forty-four hours after birth, the weakest of the six died of hyaline membrane disease, a disorder of the inner lining of the lungs. Three others remained in critical condition for five days, but eventually survived.

The suburban community of Lakewood was agog at the Staneks. Their mailman, Harry Jones, summed it up: "It makes you wonder whether we ought to be using those drugs. I think the scientists are fooling around too much. Frankly, I just don't think the doctors have a right to prescribe fertility drugs with the population explosion what it is. And having so many kids at once—that's rough on the parents. I guess the Staneks won't have too much trouble financially, though. They'll be asked to endorse all that stuff."

The predictions of prosperity for the Staneks failed to materialize. Some months after the multiple birth, a spokesman for the family declared that the commercial interest in the Staneks "has not been great—and that's putting it mildly."

The only major commercial organizations to express interest had been the local Chamber of Commerce, a department store which offered Mrs. Stanek a gift certificate, a baby shop that made a similar offer to the infants, a diaper company that wanted to sell its services, and an offer from the local Montgomery Ward department store to aid with clothing and furniture. That isn't much to weigh against the cost of five strollers, five cribs, hospital and medical expenses for five babies and, eventually, five college tuitions.

"Your life-style does change somewhat when your family size increases all at once from three to eight," noted Eugene Stanek, an accountant, philosophically.

The detectable lack of enthusiasm about the sextuplets was summed up by a nurse at the hospital, Colorado General, where the delivery took place. (Colorado General has more extensive facilities than Rose Memorial.)

She said: "You can't begin to compare the Stanek sextuplets with the Dionne quints. The Dionne quints were a natural pregnancy and they only had one doctor. When the Stanek babies were born there were two pediatricians and a pediatric nurse in attendance for each baby, not to mention the regular obstetrician. There were about thirty medical people from three hospitals crowded into that operating room."

The odds against having sextuplets naturally are about 5 billion to one, and the odds against having all six survive are beyond calculation. The latter miracle did occur, however, in Capetown, South Africa, at the Mowbray Maternity Hospital. Mrs. Susan Rosenkowitz became the mother of three boys and three girls delivered by Caesarean section.

Susan Rosenkowitz, twenty-five, already was the mother of a girl seven, and a boy five, and had asked her doctor for help in having more children. She got more help than anyone could expect. Her doctor prescribed Orciprenaline, a fertility drug. Three times she took Orciprenaline without result. On the fourth try she asked for an overdose, after which she had to report daily to her doctor for blood and urine tests until he advised her of the best time for conception. That time was the clincher.

The babies were born—weighing in order of birth, a boy at 4.4 pounds, a girl at 2.7 pounds, a boy at 4.6 pounds, a girl at 3 pounds, a boy at 4.1 pounds, and a girl at 3.5 pounds. They survived three separate crises: the actual birth, the threat of lung collapse a few hours later, and jaundice that developed forty-eight hours after birth. There might have been a fourth crisis if their rabbi had not decided to waive Jewish custom in favor of medical opinion. The three boys, according to custom, should have been circumcised when they were eight days old. Since they were spending the first six weeks of their lives in incubators, this ritual was overlooked.

Colin Rosenkowitz, the forty-year-old father, also reports that having sextuplets did not bring the fame and fortune he expected. "I'm very, very disappointed and struggling to support my family," he said on the first anniversary of the multiple birth. "I have nothing in my pocket to show for the original enthusiasm of companies here. We've had nothing but promises." Mr. Rosenkowitz had expected to make as much as $750,000 from a tour of the United States with the sextuplets, but the trip was canceled because of lack of interest.

The Rosenkowitzes were the eighth set of sextuplets to be born since fertility drugs were introduced in 1961. And they were the first in which all the babies survived. There does not seem to be a way, even for modern medical science, to guarantee the survival of all babies born as sextuplets. One of the six Stanek babies died, so did one of the six born in England in 1969. Among other cases reported in Africa, Sweden, and Italy, only a few infants survived. Of American sextuplets, those born in May 1970 to Mrs. Susan Danoff of New York died within a few hours of birth, and Mrs. Charlotte Lange, of San Jose, California, lost all but one of her six born in December 1974. This gave Mrs. Lange the tragic distinction of having lost nine babies in little more than a year, for she had also given birth to quadruplets in November 1973. All died.

No doubt, within the near future and as a result of taking fertility drugs, some woman will give birth to an unprecedented septuplets. By then, medical science may have progressed to a point where all the babies can be saved. If so, the septuplets—simply because they will be unique in human history—may become almost as famous as the Dionne quints were in their day.

But they will grow up in a world where not multiple births but birth control is the overriding issue, a world in which people are less willing to allow the number of babies to be decided by an Unseen Hand. Pregnant women, to their surprise, are finding themselves ignored or, to their bewilderment, met by open hostility. A mother of five, again pregnant, reports plaintively that when she takes her brood for an outing, she is met with such scornful remarks as, "Haven't you ever heard of birth control?"

One woman even put off having her second child until she learned that the birth rate had fallen to below replacement level. But soon after her daughter was born she began receiving anonymous letters enclosing literature on sterilization and abortion, and her husband received several pamphlets on vasectomy. "Maybe I should have had second thoughts about having a second child," she says. "But I thought, with those birth rate statistics, I was entitled to bear my 0.9 more children."

It must be hard to go through an awkward and uncomfortable nine months without the kind of sympathetic appreciation that used to be the consolation of mothers.

But the fact is that an increasing number of American women are beginning to think of children more as a burden on their freedom than the supreme justification of their lives.

THE PILL

"All of us divide our careers into two periods," says a New York gynecologist. "Much as history is divided into B.C. and A.D., we have two distinct eras: B.P. and A.P.—Before and After the Pill."

"Thanks to the Pill," says Clare Boothe Luce, "woman no longer is forced to choose between no sex or the once-inevitable nine months, nine pounds consequences of the sex act."

Shirley MacLaine, the actress, adds fervently, "The Pill was *real* emancipation for women."

The Pill, still our major contraceptive, was used by over 14 million women in 1974. Even among Catholics the birthrate continues to drop, and no one suggests that it is due either to an upsurge in abstinence or to better luck in playing Vatican roulette. In 1965 the rate had dropped from 4.5 children per woman to 3.2—or almost 30 percent. By 1970 it had plunged to 2.3.

We interviewed one hundred Catholic women of childbearing age. Fifty-seven were on the Pill, seven others had been equipped with intrauterine devices, and an even dozen relied on their husbands to use condoms.

Very few Catholic women now regard the rhythm method, so-called Vatican roulette, as a sufficient safeguard.

"The acceptance of the Pill is only a few years away," one woman told our interviewer, "so why should I keep having kids while I wait for the Pope to make up his mind? I don't even talk about it at confession. It's nobody's business but mine."

Another woman who lived in Homewood, a rather elegant Chicago suburb, told us her priest was opposed to the Pill and made her feel guilty about using it. When she heard that a priest in Olympia Fields, the next parish, was offering no objection to the Pill, she and her husband sold their house and moved there. "We're still good Catholics and have no guilt feelings now, and no fear of another unwanted baby."

There is a statistically important difference, however, between the attitudes of working-class Catholic women and those of middle and upper income. Working-class women are inclined to be more faithful to the edicts of their church, although a few sometimes practice a form of doublethink. Witness the Boston, Massachusetts, woman who said "I would never go against the Church. But I've no control over my husband. What he does about his own immortal soul is none of my business!"

Another woman of similar strong convictions told us: "I pay my debt to the Church by telling the priest about it at Confession and doing proper penance. He gets mad at me sometimes, but that's easier than having another kid squawling around the house! I've got five already!"

The lower on the economic scale, the less likely women are to approve of birth control, although opinion is still about equally divided on the question.

"I let my husband use a condom," a Scranton, Pennsylvania, woman said, "because he bought a package in the men's room at a gas station we stopped at. But I didn't feel right about it, and neither did he. God gave us sex for a reason. If we don't obey His will nothing good will come of it—and that's for sure!"

Interviews with lower-income women yielded many horror stories of deformed and stillborn babies born to those who had practiced birth control. There were frequent references to women "on the Pill" who got cancer. These stories were almost invariably cited to reinforce a religious argument, as examples of God's will working in His mysterious way.

Among higher-income families, particularly where both parents are college educated, the Church's edict on birth control is considered more as advice than commandment. There is also a feeling that high ecclesiastical authorities in Rome are simply not able to make sensible rulings about such an intimate domestic problem for the American laity.

The wife of a well-known Catholic civil rights lawyer: "It's the same with the Church as with any other kind of government. The further it's away from the people it's supposed to govern, the more irrelevant its laws become. If Pope Paul and his college of cardinals would talk more to ordinary people and find out what's really going on, they'd bring the Church more quickly into the twentieth century. In the end they'll have to anyway, so why not now before too many people decide the Church is too old fashioned for them? If His Holiness would like to know the real situation, let him listen to priests instead of telling them."

We wondered how Catholic priests feel about birth control. Many priests refused to be interviewed, and others told us they did not wish to put themselves on record, even anonymously, against a Church edict that is still in force. The results of our survey are unlike those reported by *Time* magazine in its issue of February 4, 1974. *Time* said that 60 percent to 75 percent of "U.S. priests and laity" do not consider artificial birth control to be sinful. Unless the proportion of priests in *Time*'s survey is very low, our own poll is in conflict.

Those priests willing to make a statement for the record indicate clearly that if the principle of birth control has indeed conquered the Vatican, as some liberal Catholics would like to believe, the formal surrender papers are not ready to be signed. The priests, thirty-one in all, overwhelmingly support Church policy.

Their attitude is summarized by a young St. Paul priest who conceded that young couples had moved out of his parish because of his strong stand against any form of contraception except the rhythm method. Then he ended firmly, "Yet I cannot help but condemn that which violates the teachings of Christ."

A weakly articulated opposition is best stated by a Los Angeles priest. "Mine is a poor parish, largely Chicano, and I know they believe in His Holiness. Yet I also know the cross they bear in bringing an unwanted child they cannot afford into the world. So I close my eyes. I don't attempt to practice contraception from the Confessional."

There certainly appears to be no danger of the late British writer Evelyn Waugh's nightmare coming true. Mr. Waugh, a convert to Catholicism, foresaw a day coming in which red-robed cardinals stood outside St. Peter's Basilica selling contraceptives.

IS THE PILL DANGEROUS?

Surprisingly, most gynecologists have reservations regarding the Pill, and only a minority of doctors' wives use it. A recent study published in the American Journal of Obstetricians and Gynecologists revealed only 35 percent of physicians' wives were using the Pill in 1970 and only 27 percent two years later. This report was based on responses from 355 wives of physicians in New York State in March 1972.

No gynecologist thought the Pill should be in any way barred from prescription, but all are convinced that a woman who endures any side- or after-effects should quickly find another method of contraception. And many women's experiences confirm the need for such caution.

Sylvia Dawes, a former fashion model, has a specific reason for feeling bitter about her experience with the Pill.

"I'm a 'former' fashion model because of it," she explains. "I was on the Pill for a little over a year when dark blotches started appearing on my face. At first they didn't bother me too much because I could cover them with makeup. But after a few weeks they got so dark the makeup didn't work well enough to fool the cameras and I began losing jobs. I went to my gynecologist, who told me I was one out of a hundred thousand women who had this adverse reaction to the Pill. I went off it immediately, but it's taken three years for the blotches to fade to a point where I don't look grotesque. I've been assured by skin specialists that the blotches will disappear eventually, but that is small consolation for losing what would have been the best years of my career."

This blotching—chloasma or malasma—is almost impossible to remove surgically or through peeling the skin. Time alone removes the dark patches.

"When you alter a natural function like ovulation, you can't help but disturb the metabolism," observes a Denver, Colorado, gynecologist. "I would say that three out of ten patients should not be on the Pill—they will suffer from nausea, excessive discharge during the menstrual period, occasional dizziness, headaches and/or acute nervous tension. Yet only one of the three will turn to another contraceptive. The other two will endure the discomfort because they like the convenience and the reliability."

Other doctors report that many women taking the Pill suffer a profound personality change—depression is the most common symptom. Dr. Friedrich S. Brodnitz of New York discovered yet another curious side effect. Three of his patients, all opera singers, began to complain about the loss of high tones. Brodnitz, an otolaryngologist at Mount Sinai Hospital, took the singers off the Pill and their voices returned to normal. According to a study reported in the *British Medical Journal*, healthy women from twenty to thirty-four years old who use the Pill run a risk of pulmonary or cerebral embolism which is 7 to 8 times that in non-users.

For some women there are dangerous physical consequences. Dr. Stanford Wessler, a blood specialist at Washington University School of Medicine, studied eight women who had been on the Pill and later underwent minor surgery. He compared them to a group of twelve women who had similar surgery but did not take the Pill. Three of the eight Pill users developed positive test-scans indicating thrombosis (clotting), but none of the women who did not use the Pill were similarly afflicted.

Dr. John H. Laragh, professor of clinical medicine at Columbia University's College of Physicians and Surgeons, claims that approximately three of every 100,000 women will find that use of the Pill induces hypertension, which is the underlying cause of most strokes and heart attacks. Estrogen, a hormone contained in the Pill, can set off a chain reaction that causes the body to retain a dangerously high amount of salt. And blood pressure is partially determined by the level of salt in the body.

Dr. Laragh first noted the phenomenon when a twenty-three-year-old girl came to him with dangerously high blood pressure.

"I couldn't find an apparent cause, but just before she left my office she mentioned she'd been on the Pill for five years. I told her to stop taking it, and when she came back a few months later her pressure was back to normal. When she went back on the Pill she became severely hypertensive again."

According to the New England Journal of Medicine, medical researchers are very much concerned with the growing number of strokes suffered by young women. With the assistance of neurologists in twelve major cities, case histories of nearly six hundred women between the ages of fifteen and forty-four who were hospitalized with strokes have been examined. Twice as many of the stroke sufferers had been on the Pill as women in "control" groups.

The Pill seems most strongly linked to thrombotic strokes (caused by the formation of a clot in one of the blood vessels of the brain) and hemorrhagic strokes (caused by the rupture of a cerebral blood vessel). Researchers have tentatively concluded that there is a tendency for the estrogen in oral contraceptives to increase the blood pressure of some women to a danger point where strokes result.

Dr. Martin P. Vessey, a British researcher who has done some of the most definitive research on problems related to the Pill, says that the incidence of stroke among women under forty-five years old remains small—and the chance of a woman on the Pill suffering stroke is only 1 in 10,000. However, he cautions that women taking the Pill should be careful. Dr. Vessey suggests that only pills low in estrogen should be prescribed, and that any woman who notices numbness or weakness in an arm or leg—possible signs of impending stroke—should immediately stop taking the Pill.

As a result of these findings, the officially approved labeling of oral contraceptive drugs distributed in the United States carries cautionary advice about the "statistically significant" association between these pills and blood vessel obstruction due to internal clotting.

In addition to risks to the mother, there is apparently some danger to baby too. If a woman becomes pregnant while taking birth control pills, which happens in approximately 1 percent of the cases, she has a greater chance than other women of bearing children with birth defects.

According to a New York State Department of Health study made by Dr. Dwight Janerich, the synthetic hormones in the Pill may cause birth defects. Two groups of women were studied. All of the 108 women in the first group had given birth to children with arm and leg defects. All of the 108 women in second group bore normal children. It turned out that fifteen of the women in the first group had been exposed to synthetic hormones, while only four women in the second group had been given similar exposure.

A further investigation is being conducted before any recommendation is made about the Pill. Despite the scare stories, the mortality rate from taking the Pill is less than 10 percent of that among women who become pregnant.

"ENORMOUS PROFITS"

The Pill is not the only contraceptive device under challenge. Recently, a coalition of women's groups petitioned the California State Department of Health to ban the sale of intrauterine devices until there is proof of their safety and effectiveness.

A spokeswoman said, "The IUD ought to be labeled for what it is—hazardous. It allows pregnancy that often must be terminated by surgery. It causes bleeding and pain that may require hospitalization and worsens menstruation. It may bring on pelvic infections that may cause sterility. It produces psychological problems, and the death rate is one of the big unknowns."

One representative of the Feminist Women's Health Center, observing that men do the research and make the IUDs, remarked, "No man is ever going to have an IUD inserted." This reasoning owes little to logic. By the same token, since they are unlikely to wear them, women should not be allowed to make condoms.

More serious is the accusation by Sidney Wolinsky of Public Advocates that women are allowed to take "extraordinary risks" to their health and lives because the government has failed to safeguard them from "large drug companies which have reaped enormous profits." Mr. Wolinsky said that an intrauterine device costs about 35¢ to produce, and is sold for about $3.50 to physicians, who in turn charge $35 to insert it. That would mean the IUD is marked up a hundredfold before it reaches the ultimate consumer!

A Planned Parenthood spokeswoman, asked to comment, said, "Unfortunately, the charge will scare off a lot of women intending to have a device inserted. We hope that women already using the device will not be frightened and that, if they do have any worry, they will consult their physician."

OTHER WAYS

All the controversy may hasten the introduction of more "advanced" chemical contraceptives, taken orally or injected. Research into more effective methods, although badly crippled by lack of financial support, is going forward. A Rockefeller Foundation spokesman told us that if more research money were available, scientists would quickly achieve a fundamental understanding of human reproduction. Some of the advances made in the past fifteen years are not being used to advantage because money is lacking.

"All of these advances in knowledge for improved methods of birth control are being stalled right now for lack of funds," says an officer in charge of the Ford Foundation's population office. "It's like having an expensive car ready to go and letting it sit in the garage because the gas tank is empty."

Of the new birth-control methods currently available or soon to come, these offer the most promise:

· "Morning After" pills, which must be sold or prescribed with the warning that the pill may not be safe and could trigger such side effects as blood clotting. Its use is not as simple as it should be; this pill must be taken not later than seventy-two hours after intercourse. The pill neutralizes the union of the sperm cell with the egg.

Another pill effective any time up to three days after intercourse is based on a synthetic version of prostaglandin—which is found in nature both in male semen and women's menstrual fluid. This is expected to be cleared for use before the end of 1975.

· The newest intrauterine device is the Cu-7, a copper-wrapped piece of flexible plastic that is in the shape of the numeral 7. The stem, wrapped in fine copper wire, continuously releases tiny particles of copper into the uterus, producing a contraceptive effect. The amount of copper released is so small, only a fraction of 1 percent of the amount the body normally gets from food and water, that there is apparently no danger. The Cu-7 (Cu is the chemical symbol for copper) has been tested on ten thousand women over three years in clinics, and in June 1974 was cleared for prescribing and placement by physicians. The device is smaller in size than most IUDs and can be used by women uncomfortable with larger sizes. A spokesman for Searle Laboratories, which manufactures the device, informs us that it is 99 percent effective in preventing pregnancy within a twelve-month period, and has a much lower rate of expulsion and other problems than older intrauterine devices.

· The Three-Month Contraceptive Injection, approved by the FDA in 1973. Depo Provera, produced by the Upjohn Company, can prevent pregnancy up to three months with a single injection. The precise name of the liquid is Medroxyprogesterone acetate, and it is a milky-looking fluid which is suspended in water and injected in either the hip or the arm. The dose at family planning centers is 150 milligrams every three months, although some doctors are using a 50-milligram dose once a month because their patients then have a more normal menstruation period.

One problem is that a woman who uses these birth control shots won't know exactly when the effect wears off. She might get pregnant in four months or be infertile for a year. Nevertheless, Dr. Edward A. Guess Jr., a private practitioner, says confidently: "I have no reservations about Depo Provera. It is the Cadillac of contraception."

· The Uterine Progesterone System, being used in testing programs in the United States, Hong Kong, and Red China, is a device consisting of a T-shaped piece of soft plastic which contains the hormone progesterone. It is inserted in the uterus like an intrauterine device, and the progesterone, molecularly identical to the natural hormone that women secrete, diffuses into the uterus slowly over the span of a year.

· A biodegradable birth control capsule has been developed by scientists at the Massachusetts Institute of Technology. The capsule is implanted under the skin, and the slow release delivery system makes it effective up to a year. Paul M. Newberne, professor of nutritional pathology at M.I.T., says, "The capsule, using norgestrel as the birth-control agent, is designed to be broken down and absorbed by normal body action in the same manner as absorbable sutures in surgery." So far, the capsule has only been tested on animals and will not be tested on human beings until 1978.

An oral contraceptive for men seems a strong possibility for the near future. Dr. C. Alvin Paulsen of the University of Washington in Seattle has safely tested volunteers with a drug that produces temporary infertility without affecting the sex drive. It is apparently safe, effective, and reversible. One hundred volunteers, ranging from nineteen to thirty-five years old, were given a daily pill that contained a mild dose of male hormone, plus a potent male hormone injection once a month. This treatment reduced their sperm count by 95 to 98 percent without producing any side effects.

Some questions remain: how low must the sperm count be to insure contraception? And how long will it take, after stopping use of the pill, for the sperm count to return to normal levels.

Nature, a British science magazine, reports that another birth-control pill for men has been developed. Australian biochemists Dr. Michael and Dr. Maxine Briggs of Melbourne's Alfred Hospital claim that their pill, a combination of the female hormone estrogen and the male hormone androgen, will stop the production of sperm after nine to fifteen weeks of use. There are no side effects except for a slight nausea at the beginning of the program. Men suffer no loss of sexual drive, and their sperm cells return to normal after they stop taking the pill. The return to normalcy, however, may take as long as nine to ten months.

Less credible theories about birth control have been put forward by some reputable protagonists.

Dr. Ann Chandler, a genetics researcher at Western General Hospital in Edinburgh, Scotland, claims that tight underpants reduce a man's fertility. She says tight underpants cause high temperatures in the testicles, and this brings about an abnormally low degree of sperm effectiveness. "Rabbits and gorillas produce a sperm that is ninety-eight percent effective," she says. "But no man who has been tested has sperm that is more than seventy-five percent effective. If a bull came up with a sample that was as effective as a man's, he would be shot on the spot."

Dr. Chandler is now busy comparing the sperm count of men in various stages of undress. Her subjects vary from men wearing tight underpants to kilt-wearing Scotsmen and naked African tribesmen. We have no reports on either rabbits or gorillas being tested while wearing tight underpants. Until further statistics become available, our best advice to men who want to have children is to hang loose.

Other researchers claim hot baths will reduce a man's fertility and cold baths will increase the count of active sperm. There is also some support for the theory that sexual potency and strenuous exercise are incompatible.

Dr. Robert K. Kerlan, medical director of the National Health Institute and a consultant to leading professional football, baseball, and basketball teams, tells us he has often been asked the question in reverse: whether sexual activity immediately prior to a game has a positive or negative effect on athletic performance. The question, says Dr. Kerland, is usually asked by rookies early in the game.

The doctor has a standard reply: never during halftime.

We saved for last the most delightful method of birth control. According to Dr. William H. Masters and Virginia E. Johnson, well-known sex researchers, frequent lovemaking can be an effective means of contraception.

This appears to run contrary to common sense, but Masters and Johnson cite the case of a young couple who came to their St. Louis laboratory to find out why the wife did not become pregnant.

The young couple had certainly not missed any opportunity to become parents. They engaged in intercourse regularly three times a day. When tests showed that the husband had a very low sperm count, Dr. Masters advised the couple to wait for thirty-six hours between each act of intercourse during the wife's fertile period. Within two months, she was pregnant.

"As you can imagine," Dr. Masters observed, "they immediately went back to their three-times-a-day routine, except when they wanted the wife to conceive."

They now have three children.

The only direct way of proving this theory would be too physically exhausting for the authors, but for others interested in finding out whether it works, it sounds like a good deal of fun.

FAMILY PLANNING

It's hard to believe that only in 1964 were the first federal funds allocated for a pilot birth-control center in Galveston, Texas.

Ten years later, in 1974, nearly 5 million women were receiving birth-control aid at government expense. That number will increase to 6.5 million in 1975.

For those who wonder if all this birth control activity is having any effect on the act which causes pregnancy, the answer is no. Copulation is doing better than population. In fact, according to two authoritative studies, copulation has never been more in. A poll of five thousand women by the National Fertility Study in 1965 disclosed that the frequency of sexual intercourse for U.S. women under the age of forty-five averaged 6.8 times a month. In the ensuing five years, the frequency improved by 20 percent. On the basis of four thousand interviews with women in 1971, Princeton University's Office of Population Research learned that Americans were conjugating 8.2 times monthly. Obviously, the trend is running strongly toward concupiscence.

Our government, in a rare display of wisdom, has not attempted to limit sexual activity. But it is telling millions of American women how to limit the size of their families, what kinds of birth-control devices and techniques there are, and how to use them properly. Family planning clinics are available in hospital wards, storefront buildings, farmhouses, mobile homes, and portable buildings.

Helene Gould, a family planning educator, works in a mainly Chinese community and confronts a problem with the language barrier. However, her agency has worked out a technique of visiting women in their homes. "We go door to door like the Avon lady calling, but with family planning." She has found that women who might be awed by the formalities of a clinic are easier to talk to in their home surroundings.

At the Near North Adult Center in Chicago, clients are shown films about birth control and attend lectures on the latest contraceptive methods. A woman chooses what contraceptive method she prefers. Then her medical history is taken, and she gets a complete physical checkup—including pelvic and breast examinations, Pap smear, and tests for venereal disease. Tests show whether she can safely use the method she has chosen, and the clinic supplies her with any device needed. She is examined regularly to make sure it's safe for her to continue with the technique. If she misses an appointment, she is called and urged to schedule a new visit. If she misses several visits, a staff worker may look her up to find out why.

Does it work? The number of women getting aid at the Near North Adult Center has tripled each year, and in an area of forty thousand low-income black and Spanish-speaking people, a once-burgeoning birthrate has become stabilized.

One worker said proudly, "A woman came in here the other day and didn't like the attention she was getting. She told us, 'If it wasn't for people like me using your service, you wouldn't get the money to stay open. You'd all be out of a job.' And you know something? She's right!"

WHAT "WHITEY" WANTS

The most vocal opposition to family planning is from minority groups.

A fiery young Black Muslim told us, "We're against birth control because it's part of the white man's policy for stamping out minorities. If it's just births you want to stop, start with the Kennedys and the Rockefellers. Why only ask black families to do it? Whitey wants less of us so he can handle the 'black problem'! Take all those black uteruses out of production!

"You tell me why all these clinics are starting up where the black people are poorest if it isn't aimed right at them. Of course it is aimed at them, and everybody knows it is. People read those newspaper stories about black people having to undergo enforced sterilization, and that tells them where it's really at."

A young black woman from Detroit: "Whitey ain't going to tell me whether or not I can have kids. If they only want one or two or none at all, that's their business; we like kids around, the more the better. I'm a mother, damn it, and as long as I can give my kids decent food, good clothes and an education, why shouldn't I have as many as I want?"

A U.S. government-employed doctor at a reservation hospital near Wounded Knee, South Dakota, told our interviewer why he believes the American Indian continues to record a rising birthrate: "Everything is against them. The mortality rate among Indian children is appalling. But they feel, almost all of them, that the white man has tried to exterminate them and the way to fight back is to have a large family. Birth control is just another white man's trick as far as they can see. So they go on having as many babies as they can, and with malnutrition rampant, and tuberculosis, and a whole variety of infections and illnesses, one out of three children don't survive to become six years old."

A different attitude was expressed by a Mexican-American woman in a crowded and impoverished area of East Los Angeles: "I don't know if I should have any more. My husband doesn't make much money. I've seen three of my children go into gangs before they were twelve years old, and one got in trouble, terrible trouble, when he was only sixteen. [He was arrested on a rape and assault charge.] Most of the time I think God would not think birth control is a mortal sin, like the priest says. Anyhow, it is a sin I must accept if I wish no more tragedies to happen."

Family planning clinics are open to all Americans regardless of income. Up to 90 percent of the overall cost is paid for by federal funds. There is no charge if the family income is below 150 percent of poverty level, and most others pay only part of the cost. This year, when according to law all of the nation's 3,099 counties, parishes, and districts will be required to offer family planning services to past, present, and potential recipients of welfare, the funding for the program is expected to exceed $400 million.

Those who favor subsidized birth control claim the programs pay for themselves. California State Senator Anthony C. Beilenson, author of much of the legislation that has given his state a comprehensive and well-funded planning program, defined for us what he considers to be the advantages.

"The quality of life is improved in many ways. To mention just a few:

- "One: Healthier and better cared-for children.
- "Two: Far fewer cases of child abuse and neglect.
- "Three: More stable family life and fewer illegitimate births.
- "Four: Fewer mentally disturbed children and adolescents.
- "Five: Continuing decreases in the welfare rolls.
- "Six: Fewer youthful offenders in correctional institutions.

"Health experts have estimated that for every dollar spent on family planning, government costs are reduced by twelve dollars."

Above all, there is a question of morale, of a sense of worth beyond measuring in dollars. "Without the power to control their fertility," says Joseph D. Beasley, director and founder of Louisiana's statewide family planning program, "women can't control their health, education, or their personal destiny."

Clare Boothe Luce puts it this way: "For centuries women had no control, except abortion, over nature's programming of their procreative function. Consequently, owing to successive pregnancies, they were unable to play many of the social roles that they otherwise could have performed quite ably. For the first time in history she is—*almost*—as free as man to opt for the role she wishes to play in society."

Future generations may wonder why anyone ever found Germaine Greer's proclamation controversial: "What could be more welcome than to have women sharing the unfair privilege men have enjoyed since time began—to participate in sex without having to endure pregnancy, and the rearing of a child, as a consequence. No longer are we the bovine, to be freshened at will or by accident—we can control our destiny and the destiny of the sperm cell that no longer need dominate."

BILL OF RIGHTS

Now that family planning is making headway among the poor, social workers are becoming concerned about whether help is being given in the right way.

Sally Uribe, a registered nurse who works in the family planning service of the Berkeley (California) Health Department, has produced a "consumer" bill of rights, which starts out with the premise that "the consumer has the right to know everything, even the ultimate bad news. Not telling the truth is part of the condescending attitude of health professionals." Consumers have the right to know who will see them, to be shown their charts and have them explained, to be told exactly what is going on in the examination room and what treatment and risks are involved, and to refuse treatment. They have the right to know the pros and cons of the various methods of family planning and to decide which method they prefer to use. The woman has the right to be talked to in her own language in terms she understands, to be treated as an equal, and to prevail over the doctor or whoever is attending her when picking the method of birth control she wants. "We as advisers tend to forget that the consumer has good sense," Ms. Uribe declares.

Ruth Rankin McKinnon was working in the movement in 1937 when contraceptive was a dirty word and the concept of family planning so unacceptable that her success in establishing a clinic in Knoxville was considered a major victory—even though the clinic was limited to mothers of six or more children. The very words "birth control" and "pregnancy" could not even be whispered on a radio program.

"We have to make birth control a vital priority," the eighty-one-year-old Mrs. McKinnon says today. "We need the most wide-spread education about planned parenthood methods. Ignorance, apathy, and false impressions have held us back more than anything else."

In rating recent U.S. Presidents on their attitudes toward furthering birth control research, Mrs. McKinnon gives Eisenhower low marks, Kennedy high marks (although a Catholic, he endorsed birth control), and Johnson high marks. She notes acidly that Nixon made "one statement endorsing birth control the first year he was President. Period."

Mrs. McKinnon distributed birth control information in thirty-two states and many foreign countries. She once arrived in an overpopulated and under-developed foreign country which prohibited the importation of contraceptives except for personal use. The native customs officers opened two very large cartons to discover they contained condoms. Are these for your personal use? she was asked. Yes, they are. And how long do you intend to remain in the country? Two or three weeks, she answered. Amid a gale of laughter, she triumphantly carried her cartons past the customs.

Today Mrs. McKinnon, eyes glinting humorously, says, "When I started, I never really thought we'd come as far as we have."

ABORTION AND STERILIZATION: DRASTIC REMEDIES

19

"Since I started practicing twenty years ago," a Washington, D.C., obstetrician reports, "I never failed to deliver less than twenty babies a year that weren't wanted by their mothers. The number was probably much greater, for I only include women who begged me to perform an abortion. Now, when a woman comes in who has a valid reason for not wanting her child, I'm thankful the Supreme Court rejected the idea that a fetus was a living human being with legal rights, and left the decision to the woman and her doctor."

From Tacoma, Washington, another doctor says forcefully: "We've got to become even more clinical in our attitudes. Damn it, it isn't a baby until it is delivered, cries, and *lives*. Until then it is an unknown quantity."

"One thing we can prove," adds a Des Moines gynecologist, "is that fewer women and babies are losing their lives because of unqualified professional care and/or unsanitary operating conditions. There's been a sharp drop in the infant death rate, a fall in congenital abnormalities, and a decrease in ectopic pregnancies. I've heard varying reports about pelvic inflammation, but I'm sure that's simply because cases are being reported now that weren't before. When abortions weren't legal, the parties naturally tried to cover up when anything went wrong. Sometimes the family doctor, coming into a case after the abortion had been performed, would help in the coverup. A lot of so-called inflamed appendixes were really something else, and you can bet on that!"

What are the actual risks in an abortion? Experience so far shows they are much less than in any comparable operation. In fact, it would appear that you're in more danger crossing the street. In 26,000 consecutive abortions performed in New York, there were only thirty-six perforations of the uterus and only one required a hysterectomy. Last year the death rate in legalized abortions fell below 2 per 100,000.

Abortion has become a nearly worldwide practice. Over thirty nations have legalized abortion within the first three months of pregnancy. And with the volumes of medical experience now available, the low proportion of fatalities is confirmed. Deaths during legal abortions worldwide are consistent with the United States experience—about 2 per 100,000. Illegal abortions result in deaths 50 times more frequently—about 100 per 100,000.

Fifty-five million women in the world terminated their pregnancies by either legal or illegal operations in 1971, and the number has sharply increased since then. Even in areas such as Latin America, where such operations are generally forbidden, more than half of all pregnancies are ended by illegal abortions.

LEGAL ATTACKS

In the United States the legalization of abortion has not ended the struggle against it, but merely shifted it to new battlegrounds.

In many states procedures have been made so complex that a woman trying to meet the legal requirements can pass her fourth month, after which the risks in an abortion increase. Medical authorities don't agree on the "safe" time limit for an abortion, but the consensus is that women should have it by the eighth to tenth weeks of pregnancy.

Pressure from right-to-life groups has produced an atmosphere in Louisiana, North Dakota, Mississippi, and perhaps a score of other states in which abortions have become a medical rarity—less than five per 1,000 women age fifteen to forty-four. That's only one-quarter of the national average.

Eleven states now restrict the use of federal Medicaid funds to pay for an abortion. Twenty-eight states stipulate that doctors and hospitals cannot be forced to perform abortions if this offends their ethical code, or even their better judgment. The practical result is to make abortions unobtainable in many areas. Other legislatures have passed laws that require extensive book-keeping in all abortion cases, or forbid the advertising of abortion services.

Fifteen states have passed laws requiring a woman to obtain her husband's consent before seeking an abortion. In the first test case that reached a court, the decision went in favor of the husband. A Florida judge declared, "The interest which a father has in seeing his procreation carried full term is, perhaps, at least equal to that of the mother." However, that ruling was overturned by an appeals court which declared that since the United States Supreme Court had said the state could not prohibit abortions during the first six months, "it follows inescapably that the state may not statutorily delegate to the husbands . . . an authority the state does not possess."

The judicial hot potato has now been tossed over to the Supreme Court for a further ruling, which is not expected until the summer of 1975.

Most pro-abortion forces regard the consent requirement as a ruse by state legislatures that can no longer bar abortion outright. "By making a woman get a man's consent, by invading her privacy, they make it more difficult for her to get an abortion," says a prominent civil rights lawyer. "Women of middle class and upper income can usually get around this law by forging the husband's signature, or by visiting a neighboring state that has no such law on its books. The women who are hurt are those of the poorer classes who can't afford to travel, or who are so dependent on their husbands for support they would not dare to take an action in defiance of them."

Three different constitutional amendments have been introduced to overturn the U.S. Supreme Court decision of January 22, 1973. One would give a fetus legal rights from the moment of conception and prohibit all abortions, even to save the life of the mother. Another would prohibit abortion except in a "medical emergency" threatening the life of the mother. Still another would wipe out the Supreme Court decision and let each state legislature decide what the abortion law should be.

Any one of these amendments would have to pass the Congress by a two-thirds majority and then be ratified by two thirds of the states. "But given the emotionalism of the issue," says Elizabeth D. Stengel, associate director of the Religious Coalition for Abortion Rights, "I certainly don't deny it could happen."

Her organization is battling such legislation, and other women's groups and pro-abortion forces are letting their views be heard on the question. Jan Leibman, of the National Organization for Women, says angrily, "No woman should ever be forced to be her husband's brood mare. The woman is the one who carries the fetus and gives birth to it, so she should be the only one to decide whether to carry it to term."

On the first anniversary of the Supreme Court's decision, January 22, 1974, *Time* magazine made a region-by-region survey and found that many practical obstacles to abortion remain.

In the northeastern United States, according to the report, abortions could be obtained in most states, although in some the procedure is performed only in hospitals and usually only in non-Catholic ones. New York State, which adopted an abortion-on-demand law as early as 1970, is still the best place for a woman seeking to terminate a pregnancy.

In the southern United States, *Time* reported a mixed picture. Many women in Alabama avoided a "stigma" by traveling to Georgia for a more readily available legal operation. In Louisiana, only one doctor was openly performing abortions, but at Florida and Texas hospitals, as well as at a growing number of special clinics, abortions were available.

In the midwest, women seeking abortions were advised to stick to the largest cities. Even Milwaukee and Minneapolis only had one clinic apiece. St. Louis's Mayor John Poelker had forbidden city hospitals to perform abortions. In Chicago, abortions were relatively easy to obtain.

Farther west, Utah hospitals made it very difficult to get an abortion, while Idaho women preferred to fly to Seattle where lower prices were available in hospitals and clinics. The most easily obtainable, inexpensive abortions were to be had in the state of California.

Anti-abortionists have been stepping up their campaign. They came very close to having New York's liberal abortion law repealed, and in California the Pro-Life Council, which claims a membership of fifteen thousand, is trying to persuade legislators to change the law there. Their efforts persuaded Congress to attach a rider to domestic health legislation that permits federally financed private hospitals to refuse to perform abortions.

The effect has been to make public hospitals the slowest to respond to the Supreme Court's decision. Only 17 percent of public hospitals performed any abortions in 1974. This makes the right to choose abortion much less available to low income women, who have the highest rates of unwanted pregnancy.

"The nickel-and-diming by the opposition is now as serious a threat as the proposed constitutional amendments," says Lawrence Lader, chairman of the board of the National Abortion Rights Action League.

NOTHING NEW

The late great humorist Robert Benchley used to tell about a killeyloo bird which, whenever it took off on a flight, flew backward first because it couldn't tell where it was going until it saw where it had been. At the risk of sounding like the killeyloo bird, let us again take a rapid look at the history of our subject.

Illegal abortion is known to have flourished in this country as early as 1860, although it did not become widespread until the 1920s. It was not legal in any state of the union. Only where proof could be submitted that pregnancy presented an extreme danger to the mother was abortion legally permitted, and even then the procedure was so complex that court permission usually came too late.

As a result, increasing numbers of women, usually those who did not have a husband or could not "get away for a while" to have their baby in secrecy, sought out an abortionist.

He was rarely a licensed surgeon or physician. The operations were performed in hastily improvised circumstances by unlicensed doctors, moonlighting midwives, and unqualified practitioners operating from clandestine side-street offices. The transient "offices" were usually scantily furnished and equipped so they could be abandoned at a moment's notice with nothing left behind to provide identification. Operating conditions were primitive and unhygienic.

In 1870, the price of an illegal abortion was about $20. By 1920, that was up to $100.

We shall never know the real figures on the mortality rate during these illegal abortions. The best estimates available from the U.S. Department of Health are that 750,000 abortions were performed each year from 1926 to 1972. Before that, the figures are too scanty to provide any basis for even an accurate guess. As late as 1920, it is estimated, perhaps 30 percent of aborted females died after surgery and another 30 percent were rendered sterile by inept "surgeons" who removed more than the fetus. Those staggering figures are a measure of the desperation of women willing to undertake such risks.

Of course, there have always been attempts at self-induced abortion ranging from the taking of drugs, such as bitterroot, gentian and quinine, to prolonged horseback riding. We know now that these methods did not dislodge a fetus. A prearranged fall from a horse or down a flight of stairs was far more apt to cause serious injury to the mother than to relieve her of her child, and there was a considerable risk of brain damage to the child.

From 1880 to 1930, quinine in massive doses was believed to be a likely method of inducing abortion. The use of quinine and other drugs doubtless led to a good deal of vomiting, and the havoc wrought by vomiting might conceivably have endangered a fetus by shaking it loose. But the mother would then have hemorrhaged and very likely died. Also unresolved is whether the high quinine dosages were responsible for a higher incidence of full-term stillbirths in women who used it. Laxatives were another favorite, but their only chance of dislodging a fetus would have been if the baby were located in the bowels.

As Dr. Alvarez noted, "A healthy fetus is determined to be born, and nothing short of surgery will kill it."

By 1965 only four states—New York, New Jersey, Nevada, and Wyoming—legally recognized abortion, and then only if the mother's life was in grave danger or the child would undoubtedly be born malformed or mentally deficient. This reflected a widespread abhorrence toward the forcible removal of a living fetus from the womb.

As a consequence, millions of abortions were performed illegally. Many thousands of women were rendered sterile, or died, because of unsanitary operating conditions or the abortionist's lack of skill.

Then a movement began, arising almost spontaneously in state after state, to demand the right of abortion for the pregnant woman, married or unmarried, who did not want or could not afford to have a child.

Women's organizations championed the passage of more liberal abortion laws. Welfare agencies, social workers, and politicians working in safe constituencies added their voices. Even the AMA offered tentative and qualified support. As a result, twenty-eight states approved legalized abortion to some extent.

In 1973, in an historic decision resolving the bitter controversy, the United States Supreme Court overruled all state laws that prohibit or restrict a woman's right to obtain an abortion during her first three months of pregnancy. The swift acceptance of the decision by the public was shown by that most sensitive barometer of public opinion—television. On November 21, 1973, "Maude" became the first character in a TV comedy to have an abortion.

FETAL RESEARCH

In Boston, in February 1975, a doctor was convicted of manslaughter for having caused the death of a 24-week-old male fetus.

Dr. Kenneth Edelin, a rugged-looking, moustached physician, black, and a chief resident in obstetrics and gynecology at the City Hospital, found himself in the middle of a legal controversy that may make medical and legal history and lead to a new legal definition of what constitutes a human person.

"Edelin's one of the good guys," a doctor at City Hospital told us. "There's never been any question about his skill, or his compassion, or his interest in the poor people in the ghetto community that surrounds this hospital. It's a political frame-up. They're making him a scapegoat to challenge the Supreme Court's ruling that a woman is entitled to an abortion during the first six months of pregnancy. They'd just like to push the date back to the time of conception."

We were told by medical researchers in the Boston area that the conviction of Dr. Edelin has already had adverse effects on research with fetuses. This, in turn, affects basic investigations in such fields as cancer, birth defects, aging, and viral disease. "We're cutting back for the simple reason that we don't want to get into trouble with the law," one woman researcher said. "But it's a shame. In the years I've been doing this work, I've seen research with fetal tissue lead to vaccines against polio and German measles. And also to many treatments for premature babies."

The opposition doesn't deny this. But: "The premise that what is useful is good, is destructive, and can be used to justify anything," says Dr. Mildred J. Jefferson, vice chairman of the board of directors of the national Right-to-Life Committee and assistant professor of clinical surgery at Boston University Medical School. "It is medically unethical to experiment on a live fetus because it cannot give its informed consent. And it deprives a mother of the right to change her mind about having an abortion. The doctors involved cannot allow her to change her mind, in case the agent administered has in fact caused harm to the unborn human subject."

The proponents of fetal research concede that every precaution must be taken to prevent such a tragedy. But they argue that the research with fetal tissue is simply too important to abandon. One development alone—blood transfusions for babies born with the Rh blood disease—saved 200,000 lives between 1940 and 1960. A new anti-Rh vaccine is now saving 25,000 lives a year.

As for Dr. Edelin, he says: "Obstetrics is a very, very happy specialty, seeing a woman throughout her pregnancy and delivering for her a nice, healthy baby and seeing a family develop. The concept that some people have difficulty understanding, and I feel very strongly about, is that a woman should have that choice, to continue with pregnancy or not. And my obligation is to exercise my best medical judgment to see that this outcome, whichever she wishes, is successful.

"I don't like to do abortions and I haven't met many physicians who enjoy doing abortions. Anyone who does them has to come to grips in his own mind with the problems of life and the fetus, and resolve it as best he can. But the women I take care of are poor and mostly black, and I will defend a woman's right to have abortions. I have seen the results of criminal abortions, and this helped me to decide. . . . If I don't do it, then someone else will do it, perhaps tragically."

Dr. Waldo L. Fielding, a practicing obstetrician-gynecologist in Boston and a teacher at several leading medical schools, says: "Dr. Edelin, acting within the law and hospital rules, was convicted of manslaughter—as defined by the prosecutor—and placed on a year's probation by the judge. But to many of us who live and practice medicine in Massachusetts, particularly in Boston, it is clear that he was convicted of the 'crime' of abortion—a 'crime' abolished by the Supreme Court in its 1973 ruling."

Most doctors and laymen believe that the verdict in the Edelin case was an alarming miscarriage of justice—probably with racial overtones. (Dr. Edelin is black, and his trial took place during the height of the controversy about bussing in the Boston schools.)

The conviction is already having unfortunate consequences. Hospitals in Pittsburgh, Detroit, New York City and Long Island announced they will no longer perform abortions after the third month of pregnancy, except to save the mother's life.

The impact of this change in hospital policy will be felt mostly by poor women, who must travel out of state to have abortions. Even if a hospital agrees to allow a late term abortion, the cost will rise because of sophisticated life support systems that have to be on hand to handle possibly "viable" fetuses. (In some hospitals a second physician is now required to be present in the event that intensive care of the fetus becomes necessary.) Such measures do not noticeably increase the rate of survival and add greatly to the cost of having an abortion. "It makes no sense," a Pittsburgh obstetrician points out. "A woman is having an abortion to get rid of the baby, then we're supposed to try and save it. Has anyone even considered a simple problem like who's going to take care of the baby if it lives?"

The higher cost will not deter those who can afford to have abortions. Dr.

James L. Walters, Jr., a plaintiff in the 1973 Supreme Court case, says, "College girls come bopping in when they're two weeks late for their menstrual periods. The fact that a patient gets to eighteen weeks means she has difficulty making up her mind, she has economic problems, she's not smart enough to know she's pregnant, and she's scared to death to tell her family."

These reasons apply with especial force to those in the lower income stratum.

There is a particularly unfortunate result for mothers carrying mongoloid babies or babies suffering from serious genetic defect. By removing amniotic fluid, in the process called amniocentesis, a doctor can now tell a mother if her baby is going to be seriously retarded. However, that process can only be performed after the fourteenth week and another three weeks is required for the lab study. Even if the results of the amniocentesis indicate an abortion is necessary, it cannot be done within the time limit set by some hospitals in the aftermath of the Edelin verdict.

COMMON SENSE

The Catholic war on abortion remains uncompromising. In August 1974, a priest from New York was disciplined because he baptized a baby whose mother had publicly supported a woman's right to abortion. Other Church officials, with the backing of Humberto Cardinal Medeiros, had refused to perform the baptism. The priest was not allowed to use the church for the baptism, but performed it on the doorstep.

"They're so far behind the times, it's pathetic," says a prominent Catholic layman. "They really believe they have the power to decide who will go to heaven and who won't. They think they can deny an innocent baby the right to its immortal soul because the baby's mother didn't check the bulletin board to get the latest advice from the Vatican!"

Some doctors believe that abortion increases the risk of prematurity because "rough handling" can weaken the cervix. This is not a significant risk, and only happens in the dilation and curettage technique when a general anesthetic is used. Under a local anesthetic a woman is more responsive to what is happening, and the use of the newer small plastic tubes to draw out the contents of the uterus under vacuum aspiration is a much gentler procedure.

According to a Johns Hopkins study, women who have undergone abortions show no greater depression or emotional stress than women who carry their babies to birth. They are neither more alienated nor lower in self-esteem.

The study interviewed 373 women who came to Johns Hopkins hospital for abortion or delivery. These were divided into three categories: those obtaining early abortions, late abortions, and carrying to term. Of the 373 originally questioned, 211 were questioned again about a year after abortion or delivery.

There were virtually no differences found in nine out of ten personality traits. The tenth trait: whether abortion patients or women who carried their babies to birth were more sensitive to others knowing about it. There was a most surprising result. Women who had had their babies were actually "more sensitive"!

Economics plays a large part in the decision of whether to have an abortion or a baby. The financial pressures are now heavily on the "common sense" of simply having an abortion rather than going through the expense of a full-term pregnancy.

Blue Cross in 1974 offered a comprehensive health plan at a cost to individual subscribers of $23.40 a month that covered abortions and all other health services, plus $250,000 in major medical expense benefits. Doctors usually charge private patients from $275 to $350 for abortions. A Medicaid enrollee in the state of California is billed for $265, which is paid by the state. The Cathedral Hill facility, the largest abortion center in Northern California, charges its abortion patients $160.

Dr. Louis Hellman, deputy assistant secretary with the Department of Health, Education and Welfare, estimates that Medicaid finances between 222,000 and 278,000 abortions annually, paying out up to $50 million from federal and state funds. He puts the average cost of an abortion at $180, although conceding that the price can vary widely.

Dr. Hellman says about 800,000 legal abortions were performed in 1973. An estimated 25 percent or more used Medicaid to pay for their abortions.

But, Dr. Hellman points out, this still represents a huge saving in public funds since "for each pregnancy among Medicaid-eligible women that is brought to term, the estimated first-year cost to federal, state and local governments for maternity and pediatric care and public assistance is approximately $2,200."

Obviously, the cost of an abortion whether privately or publicly financed is a good deal less than having a baby. A recent decision by the Internal Revenue Service has made it even cheaper. The IRS ruled that costs for lawful abortion can be included in medical expense when computing income tax.

DOCTOR'S VIEWPOINT

In former times most hospitals had a Tissue Committee—a group of doctors who reviewed pathology reports on D & Cs. D & C (dilation and curettage) is almost the same procedure as an abortion, for it involves dilating the cervix and scraping the lining of the uterus.

The Tissue Committee would review D & Cs to ascertain if an illegal abortion had taken place. A single suspicious report would mean a serious talk with the chief of obstetrics, a second would bring a stern censure, and a third would usually mean that the doctor was kicked off the hospital staff.

Understandably, doctors are relieved not to be subjected to that kind of scrutiny. Most agree the reason the number of miscarriages has dropped appreciably is that many were botched-up attempts at self-abortion. In any event, the mortality rate is much improved and even Catholic doctors, who are against abortion for religious reasons, are pleased with this.

Medical authorities also seem in agreement that there has been a decisive change in women's attitudes toward abortion. "They feel an abortion is their right, and we don't have to assuage their guilt," says a doctor in Riverdale, New York. "They just want the facts—about where they can go for the best and least expensive abortion. In the two years after abortion was legalized in New York, the number of births in the city dropped by thirty-seven thousand eight hundred. It's obvious that this is what women have wanted all along. They think they have a fundamental right to decide, along with their personal physicians, how many babies they'll have and when they'll have them. And if an accident happens, it doesn't mean she has to suffer for it. It isn't like being hit by a streetcar or a bus!"

Author and columnist Shana Alexander adds a more political viewpoint. "I oppose laws forbidding abortion for the same reason I oppose brainwashing. The State will please keep its cotton-pickin' hands as far away from me as possible, mind and body!"

Some doctors do not think abortion should be legal, however. A prominent obstetrician told us, "The idea of abortion should be anathema to women. I can't understand any woman taking it casually. They're killing not only a baby but an extension of themselves. How can they feel blasé about it? It's cheaper, smarter and more convenient to use appropriate birth control than to undergo suction, D & Cs, or whatever. A lot cheaper dollarwise, and psychologically cheaper too."

And a Catholic doctor in Boston, Massachusetts: "What really annoys me is the glib way so many physicians dismiss the problem. Leaving aside moral and religious questions, it is always better for the human body *not* to have to undergo any medical procedure that's unnecessary. That specifically includes abortion—even at the earliest stage."

According to the director of a family planning center, too many young women now rely on abortion rather than contraception as a means of avoiding parenthood.

"Girls are practically engaging in Russian roulette," says Mrs. Helen Steiner who directs a nonprofit clinic in Venice, California. "They figure they'll take the chance of getting pregnant because they can always have an abortion."

"That is a mistake," adds Mrs. Edward Tyler, wife of the medical director of the noted Tyler Clinic for the treatment of infertility. "Abortion is no substitute for preventive measures, for an intelligent birth control plan. Women are not aware of the physical and psychological trauma which may result from abortion. Some girls admit that they have never gotten over it."

On the other hand, to deny women the alternative of abortion will not end the practice. It will only force them into back-room surgery with all its attendant hazards. More and more people are beginning to recognize how unacceptable that option is.

PRO AND CON

Among the most recent recruits to the pro-abortion forces is the YWCA, which said in a statement announcing its position: "Our decision does not mean that we advocate abortion as the most desirable solution to the problem, but rather that a woman should have a right to make the decision."

This stance draws the support of religious organizations as various as units of the national Unitarian, Baptist, Methodist and Presbyterian churches, Church of the Brethren, American Ethical Union, B'nai B'rith Women, American Humanist Association, National Council of Jewish Women, Catholics for a Free Choice, Union of American Hebrew Congregations, and the United Church of Christ's board of homeland ministries. Recently, the conservative Southern Baptists, meeting in convention in Dallas, said that abortion should be permitted "under such conditions as rape, incest, severe fetal deformity, and danger to the emotional, mental, and physical health of the mother."

Many of these organizations are impressed by the statistics showing that maternal health has improved, that there has been a big drop in maternal deaths and also in the number of women admitted to hospitals with botched abortions and other pregnancy difficulties.

The national coalition plans to inform women of the threatening political situation through their temples and churches. "A lot of them still have the erroneous idea that their churches consider abortion sinful," says Mrs. Stengel. "It is impossible to draw liberal-conservative lines on the matter of abortion. The liberals are not all for us, and a consistent conservative would be for abortion rights because supposedly he would not sanction interference by the government in private lives."

Her last assumption is misplaced. Queried on this subject, Senator Barry Goldwater, the most prominent conservative in the country, replied, "I don't want to see promiscuous abortion. If a life is in danger, abortion is okay, but otherwise the Pill ought to be enough. If it isn't, they ought to learn to say no."

Two fellow conservatives, Senators James L. Buckley of New York and Jesse A. Helms of North Carolina, would go further and introduce constitutional amendments protecting unborn children "at every stage of their biological development" and defining the beginning of life as the moment of "fertilization."

But the tepid response from congressional leaders and the public has confirmed the verdict of the opinion polls which show that a huge majority of American men and women conclusively support a woman's right to have an abortion. The Gallup poll, for example, reported that two thirds of the public believes the decision should be left to a woman and her doctor. Among well-educated, higher-income people, the proportion rose to almost 75 percent.

More important than where it stands on the question today, however, is the direction in which public opinion appears to be moving. Here, too, the evidence seems clear.

In March 1972, a poll conducted by Opinion Research Corporation drew these responses from 1,700 interviews with persons aged sixteen and older:

Do you think that the decision to have an abortion in the early months of pregnancy should be made solely by the couple and their doctor, or do you think such abortions should be permitted only under certain circumstances?

Solely by the couple and their doctor 50%
Permitted only under certain circumstances 41%
Not permitted under any circumstances. 6%
No opinion. 3%

In March 1974, a similar poll, asking the same question, evoked these responses:

Solely by the couple and their doctor 63%
Permitted only under certain circumstances 29%
Not permitted under any circumstances. 5%
No opinion. 3%

Politicians read the polls. More importantly, they follow the election returns. In the November 1974 elections only one Congressman who favored the right of abortion was defeated. Twenty-one of the strongest supporters of so-called pro-life legislation went down to defeat. The political situation may not be as threatening as some pro-abortion forces believe.

A LOOK AHEAD

A few years ago the quickest way of finding out whether a woman was pregnant was to send a sample of her urine to a laboratory for testing. That meant days of delay. It is now possible to apply a dot of the patient's urine to a specially treated card, wait a minute or two, and find out immediately by examination under a microscope. The Prognosticon Dri-Dot manufacturers recommend the regular use of their procedure for all fertile women who may have to undergo an x ray or take immunization shots that might possibly harm a fetus.

The difficulty is that this test cannot be used until two weeks after a fertilized egg has been implanted in the uterus. That's because the hormone HCG (human chorionic gonadotrophin) is only produced by the new placenta at that time. A test now being studied would track down a different hormone and is supposedly capable of revealing pregnancy only one week after implantation.

Soon women will be able to purchase a self-test pregnancy kit now in wide use in Holland. It is called The Predictor and is said to give an answer in twenty seconds, with only 2 percent error. Self-test pregnancy kits are available in drugstores now, but their accuracy has been questioned.

For those who don't want to merely learn if they are pregnant but to prevent it, there will soon be pills (mentioned in the previous chapter) that can be taken any time within three days after intercourse. The effect can be compared to spontaneous abortion, though at such an early juncture no life is present that even resembles a fetus.

For those who forget to take their "morning after," or "three days after" pill, there will still be hope. A new procedure is a kind of cross between abortion and after-the-fact birth control. The "menstrual regulation method" can be used when a woman's period is several days late but before pregnancy can be diagnosed accurately.

Within two weeks after a woman discovers that she is "late," she visits her doctor who will insert through her undilated cervix a flexible plastic tube attached to a syringe. The syringe sucks out the menstrual lining, taking with it any fertilized egg that may be present. The procedure takes only a couple of minutes, and the cost is about $30.

No determination of pregnancy is made at the time, thereby avoiding the stigma of abortion with its attendant guilt. However, a later examination of the tissues removed by this method of suction curettage revealed that 43 percent of the women who had undergone the treatment were not pregnant.

THE PERMANENT SOLUTION

Sterilization is the most extreme form of birth control. A sterilized woman is totally unable to procreate, whereas abortion involves the removal of a single fetus and the female is able to reproduce again.

Yet the rapid growth in popularity of this "permanent solution" to the birth-control problem far exceeds all predictions. Six years ago, only 200,000 Americans were voluntarily sterilized. In 1972, about 1,100,000 were sterilized. In 1975, that number will approximately double.

Since January 1, 1970, almost 5 million Americans have been permanently sterilized as a birth-control measure.

The simplest form of sterilization is the severance of the uterine tubes. The procedure was known and practiced in America as early as 1890, when inmates of asylums in Connecticut, Georgia, and Wisconsin were rendered sterile so that while "on leave" or exposed to conjugal visitation rights, they would not add another dependent to the state's relief rolls.

By 1920, the process of sterilizing females had spread, in extra-legal form, to mental institutions in such populous states as New York, California, and Illinois. In the South, and particularly in institutions in which Negro women were kept, sterilization was conducted on a widespread scale.

The practice has endured into our own day. In 1973 you could still read news stories about young girls in Montgomery, Alabama, who were sterilized without understanding the procedure, and how in Aiken, South Carolina, welfare mothers were refused obstetrical care unless they accepted sterilization.

The Department of Health, Education and Welfare estimates that 100,000 poor persons are being sterilized each year in clinics supported by federal funds. The Department has called for new regulations to safeguard these people, to make sure that the surgical procedure is in the best interests of the patient. There is no quarrel, of course, with sterilization when it is done for medical reasons. Hysterectomies are performed for reasons such as malfunctioning ovaries, tipped uteri, or the presence of cancer. What is disturbing HEW is the number of involuntary and unwanted sterilizations that are being performed.

A more recent phenomenon has been the voluntary sterilization of young women who do not want to become mothers.

Wendy Stuart, a Sarah Lawrence college graduate, was born without one hand. She is a serious music student and felt that having a child would be an additional hardship she could not, in her situation, cope with. The intrauterine device for birth control disagreed with her metabolism, so she chose to be sterilized. The operation is called a tubal ligation: an incision is made in the abdomen, and the fallopian tubes are tied off surgically. The stitches used to close the incision make a tiny abdominal scar. "One night in the hospital and a little nausea from the anesthetic is all it took," Miss Stuart says.

Georgia Miller Graber, a thirty-year-old registered nurse in California, now the wife of a physician, decided to be sterilized when she was a twenty-eight-year-old divorcee with one child. "I adore my little boy—but I decided I didn't want to have any more children. I realized I might fall in love and get married again, but I made the decision as an individual. The man I married had to accept me as I am."

Mrs. Graber's operation was a laparoscopy, sometimes referred to as Band-Aid surgery because it requires such a small incision and leaves no scar. The surgeon made a tiny incision in her navel area and pushed an instrument called a laparoscope through it in order to see the fallopian tubes greatly magnified. Another instrument was then pushed through the laparoscope and the tubes were cut and the ends cauterized. "I didn't even take an aspirin," Mrs. Graber commented afterward.

"There's been a marked increase in sterilization," says Dr. Jack Hallatt, an obstetrician-gynecologist at Kaiser Foundation Hospital in Los Angeles. "People are becoming aware that they can be sterilized on request and that hospitals no longer have a rigid criteria. In fact, we can't turn anybody down."

Almost 25 percent of the white population over thirty who don't want children have chosen sterilization by tubal ligation or vasectomy. The Department of Health, Education and Welfare will pay 90 percent of the cost for poor people. However, a number of insurance companies still refuse to pay for the operation. Some insurance companies refuse to pay for sterilization even if there are medical reasons for it. Many such cases have been successfully appealed to the state insurance commissioner.

For most women sterilization still seems too drastic a step. Even those who ask for it often change their minds at the last minute. A recent case involved a forty-one-year-old woman who has twelve living children. She had been scheduled for a tubal ligation, but called up the night before she was due to appear at the hospital and said she didn't want to go through with it. She was pregnant again at the time, but decided to have an abortion rather than the operation that would leave her sterile. "Once it's done, there's no getting it undone," she said in explanation.

Mary Petrinovich, a board member of the National Organization for Women, says many women who come for gynecological care and counseling ask about sterilization. "Some are sure they want it, although they think it isn't available. Then they find out it is available, rap about it for hours, and finally decide to use some other form of contraception."

Norman Fleishman, executive vice president of Planned Parenthood of Los Angeles, says his organization goes to great lengths to be sure that women who want sterilization know exactly what they are asking for, and applicants are thoroughly briefed on alternative methods of birth control.

Fleishman, who has had a vasectomy, favors sterilization because, he says, all other methods of birth control have some failure rate, and a woman has such a long period of fertility—up to age fifty—that statistics favor her getting pregnant against her will at least once during the span of years.

According to the journal *Family Planning Perspectives,* 50 percent of the couples who say they do not want children are seriously considering a sterilization operation.

In a report on "The Acceptability of Contraceptive Sterilization Among U.S. Couples: 1970," authors Larry Bumpass and Harriet Presser say flatly that sterilization is gaining rapidly on the Pill as the most popular contraception method. The proportion of couples using the Pill reached a plateau in 1967, while sterilization began a sharp increase in 1969—particularly among couples previously using the Pill.

The average age of wives being sterilized is thirty-two years, and so far the operation is far more prevalent among couples in which the wife is past thirty. However, more younger women are now choosing the operation.

At first glance it may seem surprising that only 30 percent of those sterilized have been women. One reason is that the sterilization operation is much simpler for a male. It costs about $125 and involves only two small incisions on either side of the scrotum. Many physicians perform it without admitting their patients to the hospital for an overnight stay. The procedure takes about ten minutes, and the patient is free to leave the hospital or clinic as soon as the anesthetic wears off. There is only a comparatively short after-period of mild discomfort.

At one time, it was widely believed that a man could be made fertile again by a simple re-connection of the severed cords. It has proved otherwise. Only two out of every five "re-connections" prove successful. The longer a man has been rendered sterile by vasectomy, the more difficult it is to restore his fertility. Sperm continues to be produced after a vasectomy but since it can't be ejaculated, it is absorbed by the tubule walls. Eventually antibodies are formed against a man's own sperm so that even after re-connection the antibodies continue to destroy his sperm cells.

Few black men have vasectomies. The reason is not entirely clear. It may be that black males are usually low income earners and the operation is too expensive, or that they are proud of their "virility" and reject the idea of anything that might appear to diminish it.

A recent survey of black women tends to emphasize the importance of the latter explanation. Black women say overwhelmingly that their men would not, under any circumstances, consider an operation that would render them sterile.

Men who have had vasectomies give fairly predictable reasons: they simply did not plan on having children, they were glad to be relieved of the worry or the necessity for taking each-time precautions, and a vasectomy was cheap, simple, an obvious solution. Uniformly, all report themselves happier and enjoying their sex lives more since the operation.

Our mini-survey of eighteen men who have had recent vasectomies turned up only three replies that were in any way unusual.

"I had it done because I wanted to have fun," admits a middle-aged actor, "and I didn't want to get involved in a paternity suit. In any court I can prove I'm sterile, and no scheming woman can get her talons into me. Probably I sound selfish, but sex is far more important to me than fatherhood."

Another man had a vasectomy because his doctor warned him that his wife, a devout Catholic who would not take the Pill, would die if she gave birth to another baby. He hasn't told her that he had the operation. "Sure, I worry about what might happen if I have to marry again. But she's all that's important to me right now. We follow the calendar on sex and she doesn't know that I couldn't make her pregnant if I wanted to."

David Dinsmore, a vice president of Zero Population Growth, said: "Most of the things having to do with children drive me up the wall." "I have nothing in common with children. My consuming interest in life is politics, and you can't talk politics with a five-year-old!"

Public acceptance of vasectomy is clearly on the increase, although apparently not on a public forum like TV. On June 27, 1974, Foster Morgan, a television newsman in San Antonio, Texas, arranged for his vasectomy to be performed on the air. Morgan stated in advance that "no intimate parts" would be shown on the screen, and that "tasteful" diagrams would be shown to explain the process. The surgery was to take place at the Planned Parenthood Center, and TV station KENS was ready with cameras and lights to record the event.

The show was abruptly canceled. The official reason: a "misunderstanding" and not enough coordination with the doctors.

The real reason: a floodtide of angry telephone calls. The public wasn't ready to go that far yet.

DOCTORS URGE IT

A recent report from the Health Research Group, a nonprofit organization with headquarters in Washington, D.C., alleges that doctors at such hospitals as the USC Medical Center in Los Angeles, the City Hospital in Boston, and the City Hospital in Baltimore have been talking women into being sterilized. The report cites cases in which women, after agreeing to a simple sterilization, were given hysterectomies instead. In some cases, the resident physicians decided that removal of the uterus was more complicated medically and would give them better practice in the operating room!

Dr. Bernard Rosenfeld, co-author of a study on sterilization abuses, says women—often in the throes of childbirth—are cajoled and coerced into consenting to surgical sterilization.

At County-USC Hospital, Dr. Rosenfeld interviewed more than fifty physicians who came from major medical teaching hospitals around the country. Some of their replies, corroborated by two wire service reporters who accompanied Rosenfeld and posed as his assistants during the interviews:

- A doctor trained in Texas: "I used to make my pitch while sewing up the episiotomy [a small incision made to facilitate delivery of the baby]. I'd ask if she wanted any more children. If she said no, I'd say I could help her very easy. It was house staff policy. The doctors used to wear buttons saying, 'Stop at two, damn it!' "
- A doctor from a medical center in Florida: "We would just go ahead and perform a sterilization during Caesarean delivery. 'Hey, this tube is bleeding a little; better tie it off.' It got to be a standing joke."
- A physician who trained in North Carolina: "We pushed them on anyone delivering their second or more child. A resident who was up the entire night with some woman or a doctor who just got his income tax back and realized

it all went to welfare and unemployment was more likely to push it harder."
· A physician who trained at a San Diego hospital: "Some of the guys would push real hard, especially if a woman was having an illegitimate baby or if they were very hungry for surgery."

The doctors that Rosenfeld interviewed were chosen at random. He simply knocked on doors at a County-USC dormitory, identified himself as a member of the hospital's ob-gyn staff, and asked his questions.

Dr. Rosenfeld believes the answer lies in an independent "patient advocate" who would have the responsibility for making sure that a prospective sterilization candidate has been given all the information required for truly meaningful informed consent.

THE GREAT AMERICAN BIRTH BUST

20

A few years ago John B. Calhoun, a psychologist working with associates at the National Institute for Mental Health, built a laboratory paradise for mice. At the laboratory in Poolesville, Maryland, eight mice, four males and four females, were provided with all ingredients necessary for a long and happy life in a scientific environment that barred disease-bearing germs and predators. Death, except from normal aging, was banished.

The experiment began in June 1968 in an air-conditioned enclosure ten feet wide on four sides and ten feet high, containing well-stocked living and nesting quarters arranged as miniature high-rise apartments. As the colony grew, the mice tended to form social groups, and each group established a territory. When the population reached 150, all the desirable physical spaces were gone and all meaningful social roles within the groups were occupied.

"That was the beginning of the breakdown," Calhoun reported. Mother mice chased their young out of the nests before the young had a chance to learn anything of mother love. Dominant males began to break down, exhausted from the task of defending their territories. Young adult males wearied of the struggle for a territory of their own and turned to "life on the streets" on the floor of their laboratory world.

John Calhoun said, "The rejected males either became recluses or formed large, motionless aggregates in the most exposed public space, far from the housing units. The rejected females assembled in the housing units that were furthest from the food and water. They lost interest in courtship and mating."

When the population reached 2,200 two years later, rearing of young and breeding ceased, even though the elements for physical survival remained in ample supply. From then on, extinction was inevitable. The last mouse died less than five years after the experiment began.

Calhoun drew the inescapable moral: "There is no logical reason why a comparable sequence of events should not also lead to [our] species extinction."

He predicted that unless man decided quickly to reduce his numbers, the overcrowding of the planet would become so great that disruption of all social organization would follow.

His was another of the prophecies that our expanding birthrate would become the death of us all, that if world population was not curbed, the earth itself would at last glow orange-red from the accumulated "bodies heat" of all its inhabitants.

But in the last few years, the amazing downward trend of the American birthrate is what has captured the attention of economists, businessmen, and sociologists.

What caused this abrupt change? Why have we stopped breeding with such astounding suddenness?

One obvious answer is that babies have simply become too expensive. The price of rearing a baby to age one year is now conservatively estimated to be about $5,000! This includes obstetrician, hospital stay, baby and mother's wardrobe, pediatrician, diapering, food and toys, and a miscellaneous grouping of such items as baby-sitting and nursery furniture.

As Baby grows older, a parent must pay for such added items as regular visits to the dentist, nursery school and kindergarten, day care, an additional room or renovation of the nursery, birthday parties, private instruction in piano or dancing, summer camp, movies, a pet, haircuts. Because of the saving in obstetrician and hospital fees, the annual cost remains approximately the same, $5,000. But how many people in the low-to-moderate income bracket can afford that annual figure?

There are other reasons for the country's close approach to zero population growth.

"Rapid economic growth has brought about a change in most people's living patterns," says a United Nations expert on population control. "Most young people today don't believe in sacrificing their own comforts for a baby. They want a nice home or apartment, vacations, clothes, money to spend for entertainment. These competing desires have clearly caused a basic shift in the procreational habits of the average man and woman. Then add the increased use of more efficient contraceptives, the liberalized abortion laws, the women's rights movement, the increasing numbers of working women who not only have jobs but careers, the trend toward later marriages, the increasing worry about the environment, and, believe it or not, the growing popularity of television!"

The TV factor, usually underrated, was given new prominence when in December 1973 England limited TV viewing because of the energy crisis. All broadcasting ceased at 10:30 P.M., and the most vociferous protests came, not from viewers, but from the population stabilization council that was engaged in trying to keep down the rate of births. The council urged all married couples who were frustrated TV watchers to be certain to take contraceptives to bed with them after the last program ended. Nevertheless, there was a noticeable temporary increase in babies born in late 1974.

In Italy the ban on late night television actually resulted in a baby boom. There was a startling 7 percent increase in births.

This also was our experience after the electrical blackout in the northeastern United States in September 1965. Nine months later we discovered what we were doing when the lights went out.

Television viewing is clearly a contraceptive. Advocates of birth control might consider seriously the advantages of beginning prime-time TV at eleven o'clock at night and ending at two o'clock in the morning. By then, presumably, couples will be too weary to yield to the primal impulse.

The way things are going, however, birth-control advocates aren't likely to need any help. From all over the nation come continuing bulletins on the decline in human births. Hundreds of hospitals are closing down their maternity wards, elementary schools are being turned into boarding hotels, retirement and nursing homes. In Manhattan, awards are being given to the "nonParents of the year" and festivals in Central Park celebrate the non-fertility rite.

Even the results of the baby boom during that blackout backfired. Groups in favor of limiting population became alert to the influence of TV. The National Organization for Non-Parents, Zero Population Growth, and the Communication Center of the Population Institute have since been keeping a wary eye on the kinds of messages that issue from the tube.

ZPG suggests story lines to television producers in which the plots are not the kind thickened with people. The Communications Center offers prizes of up to $10,000 for scripts that most effectively dramatize the problem of overpopulation. Programs dealing with the advantages of birth control and the pleasures of small families are the ones likely to catch the approving eye of the awards committee. On the other hand, programs like "The Waltons," which show large families getting along swimmingly even during the Depression, cause members of the association to fire off indignant letters complaining about "distortions of reality" and the like.

Norman Lear, the producer of such popular TV series as "All in the Family" and "Sanford and Son," is a favorite of population-control groups, for his situation comedies feature small casts. Archie Bunker and Fred Sanford have fathered only one child apiece.

The Population Institute estimates that one fourth of the world's people see what we produce on TV, so the medium must teach the desirability of world-wide birth control and the perils of the numbers racket. As a spokesman for the Institute reminds us, "If every young couple in this country decided to have two children, the population would increase more than fifty million in the next fifty years. But if each young couple decided to have three, the population would more than double. In the year twenty twenty-five, we'd have a population of more than four hundred and thirty million!"

The trend, though, is clearly in the opposite direction. In 1800, an American woman gave birth to an average of seven children. From there on, the graph shows a fairly continuous decline until immediately following World War II, when our Johnnies came marching home. From a low of 2.1 in 1936, the rate then ascended to 3.8.

This was only a temporary bulge, however, like the swelling a bubble makes. The bubble collapsed. In 1972, the average number of children born to a family had dropped to 2.03. At the end of 1973, it had gone down to 1.9. By 1974, it sagged to a wholly unprecedented 1.7.

The effects of this are not yet fully apparent because women born in the post-World War II baby boom are now in their childbearing years. Simply because their numbers are so large, the total number of babies born remains large. There were slightly over 3 million births in 1974, and over the next few years that total number is likely to remain stable, for there will be a 7 percent increase in the number of women in the prime childbearing ages between twenty and twenty-nine.

After the next few years, though, the descent in total numbers will be abrupt. Women born in the post-World War II baby boom will be replaced as potential mothers by a much smaller group born in the middle and late 1950s. This smaller group of mothers will yield a still smaller baby group.

The full extent of the decline depends on what happens to the birthrate among minorities. Here, too, the evidence points only one way: down. Births in the U.S. are declining rapidly among the poor, black, and Mexican-American families.

Some highlights: the fertility of urban whites between the periods 1957–1960 and 1967–1970 declined by about 27 percent. But the fertility of blacks fell by 37 percent. Among Mexican-Americans and other Americans with Spanish surnames it fell 30 percent, and among American Indians the decline was a staggering 45 percent! These groups, whose fertility rate has been historically much higher than that of urban whites, are now close to the birthrate of the urban white majority.

As time moves on, potential mothers must be looked for among a much smaller group of women born during the 1960s. That means the birthrate will continue to plunge. The situation will reach its nadir when the relatively small number of babies born in the 1970s grow to childbearing age. By then, the goal of zero population growth surely will be reached. The U.S. Department of

Commerce estimates that by 1990, the population will have stabilized at about 246 million—an increase of a mere 34 million. After that, unless there is some unforeseen reversal of social trends, our actual numbers will begin to decline.

THE BABY BUSINESS BUST

The effects of the decline on the birth businesses are cataclysmic.

Companies that supply the infant and toddler markets, from baby food to nursery needs, are reeling. "If the slide in birth continues at the same precipitous rate, the effects on the makeup, the marketing practices, and the social customs of this country will be profound," says one government expert. "In a sense, more has happened in the last fifteen years to change the patterns of birth and pregnancy than took place in the millions of years man has been on the planet."

First to feel the effects were the hospitals. Officials of the American Hospital Association report a drop in births of more than 8 percent in the past five years. Hospitals have reduced their number of bassinets, cut back their nursery facilities. When cities have two or more hospitals, usually only one maintains a maternity ward. Ten New York City hospitals have closed their pediatric wards, and around the country there are fewer beds in pediatric wards.

Our schools also reflect the dwindling number of births. Nursery and elementary school construction has slowed almost to a halt. Many existing schools have closed, not for lack of funds, but for lack of pupils. Since 1966 Salt Lake City has closed twenty public schools because of a steep 37 percent drop in enrollment.

There are only 16 million preschool children in the country today, a drop of more than 4 million in little over a decade. Teachers are a glut on the labor market. In 1968 there were 81,000 new teaching jobs. There are now less than 7,000. According to the National Education Association, the surplus of beginning elementary school teachers is around 60,000 and the shortage of jobs will last for at least ten more years.

Other signs: Gerber Products Company used to proclaim its slogan, "Babies Are Our Business, Our Only Business." They have switched to "Babies Are Our Business," because they are branching out from baby food. Now they make prepackaged meals for single diners and have diversified into commercial printing and life insurance. They are also looking overseas for business and currently produce infant food for Brazilian and Greek babies.

The giants in the $400-million baby food industry are all suffering. Squibb sold its Beech-Nut baby food division because it was unprofitable and the future was unpromising. Heinz baby foods reports a decline in sales of 8 to 10 percent—a figure that almost exactly matches the percentage that births are off. Abbott Laboratories has added a food for old folks, called Ensure, to its line of infant formulas. Kellogg, with cereal sales flattening out, is establishing subdivisions to make other products such as soups, tea, waffles, and egg rolls.

Johnson & Johnson is trying to ride out the downtrend by persuading women to use their baby shampoo and powder on themselves. If the products are good for a baby's skin, shouldn't they be good for mother's too? Johnson's Baby Oil is advertised as a replacement for many of the cosmetics on a drugstore's display counter.

If this approach isn't sufficient to perk sales, the hard-pressed Johnson & Johnson executives have come up with a further gimmick: baby products are good for father too. The problem, of course, is how to sell men on the idea. The solution, they hope, is a series of commercials on TV showing unquestionably male adults, athletes and cops and telephone linemen, patting on talcum and shampooing their hair. Monkey see, monkey do.

The verdict on this sales approach is not yet clear, but while they're waiting, Johnson & Johnson isn't letting baby dust cling to its feet. Through a subsidiary they now offer a full line of diaphragms, foams, and birth-control products.

If you can't beat a trend, join it.

A stock market economist, surveying the field, reports, "Every industry connected with children will be affected as the slump in births continues. It will move through the economic spectrum—bubblegum makers, refrigerators, shoes. Buster Brown in St. Louis and Stride-Rite in Boston, big manufacturers of children's shoes, are emphasizing footwear for nine- to twelve-year-olds. They'll soon have to move into the young adult field, and probably wind up selling special shoes for the funeral casket!"

Many companies have read the chalk numbers written on the slate and are departing the children's field.

A sign of the childless times is the increasing number of new apartment developments designed to cater to the kidless set. "Most young couples are more interested in a swimming pool and a billiard room than a playground," says a prominent southern California builder. "They don't want other people's children hollering around, stampeding down the halls, playing games on the elevators or pulling pranks at Halloween. Their idea of good neighbors is neighbors who hate kids as much as they do."

CHANGING ATTITUDES

Attitudes toward parenthood are clearly undergoing a profound psychological change. This kind of change happens slowly, but there is no longer any doubt of the direction in which we are heading.

The social factors causing this new orientation are too many and too complex for the scope of this book, although they surely include the lengthening of life, the threat of population growth, the weakening of religious ties, and new, simplified, and accessible means of contraception.

Evidence of the change mounts steadily. A team of researchers for the University of Michigan reported, as a result of interviews with more than two thousand Americans, that the happiest married couples are those without children.

The survey showed that as soon as a couple has a child, contentment with life drops sharply and stress between the parents grows. The most unsatisfying marriages are those in which the couple's child is under six years of age. As the child grows, the parents become happier, and when they are alone again their general contentment is again high. "The time of the empty nest turns out to be a time of fulfillment," in the words of the report.

About 88 percent of childless wives and 73 percent of childless husbands in the eighteen to twenty-nine age groups said they were "generally happy with life as a whole." In contrast, only 65 percent of husbands and wives with children under six years of age responded affirmatively to the same question.

Business is also adopting a new attitude toward parenthood. Some loan companies and mortgage lenders now ask for assurances from young married applicants that they will practice birth control.

Mrs. Carol Lewicke of Arlington, Virginia, an assistant editor on a magazine, was made to promise she would remain childless before a loan company would approve a mortgage application. She had to sign a statement and have it notarized so the company could keep it on file. "I didn't believe something like this could happen in this country," Mrs. Lewicke says. "The whole thing was just unreal."

"We are in the business to lend money at a profit," explained an official of the loan company. "If a baby comes, her income stops, and her husband would not be able to make payments alone. A simple statement that she is practicing birth control is not legally binding."

Can you imagine, a few short decades ago, any business institution daring to put the security of profits ahead of the life of a baby? The national blast of anger would have driven the company out of business.

Mrs. Alice Lynn, who holds an M.A. in sociology and teaches courses that prepare couples for child rearing, believes the new attitudes toward childbirth and childrearing are in touch with social realities. "Parenthood is the most long-term, irreversible commitment an individual makes. You don't get to pick your child. You get no choice about the child's sex or temperament. Still, it is your child and your responsibility for life. It is difficult for parents to admit that a child is a disruptive influence on their lives. Most people subscribe to the myth that a child will fit into the couple's schedule or life-style. This is not always the case. An infant with a difficult temperament may upset the tranquility of a happy marriage, but even when the baby is perfect for the couple, they may not be prepared for the total commitment, in terms of time and energy, which a child requires. . . . This is tragic. Some couples are simply not suited for parenthood"

THE PET EXPLOSION

One business clearly destined to prosper in the babeless brave new world is the pet industry. It is currently enjoying an unprecedented boom.

Since 1941, our pet population has increased to 40 million dogs, 40 million cats, 15 million birds, 10 million other warm-blooded creatures ranging from rodents to monkeys, and 600 million fish. That is triple the human population.

Read that again in case you missed it. There are now three pets for every man, woman and child in the United States.

Three for one.

We spend an incredible 4.5 billion dollars a year on our pets. About half of this sum is for animal food alone. Dogs account for $1.12 billion in food sales, $400 million on canine health care, $350 million on accessories. Year by year the figures climb. No one who watches television can be unaware of the heavy proportion of commercial time devoted to peddling cat and dog food.

In New York, San Francisco, Chicago, and Los Angeles there are now "doggie restaurants" that serve three-course meals to canines, with prices extending from $1.50 (Biscuit, Ken-L-Ration with raw egg, Dog Yummie and skim milk) to $6.00 (Yummies, top sirloin, vegetable of choice, more Yummies, beverage of choice). Van Nuys, California, boasts a Dogmobile—a specially equipped Dodge van—that tours the community to bathe and beautify dogs on a weekly or biweekly schedule. The number of doggie shampoos, perfumes, toys, jackets and booties, slippers, etc., has proliferated almost endlessly.

"Why not?" asks the owner of a prosperous Manhattan pet store. "Pets have got it all over babies. They're easier to acquire—ever heard of a mother having birth pangs from a pet poodle? They're much less expensive—ever heard of sending a cat through college for thirty-eight thousand dollars? They don't need an obstetrician, a day-care center, music lessons or clothing.

"They're affectionate and they wouldn't think of arguing about a parent's life-style or making fun of their values. They never need a psychoanalyst to straighten them out. You can even castrate 'em. If they get really sick, nobody objects if you put 'em to sleep. When they're dead you don't have to have an expensive funeral or an elaborate tombstone to mark their resting place. How can babies compete with something like that?"

LOOKING AHEAD IN THE U.S.A.

Zero Population Growth will have an enormous impact on our health and wealth. Each American in the near future will at least theoretically have access to more goods and services. There will be less demand for housing, food supplies, hospitals, and medical care. There will be less need for nurseries, day-care centers, schools, colleges. The median age of those living in the United States will move upward, and that will have an effect on trends in fashions, sports, music, films, and even politics.

As the aging portion of the population becomes more powerful, the very look of our society will change. It is not too much to envisage, as columnist Russell Baker of *The New York Times* does, that in forty years we will inhabit a world in which almost no one has brothers or sisters, in which there are few relatives to invite to dinner, and the governing class will consist of "only children" grown to maturity.

As the proportion of older people among us increases, merchandisers will no longer devote themselves chiefly to the "young adult" market but will redirect their selling efforts to a middle-aged culture. Older people will no longer feel underprivileged. Tightness in the labor market, which will no longer be supplied by the influx of younger workers, will reverse the present trend toward early retirement and extend the productive years of the average man's lifetime.

In politics there will be conflict between the demands of the childless and the demands of those with children. The areas in which tensions will breed include taxes, military service, aid to education, social security and retirement benefits, inflation, jobs, seniority, curfew laws, housing codes, and what to do about crime.

One arena in which the conflict may be sharpest is social security. Government experts who fiddle with the birthrates, death rates, unemployment rates, and the like have come up with a startling warning. Without a huge increase in the payroll tax rate—as much as 75 percent—the social security system won't be able to pay its promised benefits in the very near future.

What most of us do not understand is that Social Security is not like insurance. The money paid to it is not saved and invested to provide a steady income during later years. Instead, the taxes that are collected are almost instantly paid out again to beneficiaries. Social Security is basically a pay-as-you-go scheme, and if there are fewer people to pay, a serious fiscal problem quickly arises.

How can it be solved? The only possibilities are to cut the steady growth of benefit payments, sharply increase the already burdensome payroll taxes that support those benefits, or shift the financing of Social Security to the income tax.

The latter course seems the most likely. The payroll tax is not equitable, for the rate is constant—5.85 percent—and only applies up to an income of $13,200. Above that point the taxpayer escapes paying Social Security tax on his income. There has been a good deal of grumbling about that from those whose income is less than $13,200. They wonder why they should pay a tax on all their income while others, better able to afford it, don't. At present, several proposals are before Congress to increase the limit.

But what will happen when those over sixty-five represent 25 percent of the working population and there isn't the base of new wage earners necessary to support them? If the Social Security system survives, it will be because the old and retired use political clout to dominate the working young, and what this portends in the way of political divisions among us is alarming to imagine.

On the ecology front the picture is brighter. Our ZPG society will have diminishing numbers of people to pollute the environment, consume natural resources, and expand cities and towns into wilderness areas. There will be an improvement in the now precarious balance between the number of United States citizens and the supply of commodities required to sustain them.

One reason for the declining birthrate may be that American families wish to have more to consume for themselves rather than to share it with children.

A psychologist says, "For a great many young parents, children were another form of diversion, grownup toys for immature people to play with—to prolong their own childhood and to fill up a vacancy in their adult lives. Now they have too many substitutes—livelier, less expensive, less trouble. If they feel a twinge of loneliness once in a while, there's always a way out. It's as near as the television set or the game room, the wet bar or the bedroom where they can try out one of the new positions in the latest best-selling sex manual—without worrying about getting a kid who'll spoil the fun!"

ZPG will be favorable for women. They will find jobs easier to get, since fewer men will be entering the labor market. Formerly male-dominated areas, including the armed forces, will welcome them. A looming shortage of eighteen- to nineteen-year-old males has already caused the Department of Defense to step up its recruiting drive to attract more women.

Women born since 1962 will have a larger supply of older men to choose from. That does not mean that they will lead them to the altar. Marriage appears to be declining in popularity. Gloria Steinem may be speaking for tomorrow's women when she says, "The surest way to be alone is to get married. Surveys show the happiest people are single women!"

The Roper poll, querying three thousand women, reports that 70 percent consider the institution of marriage weaker than ten years ago. Three out of five women found divorce an acceptable solution to a bad marriage, and a clear majority believed the children would be better off if an unhappy couple separated. Significantly, only 41 percent of women thought that having children was an important reason for marrying. And equally significant—one out of two women under the age of thirty-five is single.

In our ZPG world women will play more important roles in politics and the business world, since freedom from children will give them more time to promote their own careers and interests.

Our national economy will probably settle to a lower level. History has shown that a rapidly growing population causes an increase in the nation's gross product, and fuels the demand for more goods and still more production. Zero population growth may cause zero economic growth. But because a higher proportion of the population will be working (the number of those too young to work having sharply decreased), there will be a greater degree of savings. Savings, economists tell you, are what generate capital expansion and pay for the modernizing of present equipment and outlays for new equipment. A stationary work force in the future will produce a greater per capita gross national product. That means, simply, more for everybody.

Without a constantly expanding market, the American birth business will suffer. Infant food manufacturers will have fewer customers; so will children's garment makers and the toymakers. Charles Reich in *The Greening of America* quotes an advertisement: "Nothing makes markets like a marriage. There's new business in raising a family. All together, it's big business: appliances and house furnishings to stepped-up insurance and bigger cars." True. When the making of families slows down, so will business, at least to the degree it is dependent on the family market. The greening of America will turn to gray.

As for the children, they will undoubtedly be healthier. There will be a greater ratio of pediatricians to children, therefore assuring more children of time and better medical care. In addition, most children will have been born because their parents really wanted them, and therefore are likely to be treasured and given better care. Parents with only one or two children to look after will have more time to spend on the emotional and physical needs of each.

Children will be better educated too, for classrooms will not be so crowded. Because the supply of available teachers surpasses the demand, only the better teachers will get jobs—and will try harder to perform well.

Poor children will, of course, remain poor. The expectations of the underprivileged are disappointed time and again, but at least there will be fewer of them to be disappointed. And their condition will improve vis-à-vis the others in society.

There will be less unemployment and less mobility between classes, thereby muffling the resentment of those who fail to get ahead. In a ZPG society the only way to get ahead is by taking something away from someone else. The pie isn't getting any bigger, and the only way to increase your slice is to reduce the size of your neighbor's.

Rivalries between ethnic groups will not diminish, unless it happens from other causes than the limiting of population. In fact, because the birthrates of various groups will differ from the "average," there is likely to be a sharpened fear of "what are those people up to? Are they trying to take over?" One group, even as one individual, can only prosper in a ZPG society at the expense of another.

Immigration will become the source of our population growth. It is now totaling about 400,000 a year, with most immigrants coming from Latin America and Asia. This, too, will sharpen rivalries, as established groups may begin to fear that immigrants, and their eventual descendants, will play a disproportionately influential role in the country's future.

For more than a century, since the opening to the West, Americans have pushed on to ever-expanding frontiers. The last geographical frontier closed some years ago, and now the "frontier" of a constantly growing population is closing down. It will not reopen unless there is a calculated change in government policy—the payment of baby bonuses, or large family allowances, or such extras as a free college education. Many doubt that even these unlikely events could reverse the trend.

Will the result be a long period of stagnation? Not necessarily. Challenges will remain that will certainly demand all of our ingenuity and labor. We have to deal with the problems of improving health and education, developing technology, building a society in which more citizens have adequate housing and food, in which communities have adequate mass transportation. We will have to find ways to preserve the environment, reduce pollution, and discover new sources for our fast-depleting supplies of energy.

Mother's day will soon be over. But within a new society, where babies are more singular objects than ever before in the world's history, there will be many meaningful social roles.

Freed of demands imposed by the child-centered family, the adult may at long last be coming into his or her own.

INDEX